Asian American Literature
An Annotated Bibliography

King-Kok Cheung
Stan Yogi

The Modern Language Association of America
New York   1988

Copyright © 1988 by The Modern Language Association of America

Library of Congress Cataloging-in-Publication Data

Cheung, King-Kok, 1954–
    Asian American literature : an annotated bibliography / King-Kok Cheung,
Stan Yogi.
        p.   cm.
    Includes indexes.
    ISBN 0-87352-960-X   ISBN 0-87352-961-8 (pbk.)
    1. American literature—Asian-American authors—Bibliography.
2. Asian Americans in literature—Bibliography.   I. Yogi, Stan.   II. Title.
Z1229.A75C47 1988
[PS153.A84]
016.81'08'089507—dc19   88-5355

Published by The Modern Language Association of America
10 Astor Place, New York, NY 10003-6981

Contents

Preface

This bibliography is intended for scholars and students seeking a convenient reference guide to literature by Asian American writers in the United States and Canada. Although much has been written by Asian Americans, especially in the last two decades, this literature remains little known by the American public at large. At the same time, students and scholars in the field are sometimes befuddled by its very breadth, comprising diverse cultural groups and several generations of writers. Considering the span of Asian American writing, the body of literary criticism appears meager, partly because the field is relatively new and partly because it has not gained adequate recognition. We hope that the present bibliography will whet the appetites of the uninitiated, provide guidance to students, and inspire scholars to further research.

Aware that "Asian American literature" is a recent and controversial term, we try to be nonprescriptive despite the caveats of some prominent writers. In their introduction to *AIIIEEEEE! An Anthology of Asian-American Writers*, Frank Chin et al., for instance, distinguish sharply between Americanized Chinese authors and Chinese American authors, arguing that writers such as C. Y. Lee and Lin Yutang, whose works are often anthologized as Asian American literature, should not be classified as Chinese Americans: "[B]orn and raised in China . . . [they] are Chinese who have merely adapted to American ways and write about Chinese America as foreigners" (xxxviii). But the influence of overseas Asians—be they sojourners or immigrants with American-born offspring—cannot be ignored in a study of Asian American literary history. There are also authors who may regard themselves as expatriates or as regional writers rather than as Asian Americans. We choose to list them because national and regional allegiances, which often vary with time, cannot easily be determined.

Criteria based on "Asian American sensibility" are inevitably subjective. They cannot be applied judiciously, since the various Asian cultural groups (and even members within the same group) immigrated to North America at different periods. Moving in the direction pointed out by Elaine Kim in *Asian American Literature: An Introduction to the Writings and Their Social Context*, we try to be inclusive rather than exclusive in our selections. We list works by writers of Asian descent who have made the United States or Canada their home, regardless of where they were born, when they settled in North America, and how they interpret their experiences. Our list also includes authors of mixed descent who have one Asian parent (insofar as we can trace their parentage), as well as authors who may not be permanent North American residents but who have written specifically on the experiences of Asians in the United States or Canada. (For example, of the many travelogues by Chiang Yee—a Chinese who has settled in England—we list the three describing Boston, New York, and San Francisco.) Following the same inclusive principle we use the term "literature" in a broad sense to encompass autobiography, informal essays, and popular fiction. In short, we try to enlarge the precincts of Asian American literature. A narrow definition would stifle rather than inspire at a time when Asian American writers are still finding their voice, a voice that should be polyphonic.

The strongest reason for extending the parameters as far as we do is a practical one. Our bibliography is designed not to make a definitive statement but to facilitate research and to call attention to a group of writers who have been overlooked until recently. We believe we can best serve both specialists and general readers by omitting as little as possible. We would rather have users pass over certain entries than look for them in vain. In some instances, we include works written prior to the authors' settlement in North America. These are not strictly speaking Asian American items, but scholars specializing in immigrant writers may want to examine works written both before and after immigration. Similarly, students who want to understand fully the perspective of Chin et al. might want to read works by Lin Yutang and C. Y. Lee in order to see for themselves why the editors of *AIIIEEEEE!* dismiss these writers.

While our bibliography is in no way definitive, we do strive to make it the most comprehensive reference guide to Asian American literature possible to date. Besides providing both primary and secondary sources, we include selected fiction by non-Asians (relevant to research in comparative perspectives or in ethnic stereotypes) and selected background studies. Brief annotations accompany most prose selections. Since these annotations can do justice to neither the range nor the depth of the items annotated, we sometimes provide, as part of the primary source entry, references to selected book reviews.

To keep the bibliography to a manageable size, we establish the following limits. First, we exclude works written in Asian languages, unless they have been translated into English. Second, we do not itemize individual poems. Third, we do not list materials in archives or private collections. Fourth, we do not cover most college and university student publications. Given the broad scope of our undertaking, we have probably also overlooked some works that should have been included. Partly owing to increasing creative and critical endeavors, a bibliography of Asian American literature can never be perfectly comprehensive and up to date. Rather than lament that our text cannot keep up with this current bloom, let us rejoice that Asian American literature is flourishing and hope that our effort will further stimulate scholarship in this expanding field.

The bibliography is made possible by two research grants from the University of California, Los Angeles: one from the Academic Senate and the other from the Institute of American Cultures and the Asian American Studies Center (AASC). We would like to thank the staff of the AASC, the staff of the Asian American Studies Program at Berkeley, and the many individuals who have aided us in compiling the bibliography: Walter S. Achtert, Meena Alexander, Carlos A. Angeles, Roger J. Bresnahan, Leonard Casper, G. S. Sharat Chandra, Vijay Lakshmi Chauhan, Frank Chin, Marilyn Chin, Cheng Lok Chua, Saros Cowasjee, Charles Crow, G. V. Desani, Sean LaRoque Doherty, Theodric Feng, Gayle Fujita, N. V. M. Gonzalez, Réshard Gool, Elisabeth Gruner, Garrett Kaoru Hongo, Ruth Yu Hsiao, Yuji Ichioka, Jaime Jacinto, Elaine H. Kim, Elizabeth Kim, Kichung Kim, Teresa Kim, Maxine Hong Kingston, Chris Komai, Genny Lim, Shirley Lim, Amy Ling, David

Wong Louie, Darrell H. Y. Lum, Gerard Maré, David Mas Masumoto, Ruthanne Lum McCunn, Ved Mehta, Janice Mirikitani, P. C. Morantte, Kyoko Mori, Bharati Mukherjee, Panna Naik, Peter Nazareth, Fae Ng, Franklin Ng, Derrick Nguyễn, Ranjini Obeyesekere, Katy Oh, Seizo Oka, James Omura, Uma Parameswaran, Kristin Rieger, E. San Juan, Jr., Bienvenidos N. Santos, Yasuo Sasaki, Vasant A. Shahane, Amritjit Singh, Valerie Soe, Cathy Song, Sang Ok Song, Suwanda H. J. Sugunasiri, Stephen Sumida, Ánh Kim Trân, Linda Ty-Casper, Yoshiko Uchida, Manuel A. Viray, Nellie Wong, Sau-ling Wong, Shawn Wong, Shelley Wong, Mitsuye Yamada, Hisaye Yamamoto, J. K. Yamamoto, Wakako Yamauchi, Richard Yarborough, Sung Y. Yi, and Connie Young Yu.

Special thanks to Wing Tek Lum for alerting us to numerous Hawaiian periodicals; to Linda Nietes, president of Philippine Expressions; to Russell Leong and Glenn Omatsu, editor and associate editor of the *Amerasia Journal*; to Huỳnh Sanh Thông, editor of the *Vietnam Forum*; to M. G. Vassanji, editor of the *Toronto South Asian Review*; to Eleanor C. Au, head of special collections at the Thomas Hale Hamilton Library of the University of Hawaii; to all the librarians at the University of California, Los Angeles, particularly Marji Lee and Sereisa Milford at the AASC Reading Room and the reference librarians at the University Research Library.

We owe the greatest debt to Brian Niiya, who sacrificed countless evenings providing research assistance and moral support far beyond the call of duty.

King-Kok Cheung
Stan Yogi

Explanatory Notes

1. *Bibliographies, Anthologies, and Journals.* These sections include general works on ethnic and Asian American literature as well as works that pertain to a particular group (e.g., Japanese Americans, Korean Americans, or South Asian Americans). Items in the latter category are not listed again in the sections for the particular groups. For example, the following entry is found under "Anthologies" and not under "Filipino American Poetry":

> Ancheta, Shirley, Jaime Jacinto, and Jeff Tagami, eds. *Without Names: A Collection of Poems [by] Bay Area Pilipino American Writers.* San Francisco: Kearny Street Workshop Press, 1985.

Critical anthologies, however, are listed in the secondary sources under "General Criticism" or under specific cultural groups.

2. *Short Story and Poetry Collections.* Collections of individual authors' prose or poetry appear in the sections on cultural groups. Short stories published before their appearance in collections are listed separately, but we inform users that they have since been reprinted. In these instances we give the title (or an abbreviated title) of the collection rather than the entry number. For example:

> Mukherjee, Bharati. "The Lady from Lucknow." *Missouri Review* 8.3 (1985): 29–35. Rpt. in *Darkness* 145–58.

The full bibliographic information for the collection (*Darkness*, in this case) can easily be located under the same author.

3. *Ethnic Categories.* One of our most forbidding tasks has been determining each Asian American writer's ethnic origin. While names and subject matter provide helpful clues, they can also be sorely misleading. For example: Lensey Namioka is a Chinese American married to a Japanese American. Cathy Song has a Korean father and a Chinese mother. Paul Stephen Lim was born in the Philippines of Chinese parents. Onoto Watanna (pseud. for Winnifred Eaton Babcock) and Sui Sin Far (pseud. for Edith Maud Eaton) are Eurasian siblings, born of a Chinese mother and a British father who immigrated to America. Where Sui Sin Far writes about Chinese and Chinese American experiences, Onoto Watanna spins tales about Japan. Because of their Chinese descent, the Eaton sisters are both categorized as Chinese Americans. Many such complicated cases exist. We try to be scrupulous in checking each author's ethnic background by consulting notes on contributors, *Contemporary Authors, Who's Who, Twentieth-Century Author Biographies,* and other reference sources whenever available. Where none exist, we occasionally base inclusion on an author's Asian name. In so doing, we may

have inadvertently omitted some Asian Americans or included some non-Asians. For example, if a Betty Chang were to marry a John Smith and were to write under her married name—Betty Smith—we would have difficulty identifying her as Asian American. Conversely, non-Asians may adopt Asian pseudonyms or names: Leong Gor Yun, author of *Chinatown Inside Out*, is the Chinese pseudonym for Virginia H. Ellison; Estelle Ishigo, author of *Lone Heart Mountain*, is a Caucasian married to a Japanese American. If there are mistakes about ethnic origins in our bibliography, we accept responsibility and can only hope that they will not be considered indicative of discourtesy or disinterest.

4. *Hawaiian and Canadian Writers*. To avoid excessive crosslisting, we classify writers according to ancestral country of origin, and not place of residence. In the primary sources, however, we do identify Hawaiian writers (many of whom think of themselves as "local" rather than "Asian American") and Canadian writers by the prefix of one asterisk or two asterisks. For example, the entries below appear respectively in the Japanese American and the South Asian American sections as follows:

> *Wakayama, Mary. "1895: The Honeymoon Hotel." *Bamboo Ridge: The Hawaii Writers' Quarterly* 27 (1985): 3–10.

> **Bannerji, Himani. "Going Home." *RIKKA* 7.1 (1980): 23–26.

Users interested specifically in Hawaiian literature may also want to consult Arnold Hiura and Stephen Sumida's extensive *Asian American Literature of Hawaii: An Annotated Bibliography*. That bibliography, unlike ours, lists individual poems and works that appear in college annuals.

5. *Missing Data*. We try to provide as much bibliographic data as possible, but obtaining some international periodicals has proved difficult. Therefore, we are occasionally unable to give volume or page numbers for works that appeared in overseas publications. Considerable material was also lost during World War II. For instance, many of the Philippine periodicals in which the short stories of N. V. M. Gonzalez and Bienvenido N. Santos originally appeared were burned during the war. In addition, after the bombing of Pearl Harbor, some Japanese immigrants and their American-born children, fearing that their works in Japanese American publications might be misinterpreted as evidence of disloyalty, destroyed records of their own writing.

6. *Pseudonyms*. For authors who write under both real and assumed names, we list all their publications under their real names (with the pseudonyms in brackets). For authors who write consistently under pseudonyms, their works are listed under the pseudonyms; their real names, if known, are given in brackets.

7. *Cutoff Date and Forthcoming Works*. The cutoff date for this bibliography is July 1987, but we do include forthcoming works of which we are aware. The titles of these works, when published, may be inconsistent with our listings.

Bibliographical and Reference Works

1. Al-Bayati, Barbara Kuhn, Constance Bullock, Roberto Cabello-Argandona, Che-Hwei Lin, and Oscar L. Sims, eds. *Ethnic Serials at Selected University of California Libraries*. Los Angeles: American Indian Studies Center, Asian American Studies Center, Center for Afro-American Studies, and Chicano Studies Center, Univ. of California, 1977.

2. Alcantara, Ruben R., et al. *The Filipinos in Hawaii: An Annotated Bibliography*. Hawaii Series 6. Honolulu: Social Sciences and Linguistics Inst., Univ. of Hawaii, 1977.

3. Asian American Librarians' Caucus. Bibliography Committee. *Asian Americans: An Annotated Bibliography for Public Libraries*. Chicago: Office for Library Service to the Disadvantaged, American Library Assn., 1977.

4. Chinn, Lori, et al. *A Bibliography of Chinese and Chinese American Resource Materials*. Berkeley: Babel Lau Center, 1979.

5. Day, A[rthur] Grove. *Books about Hawaii: Fifty Basic Authors*. Honolulu: UP of Hawaii, 1977.

6. Dunn, Lynn P. *Asian Americans: A Study Guide and Sourcebook*. San Francisco: R & E Research Assoc., 1975.

7. Foronda, Marcelino A., and Cresencia R. Foronda. *A Filipiniana Bibliography, 1743–1982. A Classified Listing of Philippine Materials in the Marcelino A. and Cresencia R. Foronda Private Collection*. Manila: Philippine National Historical Soc., 1981.

8. Fujimoto, Isao, Michiyo Yamaguchi Swift, and Rosalie Zucker. *Asians in America: A Selected Annotated Bibliography*. Asian American Research Project Working Publication 5. Davis: Asian American Studies, Univ. of California, 1971. *Asians in America: A Selected Annotated Bibliography. An Expansion and Revision*. Davis: Asian American Studies, Univ. of California, 1983.

9. Gardner, Arthur L. *The Koreans in Hawaii: An Annotated Bibliography*. Hawaii Series 2. Honolulu: Social Science Research Inst., Univ. of Hawaii, 1970.

10. Hansen, Gladys C., and William F. Heintz. *The Chinese in California: A Brief Bibliographic History*. Portland, OR: Richard Abel, 1970.

11. Hiura, Arnold T., and Stephen H. Sumida. *Asian American Literature of Hawaii: An Annotated Bibliography*. Honolulu: Hawaii Ethnic Resource Center, Talk Story, 1979.

12. Ichioka, Yuji, et al. *A Buried Past: An Annotated Bibliography of the Japanese American Research Project Collection*. Berkeley: U of California P, 1974.

13. Joramo, Marjorie K. *A Directory of Ethnic Publishers and Resource Organizations*. 2nd ed. Chicago: Office for Library Service to the Disadvantaged, American Library Assn., 1979.

14. Kakugawa, Frances. "Asian-American Literature." *English Journal* 63.7 (1974): 110–11.

15. Kim, Christopher. *Annotated Bibliography on Koreans in America*. 1975. Rev. Michiko Takahashi. Los Angeles: Resource Development and Publications, Asian American Studies Center, Univ. of California, 1981.

16. Kim, Elaine H. "Asian American Writers: A Bibliographical Review." *American Studies International* 22.2 (1984): 41–78.

17. ———. "Bibliography." *Asian American Literature: An Introduction to the Writings and Their Social Context*. Philadelphia: Temple UP, 1982. 321–53.

18. Kim, Hyung-Chan, and Cynthia Mejia. *The Filipinos in America: 1898–1974: A Chronology and Fact Book*. Oceana's Ethnic Chronology Series 23. Dobbs Ferry, NY: Oceana Publications, 1976.

19. Kittelson, David J. *The Hawaiians: An Annotated Bibliography*. Hawaii Series 7. Honolulu: Social Science Research Inst., Univ. of Hawaii, 1985.

20. Kwoh, T. Jesse, and Victoria Chin. *Topical Bibliography of the Asian Experience in the United States: Material in the Cornell University Libraries*. Exchange Bibliographies 542–43. Monticello, IL: Council of Planning Librarians, 1974.

21. Lai, Him Mark. *A History Reclaimed: An Annotated Bibliography of Chinese Language Materials on the Chinese of America*. Ed. Russell Leong and Jean Pang Yip. Los Angeles: Resource Development and Publications, Asian American Studies Center, Univ. of California, 1986.

22. Library Services Section. *Multicultural Experiences in Children's Literature: An Annotated Bibliography*. Los Angeles: Los Angeles Public Library, 1978.

23. Ling, Amy. "Asian American Literature: A Brief Introduction and Selected Bibliography." *ADE Bulletin* 80 (1985): 29–33.

24. ———. "Chinamerican Literature: A Partly Annotated Bibliography." *NAIES Newsletter* 7.1 (1982): 34–48.

25. Liu, John M. "Annual Selected Bibliography." *Amerasia Journal* 5.2 (1978): 153–67.

26. ———. "Annual Selected Bibliography." *Amerasia Journal* 7.2 (1980): 155–73.

27. ———. "1979 Selected Bibliography on Asian Americans." *Amerasia Journal* 6.2 (1979): 105–20.

28. ———. "1981 Selected Bibliography." *Amerasia Journal* 8.2 (1981): 171–92.

29.   ———. "1982 Selected Bibliography." *Amerasia Journal* 9.2 (1982): 147–71.

30.   ———. "1983 Selected Bibliography." *Amerasia Journal* 10.2 (1983): 131–53.

31.   ———. "1984 Selected Bibliography." *Amerasia Journal* 11.2 (1984): 109–25.

32.   Lowe, Chuan-hua. *The Chinese in Hawaii: A Bibliographical Survey.* Taipei: China Print, 1972.

33.   Lum, William Wong, with Asian American Research Project, Univ. of California, Davis. *Asians in America: A Bibliography.* Davis: Univ. Library, Univ. of California, 1969.

34.   ———. *Asians in America: A Bibliography of Master's Theses and Doctoral Dissertations.* Davis: Asian-American Studies Div., Dept. of Applied Behavioral Sciences, Univ. of California, 1970.

35.   *Materials for Indochinese Students: An Annotated Bibliography.* 2nd ed. Los Angeles: Los Angeles County Office of Education, 1985.

36.   Matsuda, Mitsugu. *The Japanese in Hawaii: An Annotated Bibliography of Japanese Americans.* Hawaii Series 5. Rev. Dennis M. Ogawa with Jerry Y. Fujioka. Honolulu: Social Sciences and Linguistics Inst., Univ. of Hawaii, 1975.

37.   ———. *The Japanese in Hawaii, 1868–1967: A Bibliography of the First Hundred Years.* Hawaii Series 1. Honolulu: Social Science Research Inst., Univ. of Hawaii, 1968. Honolulu: East-West Inst., 1972.

38.   Matsushita, Karl K., comp. *Books-in-Print: Japanese in the Americas in English with Indexes and Glossary.* San Francisco: Japanese American Library, 1986.

39.   McCutcheon, James. *China and America: A Bibliography of Interactions, Foreign and Domestic.* Honolulu: Univ. of Hawaii, 1972.

40.   Miller, Wayne Charles, ed. *A Handbook of American Minorities.* New York: New York UP, 1976.

41.   Miller, Wayne Charles, et al., eds. *A Comprehensive Bibliography for the Study of American Minorities.* 2 vols. New York: New York UP, 1976.

42.   ———, eds. *Minorities in America: The Annual Bibliography, 1976.* University Park and London: Pennsylvania State UP, 1985.

43.   ———, eds. *Minorities in America: The Annual Bibliography, 1977.* University Park and London: Pennsylvania State UP, 1986.

44.   ———, eds. *Minorities in America: The Annual Bibliography, 1978.* University Park and London: Pennsylvania State UP, 1986.

45.   Nemenzo, Catalina A. *Southeast Asian Languages and Literature in English: An Annotated Bibliography.* Quezon City: Univ. of the Philippines, 1967.

46.   Ng, Frank. "Asian Americans in Hawaii: A Selected Bibliography." *Bridge* 7.3 (1980): 31–34.

47.   Nimura, Taku Frank. *Japanese in the United States: A Bibliography.* 1969. Sacramento: Sacramento State Coll. Library, 1978.

48.   Norell, Irene P. *Literature of the Filipino-American in the United States: A Selective and Annotated Bibliography.* San Francisco: R & E Research Assoc., 1976.

49.   Oaks, Priscilla S. *Minority Studies: A Selective Annotated Bibliography.* Boston: Hall, 1976.

50.   Okamura, Raymond. "Revisions in Japanese American History: Review of Books Published in 1976." *Journal of Ethnic Studies* 5.3 (1977): 112–15. Includes bibliographical information on fiction and nonfiction.

51.   Okihiro, Gary Y. "Annual Selected Bibliography." *Amerasia Journal* 4.2 (1977): 153–65.

52.   Omatsu, Glenn. "Annual Selected Bibliography." *Amerasia Journal* 12.2 (1985–86): 129–57.

53.   ———. "Annual Selected Bibliography." *Amerasia Journal* 13.2 (1986–87): 173–218.

54.   Patterson, Wayne. *The Koreans in North America.* Philadelphia: Balch Inst., 1976.

55.   Patterson, Wayne, and Hyung-Chan Kim. *The Koreans in America.* Minneapolis: Lerner Publications, 1977.

56.   Poon, Wei Chi. *Directory of Asian American Collections in the United States.* Berkeley: Asian American Studies Library, Univ. of California, 1982.

57.   Potasi, Larry. *Bibliography for Samoans in America.* Working Papers on Asian American Studies. Los Angeles: Asian American Studies Center, Univ. of California, 1976.

58.   Rockman, Ilene F. *Understanding the Filipino American, 1900–1976: A Selected Bibliography.* Exchange Bibliography 1178. Monticello, IL: Council of Planning Librarians, 1976.

59.   Rubano, Judith. *Culture and Behavior in Hawaii: An Annotated Bibliography.* Hawaii Series 3. Honolulu: Social Science Research Inst., Univ. of Hawaii, 1971.

60.   Saito, Shiro. *Filipinos Overseas: A Bibliography.* Staten Island, NY: Center for Migration Studies, 1977.

61.   Seriña, Loreto M., and Fe Aldave Yap. *Children's Literature in the Philippines: An Annotated Bibliography of Pilipino and English Works, 1901–1979.* Manila: National Book Store, 1980.

62.   Shinagawa, Larry Hajime. "Asian American Studies." *Critical Perspectives of Third World America* 1.1 (1983): 288–99.

63.   ———. "Ethnic Studies Bibliography." *Critical Perspectives of Third World America* 1.1 (1983): 275–88.

64. Singh, Amritjit, Rajiva Verma, and Irene M. Joshi. *Indian Literature in English, 1827–1979: A Guide to Information Sources.* Detroit: Gale, 1981.

65. Sugunasiri, Suwanda H. J.. "Bibliography: South Asian Canadian Fiction in English (–1982)." *Toronto South Asian Review* 2.2 (1983): 94–97.

66. ———. *The Literature of Canadians of South Asian Origins: An Overview and Preliminary Bibliography.* Toronto: Multicultural History Soc. of Ontario, 1987.

67. Tachiki, Dennis S. *Asians in the Americas: Resource Materials in the Social Sciences and Humanities.* Minneapolis: Asian American Studies Project, Univ. of Minnesota, 1978.

68. Tong, Te-kong. *The Third Americans: A Selected Bibliography on Asians in America with Annotations.* Oak Park, IL: CHCUS, 1980.

69. Uchida, Naosaku. "The Overseas Chinese: A Bibliographical Essay Based on the Resources of the Hoover Institution." Stanford: Hoover Inst., Stanford Univ., 1959.

70. *The Vietnamese in America.* Seattle: Asian American Studies Prog., Univ. of Washington, 1980.

71. Vohra-Sahu, Indu. *Asian Indian Ethnics in the United States: A Select Research Bibliography.* Public Administration Series P-1439. Monticello, IL: Vance Bibliographies, 1984.

72. Wall, Naomi, ed. *Children's Books for Learning: A Bibliography of Multiethnic Resources for Classroom Use.* Toronto: Cross-Cultural Communications, 1979.

73. Wang, Ling-chi. "Asian American Studies." *American Quarterly* 33.3 (1981): 339–54.
    Contains assessment of publications.

74. Women's Educational Equity Communications Network. *Asian/Pacific Women in America.* San Francisco: Far West Laboratory for Educational Research and Development, 1980.

75. Wynar, Lubomyr Roman. *Encyclopedic Directory of Ethnic Newspapers and Periodicals in the United States.* Littleton, CO: Libraries Unlimited, 1972.

76. Yabes, Leopoldo Y. *Philippine Literature in English, 1898–1957: A Bibliographical Survey.* Quezon City: U of the Philippines P, 1958.

77. Yoshitomi, Joan, et al. *Asians in the Northwest: An Annotated Bibliography.* Seattle: Asian American Studies Prog., Univ. of Washington, 1978.

78. Young, Nancy Foon. *The Chinese in Hawaii: An Annotated Bibliography.* Hawaii Series 4. Honolulu: Social Science Research Inst., Univ. of Hawaii, 1973.

79. Yuan, Tung-Li. *A Guide to Doctoral Dissertations by Chinese Students in America, 1905–1960.* Washington: Sino-American Cultural Soc., 1961.

80. Yung, Judy, et al. "Asian American Women: A Bibliography." *Bridge* 6.4 (1978–79): 49–53.

Anthologies

81. *All Aboard.* Topaz, UT: Central Utah Relocation Center, 1944.
    Prose works by Hatsuye Egami and Toshio Mori; *poetry* by Toyo Suyemoto.

82. Ancheta, Shirley, Jaime Jacinto, and Jeff Tagami, eds. *Without Names: A Collection of Poems [by] Bay Area Pilipino American Writers.* San Francisco: Kearny Street Workshop Press, 1985.
    Poems by Shirley Ancheta, Virginia R. Cerenio, Mars Estrada, Joselyn Ignacio-Zimardi, Jaime Jacinto, Norman Jayo, Orvy Jundis, Lloyd Nebres, Oscar Peñaranda, Edgar Poma, Tony Remington, Al Robles, Luis Syquia, Presco Tabios, and Jeff Tagami.
    Rev. Russell Leong, *Amerasia Journal* 13.1 (1986–87): 189–90; Marle C. Pruden, *San Francisco Sunday Examiner and Chronicle* 17 Aug. 1986, book review section: 3.

83. *Anthology: A Collection of Writings by the Youth of Chinatown.* Los Angeles: Chinatown Teen Post, 1978.

84. *Asian Women.* Berkeley: Asian Women's Journal, 1971.
    Poems by Frances Chung, Laura Ho, Joyce Kawasaki, E. H. Kim, Beverly Lee, Diane Mark, Joanne Miyamoto, Myra Moy, Juanita Tamayo, Carole Tokeshi, Kitty Tsui, Stella Wong, and Sharon Yonemura; *prose works* by Veronica Huang, Jan Masaoka, Gail Miyasaki, Kitty Tsui, and Stella Wong; *drama* by G. M. Lee.
    Rev. Lowell Chun-Hoon, *Amerasia Journal* 1.3 (1971): 69–73.

85. Balaban, John, ed. and trans. *Ca Dao Viet Nam: A Bilingual Anthology of Vietnamese Folk Poetry.* Greensville, NC: Unicorn Press, 1980. Oakville, ON: Mosaic Press, 1986.

86. Banerian, James, ed. and trans. *Vietnamese Short Stories: An Introduction.* Foreword Nguyễn Đình Hòa. Phoenix: Sphinx Publishing, 1986.
    Includes stories by Vietnamese now residing in the US.

87. Bankier, Joanna, and Deirdre Lashgari, eds. *Women Poets of the World.* New York: Macmillan, 1983.
    Contains works by Mei-Mei Berssenbrugge, Diana Chang, Laureen Mar, Janice Mirikitani, Jonny Kyoko Sullivan, and Nellie Wong.

88. Blicksilver, Edith, ed. *The Ethnic American Woman: Problems, Protests, Lifestyle.* Dubuque, IA: Kendall/Hunt Publishing, 1978.
    Multiethnic reader. *Prose works* by Teruko Ogata Daniel, Ruby Reyes Flowers, Jeanne Wakatsuki Houston, Kumi Kilburn, Maxine Hong Kingston, Uma Majmudar, Sui Sin Far, and Hisaye Yamamoto; *poems* by Diana Chang, Janice Mirikitani, and Rowena Wildin.

89.   Bruchac, Carol, Linda Hogan, and Judith McDaniel, eds. *The Stories We Hold Secret: Tales of Women's Spiritual Development.* Greenfield Center, NY: Greenfield Review Press, 1986.
        Contains works by Sharon Hashimoto, Yuri Kageyama, and Sylvia A. Watanabe.

90.   Bruchac, Joseph, ed. *Breaking Silence: An Anthology of Contemporary Asian American Poets.* Greenfield Center, NY: Greenfield Review Press, 1983.
        Brief biographical statements accompany works by Mei-Mei Berssenbrugge, Luis Cabalquinto, Virginia Cerenio, Diana Chang, Fay Chiang, Marilyn Chin, Eric Chock, Cyril Dabydeen, Jessica Hagedorn, Kimiko Hahn, Dianne Hai-Jew, Gail N. Harada, Garrett Kaoru Hongo, Patricia Y. Ikeda, Lawson Inada, Jaime Jacinto, Yuri Kageyama, Lonny Kaneko, Joy Kogawa, Tina Koyama, Geraldine Kudaka, Alex Kuo, Alan Chong Lau, Deborah Lee, George Leong, Walter Lew, Genny Lim, Stephen Shu Ning Liu, Wing Tek Lum, Laureen Mar, Diane Mei Lin Mark, Janice Mirikitani, Jim Mitsui, David Mura, Dwight Okita, Mark Osaki, Richard Oyama, Al Robles, Cathy Song, Luis Syquia, Arthur Sze, Jeff Tagami, Ronald P. Tanaka, Kitty Tsui, George Uba, Nellie Wong, Shawn Wong, Merle Woo, Traise Yamamoto, and Cyn Zarco.
        Rev. Sesshu Foster, *Amerasia Journal* 12.2 (1985–86): 126–28; Shirley Lim, *MELUS* 11.2 (1984): 85–90.

91.   ———. *The Next World: Poems by 32 Third World Americans.* Trumansburg, NY: Crossing Press, 1978.
        Contains *poems* by Mei-Mei Berssenbrugge, Jessica Tarahata Hagedorn, Lawson Fusao Inada, Geraldine Kudaka, Alex Kuo, Alan Chong Lau, and Shawn Wong.

92.   Bulkin, Elly, and Joan Larkin, eds. *Lesbian Poetry: An Anthology.* Watertown, MA: Persephone Press, 1981.
        Contains *poems* by Willyce Kim, Barbara Noda, and Kitty Tsui.

93.   Bulosan, Carlos, ed. *Chorus for America: Six Philippine Poets.* Foreword Dion O'Donnol. Los Angeles: Wagon & Star, Harvey Parker and Craftsmen, 1942.
        Poems by Cecilio Baroga, Carlos Bulosan, R. Zulueta Da Costa, R. T. Feria, C. B. Rigor, and José García Villa.

94.   ———, ed. *The Voice of Bataan.* New York: Coward-McCann, 1943.
        Poetry.
        Rev. William Rose Benét, *Saturday Review of Literature* 4 Dec. 1943: 22–24; *Booklist* 15 Jan. 1944: 79.

95.   Cachapero, Emily, et al., eds. *Liwanag: Literary and Graphic Expression by Filipinos in America.* San Francisco: Liwanag Publications, 1975.
        Includes selections by Emily Cachapero, Virginia Cerenio, Jessica Tarahata Hagedorn, Joselyn Ignacio, Nitamayo, Oscar Peñaranda, Al Robles, Luis Syquia, Serafin Syquia, Sam Tagatac, and Cyn Zarco.
        Rev. Tomas N. Santos, *Amerasia Journal* 5.2 (1978): 142–45.

96. Candelaria, Fred, et al., eds. *The Asian-Canadian and the Arts*. Spec. issue of *West Coast Review* 16.1 (1981).

Contains *prose* by Edy Goto, T. K. Higo, Roy Kiyooka, Sky Lee, Barry Wong, and Paul Yee; *poetry* by Mabel Chiu, David K. Fujino, Lakshmi Gill, Kevin Irie, Roy Kiyooka, Joy Kogawa, Helen Koyama, Carol Matsui, Suniti Namjoshi, S. Padmanab, Gerry Shikatani, Jim Wong-Chu, and Paul Yee.

97. Carroll, Dennis, ed. *Kumu Kahua Plays*. Honolulu: U of Hawaii P, 1983.

Drama by Lynette Amano, Arthur Aw, Bessie Toishigawa Inouye, Darrell H. Y. Lum, and Edward Sakamoto.

98. Casper, Leonard, ed. *New Writing from the Philippines: A Critique and Anthology*. New York: Syracuse UP, 1966.

Contains *short stories* by N. V. M. Gonzalez and Bienvenido Santos; *poems* by Carlos A. Angeles, Epifanio San Juan, José García Villa, and Manuel A. Viray.

99. Chiang, Fay, et al., eds. *American Born and Foreign: An Anthology of Asian American Poetry*. New York: Sunbury Press Books, 1979.

Poetry by Tomie Arai, Mei-Mei Berssenbrugge, Luis Cabalquinto, Laura Chan, Diana Chang, Carol Chen, George T. Chew, Fay Chiang, Frances Chung, Jessica Tarahata Hagedorn, Yuki Hartman, Lori Higa, Helen Wong Huie, Jason Hwang, Lawson Fusao Inada, Lonny Kaneko, Alan Chong Lau, Todd Lee, George Leong, Genny Lim, Willow D. Mark, Janice Mirikitani, Lane Nishikawa, Merle Okada, Richard Oyama, Oscar Peñaranda, Clarita Roja, Laura Tokunaga, Karl C. Wang, Chester Wong, Nellie Wong, Doug Yamamoto, and Susan L. Yung.

Rev. Ben Pleasants, *Los Angeles Times* 22 Aug. 1980, pt. 5: 26; Sharon Wong, *Bridge* 7.3 (1980): 46.

100. Chin, Frank, et al., eds. *AIIIEEEEE! An Anthology of Asian-American Writers*. 1974. Washington: Howard UP, 1983.

The introduction includes a brief historical review and the editors' definition of Asian American literature. *Fiction* by Carlos Bulosan, Jeffery Paul Chan, Diana Chang, Louis Chu, Wallace Lin, Toshio Mori, John Okada, Oscar Peñaranda, Sam Tagatac, Shawn Hsu Wong, Hisaye Yamamoto, and Wakako Yamauchi; *drama* by Frank Chin and Momoko Iko. The 1983 paperback edition contains an introduction by S. E. Solberg to Filipino American literature.

Rev. Bill Wong, *Bridge* 3.5 (1975): 34–35; Suzi Wong, *Amerasia Journal* 3.2 (1976): 134–42.

101. ———, eds. *The Big AIIIEEEEE! An Anthology of Asian-American Writers*. Forthcoming.

Discusses Asian American history, culture, and literature.

102. Chock, Eric, ed. *Small Time Kid Hawaii*. Spec. issue of *Bamboo Ridge* 12 (1981).

A collection of children's poetry.

Rev. Pat Matsueda, *Hawaii Literary Arts Council Newsletter* Feb.-Mar. 1982: n. pag.

103.   Chock, Eric, and Darrell H. Y. Lum, eds. *The Best of* Bamboo Ridge: The
        Hawaii Writers' Quarterly. Honolulu: Bamboo Ridge Press, 1986.
            Contains separate introductions by the editors. *Poetry* by Sheri Mae
        Akamine, Eric Chock, Herbert Chun, Wanda K. Fujimoto, Dana Naone
        Hall, Gail N. Harada, Jean Yamasaki Toyama, Jo Ann M. Uchida, and
        Tamara Wong-Morrison; *fiction* by Marshall M. Doi, Virgilio Menor Fe-
        lipe, Gail N. Harada, Violet Harada, Clara Mitsuko Jelsma, Hiroshi
        Kawakami, Jody Manabe Kobayashi, Charles M. Kong, Darrell H. Y. Lum,
        Rodney Morales, Susan Nunes, Ty Pak, Patsy S. Saiki, Wini Terada, Toshi,
        Mary Wakayama, and Sylvia A. Watanabe; *article* by Stephen H. Sumida.
            Rev. Arnold T. Hiura, *Hawaii Herald* 20 Mar. 1987: 10; Milton
        Murayama, *Literary Arts Hawaii* 85 (Summer 1987): 9.

104.   Chock, Eric, et al., eds. *Talk Story: An Anthology of Hawaii's Local
        Writers*. Foreword Maxine Hong Kingston. Honolulu: Petronium
        Press/Talk Story, 1978.
            Fiction by Koji Ariyoshi, George Gersaba, Mari Kubo, Darrell H. Y.
        Lum, Lowell Uda; *drama* by Darrell H. Y. Lum and Edward Sakamoto;
        poetry by Sheri Mae Akamine, Michael D. Among, Eric Chock, Herbert
        Chun, Fay Enos, Gail N. Harada, Mari Kubo, Wing Tek Lum, Jody
        Manabe, Dana Naone, Elizabeth Shinoda, Cathy Song, Mel Takahara, and
        Debra Thomas.

105.   Cochran, Jo, J. T. Stewart, and Mayumi Tsutakawa, eds. *Gathering
        Ground: New Writing and Art by Northwest Women of Color*. Seattle:
        Seal Press, 1984.
            Contains works by Lisa Furomoto, Sharon Hashimoto, Nancy Lee Ken-
        nel, Amy Nikaitani, Myrna Peña-Reyes, Bee Bee Tan, and Mayumi
        Tsutakawa.

106.   Croghan, Richard V., ed. *The Development of Philippine Literature in
        English (since 1900)*. Quezon City, Philippines: Alemar-Phoenix Publish-
        ing, 1975.
            Contains works by Carlos A. Angeles, N. V. M. Gonzalez, Bienvenido
        N. Santos, and José García Villa.

107.   Dabydeen, Cyril, and Rienzi Crusz, eds. *Another Way to Dance*. Toronto:
        Williams-Wallace, forthcoming.
            Works by South Asian Canadian writers.

108.   David-Maramba, Asuncion, ed. *Philippine Contemporary Literature in
        English and Pilipino*. Introd. Teodoro Evangelista. 1965. 5th ed. Rev. and
        enl. Manila: Bookmark, 1982.
            Contains works by Carlos A. Angeles, Alberto S. Florentino, N. V. M.
        Gonzalez, Bienvenido N. Santos, and José García Villa.

109.   *Dwell among Our People*. Berkeley: Asian American Studies Program,
        Univ. of California, 1977.
            Poetry by Berton Chow, Iris Cox, Kim Lee, Andy Nakaso, Edward Oda,
        Linda Sakamoto, and Carl Yee; *prose* by Berton Chow, Sharon Jeung, Kim
        Lee, and Edward Oda.

110.   Faderman, Lillian, and Barbara Bradshaw, eds. *Speaking for Ourselves: American Ethnic Writing.* 1969. 2nd ed. Glenview, IL: Scott, 1975.
        Textbook of ethnic American literature. The Asian American section has works by Carlos Bulosan, Diana Chang, Kuangchi C. Chang, Chiang Yee, Lee Yu-Hwa, Lin Yutang, Toshio Mori, Yone Noguchi, Bienvenido Santos, Toyo Suyemoto, Lloyd Tsugawa, Shiesei Tsuneishi, José García Villa, and Hisaye Yamamoto. The second edition includes Frank Chin, Lawson Inada, and Pam Koo but excludes Lee Yu-Hwa and Yone Noguchi.

111.   Farrell, E., Thomas Gage, and Raymond Rodrigues, eds. *I/You—We/They: Literature by and about Ethnic Groups.* Glenview, IL: Scott, 1976.
        Contains *prose* works by Daniel Inouye and C. Y. Lee; *poetry* by Kuangchi C. Chang, Lawson Inada, Joaquin Legaspi, and Janice Mirikitani.

112.   Fisher, Dexter, ed. *The Third Woman: Minority Women Writers of the United States.* Boston: Houghton, 1980.
        Includes works by Mei-Mei Berssenbrugge, Diana Chang, Fay Chiang, Jessica Hagedorn, Teru Kanazawa, Helen Aoki Kaneko, Maxine Hong Kingston, Geraldine Kudaka, Shirley Geok-Lin Lim, Laureen Mar, Janice Mirikitani, Gail Miyasaki, Joanne Harumi Sechi, Laura Tokunaga, Hisaye Yamamoto, Karen Tei Yamashita, Wakako Yamauchi, and Paula Yup.
        Rev. Patricia Liggins Hill, *MELUS* 7.3 (1980): 87–89.

112a.   Garcia, Mila A., Marra P. L. Lanot, and Lilia Quindoza Santiago, eds. *Filipina 1 & 2: Wo(men Writers in) Me(dia) N(ow).* 2 vols. Quezon City, Philippines: New Day Publishers, 1984. [Vol. 1: poetry, fiction, and drama; vol. 2: essays.]

113.   Gee, Emma, et al., eds. *Counterpoint: Perspectives on Asian America.* Los Angeles: Asian American Studies Center, Univ. of California, 1976.
        Literature section contains an introduction by Bruce Iwasaki. *Poems* by Mei-Mei Berssenbrugge, Emily Cachapero, Lawson Inada, Lonny Kaneko, Wing Tek Lum, Janice Mirikitani, Oscar Peñaranda, Alfred Robles, Luis Syquia, Serafin Syquia, Sam Tagatac, Ronald Tanaka, and Laura Tokunaga; *prose works* by Carlos Bulosan, Frank Chin, Momoko Iko, Toshio Mori, John Okada, Bienvenido Santos, Sui Sin Far, Shawn Hsu Wong, Hisaye Yamamoto, and Wakako Yamauchi.
        Rev. Shirley Hune, *Amerasia Journal* 5.1 (1978): 145–47; Bill Wong, *Bridge* 5.2 (1977): 51.

114.   Gill, Stephen, ed. *Green Snow: Anthology of Canadian Poets of Asian Origin.* Cornwall, ON: Vesta Publications, 1976.
        Poetry by Krishnarao V. Amembal, Rienzi Crusz, R. U. Gahun, Stephen Gill, Gurumel, Akbar Khan, Joy Kogawa, C. Lakshmi-Bai, Michael Ondaatje, S. Padmanab, Manjula Parakot, Uma Parameswaran, Gurcharan Rampuri, Ravindar Ravi, Sashikala Sankaran, Suprovat Sarkar, Brij M. Sarup, W. A. Shaheen, 'Nadan' B. N. Sinha, and Asoka Weerasinghe.
        Rev. George Bonavia, *International Corner* 49 (Oct. 1976): 2; *Canadian India Times* 2 Sept. 1976: 5; Peggy Fletcher, *Canadian Author & Bookman* 51.4 (1976): 25; *Link* 10 Aug. 1976: 6; *Quill & Quire* June 1976: 36.

115. Harris, Catherine E., and Barbara B. Robinson, eds. *Sandwich Isles U.S.A.: A Collection, Fifty Views of Hawaii by Forty-Five Authors and Four Artists.* Honolulu: Menehune Publishers, 1973.

Contains works by Darryl Cabacungan, Frankie Kam, Julienne K. Mikasa, Margaret Pai, Cynthia Quiocho, and Lowell Uda.

116. Harstad, James, and Joseph Stanton, eds. *The Ten Rules of Fishing: HERS/Bamboo Ridge Student Writing Competition Winners.* Spec. issue of *Bamboo Ridge* 26 (1985).

Works by Keith Abe, Lora Abe, Joy Asato, Alissa Fukushima, Edwin Horio, Lisa Horiuchi, Paula Kuwaye, Charles Lee, Lisa Masumoto, Byungwon Min, Darvie Miyashiro, Ryan Moon, Kyl Nakaoka, Michelle Shirasu, Kanji Takahashi, Keri Tanaka, Sathaya Tor, Darren Torres, Tracey Watada, and China Wong.

117. Harvey, Nick, ed. *Ting: The Caldron. Chinese Art and Identity in San Francisco.* San Francisco: Glide Urban Center, 1970.

A collection of short stories, essays, paintings, and poetry in both English and Chinese. Contains *prose works* by Loni Ding, Kai-yu Hsu, Lily Tom, Ling-chi Wang, J. Feisheng Wong, and Victor Wong; *poems* by Tseng Ta-yu and Nanying Stella Wong.

118. Haslam, Gerald W., ed. *Forgotten Pages of American Literature.* Boston: Houghton, 1970.

Contains works by Carlos Bulosan, S. I. Hayakawa, Richard Kim, Larry Kimura, Daisuke Kitagawa, Amy Lee, Lee Yu-Hwa, Lin Yutang, Miné Okubo, José García Villa, and Jade Snow Wong.

119. *The Hawk's Well: A Collection of Japanese American Art and Literature.* 1 vol. to date. San Jose: Asian American Art Projects, 1986.

Vol. 1 contains *poetry* by Zukin Hirasu, Jerrold Asao Hiura, Janice Mirikitani, and James Masao Mitsui; *short story* by Yoshiko Uchida. Vol. 2 forthcoming.

Rev. Stephen H. Sumida, *Amerasia Journal* 13.2 (1986–87): 245–47.

120. Hiura, Arnold T., Stephen H. Sumida, and Martha Webb, eds. *Talk Story: Big Island Anthology.* Honolulu: Talk Story and Bamboo Ridge Press, 1979.

A collection of writings by Asian Americans on the island of Hawaii. Includes works by Virgilio Felipe, Garrett Hongo, Larry Kimura, Clara Kubojiri, Kazuo Miyamoto, and Patsy Saiki.

121. Hom, Marlon K., ed. and trans. *Songs of Gold Mountain: Cantonese Rhymes from San Francisco Chinatown.* Berkeley: U of California P, 1987.

Contains a historical overview of Chinese American literature and translations of folk songs by early Chinese immigrants.

122. Hongo, Garrett Kaoru, ed. *Greenfield Review* 6.1–2 (1977).

Special issue on Asian American writers.

Rev. Tomas N. Santos, *Amerasia Journal* 5.2 (1978): 142–45.

123. Hongo, Garrett Kaoru, Alan Chong Lau, and Lawson Fusao Inada. *The Buddha Bandits down Highway 99*. Mountain View, CA: Buddhahead Press, 1978.
Poetry.
Rev. Lonny Kaneko, *Amerasia Journal* 6.2 (1979): 91–95; Sharon Wong, *Bridge* 7.3 (1980): 46.

124. Houston, James D., ed. *West Coast Fiction*. New York: Bantam, 1979.
Contains works by Maxine Hong Kingston, Shawn Hsu Wong, and Hisaye Yamamoto.

125. Hsu, Kai-yu, and Helen Palubinskas, eds. *Asian-American Authors*. 1972. Boston: Houghton, 1976.
Includes works by Chinese Americans, Japanese Americans, and Filipino Americans and provides a brief historical overview of each group included. *Poems* by Lawson Inada, Iwao Kawakami, Joaquin Legaspi, Russell C. Leong, Bayani L. Mariano, Alfred A. Robles, Samuel Tagatac, José García Villa, and Shawn H. Wong; *prose works* by Jeffery Paul Chan, Diana Chang, Frank Chin, J. C. Dionisio, N. V. M. Gonzalez, Daniel K. Inouye (with Lawrence Elliot), Virginia Lee, Pardee Lowe, Toshio Mori, Oscar Peñaranda, Bienvenido Santos, Jade Snow Wong, and Hisaye Yamamoto.
Rev. Suzi Wong, *Amerasia Journal* 2.1 (1973): 167–70.

126. Hsu, Vivian Ling, ed. *Born of the Same Roots: Stories of Modern Chinese Women*. Bloomington: Indiana UP, 1981.
Contains translated *stories* by Chen Jo-hsi, Pai Hsien-yung, and Yu Li-hua.

127. Huỳnh Sanh Thông, ed. and trans. *To Be Made Over: Tales of Socialist Reeducation in Vietnam*. New Haven: Yale Southeast Asia Studies, Yale Univ., 1987.
Contains stories by Nguyễn Mộng Giác and Nguyễn Ngọc Ngan.

128. Ifkovic, Edward. *American Letter: Immigrant and Ethnic Writing*. Englewood Cliffs, NJ: Prentice, 1975.
Textbook of ethnic American writing with *poetry* by Emmanuel Torres; *prose* by Carlos Bulosan, Robert Eng Dunn, Lin Yutang, Toshio Mori, and Ted Nakashima.

129. José, F. Sionil, ed. *Asian PEN Anthology*. Introd. Norman Cousins. New York: Taplinger, 1966.
Contains *fiction* by N. V. M. Gonzalez and Bienvenido N. Santos; *poetry* by Carlos Angeles and José García Villa.

130. Kalsey, Surjeet, ed. *Contemporary Literature in Translation* [Mission, BC] 26 (1977).
A Punjabi issue. Contains *poems* by Navtej Bharati, Jagjit Brar, Surinder Dhanjal, Gurumel, Gurnam Singh Kular, Gurcharan Rampuri, Ravinder Ravi, and Ajmer Rodey.

131. Kawaharada, Dennis, ed. *Bamboo Shoots: Stories and Poems for Kids.* Spec. issue of *Bamboo Ridge* 14 (1982).

Contains works by Dave Hagino, Violet Harada, Dennis Kawaharada, Maxine Hong Kingston, Darrell H. Y. Lum, Pat Matsueda, Oscar Peñaranda, Ramon V. Reyes, and Patsy S. Saiki.

132. Lai, Him Mark, Genny Lim, and Judy Yung, eds. and trans. *Island: Poetry and History of Chinese Immigrants on Angel Island, 1910–1940.* San Francisco: HOC DOI, 1980.

Original Chinese texts and English translations of 135 poems written by Chinese immigrants in the Angel Island immigration detention barracks. The introduction presents the history of the Angel Island Immigration Station.

Rev. Marlon Hom, *Amerasia Journal* 8.1 (1981): 133–36.

133. Lal, P., ed. *Modern Indian Poetry in English: An Anthology & A Credo.* 1969. 2nd ed. Calcutta: Writers Workshop, 1971.

Contains works by G. S. Sharat Chandra, G. V. Desani, R. de L. Furtado, Suniti Namjoshi, R. Parthasarathy, Balachandra Rajan, Tilottama Rajan, and A. K. Ramanujan.

134. Lauter, Paul, et al., eds. *The Heath Anthology of American Literature.* Lexington, MA: Heath, forthcoming.

135. Laygo, Teresito M., comp. *The Well of Time: Eighteen Short Stories from Philippine Contemporary Literature.* Los Angeles: Asian American Bilingual Center, 1978.

Includes *stories* by Carlos Bulosan, J. C. Dionisio, N. V. M. Gonzalez, and Bienvenido N. Santos.

136. Lee, Samuel S. O., ed. *75th Anniversary of Korean Immigration to Hawaii, 1903–1978.* Honolulu: 75th Anniversary of Korean Immigration to Hawaii Comm., 1978.

Contains creative writing and brief articles on the history of the Korean community in Hawaii.

137. Legaspi, Joaquin. *Joaquin Legaspi: Poet, Artist, Community Worker.* Comp. Jovina Navarro. El Verano, CA: Pilnachi Press, 1976.

Also includes *poems* dedicated to Legaspi by Robert Alan Fung, Joselyn Ignacio, Norman Jayo, Juanita Tamayo Lott, Jovina D. Navarro, Grace Wickham Odher, Al Robles, Luis Syquia, Jr., and Marge Talaugon.

138. Lumbera, Bienvenido, and Cynthia Nograles Lumbera, eds. *Philippine Literature: A History & Anthology.* Manila: National Book Store Publishers, 1982.

Contains works by Carlos A. Angeles, Alberto S. Florentino, N. V. M. Gonzalez, and Bienvenido N. Santos.

139. Martin, Patricia L., ed. *Love in Philippine Story and Verse.* Quezon City, Philippines: Bamboo Grove Assoc., 1953.

Contains works by Carlos A. Angeles, Carlos Bulosan, Bienvenido N. Santos, and Manuel A. Viray.

140.   McDowell, Jennifer, and M. Loventhal, eds. *Contemporary Women Poets: An Anthology of California Poets*. San Jose: Merlin Press, 1977.
         Includes *poems* by Norine Nishimura, Nancy Wong, Nanying Stella Wong.

141.   Mirikitani, Janice, et al., eds. *Ayumi: A Japanese American Anthology*. San Francisco: Japanese American Anthology Comm., 1980.
         A bilingual anthology of poetry, short stories, and visual arts by first-, second-, and third-generation Japanese Americans. *Poetry* by Takako Endo, Lori Reiko Higa, Garrett K. Hongo, Peter Y. Horikoshi, Momoko Iko, Lawson Fusao Inada, Lonny Kaneko, Norman M. Kaneko, Hiroshi Kashiwagi, Harue Kato, Iwao Kawakami, Toyo Kazato, Chris Kobayashi, Kisaburo Konoshima, Geraldine Kudaka, Janice Mirikitani, James Masao Mitsui, Grace Morizawa, Lane Kiyomi Nishikawa, Fumiko Ogawa, Francis Naohiko Oka, Donna Risé Omata, Alan K. Ota, Richard Oyama, Yasuo Sasaki, Jonny Kyoko Sullivan, Toyo Suyemoto, Y. J. Suzuki, Yuriko Takahashi, Ronald Tanaka, Akira Togawa, Yoshihiko Tomari, Mitsuye Yamada, Doug Yamamoto, Machiko Yamanaka, Issin Hitomi Yamasaki, Karen Tei Yamashita, Yoshio Yao, Taro Yashima, and Robert Kikuchi-Yngojo; *prose works* by Sue Kunitomi Embrey, Ryoichi Fujii, Akira Fujita, Yuriko Hoshiga, Lawson Fusao Inada, Ayako Ishigaki, Fred S. Kai, Taro Katayama, Robert H. Kono, Keiko Kubo, Tamaki Matsuno, Mitsuo Mitogawa, Toshio Mori, Setsuko Nagata, Shingo Nakamura, Shigeki Oka, Ginko Okazaki, Kazuichi Oki, Kon Oshima, Joe Oyama, Katsuma Sakai, Sasabune Sasaki, Ray K. Tsuchiyama, Hisaye Yamamoto, and Wakako Yamauchi.
         Rev. Sharon Maeda, *Amerasia Journal* 12.1 (1985–86): 116–19; Richard Oyama, *Bridge* 8.3 (1983): 43–44.

142.   ———, et al., eds. *Time to Greez! Incantations from the Third World*. Introd. Maya Angelou. San Francisco: Glide Publications/Third World Communications, 1975.
         A collection of creative writings by Afro-Americans, Asian Americans, Chicanos, and Native Americans. Contains *prose* by David Fong and *poetry* by Emily Cachapero, Curtis Choy, Dolores S. Feria, Jessica Tarahata Hagedorn, Thanh Hai, Lawson Fusao Inada, Orvy Jundis, Chris Kobayashi, Geraldine Kudaka, Kenneth Lee, George Leong, Wing Tek Lum, Bayani J. Mariano, Janice Mirikitani, Lane Nishikawa, Nitamayo, Oscar Peñaranda, Alfred Robles, Brenda Paik Sunoo, Luis Syquia, Jr., Serafin Malay Syquia, Sam Tagatac, Tsui Kit-Fan, Nanying Stella Wong, Doug Yamamoto, M. Yee, and Cyn Zarco.

143.   Moraga, Cherríe, and Gloria Anzaldúa, eds. *This Bridge Called My Back: Writings by Radical Women of Color*. Introd. Maya Angelou. Foreword Toni Cade Bambara. Watertown, MA: Persephone Press, 1981.
         Contains works by Genny Lim, Barbara Noda, Nellie Wong, Merle Woo, and Mitsuye Yamada.

144.   Mukherjee, Bharati, and Ranu Vanikar, eds. *Writing from the Indian Commonwealth*. Spec. issue of *Literary Review* 29.4 (1986).
         Contains *prose* by Neil Bissoondath, Cyril Dabydeen, Bharati Mukher-

jee, Peter Nazareth, Michael Ondaatje, and Roshni Rustomji; *poetry* by Suniti Namjoshi.

145. Nakano, Jiro, and Kay Nakano, eds. *Poets behind Barbed Wire*. Honolulu: Bamboo Ridge Press, 1983.
   Tanka written by four Hawaiian *issei*—Keiho Soga, Taisanboku Mori, Sojin Takei, Muin Ozaki—while in World War II internment camps.

146. Navarro, Jovina, comp. *Diwang Pilipino: Philippine Consciousness*. Davis: Asian American Studies, Univ. of California, 1974.
   Student-initiated anthology of short stories, essays, and poems. *Poems* by David Alcala, Simeon Doria Arroyo, Laurena Cabanero, Emily Cachapero, S. B. Garibay, Robert Kikuchi, Jeanette Lazam, Jovina Navarro, Vince Reyes, Luis Syquia, and Serafin Malay Syquia; *prose works* by Jo An Agcaoili, Kapatid Alan Gonzales, Juanita Tamayo Lott, Cynthia Maglaya, Jovina Navarro, Serafin Malay Syquia, Sid Valledor, and the Pilipino Organizing Collective.

147. ———, comp. *Lahing Pilipino: A Pilipino American Anthology*. Introd. J. D. Navarro. Davis: Mga Kapatid, Pilipino Student Assn., Univ. of California, 1977.
   Includes *poems* by Imelda Andrada, Delilia Dalit, R. A. Fung, Shirley Villalon Lewis, Theresa P. Montemayor, Marcelino Peneyra, Michael T. Peneyra, Sr., C. Rivera, M. Talaugon, and Robert Kikuchi-Yngojo.

148. Nazareth, Peter, ed., with Joseph K. Henry. *Journal of South Asian Literature* 18.1 (1983).
   Special issue on Goan literature. Contains works by Raul Furtado, Lino Leitão, Peter Nazareth, Ladis Da Silva, and Marion Da Silva.

149. Newman, Katharine D., ed. *The American Equation: Literature in a Multi-Ethnic Culture*. Boston: Allyn, 1971.
   Contains *stories* by José García Villa and Hisaye Yamamoto.

150. ———. *Ethnic American Short Stories*. New York: Washington Square Press, 1975.
   Contains works by Take Beekman, Frank Chin, and Hisaye Yamamoto.

151. Nishimura, Tomi, and Chusaburo Ito, eds. *Maple: Tanka Poems by Japanese Canadians*. Trans. Toyoshi Hiramatsu. Toronto: Continental Times, 1975.

152. Nixon, Lucille M., and Tomoe Tana, trans. *Sounds from the Unknown: A Collection of Japanese-American Tanka*. Denver: Alan Swallow, 1963.
   Tanka poems by Japanese Americans throughout the US.

153. Numrich, Charles. *Living Tapestries*. Minneapolis: Theatre Unlimited, 1986.
   Folktales and legends from the Hmong community in Minneapolis.

155. Okinawa Club of America. *History of the Okinawans in North America*. Trans. Ben Kobashigawa. Los Angeles: Okinawa Club of America and Asian American Studies Center, Univ. of California, 1988.
   Contains *poetry* by Chotei Adaniya, Seishu Aniya, Sayuri Higashi,

Ushinosuke Itomura, Hideo Kobashigawa, Jiro Kobashigawa, Shinsei Kochi, Jinkichi Matsuda, Tsuyuko Matsuda, Kazuko Matsumoto, Yosei Miyagi, Yoshino Nakama, Hana Nakamoto, Matsuji Shima, Shinsuke Taira, Toshiko Uechi, Masayuki Uema, Yoshiko Uesu, Kenden Yabe, Sumi Yabiku, Jippo Yogi, and Sadako Yogi; *prose* by Tofu Kochi, Rokumin, and Haruko Taira.

156. Okutsu, James K., project director. *Fusion '83: A Japanese American Anthology.* San Francisco: Asian American Studies Dept., San Francisco State Univ., 1984.
    Poetry and short stories by *issei, nisei,* and *sansei* writers. *Poems* by Paul K. Fujinaga, Hiroshi Kashiwagi, Lynne M. Kataoka, Kay Mainaga, Janice Mirikitani, Diane Y. Mitsuda, Taisanboku Mori, Richard Oyama, Muin Ozaki, Keiho Soga, Sojin Takei, Eugene Tashima, George Uba, Amy Uyematsu, and Doug Yamamoto; *prose works* by Gerri Igarashi, Soji C. Kashiwagi, Kevin Kato, Warren S. Kubota, Kay Mainaga, David Mas Masumoto, Toshio Mori, Carla Michie Nakata, Thalia Ohara, Welly Shibata, Eugene Tashima, and Sheridan Tatsuno.

157. ———. *Fusion-San.* San Francisco: Asian American Studies Dept., San Francisco State Univ., 1986.
    Prose by Thomas Arima, Clyde Fugami, Michiyo Fukaya, Richard Haratani, Lynne M. Kataoka, Gary Kawaguchi, I. S. Nakata, Linda Matsumoto, Joe Oyama, Richard Oyama, Gregory Mark Uba, Yachiyo Uehara, Yori Wada, Jennifer Y. Yazawa, and Gerri Igarashi Yoshida; *poetry* by Denise Okamoto and Jennifer Y. Yazawa.

158. ———. *Fusion Too: A Japanese American Anthology.* San Francisco: Asian American Studies Dept., San Francisco State Univ., 1985.
    Poems by Dina M. Harada, Ernest Michio Matsunaga, J. Moriyama, Richard Oyama, Susan Sugawara, Eugene Tashima, and Gregory Mark Uba; *prose* works by Candace Nosaka Ames, Clyde Fugami, Sumio Kubota, David Mas Masumoto, Louann Nosaka, Yoshie Tao, and Eugene Tashima.

159. Oyama, David, ed. *Bridge: An Asian American Perspective* 4.4 (1976).
    Special issue on Asian American poetry.

160. *The Pen.* Rowher, AK: The Outpost, 6 Nov. 1943.
    Collection of writing by individuals interned in the Rowher concentration camp. *Prose* by George Akimoto, Ichiro Hori, Jobo Nakamura, B. Saiki, Mort Shimabukuro, and Mitsu Yamada.

161. Planas, Alvin, et al., eds. *Hanai: An Anthology of Asian American Writings.* Berkeley: Asian American Studies, Dept. of Ethnic Studies, Univ. of California, 1980.
    A collection of creative writing by Asian Pacific Americans at the Univ. of California, Berkeley. *Poetry* by Marshall Lee, Cindy Leong, Barbara Maruoka, and Fae Ng; *prose works* by Diana Chow, Tim Fukai, Kimberly Kitano, Fae Ng, and Kevin Yuen; *drama* by Elaine Becker, Spencer Nakasako, and Merle Woo.

162. Reed, Ishmael, ed. *CALAFIA: The California Poetry*. Berkeley: Y'Bird Books, 1979.

    Poems by Carlos Bulosan, Jessica Hagedorn, Sadakichi Hartmann, Lawson Inada, Bunichi Kagawa, Iwao Kawakami, Geraldine Kudaka, Alan Chong Lau, George Leong, Oscar Peñaranda, Al Robles, Karen Yamashita, Connie Young Yu, and Cyn Zarco; *essays* by Shawn Wong and Wakako Yamauchi.

163. Reed, Ishmael, and Al Young, eds. *Quilt*. See *Quilt* in the Journals and Periodicals section.

164. ———. *Yardbird Lives!* New York: Grove, 1978.

    Includes *poems* by Mei-Mei Berssenbrugge, Lawson Fusao Inada, Wing Tek Lum, Merceditas Manabat, and Cyn Zarco; *prose works* by Jeffery Paul Chan, Doug Matsui, and Shawn Wong.

Reed, Ishmael, et al., eds. *Yardbird Reader*. See *Yardbird Reader* in the Journals and Periodicals section.

166. Reese, Lyn, Jean Wilkinson, and Phyllis Sheon Koppelman, eds. *I'm on My Way Running: Women Speak on Coming of Age*. New York: Avon, 1983.

    Contains *prose* by Maxine Hong Kingston, Aimee Liu, and Jade Snow Wong; *poetry* by Janice Mirikitani and Nellie Wong.

167. Roseburg, Arturo G., ed. *Pathways to Philippine Literature in English: An Anthology with Biographical and Critical Introductions*. Rev. ed. Quezon City, Philippines: Alemar-Phoenix Publishing, 1966.

    Contains works by Carlos Bulosan, N. V. M. Gonzalez, Bienvenido N. Santos, and José García Villa.

168. Shikatani, Gerry, and David Aylward, eds., with translations by David Aylward. *Paper Doors: An Anthology of Japanese-Canadian Poetry*. Toronto: Coach House, 1981.

    Poetry by David Fujino, Minoru Furusho, Kevin Irie, Chusaburo Koshu Ito, Midori Iwasaki, Roy Kiyooka, Joy Kogawa, Takeo Ujo Nakano, Hidetaro Shuzan Nishi, Tomi Nishimura, Sukeo Mokujin Sameshima, Gerry Shikatani, and Choichi Hando Sumi.

    Rev. Tara Cullis, *Canadian Literature* 97 (1983): 150–52; Momoye Sugiman, *Asianadian* 4.4 (1982): 21+.

169. Simone, Carol A., ed. *Networks: An Anthology of San Francisco Bay Area Women Poets*. Foreword Bonnie Lateiner. Introd. Carol A. Simone. Palo Alto: Vortex Editions, 1979.

    Contains *poems* by Jessica Hagedorn, Chris Kobayashi, and Genny Lim.

170. Stewart, Frank, ed. *Passages to the Dream Shore: Short Stories of Contemporary Hawaii*. Honolulu: U of Hawaii P, 1987.

    Contains works by Lanning Lee, Darrell H. Y. Lum, Susan Nunes, Patsy S. Saiki, Mary Wakayama, Sylvia Watanabe, and Cedric Yamanaka.

171. Stewart, Frank, and John Unterecker, eds. *Poetry Hawaii: A Contemporary Anthology*. Honolulu: U of Hawaii P, 1979.

    Includes *poetry* by Fred Caparoso, Laban Chang, Eric Chock, Sheryl Dare, Glenn John Kim, Leonard Kubo, Mari Kubo, Wing Tek Lum, Jody Manabe, Dana Naone, Elizabeth Shinoda, Cathy Song, Mel Takahara, and Reuben Tam.

    Rev. Marvin Bell, *Hawaii Review* 10 (1980): 186–87; Ilima Piianaia, *Mana* 6.1 (1981): 84–87.

172. Sunoo, Brenda Paik, ed. *Korean American Writings*. New York: Insight, 1975.

    Includes *poems* by John Sukjun Burke, Natalie Cha, Sungsook Choi, Gail Whang Desmond, Sim Hoon, Tong Il Kim, Edward Koh, Jai Lee, Sebastian R. Lee, Soon Ok, Suzie Park, Yun Am Park, Brenda Paik Sunoo, Chris Yim, Young Yoo, and Grace Yun.

173. Tachiki, Amy, et al., eds. *Roots: An Asian American Reader*. Los Angeles: Asian American Studies Center, Univ. of California, 1971.

    A collection of essays, reviews, and creative writing concerning Asian Americans. Divided into sections on identity, history, and community. Contains *poems* by Marie Chung, Lawson Inada, Shin'ya Ono, Al Robles, Ron Tanaka, Tomi Tanaka, and Mary Uyematsu; *essays* by Bruce Iwasaki and Ron Low.

174. *Third World Women*. San Francisco: Third World Communications, 1972.

    Literature by minority women. Contains *poetry* by Emily Cachapero, Connie Chan, Leslee Kimiko Inaba, Geraldine Kudaka, Diane Mark, Janice Mirikitani, Kitty Tsui, and Nanying Stella Wong; *prose* by Diana Lin; *drama* by Jessica Hagedorn.

175. Tsutakawa, Mayumi, and Alan Chong Lau, eds. *Turning Shadows into Light: Art and Culture of the Northwest's Early Asian/Pacific Community*. Seattle: Young Pine, 1982.

    Works by Carlos Bulosan, Garrett Kaoru Hongo, Lawson Fusao Inada, Shizue Iwatsuki, Lonny Kaneko, Alan Chong Lau, Laureen Mar, James Masao Mitsui, S. E. Solberg, and Sui Sin Far.

    Rev. Esther Sugai, *East Wind* 1.2 (1982): 62.

176. Unbound Feet (A Chinese American Women Writers Collective). *Unbound Feet: A Collective of Chinese American Women Writers*. San Francisco: Isthmus Press, 1981.

177. Wand, David Hsin-Fu, ed. *Asian-American Heritage: An Anthology of Prose and Poetry*. New York: Washington Square Press, 1974.

    A collection of stories, poems, essays, novel excerpts, and oral poetry with commentary for each section. *Short stories* by Richard E. Kim, Kim Yong Ik, Toshio Mori, and Hisaye Yamamoto; *poetry* by Diana Chang, Ling Chung, John Hideyo Hamamura, Sadakichi Hartmann, Alexander Kuo, Stephen S. N. Liu, Wing Tek Lum, Suzi Mee, Janice Mirikitani, Paul Motoyoshi, Jr., Francis Naohiko Oka, José García Villa, and David Rafael Wang; *essays* by Daniel Iwao Okimoto and Irvin Paik; *prose excerpts* from

works by Carlos Bulosan, Diana Chang, Younghill Kang, Pardee Lowe, and John Okada; *oral poetry* from Samoa and Hawaii.
Rev. Bill Wong, *Bridge* 4.2 (1976): 47; Suzi Wong, *Amerasia Journal* 3.2 (1976): 134–42.

178. *We Won't Move: Poems and Photographs of the International Hotel Struggle.* San Francisco: Kearny Street Workshop Press, 1977.

179. Wong, Shawn, and Frank Chin, eds. *Yardbird Reader* 3 (1974).
A special Asian American issue.
Contains *poetry* by Mei-Mei Berssenbrugge, Ben Fee, Lawson Fusao Inada, Alexander Kuo, Alan Chong Lau, George Leong, Wing Tek Lum, Al Robles, and Cyn Zarco; *prose* by Jeffery Paul Chan, Shawn Hsu Wong, Hisaye Yamamoto, and Wakako Yamauchi.
Rev. Suzi Wong, *Amerasia Journal* 3.2 (1976): 134–42.

180. Yabes, Leopoldo Y., ed. *Philippine Short Stories 1925–1940.* Quezon City: U of the Philippines P, 1975.
Contains *fiction* by N. V. M. Gonzalez, Bienvenido N. Santos, and José García Villa.

181. ———. *Philippine Short Stories 1941–1955.* 2 vols. Quezon City: U of the Philippines P, 1981.
Contains *fiction* by Carlos Bulosan, N. V. M. Gonzalez, Maximo Ramos, Bienvenido N. Santos, and Manuel A. Viray.

182. *Yellow Peril.* New York: Basement Workshop, 1972.
An anthology with *poetry* by Henri Chang, George T. Chew, Fay Chiang, Betty Chin, Lois Chin, Curtis Choy, John Chu, Frances Chung, Pamela Eguchi, John Eng, Lova Eng, Bob Fong, Larry Hama, Isomi Handrych, Dennis Hirota, Chris Iijima, Koon Jo, Yasunori Gene Kita, Wally Lim, Lili Liu, Alice Look, Joanne Miyamoto, Toyo Obayashi, Tomi Tanaka Ohta, Shin'ya Ono, John Saka, Dorothy Suzuki, Serafin Syquia, Takashi Yanagida, Aileen Yip, Bun Yoshikami, and Richard Young; *prose* by Pamela Eguchi.

183. *Yoisho! An Anthology of the Japantown Arts and Media Workshop.* San Francisco: Japantown Art and Media Workshop, 1983.
Contains *prose works* by Keiko Kubo, Warren Kubota, Presco Tabios, Sheridan Tatsuno, and John Togashi; *poems* by Jeff Leong, Hayami Miyasato, Grace Morizawa, Richard Oyama, Sheridan Tatsuno, and Doug Yamamoto.

Journals and Periodicals

184.   *Aion*. San Francisco: Asian American Publications.
       Arts and political journal. Irregular publication dates. 1970–71.

185.   *Aloha*. Formerly *Hawaiian Digest* (1947–48). Honolulu: Pacific Publication.
       Quarterly. Published a selection of articles from Honolulu publications and original articles about Hawaii. 1949–51.

186.   *Aloha: The Magazine of Hawaii and the Pacific*. Honolulu: Davick Publications.
       Bimonthly. 1977–.

187.   *Amerasia: A Review of America and the Far East*. New York: American Friends of the Chinese People.
       1937–47.

188.   *The Amerasia Journal*. Los Angeles: Asian American Studies Center, Univ. of California.
       Semiannual interdisciplinary journal that often includes creative writing. Special issue on Carlos Bulosan: 6.1 (1979); special issue on Asian American literature 1910–82: 9.2 (1982). Originally published at Yale Univ. 1971–.

189.   *The Antigonish Review*. Antigonish, NS: St. Francis Xavier Univ.
       Quarterly. Publishes poetry, short stories, criticism, and book reviews. Frequently includes works by South Asian Canadians. 1970–.

190.   *Archipelago: The International Magazine of the Philippines*. Manila: Dept. of Public Information, Bureau of National and Foreign Information.
       Monthly.

191.   *Ariel*. Calgary: U of Calgary P.
       Quarterly. Review of international literature in English. 1970–.

192.   *Asianadian*. Toronto: Asianadian Resource Workshop.
       Quarterly. Arts and political journal dealing with Asians in Canada. 1978–.

193.   *Asian American Review*. Berkeley: Asian American Studies, Dept. of Ethnic Studies, Univ. of California.
       Interdisciplinary journal. 1972–76.

The Asterisk. See *Hawaii Review*.

194.   *Bamboo Ridge: The Hawaii Writers' Quarterly*. Honolulu: Bamboo Ridge Press and the Hawaiian Ethnic Resource Center, Talk Story.
       Creative writing journal. 1978–.

195. *Bridge: Asian American Perspectives*. New York: Basement Workshop/Asian Cinevision.
     Quarterly. Politics and culture of Asian Americans. Poetry issue: 4.4 (1976); literature issue: 8.4 (1983). 1971–85.

196. *Bulletin of Concerned Asian Scholars*. Berthoud, CO: Comm. of Concerned Asian Scholars.
     Quarterly. Special Asian American issue: 4.3 (1972). 1968–.

197. *Bulletin of the Chinese Historical Society of America*. San Francisco: Chinese Historical Soc. of America.
     Published ten times a year. 1966–.

198. *Caliban*. Ann Arbor: Caliban.
     Prose, poetry, and art. Published twice a year. 1986–.

199. *CALYX: A Journal of Art and Literature by Women*. Corvallis, OR: Calyx.
     Triannual. Literary magazine. Special issue on Asian American women is forthcoming. 1976–.

200. *Canadian Ethnic Studies*. Calgary: Research Centre for Canadian Ethnic Studies, Univ. of Calgary, for the Canadian Ethnic Studies Assn.
     Interdisciplinary journal devoted to the study of ethnicity, immigration, intergroup relations, and the cultural life of ethnic groups in Canada. 1969–.

201. *Canadian Literature/Littérature Canadienne*. Vancouver: Univ. of British Columbia.
     Quarterly. Occasionally publishes articles on Asian Canadians. 1959–.

201a. *Chelsea*. New York: Chelsea Assoc.
     International and interethnic journal. Publishes poetry, fiction, and art. Irregular publication dates. 1958–.

202. *Clay: A Literary Notebook*. Albuquerque: Univ. of New Mexico.
     Quarterly. Frequently published short stories and poems by Asian Americans. 1931–32.

203. *Common Ground*. New York: Common Council for American Unity.
     Quarterly. Journal focusing on the various cultures of America. 1940–49.

204. *Contact II*. Formerly *Contact*. New York: Contact II Publications.
     Bimonthly poetry review. Special issue on Asian American poetry: 7.38–40 (1986). 1976–.

205. *Critical Perspectives of Third World America*. Berkeley: Ethnic Studies Student Union and Editorial Board Council, Univ. of California.
     Semiannual interdisciplinary journal. 1983–84.

206. *East/West: The Chinese American Journal*. San Francisco: East/West Chinese-American Journal.
     Weekly newspaper. In English and Chinese. 1967–.

207. *East Wind: Politics and Culture of Asians in the U. S.* Oakland: Getting Together Publications.

Semiannual. Special issue on art and literature, ed. Fred Wei-han Houn: 5.1 (1986). 1982–.

208. *Echoes.* Formerly *Echoes from Gold Mountain* (1978–82). Long Beach: California State Univ.
Literature and arts journal. Irregular publication dates. 1987–.

Echoes from Gold Mountain. See *Echoes.*

209. *Ethnic Forum: Journal of Ethnic Studies and Ethnic Bibliography.* Kent: Center for the Study of Ethnic Publications, Kent State Univ./Intercollegiate Academic Council on Ethnic Studies Serving Ohio.
Semiannual interdisciplinary journal. 1980–.

210. *Ethnic Groups: An International Periodical of Ethnic Studies.* London: Gordon & Breach.
Quarterly interdisciplinary journal. 1976–.

211. *Explorations in Ethnic Studies: The Journal of the National Association of Interdisciplinary Ethnic Studies.* Claremont, CA: National Assn. of Interdisciplinary Ethnic Studies.
Semiannual interdisciplinary journal. 1978–.

Gidra. See *Pacific Ties.*

212. *The Greenfield Review: A Magazine of Contemporary Poetry.* Greenfield Center, NY: Greenfield Review Press.
Semiannual journal of creative writing. Special issue on Asian American literature: 6.1–2 (1977). 1970–.

213. *Hanai.* Honolulu: State Foundation on Culture and the Arts.
One issue only: 1 (1977). Literary contributions from Hawaiian writers.

214. *Hapa.* Wailuku, HI: Xenophobia Press.
Literary journal. 1981–83.

Hawaiian Digest. See *Aloha.*

Hawaii Literary Arts Council Newsletter. See *Literary Arts Hawaii.*

Hawaii Literary Review. See *Hawaii Review.*

The Hawaii Quill Magazine. See *Hawaii Review.*

215. *Hawaii Review* (1973–). Formerly *The Hawaii Quill Magazine* (1928–37), *The Lit* (1951–52), *Ka Lama* (1952–54), *The Asterisk* (1955–61?), *Kapa* (1963–1972), and *Hawaii Literary Review* (1973). Honolulu: Univ. of Hawaii, Manoa.
Semiannual creative journal. For entries from *The Hawaii Quill Magazine*, *The Lit*, *Ka Lama*, *The Asterisk*, and *Kapa*, all of which are student publications, see *Asian American Literature of Hawaii* [#11].

216. *Hokubei Mainichi.* San Francisco.
Japanese American daily that occasionally prints creative writing.

217. *Honolulu.* Formerly *Paradise of the Pacific* (1888–1966). Honolulu: Honolulu Publishing.
Monthly. 1966–.

218.   *Insights*. New York: Insights.

        Bimonthly Korean American publication. Discontinued.

219.   *Interracial Books for Children Bulletin*. Formerly *Interracial Books for Children* (quarterly, 1966–75). New York: Council on Interracial Books for Children.

        Analyzes children's books and other learning materials for racism, sexism, and ageism. Published eight times a year. Special double issue, *The Portrayal of Asian Americans in Children's Books*: 7.2–3 (1976). 1976–.

220.   *José: The Literary Quarterly of the Philippines*. Manila: Philippine Writers' Foundation.

        1982–.

221.   *The Journal of Ethnic Studies*. Bellingham: Western Washington State Coll.

        Quarterly interdisciplinary journal. Special issue on the Asian experience in America: 4.1 (1976). 1973–.

222.   *Journal of South Asian Literature*. Formerly *Mahfil*. East Lansing: Asian Studies Center, Michigan State Univ.

        Semiannual. 1963–.

Ka Lama. See *Hawaii Review*.

Kapa. See *Hawaii Review*.

223.   *Kashu Mainichi*. Los Angeles.

        Japanese American daily newspaper. Occasionally prints creative writing. 1931–41; 1947–.

224.   *Korean Culture*. Los Angeles: Korean Cultural Service.

        Quarterly. Occasionally publishes fiction and poetry by Korean Americans. 1980–.

225.   *Likhaan: Multi-Lingual Creative Writing Journal*. Diliman, Quezon City: Univ. of the Philippines Creative Writing Center.

        Semiannual. 1979–.

The Lit. See *Hawaii Review*.

226.   *Literary Arts Hawaii*. Formerly the *Hawaii Literary Arts Council Newsletter* (bimonthly, 1975–83). Honolulu: Hawaii Literary Arts Council.

        Quarterly, though frequently irregular. 1983–.

Mahfil. See *Journal of South Asian Literature*.

227.   *Mana: South Pacific Journal of Language and Literature*. Formerly *Mana Annual of Creative Writing*. Hawaii Edition. Suva, Fiji: South Pacific Creative Arts Soc., Mana Publications, and *Seaweeds and Constructions*. Biannual. 1973–.

228.   *The Manila Review: Philippines Journal of Literature and the Arts*. Manila: Dept. of Public Information, Bureau of National and Foreign Information.

        Quarterly. 1975–.

229. *MELUS: The Journal of the Society for the Study of the Multi-Ethnic Literature of the United States.*
   Quarterly. Irregular place of publication. Literary criticism and book reviews of ethnic American literature. Vol. 3-, 1975-.

230. *Nisei: In Hawaii and the Pacific.* Honolulu: Hawaii Circulation.
   Quarterly. Published fiction occasionally. 1947-56.

231. *Overland Monthly.* Interim journal: *Californian* (1880-82). San Francisco.
   Frequently published short stories about Chinese immigrants. 1868-75, 1883-1935.

232. *The Pacific Citizen.* Los Angeles.
   Weekly official newspaper of the Japanese American Citizens League. Holiday issues feature Japanese American writers. 1930-.

233. *Pacific Ties: The Voice of the Asian Pacific Community.* Formerly *Gidra* (1969-74). Los Angeles: ASUCLA Communications Board.
   Published six times yearly. Frequently includes creative writing. 1974-.

234. *The Paper.* Independent publication. Ed. Pat Matsueda. Honolulu: Petronium Press.
   Bimonthly. Literary magazine. 1980-86.

Paradise of the Pacific. See *Honolulu.*

235. *Poetry East & West.* Honolulu: East-West Center.
   Irregular publication dates. 1981-?

236. *Quilt.* Berkeley.
   Semiannual. A multicultural literary journal. 1980-.

237. *The Rafu Shimpo.* Los Angeles.
   Japanese American daily newspaper. Holiday issues feature Japanese American creative writers. 1903-.

238. *Ramrod.* Wahiawa, HI: Iron Bench Press.
   Poetry and art annual. 1980-.

239. *Reimei.* Salt Lake City: Reimei Club.
   Japanese American literary magazine. 1931-33.

240. *RIKKA.* Manitoulin Island, ON: Plowshare Press.
   Quarterly. Devoted to Asian Canadian studies. 1974-.

241. *Rising Waters.* Santa Cruz: Asian American Student Alliance, Univ. of California.
   Annual creative arts journal. 1975-76.

242. *Seaweeds and Constructions: Honolulu's Art and Literary Magazine.* Honolulu: Elepaio Press.
   Semiannual. Special issue, *Anthology Hawaii*: 6.1 (1979). 1976-79.

243. *Short Story International.* Great Neck, NY: International Cultural Exchange.
   Switches from monthly (1963-65) to bimonthly. 1977-.

244. *Solidarity: Current Affairs, Ideas and the Arts.* Manila: Solidaridad Publishing House.
     Irregular frequency of publication. 1965–.

245. *The Toronto South Asian Review.* Toronto.
     Triannual. 1982–.

246. *Trek.* Topaz: Central Utah Relocation Center.
     Journal published by Japanese Americans interned at the Topaz concentration camp. 1943–44.

247. *Tulean Dispatch Magazine.* Newell, CA: *Daily Tulean Dispatch.*
     Published by Japanese American internees in the Tule Lake concentration camp. 1942–43.

248. *The Vietnam Forum: A Review of Vietnamese Culture.* New Haven: Yale Southeast Asia Studies.
     Semiannual. 1983–.

249. *Yardbird Reader.* Variant title: *Y'bird.* Berkeley: Yardbird Publishing.
     A multiethnic annual. Special Asian American issue, ed. Shawn Wong and Frank Chin: 3 (1974). 1971–76.

Primary Sources

Chinese American Literature

Prose

250. Abbott, Jack Henry. *In the Belly of the Beast: Letters from Prison*. Introd. Norman Mailer. New York: Random, 1981.
    Describes the atrocity of prison.
    Rev. John A. Barnes, *National Review* 21 Aug. 1981: 974; Jack Beatty, *New Republic* 1–8 Aug. 1981: 38–39; James Boatwright, *Book World* 12 June 1981: 1–2; Anatole Broyard, *New York Times* 20 June 1981: 15; John McCarthy, *Times Literary Supplement* 22 Jan. 1982: 74; Terrence Des Pres, *New York Times Book Review* 19 July 1981: 3+.

251. *Au, Wanda Kulamanu Ellis. "My Manoa Ghetto." *Sandwich Isles U.S.A.* [#115] 18–20.
    Describes the author's old neighborhood.

252. *Au, Yat Cho. "Hawaiian Tragedy." *Paradise of the Pacific* Nov. 1946: 27.
    Two young boys take a night swim during which one of them dies.

Babcock, Winnifred Eaton. See Watanna, Onoto.

253. Chan, Jeffery Paul. "Auntie Tsia Lays Dying." *Aion* 1.2 (1971): 82–87.
    Rpt. in *Asian-American Authors* [#125] 77–85.
    Describes an old aunt who fabricates tall tales about China.

254. ———. "Cheap Labor." *Amerasia Journal* 9.2 (1982): 99–116.
    Rpt. in *Bamboo Ridge* 17 (1982–83): 51–67.
    Depicts the incongruity among the immigrant and American-born members of a family.

255. ———. "The Chinese in Haifa." *AIIIEEEEE!* [#100] 12–29.
    Centers on a recently divorced Chinese American who has an affair with his Jewish neighbor's wife.

256. ———. "Jackrabbit." *Yardbird Reader* 3 [#179] 217–38.
    Rpt. in *Yardbird Lives!* [#164] 71–93.
    Two Chinese American men suffer racist abuse in Nevada.

257. ———. "Sing Song Plain Song." *Amerasia Journal* 3.2 (1976): 23–37.
    A Chinese American seeks a pattern of existence amid disparate experiences.

258. Chan, Leonard. "Green Striped Pajamas." *Clipper* 2.3 (1941): 27–29.
    About a soldier fighting in World War II.

259. Chan, Richard C. "Mr. Chan, the Tailor." *Bridge* 5.3 (1977): 22–28.

A tailor who is constantly being stereotyped describes his inner thoughts about various customers.

260.　Chang, Diana. *Eye to Eye.* New York: Harper, 1974.
　　　A satirical novel about an artist who discovers his art while undergoing psychotherapy.
　　　Rev. Blanche H. Gelfant, *Hudson Review* 28 (1975): 312–13.

261.　———. "[Excerpt] From *Intimate Friends* [forthcoming novel]." *The Third Woman* [#112] 501–04.
　　　Describes a love-making scene.

262.　———. *The Frontiers of Love.* New York: Random, 1956. Excerpts in *AIIIEEEEE!* [#100] 31–48; *Asian-American Heritage* [#177] 255–58.
　　　A novel about a group of Eurasians and their families living in Shanghai during the Japanese occupation.
　　　Rev. Kay Boyle, *American Scholar* 26 (1957): 226–28; Kenneth Rexroth, *Nation* 29 Sept. 1956: 271–73.

263.　———. "Getting Around." *North American Review* Dec. 1986: 46–49.
　　　Describes a woman's numerous short-term relationships with men.

264.　———. *The Gift of Love.* New York: Ballantine, 1978.
　　　Based on a teleplay by Caryl Ledner.

265.　———. *The Only Game in Town.* New York: New American Library, 1963.
　　　A political satire about the love between a Caucasian Peace Corps volunteer and a Communist Chinese dancer.

266.　———. *A Passion for Life.* New York: Random, 1961.
　　　A Caucasian woman impregnated by a rapist hesitates to report the crime.

267.　———. *A Perfect Love.* New York: Jove, 1978.
　　　A novel about a designer who feels sexually frustrated in her marriage and who develops a crush on a younger man.

268.　———. "The Story That Swallowed Itself." *Confrontation* 30–31 (1985): 81–86.
　　　Describes a painter's artistic response to marital conflict.

269.　———. "Why Do Writers Write?" *American Pen* 1.1 (1969): 1–3.
　　　Describes the drive to write.

270.　———. *A Woman of Thirty.* New York: Random, 1959.
　　　Describes an unhappy love affair between a divorced woman and a married man; set in the publishing world of New York City.

271.　Chang, Eileen [Chang Ai-ling]. "The Golden Cangue." Trans. author. *Twentieth Century Chinese Stories.* Ed. C. T. Hsia, with Joseph S. M. Lau. New York: Columbia UP, 1971. 138–91.
　　　Rpt. in *Modern Chinese Stories and Novellas: 1919–1949.* Ed. Joseph S. M. Lau, C. T. Hsia, and Leo Ou-fan Lee. New York: Columbia UP, 1981. 530–59.

The novella traces the career of a willful woman in a decadent feudal family.

272. ———. *Naked Earth*. Trans. author. Kowloon, Hong Kong: Union Press, 1956.
A novel about China.

273. ———. *The Rice-Sprout Song*. Trans. author. New York: Scribner's, 1955.
Describes the effect of the Communist regime on a peasant family.

274. ———. *The Rouge of the North*. London: Cassell, 1967.

275. ———. "Shame, Amah!" Trans. author. *Eight Stories by Chinese Women*. Ed. Nieh Hua-ling. Taipei: Heritage Press, 1962. 91–114.
Describes a day in the life of a Chinese maid employed by a foreigner in Shanghai.

276. ———. "Stale Mates: A Short Story Set in the Time When Love Came to China." *Reporter* 20 Sept. 1956: 34–38.

277. Chang, Glenn. "In the Blood." *The Edge of Space: Three Original Novellas of Science Fiction by Glenn Chang, Phyllis Gotlieb, Mark J. McGarry*. Ed. Robert Silverberg. New York: Elsevier/Nelson Books; Don Mills, ON: Thomas Nelson, 1979. 75–143.

278. ———. "Stars and Darkness." *Universe 6*. Ed. Terry Carr. Garden City: Doubleday, 1976. 130–50.
A sadistic man offers dream sessions to the inmates of a spaceship.

279. Chang, Hsin-Hai. *The Fabulous Concubine*. New York: Simon, 1956.
Set in China and Europe, the novel reveals the Chinese official mind during the Boxer Rebellion of 1900.
Rev. Chiang Yee, *New York Times* 16 Sept. 1956: 40.

280. ———. *Letters from a Chinese Diplomat*. Shanghai: Chinese American Publishing, 1948.

281. ———. *Within the Four Seas: Being the Views of a Disciple of Confucius on the Prospects of Peace on Earth*. New York: Twayne, 1958.

282. Chang, Lily. "What It's Like to Be a Chinese-American Girl." *Cosmopolitan* Oct. 1978: 206+.
Autobiographical essay.

283. Chao, Buwei Yang. *Autobiography of a Chinese Woman*. Trans. Yuen-ren Chao. 1947. Westport, CT: Greenwood, 1970.

284. Chao, Evelina. *Gates of Grace*. New York: Warner, 1985.
A novel about a young Chinese woman who immigrates to New York Chinatown after the Chinese Revolution of 1949.
Rev. Don Lau, *Asian Week* 18 Oct. 1985: 24; Mao-chu Lin, *Minnesota Daily* 25 Nov. 1985: 14+.

285. Chao, Ming-Heng Thomas. *Shadow Shapes: Memoirs of a Chinese Student in America*. Peking: Peking Leader Press, 1928.
Autobiography.

Chen Hsiu-mei. See Chen Jo-hsi.

286.   Chen Jo-hsi [Lucy Hsiu-mei Chen Tuan]. Also Chen Ruoxi. *"The Execu-tion of Mayor Yin," and Other Stories from the Great Proletarian Cul-tural Revolution.* Trans. Nancy Ing and Howard Goldblatt. London: Allen, 1979.

287.   ———. "The Last Performance." Trans. Timothy A. Ross and Joseph S. M. Lau. *Chinese Stories from Taiwan: 1960–1970.* Ed. Joseph S. M. Lau, with Timothy A. Ross. New York: Columbia UP, 1976. 3–12.
         Describes the effect of narcoticism on an opera singer.

288.   ———. "A Morning for Chao-ti." Trans. Nieh Hua-ling. *Eight Stories by Chinese Women.* Ed. Nieh Hua-ling. Taipei: Heritage Press, 1962. 43–52.

289.   ———. "My Friend Ai Fen." Trans. Richard Kent and Vivian Hsu. *Born of the Same Roots* [#126] 277–302.
         Rpt. in *The Old Man and Other Stories* 81–111.
         Describes the checkered love life of a gynecologist during the Cultural Revolution.

290.   ———. *The Old Man and Other Stories.* Hong Kong: Renditions Paper-backs, 1986.

291.   ———. *Spirit Calling: Five Stories of Taiwan.* Taipei: Heritage Press, 1962.
         "Spirit Calling" is rpt. in *New Voices: Stories and Poems by Young Chi-nese Writers.* Trans. and ed. Nancy Ing. 2nd ed. San Francisco: Chinese Materials Center, 1980.

292.   ———. "Ting Yun." Trans. Chi-Chen Wang. *Renditions* [Hong Kong] 10 (1978): 93–100.
         Rpt. in *Two Writers and the Cultural Revolution.* Ed. George Kao. Hong Kong: Chinese UP, 1980. 133–40. Rpt. as "Ding Yun" in *The Old Man and Other Stories* 63–79.

293.   ———. "The Tunnel." Trans. Chi-Chen Wang. *Renditions* [Hong Kong] 10 (1978): 101–09.
         Rpt. in *Two Writers and the Cultural Revolution.* Ed. George Kao. Hong Kong: Chinese UP, 1980. 141–49; *Canadian Fiction Magazine* 36–37 (1980): 108–20; *The Old Man and Other Stories* 45–62.
         Because of political reasons, a retired factory worker in Nanking is un-able to marry a woman he loves.

Chen, Lucy H. M. See Chen Jo-hsi.

Chen Ruoxi. See Chen Jo-hsi.

294.   Chen, Yuan-tsung. *The Dragon's Village.* New York: Pantheon, 1980.
         An autobiographical novel about land reform in China.
         Rev. Jonathan Spence, *New York Review of Books* 17 Apr. 1980: 20.

295.   Cheng, Josephine. "Forgive and Remember." *Quilt* 2 (1981): 32–38.
         Describes a homecoming.

296. Cheng, Nien. *Life and Death in Shanghai*. New York: Grove, 1987.
An autobiographical account of life during the Chinese Cultural Revolution.

297. Chennault, Anna [Chan]. *Chennault and the Flying Tigers*. New York: Paul S. Eriksson, 1963.
Biography.

298. ———. *The Education of Anna*. New York: Times Books, 1980.
Autobiography.

299. ———. *A Thousand Springs: The Biography of a Marriage*. Introd. Lin Yutang. New York: Paul S. Eriksson, 1962.
Describes the author's marriage with Claire Chennault, US Air Force general who organized the Flying Tigers in China during World War II.

Chiang I. See Chiang Yee.

300. Chiang, Monlin. *Tides from the West: A Chinese Autobiography*. New Haven: Yale UP, 1947.
The author was a Chinese statesman who had been minister of education and secretary-general of the cabinet under Chiang Kai-Shek.

301. Chiang Yee. Also Chiang I. *The Silent Traveller in Boston*. New York: Norton, 1959.
Prose, poetry, and painting recording the author's impressions of Boston.

302. ———. *The Silent Traveller in New York*. New York: Day, 1950.
Prose, poetry, and painting about the author's impressions of New York.

303. ———. *The Silent Traveller in San Francisco*. New York: Norton, 1964.
Contains comparisons between San Francisco and China.

304. Chiao, Brenda. "New Country." *Hokubei Mainichi* 7 June 1984: 1.
Focuses on the immigrant experiences of a girl from China.

305. Chin, Frank. *Chinaman Pacific and Frisco R.R. Co.* Minneapolis: Coffee House Press, forthcoming.
A collection of short stories.

306. ———. "Chinaman's Chance." *WCH Way* 4 (Summer 1982): 167–81.
Essay.

307. ———. "Confessions of a Chinatown Cowboy." *Bulletin of Concerned Asian Scholars* 4.3 (1972): 58–70.
Essay.

308. ———. "Confessions of a Number One Son." *Ramparts* Mar. 1973: 41–48.
Rpt. in *Speaking for Ourselves* [#110] 2nd ed.: 218–27.
Essay.

309. ———. "Food for All His Dead." *Asian-American Authors* [#125] 48–61.
Short story.

310. ———. "Goong Hai Fot Choy." *19 Necromancers from Now.* Ed. Ishmael Reed. New York: Doubleday, 1970. 31–54.
      Excerpt from *A Chinese Lady Dies,* an unpublished novel.

311. ———. "How to Watch a Chinese Movie with the Right 'I.'" *Bamboo Ridge* 5 (1979–80): 57–65.
      Essay.

312. ———. "The Most Popular Book in China." *Quilt* 4 (1984): 6–12.
      A parody of *The Woman Warrior* and *FOB.*

313. ———. "The Only Real Day." *Counterpoint* [#113] 510–24.
      Short story.

314. ———. "Remembrances of a Railroad Man." *Weekly* [Seattle] 21 July 1976: 9–10.

315. ———. "Yes, Young Daddy." *In Youth.* Ed. Richard Kostelanetz. New York: Ballantine, 1972. 39–52.
      Rpt. in *Ethnic American Short Stories* [#150] 187–200; *RIKKA* 7.2 (1980): 37–44.
      Short story.

316. Chin, Frank, and Jeffery Paul Chan. "Racist Love." *Seeing through Shuck.* Ed. Richard Kostelanetz. New York: Ballantine, 1972. 65–79.
      Essay.

317. Chin, M. Lucie. "Lan Lung." *Masterpieces of Terror and the Supernatural: A Treasury of Spellbinding Tales Old and New.* Ed. Marvin Kaye with Saralee Kaye. Garden City: Doubleday, 1985. 86–105.
      A man born in Boston but transported to ancient China encounters a Taoist priest and dragons.

318. Chiu, Tony. *Port Arthur Chicken.* New York: Morrow, 1979.
      Political novel.

319. *Chong, Claire. "Blah and Tita." *Paradise of the Pacific* July 1952: 37.
      A retelling of *Romeo and Juliet* written in pidgin English.

320. *Chong, Kalynn. "Nasus." *Seaweeds and Constructions* 4 (Dec. 1977): 57–59.
      Centers on relationships between Asian women and white men.

321. Chou, Cynthia L. *My Life in the United States.* North Quincy, MA: Christopher Publishing House, 1970.
      Autobiography.

322. Chow, Berton. "The Fimmans." *Dwell among Our People* [#109] 29–30.
      A mythical account of how selfishness contributes to the evolution of slugs.

323. ———. "When Mosquitoes Were Teachers." *Dwell among Our People* [#109] 31–32.
      A fable concerning power and control.

324. Chow, Diana. "The Village." *Hanai* [#161] 27–30.
      Depicts a raid by brutal soldiers.

325.   Choy, Craig. "All Men Are Dogks!" *Rising Waters* 1976: n. pag.
         A mother advises her son on sexual matters.

326.   ———. "Untitled." *Rising Waters* 1976: n. pag.
         Describes Chinese funeral customs.

327.   **Choy, Wayson S. "The Sound of Waves." *Prism* (1961).
         Rpt. in *The Best American Short Stories of 1962*. Boston: Houghton,
         1962. 16–31.
         Describes the interaction between two youths in their late teens, one
         of whom wants to try his strength by swimming across a dangerous river.

328.   Chu, Louis. "Bewildered." *East Wind* 1.1 (1982): 53–57.
         Depicts the anxiety of a newcomer detained by the US immigration
         service.

329.   ———. *Eat a Bowl of Tea*. New York: Lyle Stuart, 1961. Introd. Jeffery
         Paul Chan. Seattle: U of Washington P, 1979. Secaucus, NJ: Lyle Stuart,
         1986.
         Excerpt in *AIIIEEEEE!* [#100] 1983: 76–87.
         Set mostly in the bachelor society of New York Chinatown during the
         1940s, the novel depicts the interaction between two generations of Chi-
         nese Americans.
         Rev. Cheng Lok Chua, *Explorations in Ethnic Studies* 3.1 (1980): 67–69;
         Carol Field, *New York Herald Tribune* 19 Feb. 1961: 33; Marlon Hom,
         Amerasia Journal 6.2 (1979): 95–98; Curtis W. Stucki, *Library Journal* 15
         Mar. 1961: 1156.

330.   Chua, C[heng] Lok. "Down by the Sea." *Twenty-Two Malaysian Stories:
         An Anthology of Writing in English*. Ed. Lloyd Fernando. Singapore:
         Heinemann, 1968. 141–45.
         Describes a young boy's reaction to death and sex.

331.   ———. "An Exorcism: Two Asians in America." *Massachusetts Review*
         22.2 (1981): 361–67.
         A memoir about how a Chinese and a Japanese immigrant eventually
         exorcise "personal and tribal ghosts."

332.   Chuang Hua [pseud.]. *Crossings*. New York: Dial, 1968. Foreword Amy
         Ling. Boston: Northeastern UP, 1986.
         A blend of autobiography and fiction about a Chinese American
         woman's adventure in Paris.

333.   Deng Ming-Dao [Mark Ong]. "Broken Faith." *Amerasia Journal* 3.2
         (1976): 82–94.
         Describes the interaction and secret thoughts of a widower, his second
         wife, and her stepson.

334.   ———. *Seven Bamboo Tablets of the Cloudy Satchel*. San Francisco:
         Harper, 1987.
         Describes a young Taoist's experiences during the Sino-Japanese war.

335.   ———. "Snake Dreams." *Asian American Review* 1 (1976): 79–82.
         Describes a Chinese American's anxiety over falling in love with a white
         woman.

336. ————. *The Wandering Taoist*. San Francisco: Harper, 1983.
Describes a Taoist ascetic from China.

337. **Duh, Eileen. "Thoughts in the Suburbs: The Journey Home." *Asianadian* 1.3 (1978): 20–23.
An elderly Chinese woman reminisces about her life in China and in a Canadian suburb.

338. Dunn, Ashley Sheun. "No Man's Land." *Amerasia Journal* 5.2 (1978): 109–33.
Reveals the psychological trauma of an Asian American Vietnam veteran.

339. Dunn, Robert Eng. "China or America?" *American Letter* [#128] 324–26.
An autobiographical essay describing the conflict of being a second-generation Chinese American.

Eaton, Edith. See Sui Sin Far.

Eaton, Winnifred. See Watanna, Onoto.

Engle, Hua-ling Nieh. See Nieh Hua-ling.

340. Fong, David. "As Opposed to the Prayer Box." *Time to Greez!* [#142] 24–28.
On suicidal impulses.

341. *Fong, Tina. "Goddess." *Bamboo Ridge: The Hawaii Writers' Quarterly* 6 (1980): 2–6.
Short story.

342. Gong, Eddie. "I Want to Marry an American Girl." *American Magazine* Sept. 1955: 15+.

343. Goo, Thomas York-Tong. *Before the Gods*. Ed. and introd. James T. Goo [author's son]. New York: Helios Book Publishing, 1976.
An autobiographical novel of a Chinese American who discovers his roots during an extensive stay in China.

344. Howe, Joyce. "A Nice 'Lo Fang' Boy." *Village Voice* 6 Dec. 1983: 29+.
A Chinese American woman analyzes her feelings for Asian and Caucasian men.

345. Hsia, T. A. "The Birth of a Son." *Literature East and West* 9.4 (1965): 291–309.

346. Hsiao, Ellen. *A Chinese Year*. Philadelphia: Lippincott, 1970.
A Chinese American describes her childhood experiences in her grandfather's house.

347. Hsiung, S[hih] I. *The Bridge of Heaven*. New York: Putnam's, 1943.
A historical novel set in China at the turn of the century.
Rev. Chen Yi, *New York Times* 25 July 1943: 5; *Times Literary Supplement* 30 Jan. 1943: 53.

348.   ———. *The Story of Lady Precious Stream*. London: Hutchinson, 1950.
A rendering of an old Chinese tale.

349.   Huang, Ken. *Citizen Tyrone Han*. Forthcoming in 1988. Excerpts in
AsiAm Dec. 1986: 34+; Jan. 1987: 33+; Feb. 1987: 33–37.
Set in Los Angeles Chinatown.

350.   Huang, Veronica. "Backstage." *Asian Women* [#84] 52–55.
An isolated Chinese American girl is haunted by a sense of invisibility.

351.   ———. "The Maid and the Mistress." *Asian Women* [#84] 64–67.
After coming to America with her Caucasian husband, a former maid
and bargirl from Taiwan gradually goes insane out of loneliness.

352.   Hui, Kin. *Reminiscences*. Peiping: San Yu Press, 1932.
An autobiography of a Chinese immigrant who becomes a Presbyterian
minister in New York.

353.   Jeung, Sharon. "The Butterfly." *Dwell among Our People* [#109] 10–11.
Describes the angst of a young Asian American woman.

354.   *Kingston, Maxine Hong. *China Men*. New York: Knopf, 1980. Portions
of the book appear as follows: "Gold Mountain Heroes." *Bamboo Ridge:
The Hawaii Writers' Quarterly* 2 (1979): 20–21; "'How Are You?' 'I Am
Fine, Thank You. And You?'" *The State of the Language*. Ed Leonard
Michaels and Christopher Ricks. Berkeley: U of California P, 1980. 152–57;
"The Making of More Americans." *New Yorker* 11 Feb. 1980: 34+; "The
Making of More Americans." *Interchange: A Symposium on Regional-
ism, Internationalism, and Ethnicity in Literature*. Ed. Linda Spalding
and Frank Stewart. Honolulu: InterArts, 1980. 81–93; "On Understand-
ing Men." *Hawaii Review* 7 (1977): 43–44.
A blend of autobiography and fiction about three generations of Chi-
nese American men and their contributions to America.
Rev. Patricia Lin Blinde, *Amerasia Journal* 8.1 (1981): 139–43; Mary
Gordon, *New York Times Book Review* 13 June 1980: 1+; Oggie Kim,
Bridge 8.2 (1982): 27–28; Loretta Petrie, *Paper* Nov. 1980: 11; Jean Strouse,
Newsweek 16 June 1980: 88; Frederic Wakeman, Jr., *New York Review
of Books* 14 Aug. 1980: 42–44.

355.   ———. "The Coming Book." *The Writer on Her Work*. Ed. Janet Stern-
burg. New York: Norton, 1980. 181–85.
An essay delineating the creative-writing process.

356.   ———. "Duck Boy." *New York Times Magazine* 12 June 1977: S4+.
A true story about an abandoned boy who cannot read.

357.   ———. *Hawai'i One Summer*. Illus. Deng Ming-Dao. San Francisco:
Meadow Press, 1987.
A collection of sketches.

358.   ———. "San Francisco's Chinatown: A View from the Other Side of
Arnold Genthe's Camera." *American Heritage* Dec. 1978: 36+.
Describes how Genthe's photographs of Chinatown give only an incom-
plete image.

359.   ———. "[Chapter 1] from [forthcoming] *Tripmaster Monkey — His Fake Book." Caliban* 1 (1986): 35–39.
           A man who contemplates suicide takes a walk in San Francisco.

360.   ———. *The Woman Warrior: Memoirs of a Girlhood among Ghosts.* New York: Knopf, 1975. Portions of the book appear as follows: "Moon Orchid Comes to the Gold Mountain." *New West* 13 Sept. 1976: 32–46; "No-Name Woman." *The Third Woman* [#112] 460–69; "No Name Woman." *The Ethnic American Woman* [#88] 18–26; "No Name Woman." *West Coast Fiction* [#124] 152–64; "The Other End of the String." *I'm On My Way Running* [#166] 287–88.
           A blend of autobiography and fiction about growing up between two cultures in America.
           Rev. Sara Blackburn, *Ms.* Jan. 1977: 39–40; *Booklist* 1 Nov. 1976: 385; Jeffery Paul Chan, *New York Review of Books* 28 Apr. 1977: 41+ (a response to Diane Johnson's review); Kathryn M. Fong, *Bulletin of Concerned Asian Scholars* 1977: 67–69, rpt. in *San Francisco Journal* 25 Jan. 1978: 6 and *RIKKA* 6.4 (1979): 33–36; Paul Gray, *Time* 6 Dec. 1976: 91; Diane Johnson, *New York Review of Books* 3 Feb. 1977: 19+; Jane Kramer, *New York Times Book Review* 7 Nov. 1976: 1+; John Leonard, *New York Times* 17 Sept. 1976: C21; Audrey Levy, *Books West* 1.4 (1977): 27; Louise Liew, *Bridge* 5.1 (1977): 47–48; Michael Malloy, *National Observer* 9 Oct. 1976: 25; Ruth Mathewson, *New Leader* 6 June 1977: 14–15; William McPherson, *Washington Post Book World* 10 Oct. 1976: E1; Jacob Muller, *RIKKA* 6.4 (1979): 32–33; Elizabeth Pomada, *San Francisco Sunday Examiner and Chronicle* 17 Oct. 1976: 41, and *New York Times Book Review* 14 Aug. 1977: 31; *Publisher's Weekly* 9 Aug. 1976: 80; Nan Robertson, *New York Times* 12 Feb. 1977: 26; Lois Taylor, *Honolulu Star-Bulletin* 1 Sept. 1976: B1; Benjamin R. Tong, *San Francisco Journal* 11 May 1977: 6 (a response to Diane Johnson's review); Nellie Wong, *Bridge* 6.4 (1978–79): 46–48; Sharon Wong, *Equality* (Asian Americans for Equality) 1.3 (1978): 1, and *Library Journal* 15 Sept. 1976: 1849; Suzi Wong, *Amerasia Journal* 4.1 (1977): 165–67.

361.   ———. "A Writer's Notebook from the Far East." *Ms.* Jan. 1983: 85–86.
           Discusses the issue of free press.

362.   *Kong, Charles. "Hard Head." *Aloha* 4.23 (1950–51): 17–21.
           Two women in a hospital hate each other.

363.   ———. "Pele's Own." *Paradise of the Pacific* 63 (1952): 70+.
           Rpt. in *Bamboo Ridge* 3 (1979): 35–43; *The Best of* Bamboo Ridge [#103] 159–66.
           Describes a rural Hawaiian girl's infatuation with a sophisticated Hawaiian boy.

364.   ———. "Proof." *Aloha* 4.24 (1951): 3–6.
           A man drowns while trying to prove his love for a woman.

365.   ———. "Well, Then?" *Aloha* 5.25 (1951): 13–16.
           A sketch of a bully, written in pidgin English.

366. *Koo, Alvin [R.]. "The Fable of Li-Ling." *AsiAm* July 1987: 33+.
A father attempts to teach his daughters about sex.

367. ———. "Fresh Akule." *Hawaii Review* 1.2 (1973): 35–41.
Describes an old fisherman.

368. Kuo, Alex. "A Story." *Journal of Ethnic Studies* 12.4 (1985): 65–86.
A prose poem about various unfulfilled relationships.

369. Kuo, Ching Ch'iu [Helena Kuo]. *I've Come a Long Way*. New York: Appleton, 1942.
An autobiography of a young Chinese woman who has come from Canton to America.

370. ———. *Peach Path*. London: Methuen, 1940.
A collection of essays about women in China.

371. ———. *Westward to Chungking*. New York: Appleton, 1944.
Describes the hardship encountered by a Chinese family moving from their home in Soochow to Chungking, the provisional capital during the Sino-Japanese War.

Kuo, Helena. See Kuo, Ching Ch'iu.

372. *Kwock, Laureen. "Wedding Day." *AsiAm* Aug. 1987: 74+.
A man marries to avoid being drafted.

373. Lai, Ivan F. "Homecoming." *AsiAm* June 1987: 33+.
An immigrant returns to Los Angeles, the city where he first landed 25 years ago as a boy.

374. *Lai, Kum Pui. "Alma Jaded Lotus Blossom." *Common Ground* 2.3 (1942): 56–58.
Describes the Chinese ways of celebrating the birth of a child.

375. *Lai, Violet Lau. "Consum." *Aloha* 3.18 (1949): 15–16.
A comic sketch about thrift and ignorance.

376. *Lau, Terry. "The Opening." *Bamboo Ridge* 25 (1985): 3.
A prose poem about encountering a woman.

377. Lee, C. Y. [Chin-Yang Lee]. *China Saga*. New York: Weidenfeld, 1987.
A semiautobiographical novel describing four generations of a Chinese family and spanning the Boxer Rebellion, Sun Yat-Sen's revolution, Mao's regime, and the Cultural Revolution.

378. ———. *Cripple Mah and the New Order*. New York: Farrar, 1961.
A satirical novel about a man who stumbles from one misfortune to another in the People's Republic of China.

379. ———. *Days of the Tong Wars*. New York: Ballantine, 1974.
Set in California. *Tong*, or "hall" in Chinese, is a sort of vigilance committee that offers protection to members.

380. ———. *The Flower Drum Song*. New York: Farrar, 1957.
A portion of the work appears as "A Man of Habit" in *New Yorker* 30 Mar. 1957: 33–38 and is rpt. in *I/You-We/They* [#111] 54–63.
Set in San Francisco Chinatown.

381.   ———. *The Land of the Golden Mountain*. New York: Meredith, 1967.

382.   ———. *Lover's Point*. New York: Farrar, 1958.
A refugee from the People's Republic of China becomes a teacher of Mandarin in Monterey, California, and falls in love with a Japanese divorcée.

383.   ———. *Madame Goldenflower*. New York: Farrar, 1960. Westport, CT: Green World, 1975.
A novel about a high-class Chinese concubine during the Boxer Rebellion.

384.   ———. "Mr. Weng's Last Forbidden Dollar." *Anthology of Best Short-Short Stories: Volume 5*. Ed. Robert Oberfirst. New York: Frederick Fell, 1957. 53–57.
An anecdote about how a Confucian scholar makes use of an illegal silver dollar.

385.   ———. *The Sawbwa and His Secretary: My Burmese Reminiscences*. New York: Farrar, 1959.
A blend of fiction and autobiography about life in Burma.

386.   ———. *The Virgin Market*. Garden City: Doubleday, 1964.
Cannot locate.

387.   Lee, Jon, comp. *Chinese Tales Told in California*. Rev. Paul Radin. San Francisco: California State Library, 1940.
Mimeographed.

388.   *Lee, Lanning. "Born and Bred." *Hawaii Review* 17 (1985): 33–43.
Rpt. in *Passages to the Dream Shore* [#170] 84–94.
A boy reminisces about a Chinese woman and an Indian who courts her with pigeon manure.

389.   **Lee, Sharon. "Sweatshop." *Asianadian* 3.2 (1980): 3–4.
Registers the thoughts of a Chinese garment worker.

390.   **Lee, Sky. "Broken Teeth." *The Asian-Canadian and the Arts* [#96] 20–23.
A mother tells her Canadian-born son about an unsettling childhood experience in China.

391.   ———. "Gig Goes Island Crazy." *Asianadian* 3.2 (1980): 10–13.
A psychiatrist decides to take an expensive vacation.

392.   Lee, Virginia Chin-lan. *The House That Tai Ming Built*. New York: Macmillan, 1963.
A novel about the interaction of a Chinese American family.

393.   Lee Yan Phou. *When I Was a Boy in China*. Boston: D. Lothrop Co., 1887.
Autobiography.

394.   Lee Yu-Hwa. "An Afternoon of Surmises." *Southwest Review* 52.4 (1967): 344–51.
Rpt. in *"The Last Rite"* 61–71.
A couple watch attentively while their neighbors are robbed.

395. ———. "The Bomb-Proof Inn." *Literary Review* 11.3 (1968): 306–18. Rpt. in *"The Last Rite"* 72–89.

396. ———. "Dinner with Father." *Arizona Quarterly* 34.1 (1978): 44–54. Rpt. in *"The Last Rite"* 125–38.

397. ———. "The Fresh Start." *Arizona Quarterly* 27.4 (1971): 321–34. Rpt. in *"The Last Rite"* 90–106.

398. ———. "The Last Rite." *Literary Review* 7.4 (1964): 533–47.
Rpt. in *The Best American Short Stories: 1965.* Ed. Martha Foley. Boston: Houghton, 1965. 371–84; *The Last Rite* 1–20; *The Other Woman: Stories of Two Women and a Man.* Ed. Susan Koppelman. Old Westbury, NY: Feminist Press, 1984. 256–69; *Stories from the* Literary Review. Ed. Charles Angoff. Rutherford: Fairleigh Dickinson UP, 1969. 35–53; *Speaking for Ourselves* [#110] 1969: 178–87.
A progressive Chinese is pressured by his family into an arranged marriage.

399. ———. *"The Last Rite" and Other Stories.* San Francisco: Chinese Materials Center, 1979.
Contains original stories and retold tales.

400. ———. "The Monument." *Arizona Quarterly* 23.1 (1967): 45–60.
Rpt. in *Forgotten Pages of American Literature* [#118] 146–59; *The Last Rite* 41–60.
A satire on human imperfection.

401. ———. "The Scholar's Woman." *Massachusetts Review* 6 (Autumn 1965): 785–800.
Rpt. in *"The Last Rite"* 21–40.

402. ———. "Void-and-Nihil." *Literature East and West* 15.3 (1971): 432–46. Rpt. in *"The Last Rite"* 107–24.

403. Leong, Charles L. "Ten Hours: Union Street." *Rising Waters* 1976: n. pag.
A revisit to an old haunt evokes memories of youth.

404. Leong, Monfoon. *Number One Son.* San Francisco: East/West, 1975.
A collection of short stories about the clash between Chinese and Chinese American points of view.

405. Leong, Russell. "Take Only the Essentials." *Echoes from Gold Mountain* 1 (1978): 10–11.
Recounts how a couple in China is uprooted by war.

406. ——— [under pseud. Wallace Lin]. "Rough Notes for Mantos." *AIIIEEEEE!* [#100] 116–22.
A prose poem registering a son's impressions of a father.

407. Leung, Lincoln. "The Twain Meet." *Common Ground* 2.2 (1942): 100–03.
Describes how the upbringing of Chinese Americans prepares them for promoting understanding between East and West.

408. *Li, Ling-Ai. *Life Is for a Long Time: A Chinese Hawaiian Memoir.* New York: Hasting House, 1972.
      An account of the author's childhood.

409. Li, Yao-wen. "Uprooted." *Confrontation* 33–34 (1986–87): 94–101.
      To please his father, a wealthy Hong Kong student dates various US citizens with the intent of becoming one himself.

410. Lim, Genny. "Journey to Death Valley." *Bridge* 8.1 (1982): 13+.
      Prose poem.

411. ———. "Sunday minus Seven." *Y'Bird Magazine* 1.1 (1977): 108–12.
      A prose poem about prostitutes and drug addicts in Louisiana.

412. Lim, Paul Stephen. *Some Arrivals, but Mostly Departures.* Quezon City, Philippines: New Day Publishers, 1982.
      A collection of short stories.
      Rev. Roger J. Bresnahan, *Asiaweek* [Hong Kong] 23 Sept. 1983: 59.

413. ———. "Taking Flight." *Solidarity* 10.6 (1975): 82–97. Rpt. in *Amerasia Journal* 3.2 (1976): 38–62.
      Describes the thoughts of a young Asian student in America and his relationship with his family in the Philippines.

414. ———. "Victor and Other Issues." *Bridge* 6.4 (1978): 6+.
      Centers on adopted children.

415. Lim, Shirley [Geok-lin]. *"Another Country" and Other Stories.* Singapore: Times Books International, 1982. "All My Uncles" is rpt. in *Asia* [New York] Feb. 1983: 14–15.
      Rev. Peter Nazareth, *World Literature Today* 58.1 (1984): 167.

416. ———. "Blindness." *Her World* [Kuala Lumpur] May 1982: 154–55. Rpt. in *"Another Country"* 63–80.
      A high school teacher learns that her brother, an obsessive reader, has gone blind.

417. ———. "The Dispossessing Eye: Reading Wordsworth on the Equatorial Line." *Discharging the Canon: Cross-Cultural Readings in Literature.* Ed. Peter Hyland. Singapore: Singapore UP, National U of Singapore, 1986. 126–32.

418. ———. "Haunting." *Her World* [Kuala Lumpur] Apr. 1982: 132–33. Rpt. in *"Another Country"* 126–37.
      A woman feels that the house of her mother-in-law is haunted.

419. ———. "Journey." *Twenty-Two Malaysian Stories: An Anthology of Writing in English.* Ed. Lloyd Fernando. 1968. Singapore: Heinemann, 1974. 106–12. Rpt. in *"Another Country"* 36–41.
      Describes a preadolescent girl's initiation.

420. ———. "Mr. Tang's Girls." *Asiaweek* [Hong Kong] 1 Oct. 1982: 42–51. Rpt. in *"Another Country"* 110–25.

421. ———. "On Christmas Day in the Morning." *Malaysian Short Stories.* Ed. Lloyd Fernando. Heinemann Writing in Asia. Kuala Lumpur: Heinemann, 1981. 131–40.

422. ———. "The Touring Company." *Malaysian Short Stories*. Ed. Lloyd Fernando. Heinemann Writing in Asia. Kuala Lumpur: Heinemann, 1981. 198–205. Rpt. in *"Another Country"* 14–21.
   The narrator recalls acting in *A Midsummer Night's Dream* when a Shakespearean touring company visits her school.

423. Lin, Adet [under pseud. Tan Yun]. *Flame from the Rock*. New York: John Day, 1943.
   A love story set in war-torn China.

424. Lin, Adet, and Anor Lin. *Our Family*. Introd. Pearl S. Buck. New York: John Day, 1939.
   The authors, daughters of Lin Yutang, describe their impressions of the Lin family.

425. Lin, Adet, Anor Lin, and Meimei Lin. *Dawn over Chungking*. New York: John Day, 1941.
   Three young girls describe their journey to China during the Sino-Japanese War.

426. Lin, Anor [under pseud. Lin Tai-yi]. *The Eavesdropper*. 1958. Cleveland: World, 1959.
   Describes the inner conflict of a Chinese novelist who moves between China and America.

427. ———. *The Golden Coin*. New York: John Day, 1946.
   Describes an incompatible couple in Shanghai.

428. ———. *Kampoon Street*. Cleveland: World, 1964.
   Describes a family of Chinese refugees in Hong Kong slums.

429. ———. *The Lilacs Overgrow*. New York: World, 1960.
   A novel set in China during the turmoil of the late 1940s.

430. ———. *War Tide*. New York: John Day, 1943.
   Describes war-torn China between the end of the Japanese occupation and the success of the Chinese communists.

431. Lin, Diana. "Encounter." *Third World Women* [#174] 148–50.
   Set in Hong Kong, the story describes an encounter between a drug addict and his son.

432. Lin, Hazel. *The Physicians*. New York: John Day, 1951.
   A Chinese woman studies Western medicine against her grandfather's wishes.

433. Lin, Hwai-min. "Homecoming." *Bridge* 1.1 (1971): 20–26.
   A sketch about the changes that have occurred in a rural village in Taiwan.

Lin Tai-yi. See Lin, Anor.

Lin, Wallace. See Leong, Russell.

434. Lin Yutang. *Between Tears and Laughter*. New York: John Day, 1943.
   A collection of essays on the prerequisites for peaceful relations between Asia and the Western world.

435. ———. *Chinatown Family.* New York: John Day, 1948. Excerpts in *Speaking for Ourselves* [#110] 189–94; *American Letter* [#128] 165–70.
A novel about how immigrants experience the clash of Chinese and American values.

436. ———. *"Confucius Saw Nancy" and Essays about Nothing.* Shanghai: Commercial Press, 1937.
A collection of drama, essays, and satires.

437. ———. *The Flight of the Innocents.* New York: Putnam's, 1964.
A novel about refugees from the People's Republic of China.

438. ———. *Imperial Peking: Seven Centuries of China.* New York: Crown, 1962.
Discusses the growth of Peking over centuries.

439. ———. *The Importance of Living.* New York: John Day, 1937.
Nonfiction. Outlines a Chinese philosophy of life for Western readers.

440. ———. *Lady Wu: A True Story.* London: Heinemann, 1957. Also published as *Lady Wu: A Novel.* New York: Putnam's, 1965.
A historical biography about a self-made Chinese empress.

441. ———. *A Leaf in the Storm: A Novel of War-Swept China.* New York: John Day, 1941.
Set during the Sino-Japanese conflict.

442. ———. *"Letters of a Chinese Amazon," and War-Time Essays.* Shanghai: Commercial Press, 1934.

443. ———. *The Little Critic: Essays, Satires, Sketches on China* [First series, 1930–32; second series, 1933–35]. Shanghai: Commercial Press, 1937. Westport, CT: Hyperion Press, 1983.

444. ———. *Looking Beyond.* New York: Prentice-Hall, 1955. Also published as *The Unexpected Island.* Melbourne: Heinemann, 1955.
A woman from America is stranded on a Greek island.

445. ———. *Memoirs of an Octogenarian.* Taipei: Mei Ya Publications, 1975.

446. ———. *Moment in Peking: A Novel of Contemporary Chinese Life.* New York: John Day, 1939.

447. ———. *My Country and My People.* New York: Reynal & Hitchcock, 1937.
Nonfiction. The author expresses his opinions on China and the Chinese.

448. ———. *On the Wisdom of America.* New York: John Day, 1948.
The author comments on Jefferson, Emerson, Franklin, Santayana, Thoreau, and other Americans.

449. ———. *The Pleasures of a Nonconformist.* Cleveland: World, 1962.
A collection of essays, sketches, and lectures.

450. ———. *The Red Peony*. Cleveland: World, 1961.
Widowed at 22, a Chinese woman conducts a series of unhappy love affairs.

451. ———. *The Vermilion Gate: A Novel of a Far Land*. New York: John Day, 1953.

452. ———. *The Vigil of a Nation*. New York: John Day, 1944.
Describes the author's travels in wartime China.

453. ———. "When East Meets West." *Atlantic Monthly* Dec. 1942: 43–48.
Discusses the state of philosophy in Asia and in America.

454. ———. *With Love and Irony*. Introd. Pearl S. Buck. New York: John Day, 1940.
A collection of familiar essays.

455. Liu, Aimee. *Solitaire: A Narrative*. New York: Harper, 1979. Excerpt entitled "Thin Fever" in *I'm on My Way Running* [#166] 156–60.
An autobiography of a woman who suffers from anorexia.

456. **Liu, Richard. "From *Return of the Wild Good*." Trans Mr. Lin. *Canadian Fiction Magazine* 36–37 (1980): 90–93.
An excerpt from a novel in Chinese published under the pseudonym Wen Zhao.

457. Lord, Bette [Bao] (with sister Sansan). *Eighth Moon: The True Story of a Young Girl's Life in Communist China, by Sansan as Told to Bette Lord*. New York: Harper, 1964.
Sansan escapes from China in 1962.

458. ———. *Spring Moon: A Novel of China*. New York: Harper, 1981.
The novel traces the decline of a prominent Chinese family from 1892 to 1927.
Rev. Charlotte Curtis, *New York Times Book Review* 25 Oct. 1981: 15; Ann Rice, *San Francisco Sunday Examiner and Chronicle* 3 Jan. 1982: 5.

459. Louie, David Wong. "Birthday." *Agni Review* 24–25 (1987): 72–83.

460. ———. "Bottles of Beaujolais." *Iowa Review* 13.3–4 (1982–83): 102–15.
Describes a strange rendezvous.

461. ———. "Disturbing the Universe." *Colorado State Review* 10.2 (1983): 66–79.

462. ———. "Growing Up West." *Bridge* 7.1 (1979): 51+.

463. ———. "In a World Small Enough." *Chicago Review* 35.4 (1987): 90–102.

464. ———. "Love on the Rocks." *Quarry West* 18 (1983): 30–43.

465. ———. "The Movers." *Mid-American Review* 5.1 (1985): 45–53.

466. ———. "One Man's Hysteria—Real and Imagined—in the 20th Century." *Iowa Review* 12.4 (1981): 69–85.
A paranoid man tries to get ready for nuclear war.

467. ———. "Warming Trends." *Kansas Quarterly* 18.1–2 (1986): 149–60.

469.   Low, David. "Winterblossom Garden." *The Ploughshares Reader: New Fiction for the Eighties*. Ed. and introd. DeWitt Henry. Wainscott, NY: Pushcart Press, 1985. 375–90.
        A photographer portrays his aging parents, restaurant owners in San Francisco Chinatown.

470.   Low, Ron. "A Brief Biographical Sketch of a Newly-Found Asian Male." *Roots: An Asian American Reader* [#173] 105–08.
        Describes an identity crisis.

471.   Lowe, Pardee. *Father and Glorious Descendant*. Boston: Little, 1943. Excerpts in *Asian-American Authors* [#125] 16–23; *Asian-American Heritage* [#177] 259–67; *The Ethnic Image in Modern American Literature: 1900–1950*. 2 vols. Washington: Howard UP, 1984. 1: 88–91, 2: 74–75.
        An autobiography that centers on the interaction between a son and his father, a Chinese immigrant.
        Rev. *Common Ground* 3.4 (1943): 118; Rose Feld, *New York Herald Tribune Weekly Book Review* 11 Apr. 1943: 4; Helena Kuo, *New York Times Book Review* 11 Apr. 1943: 19; *Library Journal* 1 Apr. 1943: 287; Edward Skillin, *Commonweal* 23 Apr. 1943: 18–19.

472.   *Lum, Darrell H. Y. "Burn Too Much." *Hawaii Herald* 14 Dec. 1984: 8+.
        Centers on two brothers, a Boy Scout and a Cub Scout.

473.   ———. "Da Beer Can Hat." *Bamboo Ridge: The Hawaii Writers' Quarterly* 8 (1980): 67–71.
        Rpt. in *The Best of* Bamboo Ridge [#103] 175–83.
        A boy describes his relationship with an old man who sells newspapers.

474.   ———. "Hadashi." *Hanai* 1 (1977): 39–43.
        Rpt. in *Sun* 7–9.
        Two boys cut class in order to sniff paint.

475.   ———. "J'like Ten Thousand." *Landmarks* [Seattle] 4.3–4 (1986): 30–31.
        Rpt. in *Literary Arts Hawaii* 84 (Spring 1987): 6–7.

476.   ———. "The Moiliili Bag Man." *Hawaii Review* 13 (1982): 84–87.
        Rpt. in *Passages to the Dream Shore* [#170] 105–08.
        A boy encounters a clever street person.

477.   ———. "No Pass Back." *Hawaii Review* spec. supp. (Fall 1983): 9.
        Short story.

478.   ———. "Paint." *Bamboo Ridge* 27 (1985): 54–60.
        Rpt. in *The Best of* Bamboo Ridge [#103] 189–94.
        A boy tries to be somebody by regularly spraying paint on a wall.

479.   ———. "Primo Doesn't Take Back Bottles Anymore." *Talk Story* [#104] 33–38.
        Rpt. in *Sun* 20–25; *The Best of* Bamboo Ridge [#103] 184–88; *Passages to the Dream Shore* [#170] 100–04.
        Focuses on a man who collects Primo beer bottles for a living.

480.   ———. "Sun." *Kapa* (Spring 1972): 54–55.
        Rpt. in *Sun* 74–76.

A man sunbathes at the beach while his mother suffocates at home in an accidental fire.

481.   ———. *Sun: Short Stories and Drama*. Spec. issue of *Bamboo Ridge* 8 (1980).
Includes local pidgin English fiction and stories about growing up Chinese American in Hawaii.
Rev. Loretta Petrie, *Paper* Jan. 1981.

482.   ———. "Yahk Fahn, Auntie." *Echoes from Gold Mountain* 1978: 37–39.
Rpt. in *Sun* 38–43; *Paper* 2.3 (1983): 12–13; *Passages to the Dream Shore* [#170] 95–99.
A Chinese American recalls how he was influenced by an aunt who encouraged him to follow Chinese traditions.

483.   Mar, Laureen. "3-D." *Quilt* 5 (1986): 109–18.
Two women who need to move to pursue new careers are deserted by their lovers.

484.   McCunn, Ruthanne Lum. "The Long Journey." *Echoes from Gold Mountain* 1982: 61–75.
Describes the inner thoughts of an old Chinese immigrant.

485.   ———. *Sole Survivor*. San Francisco: Design Enterprises, 1985.
A biographical novel about a Chinese seaman who holds the Guinness world record for survival at sea.
Rev. John Kenny, *Library Journal* 1 Oct. 1985: 113; Don Keown, *San Francisco Chronicle* 25 Sept. 1985: 55; Genny Lim, *East Wind* 5.1 (1986): 28; *Publisher's Weekly* 11 Oct. 1985: 61–62; Judy Yung, *East/West* 11 Sept. 1985: 10.

486.   ———. *Thousand Pieces of Gold*. San Francisco: Design Enterprises, 1981.
A biographical novel about a Chinese woman who is sold to America as a slave.
Rev. Lorraine Dong, *Amerasia Journal* 9.1 (1982): 113–14; Kathleen Hirooka, *Bridge* 8.1 (1982): 39–40; Judy Yung, *East Wind* 1.2 (1982): 60.

487.   Mei, June, and Jean Pang Yip, with Russell Leong. "The Bitter Society: *Ku Shehui*. A Translation, Chapters 37–46." *Amerasia Journal* 8.1 (1981): 33–67.
Depicts the suffering of early Chinese immigrants.

488.   Ng, Fae [Myenne]. "The First Dead Man." *Crescent Review* 4.2 (1986): 147–54.
After seeing a dead man for the first time, a woman remembers the various tales of death her mother has told her.

489.   ———. "Last Night." *City Lights Review* 5.1 (1987): 24–29.
A Chinese couple rescue their Italian landlady.

490.   ———. "Pressed Petals." *Hanai* [#161] 2–6.
Rpt. in *Quilt* 2 (1981): 163–67.
Illustrates the oppression of Chinese women through the juxtaposed

descriptions of a Chinese American seamstress and a famed Chinese courtesan.

491. ———. "A Red Sweater." *American Voice* 4 (Fall 1986): 47–58.
A woman tries to help her sister break away from their quarrelsome parents by giving her a sexy sweater.

492. ———. "Tea Leaves." *Echoes from Gold Mountain* 1979: 48–52.
A girl who has been serving tea to her grandfather every morning discovers his suicide.

493. Nieh Hua-ling. [Also Engle, Hua-ling Nieh.] "Camellia." Trans. author.
Eight Stories by Chinese Women. Ed. Nieh Hua-ling. Taipei: Heritage Press, 1962. 129–48.
Rpt. in *Short Story International* Oct. 1977: 123–34.

493a. ———. "Never Again, Again." *Short Story International* Nov. 1963: 137–48.

494. ———. *The Purse, and Three Other Stories of Chinese Life.* Taipei: Heritage Press, 1962.

495. ———. "The Several Blessings of Ta-nien Wang." *Atlantic Monthly* Dec. 1966: 91–94.
Rev. and rpt. as "The Several Blessings of Wang Ta-nien" in *Twentieth Century Chinese Stories.* Ed. C. T. Hsia, with Joseph S. M. Lau. New York: Columbia UP, 1971. 194–201; *Short Story International* Feb. 1978: 117–24.
In this political satire, a high school teacher shares with his friend his unfeasible plan for the future.

496. ———. *Two Women of China: Mulberry and Peach.* Trans. Jane Parish Yang and Linda Lappin. New York: Sino Publishing, 1981. Boston: Beacon, 1988.
An epistolary novel depicting the dual personalities of the heroine, a Chinese woman in exile in America.
Rev. Peter Nazareth, *World Literature Today* 56.2 (1982): 403–04.

497. Pai Hsien-yung [Kenneth]. "A Day in Pleasantville." *Born of the Same Roots* [#126] 184–92.
Describes the adjustment of a Chinese housewife in a white neighborhood.

498. ———. "The Elder Mrs. King." *New Voices: Stories and Poems by Young Chinese Writers.* Trans. and ed. Nancy Ing. 2nd ed. San Francisco: Chinese Materials Center, 1980. 21–38.

499. ———. "Hong Kong 1960." Trans. author. *Literature East and West* 9.4 (1965): 362–69.

500. ———. "Li T'ung: A Chinese Girl in New York." Trans. author and C. T. Hsia. *Twentieth Century Chinese Stories.* Ed. C. T. Hsia, with Joseph S. M. Lau. New York: Columbia UP, 1971. 220–39.
Centers on a proud and defiant Chinese beauty who drinks and gambles recklessly.

501. ———. *Wandering in the Garden, Walking from a Dream: Tales of Tai-*

pei Characters. Trans. author and Patia Yasin. Ed. George Kao. Foreword Patrick Hanan. Bloomington: Indiana UP, 1982.

502.   ———. "Winter Nights." Trans. John Kwan-Terry and Stephen Lacey. *Chinese Stories from Taiwan: 1960–1970.* Ed. Joseph S. M. Lau, with Timothy A. Ross. New York: Columbia UP, 1976. 337–54.

503.   *Pai, Margaret K. "Plumeria Litter." *Sandwich Isles U.S.A.* [#115] 81.

504.   ———. "Red Waters at Papaloa." *Bamboo Ridge* 6 (1980): 24–27.
Short story.

Park, No Yong. See Korean American section.

505.   Pei, Lowry [Cheng-Wu]. "Barranca, King of the Tree Streets." *Edges: Thirteen New Tales from the Borderlands of the Imagination.* Ed. Ursula K. Le Guin and Virginia Kidd. New York: Pocket, 1980. 108–13.
A man looking for an apartment has a strange romantic adventure.

506.   ———. "The Cold Room." *Stories* 4 (Mar.-Apr. 1983): 41–56.
Rpt. in *Best American Short Stories.* Boston: Houghton, 1984. 223–37.
A technician who works in an animal lab must choose between two lovers.

507.   ———. *Family Resemblances.* New York: Random, 1986.
In this novel of initiation, an unconventional aunt imparts cynical wisdom to her fifteen-year-old niece.
Rev. Lee Smith, *New York Times Book Review* 20 Apr. 1986: 9+.

508.   ———. "Naked Women." *Story Quarterly* 20 (1985): 1–12.
A jealous wife discovers the nude pictures of her husband's ex-lovers.

509.   **Po, Tonfang [Wender Lin]. "The Slave." Trans. Rosemary Haddon. *Canadian Fiction Magazine* 36–37 (1980): 94–107.
A Chinese man who was a slave by birth continues to behave like one after going abroad.

510.   *Shen, Yao. "An Hour with a Hawaiian Queen." *Bamboo Ridge* 7 (1980): 46–57.

*Song, Cathy. See Korean American section.

511.   **Sui Sin Far [also Sui Sin Fah; pseuds. for Edith Maud Eaton]. "Alutch." *Chautauquan* 42.4 (1905): 338–42.
A young woman saves a mandarin who is unjustly accused.

512.   ———. "Autumn Fan." *New England Magazine* Aug. 1910: 700–02.
"Autumn fan" refers to a jilted wife.

513.   ———. "Bird of Love." *New England Magazine* Sept. 1910: 23–37.
Love between a couple finally overcomes their parents' hate.

514.   ———. "Candy That Was Not Sweet." *Delineator* July 1910: 76+.
Rpt. in *Mrs. Spring Fragrance* 303–08.
A child steals money to buy candy.

515.   ———. "Chan Hen Yen, Chinese Student." *New England Magazine* Jan. 1912: 462–66.
           A student from China falls in love with a white Christian woman.

516.   ———. "A Chinese Boy-Girl." *Century* ns 45.6 (1904): 828–31.
           Rpt. in *Mrs. Spring Fragrance* 323–33.
           A sketch of a mischievous girl.

517.   ———. "A Chinese Feud." *Land of Sunshine* Nov. 1896: 236–37.
           Two Chinese American lovers come to grief because of a feud between Chinese from two Kwangtung districts.

518.   ———. "A Chinese Ishmael." *Overland Monthly* July 1899: 43–49.
           Describes the ordeals of an abused slavegirl.

519.   ———. "The Chinese Woman in America." *Land of Sunshine* 6.2 (1897): 59–64.

520.   ———. "Chinese Workman in America." *Independent* 31 July 1913: 56–58.

521.   ———. "Half Moon Cakes." *Good Housekeeping* May 1909: 584–85.
           A comic story about how the appearances of two boys are transformed after each has tasted the moon cakes baked by the other's mother.

522.   ———. "Her Chinese Husband." *Independent* 18 Aug. 1910: 358–61.
           Rpt. in *Mrs. Spring Fragrance* 132–43.
           Sequel to "White Woman Who Married a Chinaman."

523.   ———. "Inferior Woman." *Hampton* May 1910: 727–31.
           Rpt. in *Mrs. Spring Fragrance* 21–47.
           Describes prejudices against a "self-made" woman.

524.   ———. "In the Land of the Free." *Independent* 2 Sept. 1909: 504–08.
           Rpt. in *Mrs. Spring Fragrance* 161–78.
           A Chinese family runs into many difficulties with immigration officers.

525.   ———. "Kitten-Headed Shoes." *Delineator* Feb. 1910: 165.
           A little girl exchanges her kitten for a pair of shoes.

526.   ———. "Ku Yum and the Butterflies." *Good Housekeeping* Mar. 1909: 299.
           An anecdote about Asian obedience.

527.   ———. "Leaves from the Mental Portfolio of an Eurasian." *Independent* 7 Jan. 1909: 125–32.
           Excerpts rpt. in *Turning Shadows into Light* [#175] 88–90; *The Ethnic American Woman* [#88] 187–89.
           An autobiographical essay about the experience of growing up Eurasian in 19th-century England and America.

528.   ———. "Love Story from the Rice Fields of China." *New England Magazine* Dec. 1911: 343–45.
           A woman tells a friend about her romance.

529.   ———. "Mrs. Spring Fragrance." *Hampton* Jan. 1910: 137–41.
           Rpt. in *Mrs. Spring Fragrance* 1–21.
           An immigrant describes various anecdotes.

530. ———. *Mrs. Spring Fragrance*. Chicago: A. C. McClurg, 1912.
"Lin John" is rpt. in *Counterpoint* [#113] 534–35.
A collection of short stories; the first half focuses on adults, the second half on children.
Rev. *Independent* 15 Aug. 1912: 388; *New York Times Book Review* 7 July 1912: 405.

531. ———. "O Yam—A Sketch." *Land of Sunshine* Nov. 1900: 341–43.
A sketch of a six-year-old Chinese American girl.

532. ———. "The Smuggling of Tie Co." *Land of Sunshine* July 1900: 100–04.
Rpt. in *Mrs. Spring Fragrance* 184–93.
A white man engages in smuggling Chinese from Canada into the US.

533. ———. "Sugar Cane Baby." *Good Housekeeping* May 1910: 570–72.
A baby is taken away from his mother by two strangers.

534. ———. "White Woman Who Married a Chinaman." *Independent* 10 Mar. 1910: 518–23.
Rpt. in *Mrs. Spring Fragrance* 111–32.
Describes a white woman's two marriages, the first with a white man and the second with a Chinese man.

535. ———. "Who's Game?" *New England Magazine* Feb. 1912: 573–79.
Two ladies try to convert a man to Christianity.

536. Sun, Patrick Pichi. *Recollections of a Floating Life*. N.p.: n.p., 1972. 2nd ed. Taipei: China Post Publishing, 1973.

537. Sze, Mai-mai. *Echo of a Cry: A Story Which Began in China*. New York: Harcourt, 1945.
Memoirs written by the daughter of a Chinese diplomat to London and Washington; she stresses the similarities of different civilizations.
Rev. R. A. H., *Saturday Review of Literature* 10 Nov. 1945: 76.

538. ———. *Silent Children*. New York: Harcourt, 1948.
A novel about a band of uprooted children who establish their own furtive society.

539. Tsiang, H[si] T[seng]. *And China Has Hands*. New York: Robert Speller, 1937.
Describes the struggle of immigrants in New York Chinatown.

540. ———. *China Red*. New York: privately printed, 1931.
A novel consisting of a series of letters between a female college student in China and her fiancé, an overseas student in the US.

541. ———. *The Hanging on Union Square*. New York: privately printed, 1935.
A satire on capitalist society.

542. Tsui, Kitty. "Going Home." *Asian Women* [#84] 35.
A prose poem in which a Chinese immigrant reveals her nostalgia for China.

543. ———. "Pao Pao Is Living Breathing Light." *Lesbian Fiction: An Anthology*. Ed. Elly Bulkin. Watertown, MA: Persephone Press, 1981. 168–74.
   Describes a dying grandmother.

544. Wang, C. H. "Poetry Ablaze, and Ambiguous." *Caliban* 1 (1986): 50–55.
   An autobiographical sketch.

545. **Watanna, Onoto [Winnifred Eaton Babcock]. *Diary of Delia*. Garden City, NY: Doubleday, 1907.
   Delia is a maid for a family of six.

546. ———. *The Heat of the Hyacinth*. New York: Harper, 1903.

547. ———. *Honorable Miss Moonlight*. New York: Harper, 1912.
   Describes a geisha.

548. ———. *Japanese Blossom*. New York: Harper, 1906.
   A Japanese goes to America to retrieve his shattered fortunes.

549. ———. *A Japanese Nightingale*. New York: Harper, 1901.
   Novella.

550. ——— [Anonymous]. *Me: A Book of Remembrance*. New York: Century, 1915.
   An autobiographical novel about the struggle of a Canadian writer.

551. ———. *Miss Numè of Japan: A Japanese American Romance*. Chicago: Rand, McNally, 1899.

552. ———. *Sunny-San*. New York: George H. Doran, 1922.
   Four American students in Japan encounter a geisha.

553. ———. *Tama*. New York: Harper, 1910.
   A love story about a Western professor and a blind girl in Japan.

554. ———. *The Wooing of Wistaria*. New York: Harper, 1902.

555. *Way, Frances M. "A Tea House Tale: The Haunted Hall of Lingering Fragrance." *Paradise of the Pacific* Sept. 1949: 26–27.
   A romantic tale set in China.

556. Wei, Katherine, and Terry Quinn. *Second Daughter: Growing Up in China, 1930–1949*. Boston: Little, 1984.
   Autobiography.
   Rev. Michiko Kakutani, *New York Times* 3 Aug. 1984: C24.

557. *Wong, Barry. "The Interview." *The Asian-Canadian and the Arts* [#96] 14.
   An old Chinese American reveals his unwritten history while claiming ignorance.

558. ———. "The Poetry in His Eyes." *The Asian-Canadian and the Arts* [#96] 12.
   Recalls a glimpse into an old Chinese Canadian's eyes.

559. **Wong, Gina. "Learning English." *Asianadian* 4.4 (1982): 7+.
   Describes the women who attend an English class.

560. Wong, Jade Snow. "Daddy." *Common Ground* 5.2 (1945): 25–29.
The author's sketch of her Confucian father.

561. ———. "Dinner with the Wongs." *Holiday* Dec. 1956: 48+.
An essay about the author's tour in Hong Kong.

562. ———. *Fifth Chinese Daughter.* New York: Harper, 1945.
Excerpts: "The Sanctum of Harmonious Spring" in *Common Ground*
8.2 (1948): 84–91; "All but Jade Snow" in *I'm On My Way Running* [#166]
185–86; "A Measure of Freedom" in *Asian-American Authors* [#125] 1976:
25–36.
An autobiographical novel about growing up between two cultures in
San Francisco Chinatown.

563. ———. "Growing Up between the Old World and the New." *Horn Book
Magazine* Dec. 1951: 440–45.
Text of a talk given at the American Library Assn. Conference, Chicago,
July 1951.

564. ———. "Jon." *Common Ground* 6.1 (1945): 39–44.
The author's sketch of her youngest brother.

565. ———. *No Chinese Stranger.* New York: Harper, 1975.
Autobiography.

566. ———. "Puritans from the Orient: A Chinese Evolution." *The Immigrant Experience: The Anguish of Becoming American.* Ed. and introd. Thomas C. Wheeler. New York: Dial, 1971. 107–31.
A personal narrative that centers on the author's parents, Chinese immigrants in San Francisco.

567. *Wong, Marcellina. "Ipu O Lono: Legend of the Pali Rock." *Paradise of
the Pacific* 61, holiday ed. (1949): 26–27.
A retelling of a legend explaining the origin of a large upright boulder in Hawaii.

568. Wong, Nellie. "In Search of the Self as Hero: Confetti of Voices on New
Year's Night." *This Bridge Called My Back* [#143] 177–81.
The author addresses a letter to herself explaining why she must write.

569. ———. "Long Steam." *Asian Week* 26 Dec. 1986: 2+.
Reflections upon attending an old lady's funeral.

570. Wong, Shawn H. *Homebase.* New York: I. Reed Books, 1979. Portions
of the novella appear as follows: "All in the Night without Food." *Yardbird Reader* 5 (1976): 255–65, rpt. in *Yardbird Lives!* [#164] 28–38 and
West Coast Fiction [#124] 335–45; "Each Year Grain." *AIIIEEEEE!* [#100]
1983: 170–75; "Good Luck, Happiness, and Long Life." *Counterpoint*
[#113] 464–70; "Night Driver." *Yardbird Reader* 3 [#179] 193–99.
A novella about the search for Chinese American identity.
Rev. Diana Chang, *Amerasia Journal* 8.1 (1981): 136–39; Oggie Kim,
Bridge 8.2 (1982): 27–28.

571. Wong, Stella. "The Paper Son." *Asian Women* [#84] 36–39.
A man gets into trouble for claiming his nephew as his son.

572.   Wong, Su-Ling [pseud.], and E. H. Cressy. *Daughter of Confucius: A Personal History*. New York: Farrar, 1952.
        An autobiography set in both China and the US.

573.   Wong, Victor. "Childhood 1930's." *Ting* [#117] 15–24.
        The author reminisces about growing up in Chinatown.

574.   ———. "Childhood II." *Ting* [#117] 69–72.
        Reminiscences about the conflicts resulting from attending Chinese and English schools simultaneously.

575.   Woo, Merle. "Letter to Ma." *This Bridge Called My Back* [#143] 140–47.
        Describes the chasm and connection between a mother and daughter.

576.   ———. "Recovering." *Bridge* 6.4 (1978): 42–45.
        Describes a female alcoholic.

577.   Wu Ting Fang. *America through the Spectacles of an Oriental Diplomat*. New York: Frederick A. Stokes, 1914.
        The author describes his impressions of America and compares the American and Chinese civilizations.

578.   **Yee, Paul. "Morning Heat." *Asianadian* 3.2 (1980): 14–15.
        A young painter encounters a bewitching woman.

579.   ———. "Prairie Night 1939." *The Asian-Canadian and the Arts* [#96] 24–28.
        A café owner in Saskatchewan tries to understand his reluctance to return to China.

580.   ———. "Prairie Widow." *West Coast Review* 18.3 (1984): 7–18.
        A widow left with two sons in Saskatchewan thinks about her past in China and her future in Canada.

581.   Yep, Laurence. "In a Sky of Daemons." *Protostars*. Ed. David Gerrold with Stephen Goldin. New York: Ballantine, 1971. 32–69.
        Science fiction.

582.   ———. "Looking-Glass Sea." *Strange Bedfellows: Sex and Science Fiction*. Ed. Thomas N. Scortia. New York: Random, 1972. 166–77.
        A space explorer recalls his numerous love affairs with women from other planets.

583.   ———. *Seademons*. New York: Harper, 1977.
        Science fiction.

584.   Yih, Chia-Shun. "Old China Remembered." *Ohio Review* 18.2 (1977): 69–77.
        Autobiographical reminiscences.

585.   Yu, Connie Young. "Notes from an Extra in the American Moving Picture Show." *Working It Out: 23 Women Writers, Artists, Scientists, and Scholars Talk about Their Lives and Work*. Ed. Sara Ruddick and Pamela Daniels. New York: Pantheon, 1977. 179–95.
        Autobiographical essay.

586. Yu Li-hua [Helen]. "In Liu Village." Trans. author and C. T. Hsia. Pt. 1 in *Literature East and West* 15.2 (1971): 219–43; pt. 2 in *Literature East and West* 15.3 (1971): 432–46.
   Entire story rpt. in *Chinese Stories from Taiwan: 1960–1970*. Ed. Joseph S. M. Lau, with Timothy A. Ross. New York: Columbia UP, 1976. 101–42.
   A woman who is raped confronts members of an extended family.

587. ———. "Nightfall." Trans. Vivian Hsu and Julia Fitzgerald. *Born of the Same Roots* [#126] 194–209.
   The sight of her aging father evokes in the daughter memories of heated parental disputes.

588. ———. "Sorrow at the End of the Yangtze River." *Uclan Review* 3.2 (1957): 5–13.

589. *Yuen, Kevin. "Looking for Mana." *Hanai* [#161] 15–24.
   A young man who returns to his native Hawaii for a visit discovers how much he has changed.

Yun, Tan. See Lin, Adet.

590. Yung, Shau May. "The Tea Party." *Transfer Magazine* Fall 1977: 63–70.
   A woman reflects on people in the medical profession and their neglected spouses.

591. Yung Wing. *My Life in China and America*. New York: Holt, 1909. New York: Arno, 1978.
   An autobiography by the first Chinese student to study in America.

592. Yup, Paula. "My Mother Used to Dream." *Echoes from Gold Mountain* 1982: 91–93.
   A girl describes her estrangement from her family and environment.

Poetry

593. Berssenbrugge, Mei-Mei. *Fish Souls*. New York: Greenwood, 1971.

594. ———. *The Heat Bird*. Providence: Burning Deck Press, 1983.
   Rev. Jesse Hiraoka, *Contact II* 7.38–40 (1986): 56; Carolyne Wright, *Northwest Review* 23.1 (1985): 118–33.

595. ———. *Packrat Sieve*. New York: Contact II, 1983.

596. ———. *Random Possession*. New York: I. Reed Books, 1979.

597. ———. *Summits Move with the Tide*. Greenfield Center, NY: Greenfield Review Press, 1974.
   Rev. Fred Wei-han Houn, *East Wind* 2.2 (1983): 65–67.

598. Chang, Diana. *The Horizon Is Definitely Speaking*. New York: Backstreet Editions Press, 1982.
   Rev. Shirley Lim, *Contact II* 7.38–40 (1986): 55–56.

599. ———. *What Matisse Is After*. New York: Contact II, 1984.
   Poems and drawings.

600. **Cheng, Sait Chia. *Turned Clay*. Fredericton, NB: Fiddlehead Poetry Books, 1981.
Rev. Connie Young Yu, *Contact II* 7.38–40 (1986): 24.

601. Chiang, Fay. *In the City of Contradictions*. Bronx, NY: Sunbury Press, 1979.

602. ———. *Miwa's Song*. Bronx, NY: Sunbury Press, 1982.
Rev. Fred Wei-han Houn, *East Wind* 2.2 (1983): 65–67.

603. Chin, Marilyn. *Dwarf Bamboo*. Greenfield Center, NY: Greenfield Review Press, 1987.

604. *Chock, Eric. *Ten Thousand Wishes*. Honolulu: Bamboo Ridge Press, 1978.

605. Hsia, Wei Lin. *The Poetry of English and Chinese*. New York: Vantage, 1978.
Forty-two poems are in English.

606. Kuo, Alexander. *Changing the River*. Berkeley: Reed & Cannon, 1986.

607. ———. *"New Letters from Hiroshima" and Other Poems*. Greenfield Center, NY: Greenfield Review Press, 1974.

608. ———. *The Window Tree*. Peterborough, NH: Windy Row Press, 1971.

609. Kwan, Moon. *A Chinese Mirror: Poems and Plays*. Introd. Manly Hall. Los Angeles: Phoenix Press, 1932.

610. Lau, Alan Chong. *Songs for Jadina: Poems by Alan Chong Lau*. Greenfield Center, NY: Greenfield Review Press, 1980.
Rev. Diana Chang, *Contact II* 7.38–40 (1986): 97–98.

611. Lee, Li-Young. *Rose*. Foreword Gerald Stern. Brockport, NY: Boa Editions, 1986.

612. Lee, Mary. *The Guest of Tyn-y-Coed Cae: Poems and Drawings*. Pref. Anaïs Nin. Santa Monica, CA: Hightree Books, 1973.

613. ———. *Hand in Hand*. Illus. author. New York: Crown, 1971.

614. ———. *Tender Bough*. Photos. Alice Gowland and Peter Gowland. New York: Crown, 1969.

615. Lee, Mary Wong. *Through My Windows*. Stockton, CA: Roxene Lee Publishing, 1979.

616. ———. *Through My Windows, Book II*. Stockton, CA: Mills Press, 1980.

617. Lem, Carol. *Don't Ask Why*. Los Angeles: Peddler Press, 1982.
Rev. Dianne Hai-Jew, *Contact II* 7.38–40 (1986): 65.

618. ———. *Grassroots*. Los Angeles: Peddler Press, 1975.

619. Leong, George. *A Lone Bamboo Doesn't Come from Jackson Street: History, Poetry, Short Story*. San Francisco: Isthmus, 1977.
Rev. Tomas N. Santos, *Amerasia Journal* 5.2 (1978): 142–45; Sharon Wong, *Bridge* 6.1 (1978): 64; Connie Young Yu, *Contact II* 7.38–40 (1986): 11.

620.   Lim, Shirley [Geok-lin]. *Crossing the Peninsula and Other Poems.* Kuala Lumpur: Heinemann, 1980.
      Rev. Peter Nazareth, *World Literature Today* 55.3 (1981): 534.

621.   ———. *Modern Secrets.* London: Dangaroo Press, forthcoming.

622.   ———. *No Man's Grove.* Singapore: Dept. of English Lang. and Lit., National Univ. of Singapore, 1985.

623.   Ling, Amy. *Chinamerica Reflections: A Chapbook of Poems and Paintings.* Lewiston, ME: Great Raven Press, 1984.

624.   Liu, Stephen Shu Ning. *Dream Journeys to China.* Beijing: New World Press; San Francisco: China Books, 1982.
      In Chinese and English.
      Rev. Jesse Hiraoka, *Contact II* 7.38–40 (1986): 63–64.

625.   *Lum, Wing Tek. *Expounding the Doubtful Points.* Spec. double issue of *Bamboo Ridge* 34–35 (1987).
      Rev. Pat Matsueda, *Literary Arts Hawaii* 85 (Summer 1987): 6–8.

626.   Mar, Laureen. *Living Furniture.* San Francisco: Noro Press, 1982.

Song, Cathy. See Korean American section.

627.   Sze, Arthur. *Dazzled.* Point Reyes Station, CA: Floating Island Publications, 1982.
      Rev. Gayle Kimi Fujita, *Literary Arts Hawaii* 80–81 (Summer 1986): 8–11; Jeff Tagami, *Contact II* 7.38–40 (1986): 20.

628.   ———. *Two Ravens.* 1976. Santa Fe: Tooth of Time Books, 1984.
      Contains translations of Chinese poetry and the author's own poetry.
      Rev. Oliver Conant, *Contact II* 7.38–40 (1986): 62–63.

629.   ———. *The Willow Wind.* 1972. Guadalupita, NM: Tooth of Time Books, 1981.
      Contains translations of Tang poems.

630.   Ting, Walasse. *Chinese Moonlight: 63 Poems by 33 Poets.* Introd. Irving Groupp. Trans. and recomposed by Walasse Ting. Copenhagen: Permild & Rosengreen; New York: Wittenborn, [1967].

631.   ———. *Hot and Sour Soup.* N.p.: Sam Francis Foundation, 1969.

632.   ———. *My Shit and My Love: 10 Poems.* Bruxelles: Galerie Smith, [1961].

633.   ———. *1¢ Life.* Ed. Sam Francis. Bern: E. W. Kornfield, 1964.
      Poems and drawings.

634.   Tsiang, H[si] T[seng]. *Poems of the Chinese Revolution.* New York: privately printed, 1929.

635.   Tsui, Kitty. *The Words of a Woman Who Breathes Fire.* San Francisco: Spinsters, Ink., 1983.
      Rev. Dianne Hai-Jew, *Contact II* 7.38–40 (1986): 15.

636.   **Wah, Fred. *Among.* Toronto: Coach House Press, 1972.

637.   ———. *Breathin' My Name with a Sigh.* 1978. Vancouver: Talonbooks, 1981.

638.   ———. *Earth.* Canton, NY: Inst. of Further Studies, 1974.

639.   ———. *Grasp the Sparrow's Tail.* Kyoto, 1982.

640.   ———. *Lardeau.* Toronto: Island Press, 1965.

641.   ———. *Loki Is Buried at Smoky Creek: Selected Poems.* Introd. George Bowering. Vancouver: Talonbooks, 1980.
        Rev. Judith Roche, *Contact II* 7.38–40 (1986): 18–19.

642.   ———. *Mountain.* Buffalo, NY: Audit, 1967.

643.   ———. *Music at the Heart of Thinking.* Red Deer, AB: Red Deer Coll. Press, 1987.

644.   ———. *Owners Manual.* Lantzville, BC: Island Writing Series, 1981.

645.   ———. *Pictograms from the Interior of B. C.* Vancouver: Talonbooks, 1975.

646.   ———. *Rooftops.* South Harpswell, ME: Blackberry—Salted in the Shell, 1987.

647.   ———. *Tree.* Vancouver: Vancouver Community Press, 1972.

648.   ———. *Waiting for Saskatchewan.* Winnipeg: Turnstone Press, 1985.

649.   **Wah, Fred, et al. *Pictures and Words.* Castlegar, BC: Cotinneh Books (dist.), 1973.

650.   Wang, David Rafael. *The Goblet Moon.* Lunenburg, VT: Stinehour Press, 1955.

651.   ———. *The Intercourse.* Greenfield Center, NY: Greenfield Review Press, 1975.
        Rev. Bill Wong, *Bridge* 4.2 (1976): 47.

652.   ———. *Rivers on Fire.* New York: Basilisk Press, 1977.

653.   Wong, May. *A Bad Girl's Book of Animals.* New York: Harcourt, 1969.

654.   ———. *Reports.* New York: Harcourt, 1972.
        Rev. Norman Rosten, *Saturday Review* 12 Aug. 1972: 58.

655.   ———. *Superstitions: Poems.* New York: Harcourt, 1978.

656.   Wong, Nanying Stella. *Man Curving to Sky.* San Francisco: Anthelion Press, 1976.

657.   Wong, Nellie. *The Death of a Long Steam Lady.* Los Angeles: West End Press, 1986.
        Rev. David Volpendesta, *San Francisco Sunday Examiner and Chronicle* 8 Feb. 1987, rev. sec.: 8.

658.   ———. *Dreams in Harrison Railroad Park.* Berkeley: Kelsey Street Press, 1977.
        Rev. Tina Koyama, *Contact II* 7.38–40 (1986): 17; Amy Ling, *MELUS*

6.1 (1979): 91–93; Judy Yung, *Bridge* 5.4 (1977): 28.

659. Yau, John. *Broken Off by the Music.* Providence: Burning Deck Press, 1981.

660. ———. *Corpse and Mirror.* 1977. National Poetry Ser. Selected by John Ashbery. New York: Holt, 1983.
Poetry and prose poems.
Rev. Joseph Keppler, *Contact II* 7.38–40 (1986): 64–65.

661. ———. *Crossing Canal Street.* Binghamton, NY: Bellevue Press, 1976.

662. ———. *Notarikon.* New York: Jordon Davies, 1981.

663. ———. *The Reading of an Ever-Changing Tale.* New York: Nobodaddy Press, 1977.
Chapbook.

664. ———. *The Sleepless Night of Eugene Delacroix.* New York: Release Press, 1980.

665. ———. *Sometimes: Poems.* New York: Sheep Meadow Press, 1979.

666. Yup, Paula. *Love Poems.* East Talmouth, MA: Peka Boo Press, 1984.

Drama

667. *Aw, Arthur. *All Brand New Classical Chinese Theatre.* *Kumu Kahua Plays* [#97] 83–122.

668. Berssenbrugge, Mei-Mei. *One, Two Cups.* *Summits Move with the Tide* [#597] 51–68.
A one-act play about the relationship between daughters and mothers.

669. Chin, Frank. The Chickencoop Chinaman *and* The Year of the Dragon. Introd. Dorothy Ritsuko McDonald. Seattle: U of Washington P, 1981.
Act 1 of *The Chickencoop Chinaman* in *AIIIEEEEE!* [#100] 1983: 51–74; act 2 of *The Chickencoop Chinaman* in *Yardbird Reader* 3 [#179] 259–91.

670. Chong, Ping. *I Flew to Fiji; You Went South.* *Bridge* 5.2 (1977): 24–26.

671. Chow, Diana W. *An Asian Man of a Different Color.* *Quilt* 2 (1981): 39–50.
A comedy about an Asian man who literally turns Caucasian.

672. Hsiung, S[hih] I. *Wang Pao-Chuan: Lady Precious Stream.* London: Methuen, 1934. New York: French, 1962.
An old Chinese play adapted into English according to traditional style.

673. Hwang, David Henry. *Broken Promises: Four Plays.* New York: Avon, 1983.
Family Devotions, *The Dance and the Railroad*, *FOB*, and *The House of Sleeping Beauties.*

674. ———. *The Sound of a Voice.* New York: Dramatists Play Service, 1984.

Kwan, Moon. See #609.

675. Lee, G. M. *One in Sisterhood. Asian Women* [#84] 119–21.
   Five women debate on whether their identity as women or as Asians is more important.

676. Lim, Genny. *The Only Language. Bamboo Ridge* 30 (1986): 34–41.
   A dialogue from "The Only Language She Knows," a 20-minute feature film about a mother-daughter conflict.

677. ———. *Pigeons. Bamboo Ridge* 30 (1986): 57–79.
   One-act play.

678. Lim, Paul Stephen. *Points of Departure. Bridge* 5.2 (1977): 27–29.
   One-act play.

Lin Yutang. See #436.

679. *Lum, Darrell H. Y. *Magic Mango. Bamboo Shoots* [#131] 4–13.
   One-act children's play.

680. ———. *My Home Is Down the Street.* Act 1, scene 1 in *Literary Arts Hawaii* 78–79 (Spring 1986): 16–20; act 2, scene 1 in *Literary Arts Hawaii* 80–81 (Summer 1986): 20–22.
   Rev. Bev Fujita, *Literary Arts Hawaii* 83 (New Year 1987): 10–11.

681. ———. "Oranges Are Lucky." *Talk Story* [#104] 139–56.
   Rpt. in *Sun* [#481] 44–61; *Asian-Pacific Literature.* Ed. James Harstad and Cheryl A. Harstad. Honolulu: Hawaii English Program–Secondary, Curriculum Research and Development Group of the Univ. of Hawaii and the Dept. of Education, State of Hawaii, 1981. 1: 342–53; *Kumu Kahua Plays* [#97] 63–82.
   Set in a Chinese restaurant, this one-act play depicts a family gathering to celebrate the eightieth birthday of their grandmother.
   Rev. Mary Wakayama, *Hawaii Literary Arts Council Newsletter* Feb.-Mar. 1982: n. pag.

———. *Sun: Short Stories and Drama.* See #481.

682. Woo, Merle. *Balancing* [act 1]. *Hanai* [#161] 67–73.
   A mother disparages her daughter's white boyfriend while the daughter casts aspersions on the mother's lesbianism.

683. Yep, Laurence. *Daemons. Bamboo Ridge* 30 (1986): 80–94.
   One-act play.

Japanese American Literature

The following terms appear frequently in this section: *nikkei* (people of Japanese ancestry living in North or South America), *issei* (Japanese immigrants to the US or Canada), *nisei* (second-generation Japanese Americans, children of the *issei*), *kibei* (*nisei* who lived in Japan for a substantial portion of their childhood and/or adolescence), *sansei* (third-generation Japanese Americans, children of the *nisei*).

Prose

684. Abe, Yoshio. "[Excerpt from] *The Man of Dual Nationality*." Trans. Fumio Takemae. Introd. Kazuo Yamane. *Journal of Ethnic Studies* 12.4 (1985): 87–99.

    An excerpt from the first volume of a three-volume novel. Introduces the *kibei* protagonist and his *nisei* girlfriend who are interned in the Santa Anita racetrack.

685. Adachi, Jeffrey. *Maniwala Boy: The Adventures of a Walnut Grove Country Boy*. Sacramento: Yancha Productions, 1982.

    The story of a Japanese country bumpkin who lives in Walnut Grove, California, during the early 1900s.

686. ———. *Yancha!* Sacramento: Jeff Adachi, 1981.

    Short stories and poetry by a *sansei*.

687. Airan, Hoshina. "Enlightenment." *Reimei* ns 1.1 (1932): 5–10.

    A short story about a cynical student who eventually becomes a priest.

688. Akagi, James. "He Will Be Equal." *Rafu Shimpo* 18 Dec. 1976: 14 + .

    The author describes his grandfather's power and lack of power over others.

689. Akagi, Richard. "Two Fables for Today." *Pacific Citizen* 22 Dec. 1951: 20–21.

    Two comic sketches.

690. Akashi, Hama. "Johnny's Uncle." *Tulean Dispatch Magazine* Feb. 1943: 21–23.

    Uncle Sam is personified in this short story describing the relationship between Japanese Americans and the US.

691. Akimoto, George. "Daggers in the Wallboard." *The Pen* [#160] 59–60.

    A Japanese American man is disturbed by his loud neighbors.

692. *Akutagawa, Jill K. "Obake Bite You." *Bamboo Ridge* 20 (1983): 17–18.

    About the relationship between a girl and her grandmother. *Obake* means "ghost" or "spirit" in Japanese.

693. Amano, Alfred. "Prelude." *Reimei* ns 1.3 (1933): 21–23.

    In this essay, the author rejoices in living.

694. Ames, Candace Nosaka, and Louann Nosaka. "Nasakenai." *Hokubei Mainichi* 1 Jan. 1984: 1–2.
Rpt. in *Fusion Too* [#158] 57–62.
Describes the lives of an *issei* couple during the days immediately following the bombing of Pearl Harbor.

695. Ando, Mariane. "Fallen Angel." *Rafu Shimpo* 20 Dec. 1956: 15.
A missing Christmas-tree angel causes problems for a family.

696. Arakawa, Jeanette. "A Pearl Harbor Survivor." *Hokubei Mainichi* 1 Jan. 1979, supplement: 2–3.

697. Arima, Thomas. "The Humble Road." *Hokubei Mainichi* 1 Jan. 1979, supplement: 2–3.
Rpt. in *Fusion-San* [#157] 46–48.
A woman who has tried to break away from her past rediscovers it.

698. ———. [under pseud. Manzen]. "The Eve." *Hokubei Mainichi* 1 Jan. 1987: 1.

699. *Ariyoshi, Koji. "The Sinner." *Paradise of the Pacific* July 1940: 20+.
Rpt. in *Talk Story* [#104] 55–63.
A woman recalls scenes from her troubled family life while attending her son's college graduation.

700. Asai, Hisayo M. "Michael, a Poor Boy." *Pacific Citizen* 19 Dec. 1986: B24.
A short sketch about a boy who cannot afford to buy shoes.

701. *Asakura, Ben. "The Funa, the Dojo, and the Namazu." *Bamboo Ridge* 20 (1983): 5–10.
Describes various extinct species of fish.

702. ———. "A Visitor from Alaska." *Bamboo Ridge* 20 (1983): 9–10.
The narrator observes the migration pattern of a one-legged bird.

703. *Au, Joy Mitsui. "A Distant World." *Bamboo Ridge* 11 (1981): 21–25.
Short story.

704. Beekman, Take, and Allan Beekman. "No Place beneath the Rising Sun." *Pacific Citizen* 22 Dec. 1961: B9–B10.
Rpt. in *Hawaiian Tales*. Detroit: Harlo Press, 1970. 50–70; *Ethnic American Short Stories* [#150] 145–65.
Describes a young boy's experiences immediately after the bombing of Pearl Harbor.

705. ———. "The World That Then Was." *Pacific Citizen* 21 Dec. 1962: C1–C3.

706. Burns, Vivian. "Rose." *Rafu Shimpo* 20 Dec. 1977: 13.
A sketch of an old woman whose life is transformed after taking in a stray kitten.

708. Chinen, Jon. "Good Luck, Sergeant." *Paradise of the Pacific* 66 (1954): 21.
A young Hawaiian soldier who has served in Japan plans to return in order to locate a childhood friend.

709.   ———. "The Old and the New." *Aloha* 4.21 (1950): 2–6.
A version of this story is rpt. as "Christmas Reunion" in *Pacific Citizen* 22 Dec. 1951: 68–69.
An *issei* mother laments her son's death in the Korean War but discovers that he married and fathered a son while in Hawaii.

710.   ———. "A Special Lei." *Aloha* 4.20 (1950): 7–9.
A young boy is ashamed of a lei his mother makes for him.

711.   ———. "They Were So Young, Part I: Anzio Beachhead." *Hawaiian Digest* Mar. 1948: 49–55.
A serialized novella about Hawaii's famed 100th Battalion.

712.   ———. "They Were So Young, Part II: Combat Patrol." *Hawaiian Digest* Apr. 1948: 49–55.

713.   ———. "They Were So Young, Part III: An Unknown German." *Aloha* 3.17 (1949): 35–40.

714.   ———. "They Were So Young, Part IV: Conclusion." *Aloha* 3.18 (1949): 32–38.

715.   Daniel, Teruko Ogata. "Such, Such Were the Joys." *The Ethnic American Woman* [#88] 182–85.
An autobiographical account about a family's fear and frustration immediately after the bombing of Pearl Harbor and the author's subsequent attempts to assimilate.

716.   ———. "We Wise Children." *The Ethnic American Woman* [#88] 107–08.
Portrait of a troubled and abused *issei* woman.

DeSoto, Hisaye Yamamoto. See Yamamoto [DeSoto], Hisaye.

717.   "Diary of a Soldier in the '442' Combat Team." *Rafu Shimpo* 21 Dec. 1974: 18+.
A nonfictional account by a member of the 442nd Regimental Combat Team, tracing his experiences from volunteering in Hawaii, to fighting in Europe, where he is injured, to returning home.

718.   Doi, Amy Tamaki. "Mama and the Great Tokyo Earthquake." *Rafu Shimpo* 20 Dec. 1977: 14+.
The author recounts her mother's experience in the Tokyo earthquake of 1923 and describes the devastating death and destruction.

719.   *Doi, Marshall M. "The Luna of the Landing." *Bamboo Ridge* 1 (1978): 24–31.
Rpt. in *The Best of* Bamboo Ridge [#103] 115–21.
Focuses on the relationship between an old man and a retarded boy.

720.   Doi, Roy. "Rabbit Hunt." *Hokubei Mainichi* 1 Jan. 1975, supplement: 1.

721.   Egami, Hatsuye. "Wartime Diary." *All Aboard* [#81] 34–39.
Diary entries concerning internment.

722. Eguchi, Pamela. "Childhood." *Bridge* 1.6 (1972): 31.
     Rpt. in *Yellow Peril* [#182] n. pag.
     After a happy birthday, a seven-year-old girl, along with her family, is sent to a relocation center.

723. Embrey, Sue Kunitomi. "Some Lines for a Younger Brother. . . ." *Ayumi* [#141] 103–05.
     An autobiographical sketch tracing the life and death of the author's brother.

724. Endo, Ellen. "The Pathetic Picket." *Rafu Shimpo* 20 Dec. 1965: 20+.
     A comic interior monologue of a picketer who has some mental problems.

725. Fugami, Clyde. "The Fisherman's Wife." *Fusion Too* [#158] 46–51.
     A character study of an old *nisei* fisherman and his reaction to his wife's death.

726. ———. "Medicine Man." *Fusion-San* [#157] 50–52.
     A Native American medicine man counsels a Japanese American railroad worker.

727. Fujii, Ryoichi. "Autobiography, an Excerpt." *Ayumi* [#141] 3–4.
     An account of the author's involvement in radical politics while studying in the US.

728. *Fujimoto, Alan S. "Flakes of Snow." *Hawaii Review* 2.2 (1974): 48–59.
     Short story.

729. Fujimura, Bunya. *Though I Be Crushed: The Wartime Experiences of a Buddhist Priest.* Los Angeles: Nembutsu Press, 1985.

730. Fujita, Akira. "Season of Repatriation: Diary of a Renunciant." *Ayumi* [#141] 7–8.
     Excerpts from the diary of a Tule Lake internee that comment on the various reasons why Japanese Americans would renounce their citizenship and why *issei* would choose to return to Japan.

731. *Fujita, Fumiko. "Grandmother's White Hands." *Paradise of the Pacific* Nov. 1946: 26.
     A woman develops a phobia after seeing her grandmother's corpse.

732. *Fujita, Gerald. "The Christmas Jinx." *Daylight.* Pearl City: Hawaii Writers Club, 1969. 53–56.
     A personal sketch describing how the author's father broke his nose on four different Christmas Eves.

733. Fukai, Tim. "Growing Out." *Hanai* [#161] 7–14.
     Autobiographical essay.

734. Fukaya, Michiyo. "The New Land." *Fusion-San* [#157] 38–44.
     Follows the immigration experiences of an *issei* woman.

735. Fukei, Arlene. "A Christmas Miracle." *Pacific Citizen* 20 Dec. 1957: C20+.
     A Christmas delivery mixup results in understanding between a Buddhist minister and a Catholic priest.

736.   Fukuzawa, Yukichi. *The Autobiography of Yukichi Fukuzawa*. Trans. Eiichi Kiyooka. New York: Columbia UP, 1966.

737.   Goto, A. "A Reverse Climbing Coiled Rope Trick: An Interview." *Rising Waters* 1976: n. pag.
       A series of flashbacks and interior monologues.

738.   **Goto, Edy. "The Dream." *The Asian-Canadian and the Arts* [#96] 5–8.
       A Japanese Canadian woman dreams about Japan.

739.   *Hamabata, Marla. "Oh Wow." *Hawaii Review* 13 (1982): 99–104.
       Describes the sexual awakening of a young Hawaiian woman at a boarding school.

740.   Hamada, James T. *Don't Give Up the Ship*. Boston: Meador Publishing, 1933.
       A man sets out to find a missing ship in the South Pacific.

741.   *Harada, Gail N. "Waiting For Henry." *Bamboo Ridge* 13 (1981–82): 45–50.
       Rpt. in *The Best of* Bamboo Ridge [#103] 131–36.
       A woman loses her lover and her cat in succession.

742.   Harada, Margaret. *The Sun Shines on the Immigrant*. New York: Vantage, 1960.
       A novel about a Japanese immigrant.

743.   *Harada, Violet. "The Shell Gatherer." *Behold Hawaii*. Ed. Barbara B. Robinson and Catherine E. Harris. Honolulu: Menehune Publishers, 1975. 53–55.
       Rpt. in *Bamboo Ridge* 14 (Mar. 1982): 43–46; *The Best of* Bamboo Ridge [#103] 137–40.
       Describes a Japanese American man's deep-seated prejudice against Filipinos.

744.   Haratani, Richard. "Attention to Detail." *Fusion-San* [#157] 70–73.
       A *nikkei* man working on a military base faces problems after the bombing of Pearl Harbor.

745.   Hartmann, [Carl] Sadakichi. *The Last Thirty Days of Christ*. New York: privately printed, 1920.
       Purports to be the diary of St. Lebbeus, describing Christ's journey through Galilee, Samaria, and Jordan.
       Rev. George Knox, *Los Angeles Free Press* 7 Apr. 1972, sec. 2: 2.

746.   ———. *My Crucifixion; Asthma for 40 Years*. Tujunga, CA: Cloister Press of Hollywood, for the author, 1931.

747.   ———. *Passport to Immortality*. Beaumont, CA: privately printed, [1927].
       Personal reflections on the state of the soul.

748.   ———. *Permanent Peace: Is It a Dream?* New York: G. Bruno, 1915.

749.   ———. *Schopenhauer in the Air: Seven Stories*. New York: privately printed, 1894.

750. ———. *Schopenhauer in the Air: Twelve Stories*. Rochester, NY: Stylus Publishing, 1908.

751. ———. *Seven Short Stories*. Beaumont, CA: privately printed, 1930.
Contains "Dispossessed," "An Old-Fashioned Garden," "The Little Wayside Station," "Nancy Penington," "Old People's Home," "The Balalaika Man," "The Panther Girl."

752. ———. *White Chrysanthemums: Literary Fragments and Pronouncements*. Ed. George Knox and Harry Lawton. New York: Herder, 1971.
A collection of essays.

753. ———. *"The Whitman-Hartmann Controversy including Conversations with Walt Whitman" and Other Essays*. Ed. and introd. George Knox and Harry Lawton. Bern: Lang, 1976.

754. Hashimoto, Sharon. "The Last Inari and Makizushi Stand." *Echoes from Gold Mountain* 1979: 53–59.
Rpt. in *The Stories We Hold Secret* [#89] 216–23.
A sketch of an *issei* woman's relationship with her family.

755. ———. "When the World Winds Down." *Echoes from Gold Mountain* 1978: 50–55.
While repairing the watch of a *sansei* man, an older *nisei* is reminded of his younger brother who died in World War II.

756. Hatsutaro. *Kaigai Ibun: A Strange Tale from Overseas: Or, A New Account of America*. Comp. Bunzo Maekawa and Junzo Sakai. Trans. Richard Zumwinkle. Los Angeles: Dawson's Book Shop, 1970.
A Japanese castaway in 1841 is picked up by a Spanish ship and taken to Mexico.

757. *Hattori, Raymond. "Gateway to Christmas." *Nisei: In Hawaii and the Pacific* 4 (holiday issue 1950): 6+.
Chronicles the events that lead a Japanese man to overcome his bitterness toward Americans.

758. Hayakawa, Sessue Kintaro. *The Bandit Prince*. New York: Macaulay, 1926.
Focuses on political events in Asia.

759. ———. *Zen Showed Me the Way — to Peace, Happiness and Tranquility*. Indianapolis: Bobbs, 1960. Introd. Croswell Bowen. London: Allen, 1961.

760. Hickel, Martin. "Tree." *Hokubei Mainichi* 1 Jan. 1981, supplement: 1–2.

761. Hicks, J. A. "Untitled." *Fusion-San* [#157] 32–33.
Describes the author's childhood trips to San Francisco Japantown.

762. Hifumi, A. [pseud.]. "Scenes from a Sansei Life." *Pacific Citizen* 21–28 Dec. 1979: 53.
Autobiographical piece.

763. Higa, Lori R. "Homecoming." *Rising Waters* 1975: n. pag.
A sketch about a soldier returning home to his wife and daughter.

764. *Higashi, Mary S. "A Day in the Fields." *Paradise of the Pacific* Jan. 1950: 19.
      A sketch of an *issei* plantation laborer.

765. **Higo, T. K. "Egg Whites and Yolks." *The Asian-Canadian and the Arts* [#96] 69–72.
      Describes a confrontation between a practical mother and a daughter who wants to be an artist.

766. Hijikata, Frank. "Mandy's Dream." *Tulean Dispatch Magazine* Apr. 1942: 2+.
      A black slave dreams of her home in heaven.

767. Hirabayashi, Lane Ryo. "'The Best of Both Worlds?': Reflections on the Bi-Cultural Experience." *Echoes from Gold Mountain* 1982: 77–90.

768. Hirahara, Naomi. "The Bath." *Rafu Shimpo* 22 Dec. 1984: 4+.
      A story about a Japanese American woman in Japan.

769. Hirano, Kiyo. *Enemy Alien*. Trans. George Hirano and Yuri Kageyama. San Francisco: Japantown Art and Media Workshop, 1984.
      An *issei* woman recalls the outbreak of World War II.

770. Hirooka, Kats. "Summer Afternoon." *Pacific Citizen* 24 Dec. 1949: 10.

771. *Hongo, Bob Nobuyuki. *Hey, Pineapple!* Tokyo: Hokuseido Press, 1958.
      Describes the adventures of a group of Hawaiian soldiers who fight in the Korean War.

772. Hori, Ichiro. "Hard to Choose." *The Pen* [#160] 55–57.
      A *nisei* woman chooses between two men who have proposed—a *nisei* who wishes to expatriate and a *kibei* who wishes to remain in the US.

773. ———. "A Young Evacuee." *The Pen* [#160] 52–53.
      A *nisei* high school student explains his frustration and disappointment over the internment.

774. Hoshiga, Yuriko. "Ginza Memories." *Ayumi* [#141] 13–14.
      The author describes her first trip to the Ginza and recounts a second trip she makes 10 years later.

775. Hoshizaki, Tomi. "Flashback to 1955." *Hokubei Mainichi* 13 Jan. 1979: 1; 16 Jan. 1979: 1–2.

776. Hosokawa, Bill. "The Service Flags." *Pacific Citizen* 22 Dec. 1945: 27+.
      A *nisei* woman and her young son must cope with prejudice while resettling in a large city after leaving a wartime concentration camp.

777. Houston, Jeanne Wakatsuki. *Beyond Manzanar: View of Asian American Womanhood*. Santa Barbara: Capra Press, 1985.
      An autobiographical essay.

778. ———. "One Self: Two Cultures." *Common Ground: A Thematic Reader*. Ed. Jane K. Epstein and Laury Magnus. Glenview, IL: Scott, 1982. 69–74.
      Describes the efforts to shape an independent personal and cultural identity.

779. Houston, Jeanne Wakatsuki, and James Houston. *Farewell to Manzanar.* Boston: Houghton, 1973. Excerpt entitled "Whatever He Did Had Flourish" in *The Ethnic American Woman* [#88] 63–68.

An autobiographical account of growing up in Manzanar, one of the biggest concentration camps that confined Japanese Americans during World War II.

Rev. Dorothy Bryant, *Nation* 9 Nov. 1974: 469; Forrest E. LaViolette, *Pacific Affairs* 47 (1974): 405–06; David Oyama, *Bridge* 3.3 (1974): 32–33; Dorothy Rabinowitz, *Saturday Review World* 6 Nov. 1973: 34; Lee Ruttle, *Pacific Citizen* 4 Jan. 1974: 5; Robert A. Wilson, *Pacific Historical Review* 43 (Nov. 1974): 621–22.

780. Houston, Velina Hasu. "On Being Mixed Japanese in Modern Times." *Pacific Citizen* 20–27 Dec. 1985: B1–B3.

An autobiographical account by a playwright whose mother was Japanese and whose father was part Native American and part black.

781. *Ichida, Karl. "Babachan." *Bamboo Ridge: The Hawaii Writers' Quarterly* 7 (1980): 16–20

Short story.

782. Ichinaga, Mike. "One Day on a Tokyo Commute." *Hokubei Mainichi* 1 Jan. 1976: Supplement, 1–2.

783. Ide, Joseph Patrick. "Are You Going, Too?" *Rafu Shimpo* 20 Dec. 1965: 16–17.

The memory of a summer camping trip leads the author to ponder about both physical and emotional maturation.

784. ———. "Backtalk." *Rafu Shimpo* 20 Dec. 1961: 23+.

A dialogue between a father and his teenage son about childrearing practices.

785. ———. "Blue Smoke . . . Night Air." *Rafu Shimpo* 20 Dec. 1960: 21+.

Chronicles the problems of an arrested teenager.

786. ———. "But for the Grace of God." *Rafu Shimpo* 19 Dec. 1959: 15–16.

Relates the experience of counseling a troubled teenager.

787. ———. "Drumbeats." *Rafu Shimpo* 18 Dec. 1971: 19+.

The author describes one of his sons.

788. ———. "Hours That Are No More." *Rafu Shimpo* 19 Dec. 1967: 16+.

Describes the various characters at a class reunion.

789. ———. "My Life in America." *Rafu Shimpo* 22 Dec. 1952: 18.

A short story concerning an *issei* man who works at various jobs throughout California.

790. ———. "What's That, Dad?" *Rafu Shimpo* 19 Dec. 1964: 9.

The author recounts his experiences after returning to college at the age of forty-five.

791. ———. "When a Man Is Middle-Aged." *Rafu Shimpo* 20 Dec. 1975: 17+.

Selections from the author's wartime journal.

792.   ———. "Whistling in the Dark." *Rafu Shimpo* 20 Dec. 1972: 10+.
         The author describes the family who took him in after his mother and siblings died of tuberculosis.

793.   *Ige, Philip K. "The Forgotten Flea Powder." *Paradise of the Pacific* Nov. 1946: 24–25.
         Rpt. in *Bamboo Ridge: The Hawaii Writers' Quarterly* 1 (Dec. 1978): 56–59.
         A short story written in pidgin English about two brothers.

794.   ———. "The Great Depression." *Nisei: In Hawaii and the Pacific* 5 (Spring 1951): 14+.
         A short story about two boys who attempt to swindle another boy.

795.   ———. "Two Boys and a Kite." *Paradise of the Pacific* Nov. 1945: 20–21.
         A short story about the friendship between two boys.

796.   Iko, Momoko. "And There Are Stories, There Are Stories." *Greenfield Review* 6.1–2 (1977): 39–46.
         Rpt. in *Rafu Shimpo* 20 Dec. 1980: 20–21.
         Autobiographical prose poem.

797.   ———. "A Memorial Service Is Not a Story." *Pacific Citizen* 19–26 Dec. 1986: B24+.
         An autobiographical account chronicling the author's development as a writer.

798.   ———. "Second City Flat." *Counterpoint* [#113] 526–30.
         While taking a bath, a young Japanese American woman thinks about her parents' deaths and her recent sexual encounter.

799.   Imahara, James, with Anne Butler Poindexter. *James Imahara: Son of Immigrants*. Baton Rouge, LA: Imahara Nursery, 1982
         Autobiography.

800.   Inaba-Wong, Leslee. "The Phoenix." *East Wind* 3.1 (1984): 32–39.
         Portraits of the author's grandmother, an elderly Chinese American woman, and the individuals who struggled to save the International Hotel in San Francisco.

801.   Inada, Lawson Fusao. "The Flower Girls." *Pacific Citizen* 20–27 Dec. 1985: B48–B49.
         A tale concerning a friendship between a *nikkei* girl and a Caucasian girl that is ended by the onset of World War II.

802.   ———. "The Model Minority." *Pacific Citizen* 19 Dec. 1986: B19.
         An autobiographical piece.

803.   *Inouye, Daniel, with Lawrence Elliot. *Journey to Washington*. Englewood Cliffs, NJ: Prentice, 1967.
         Excerpts entitled "One Sunday in December" in *Asian-American Authors* [#125] 1976: 100–07; *I/You — We/They* [#111] 183–89.
         Autobiography.

804.   Inouye, Frank. "In Memoriam." *Echoes from Gold Mountain* 1979: 60–64.
         A *nisei* man eulogizes his mother.

805.   Inouye, Jon. "Lost Art." *Rafu Shimpo* 20 Dec. 1975: 14+.
         A short story that chronicles the adventures of a space-age samurai.

806.   ———. "S. F." *Rafu Shimpo* 21 Dec. 1974: 12.
         A science-fiction sketch about a brother and sister who travel to the moon.

807.   *Ishida, Lyle Stanley. "An Apology to Kathryn." *Bamboo Ridge: The Hawaii Writers' Quarterly* 15 (1982): 42–47.
         A man is haunted by his past relationships.

808.   Ishigaki, Ayako. "America after Twenty-Five Years." *Ayumi* [#141] 16–17.
         A personal account of the McCarthy Era and the author's problems, which developed from her involvement with liberal politics.

809.   Ishimaru, Haruo. "A Son Writes of the Issei He Knew Best—His Father." *Pacific Citizen* 18 Dec. 1953: A10–A11.
         Biography.

810.   Ishimoto, Shidzue. *Facing Two Ways: The Story of My Life.* New York: Farrar, 1935.
         Pt. 1 republished as *East Way West Way: A Modern Japanese Girlhood.* New York: Farrar, 1937.
         Autobiography.

811.   Itaya, Paul. "The Set-Up." *Pacific Citizen* 19 Dec. 1952: 38.
         A *nisei* man thinks of forging a check but at the last moment changes his mind.

812.   ———. "Why Not?" *Pacific Citizen* 24 Dec. 1949: A4.
         An author acts out a domestic quarrel with his wife in order to include it in a short story he is writing.

813.   Iwamatsu, Mako. "Mako Discovers America." *Pacific Citizen* 22 Dec. 1951: 25+.
         In this letter to a friend, the author recounts his adjustment to American life by describing his experiences in school and at work.

814.   Iwata, Buddy T. *Portrait of One Nisei: His Family and Friends.* Modesto, CA: Ink Spot, 1986.

815.   Iwata, Eddie. "The Old Man and the Swords." *Rafu Shimpo* 20 Dec. 1977: 12+.
         Describes the relationship between a collector and an older Japanese American man who passes on to him the swords of his samurai grandfather.

816.   *Jelsma, Clara Mitsuko. "The Cave at Kalapana." *Bamboo Ridge* 6 (1980): 18–23.
         Rpt. in *Hawaii Herald* 15 June 1985.
         A woman remembers a childhood experience.

817.   ———. *Teapot Tales*. Honolulu: Bamboo Ridge Press, 1981.
Excerpt in *Bamboo Ridge* 4 (1979): 3–8; *The Best of* Bamboo Ridge [#103] 141–46.
Biography of the author's mother.

818.   Kadohata, Cynthia. "Marigolds." *New Yorker* 9 Feb. 1987: 36–39.
A woman recalls a childhood experience in which she comes to understand adult realities.

819.   Kageyama, Yuri. "Asian American Art Story." *The Stories We Hold Secret* [#89] 114–24.
Challenges the dogmatic definitions of Asian American art.

820.   ———. "March 8th." *Echoes from Gold Mountain* 1978: 15–17.
Describes the complex feelings after an abortion.

821.   ———. "Shizuka: A Love Tale." *Bridge* 9.1 (1984): 30–34.
A court dancer raped by a young samurai falls in love with him.

822.   Kai, Fred S. "Last Farewell." *Pacific Citizen* 18 Dec. 1953: B20–B21.
Before returning to Japan, an *issei* confronts his Eurasian daughter.

823.   ———. "A Mid-Summer Incident." *Pacific Citizen* 17 Dec. 1954: B14–B15.
Rpt. in *Ayumi* [#141] 109–12.
A short story describing a young *nisei*'s experiences as a dishwasher at a Massachusetts summer resort and his encounter with a mentally ill *issei* man.

824.   ———. "The Walk Home." *Pacific Citizen* 19 Dec. 1952: 41–43.
Set in feudal Japan, this short story describes the dangers a Japanese man faces when he agrees to harbor in his home an outlawed Christian missionary.

825.   *Kakugawa, Frances. "The Enemy Wore My Face." *Bamboo Ridge* 9 (1980): 25–33.
Short story.

826.   Kameda, Yoshie. "Christmas at the Hamada's." *Hokubei Mainichi* 1 Jan. 1976, supplement: 1–2.

827.   ———. "Funeral for a Goldfish." *Hokubei Mainichi* 1 Jan. 1975, supplement: 3.

828.   ———. "A Legacy for Yasumasa." *Hokubei Mainichi* 1 Jan. 1977, supplement: 1+.

829.   Kamiya, Marcia. "A Visit for Grandma." *Rising Waters* 1975: n. pag.
Describes the tension between a woman and her son's family.

830.   Kanazawa, Joy Kimi. "The Legacy." *East Wind* 2.1 (1983): 58–62.
The granddaughter of a strong-willed *issei* woman recounts her grandmother's last months.

831.   ———. "Rites of Innocence." *RIKKA* 10.2 (1985): 24–30.
A short story about a *nikkei* family troubled by guilt over the past.

832.   Kanazawa, Tooru. "After Pearl Harbor—New York City." *Common Ground* 2.3 (1942): 13–14.
        A personal account of New York City's reaction to the bombing of Pearl Harbor.

833.   ———. *Sushi and Sourdough*. Seattle: U of Washington P, forthcoming.
        Follows the adventures of an *issei*.

834.   Kaneko, Hisakazu. *Manjiro: The Man Who Discovered America*. Boston: Houghton, 1956.
        A Japanese fisherboy is rescued by a Yankee whaler, who brings the boy to America.

835.   Kaneko, Lonny. "The Shoyu Kid." *Amerasia Journal* 3.2 (1976): 1–9.
        Rpt. in *Yardbird Reader* 5 (1976): 273–83.
        Describes a group of boys in an internment camp.

836.   *Kanemoto, Gale. "Expecting Amy." *Hawaii Review* 6 (1976): 66–75.
        Focuses on the conflicts brought out by the funeral of an *issei* man.

837.   Kaneshiro, Takeo. *Internees: War Relocation Center Memoirs and Diaries*. New York: Vantage, 1976.
        Presents in memoir and diary form the firsthand observations of Japanese American civilians held in concentration camps during World War II.

838.   Kashiwagi, Hiroshi. "Dominguez." *Echoes from Gold Mountain* 1979: 70–77.
        A *nisei* teenager witnesses discrimination against a Filipino farmworker.

839.   ———. "The Eyes." *Ayumi* [#141] 118–19.
        Recounts a couple's troubled relationship.

840.   ———. "The Map." *Pacific Citizen* 19 Dec. 1952: D37.
        A Japanese American hobo fascinates a young Japanese American boy.

841.   Kashiwagi, Soji C. "It's All in a Name." *Fusion '83* [#156] 19–20.
        The author jokes about the various mispronunciations of his first name.

842.   ———. "Three of a Kind." *Fusion '83* [#156] 16–19.
        While visiting the graves of two childhood friends, a *nisei* remembers their experiences together and the eventual deaths of his two friends while fighting in World War II.

843.   Kataoka, Lynne M. "The Unforgettable Memorial Day." *Fusion-San* [#157] 31–32.
        The author discovers a spiritual link with her dead ancestors.

844.   Katayama, Taro. "Haru." *Reimei* ns 1.3 (1933): 7–18.
        Rpt. in *Ayumi* [#141] 120–29.
        An account of a young Japanese American woman's arranged marriage.

845.   Kato, Kevin. "Return of the Native: A Sansei's Return to Japan." *Fusion '83* [#156] 89–92.
        An autobiographical account of how the author's trip to Japan aided him in synthesizing his Japanese and American heritages.

846. Kawachi, Asami. "Stranger's Rice." *Common Ground* 2.4 (1942): 73–76.
An autobiographical essay that highlights the author's positive experiences in the US.

847. Kawaguchi, Gary. "Face and Moon." *Fusion-San* [#157] 61–67.
A Vietnamese American man is infatuated with a Caucasian co-worker.

848. Kawahara, Ray. "A Biography of an Issei Woman." *Hokubei Mainichi* 1 Jan. 1978, supplement: 1–2.

849. *Kawakami, Hiroshi. "Excerpt from *Who Da Guy?*" *Bamboo Ridge* 25 (1985): 27–32.
Rpt. in *The Best of* Bamboo Ridge [#103] 147–53.
A prose poem written from the points of view of both man and dog.

850. Kawakami, Iwao. "Out of the Cradle Endlessly Rocking." *Reimei* ns 1.1 (1932): 11–12.
Rpt. in *Hokubei Mainichi* 1 Jan. 1986: 3.
A dying Japanese American woman recalls the early years of her marriage.

851. Kawamoto, Deanna. "Natsu Sukuwashi." *Hokubei Mainichi* 1 Jan. 1975, supplement: 1.

852. ———. "The Tablecloth." *Hokubei Mainichi* 1 Jan. 1976, supplement: 1.

853. *Kawano, Doris. *Harue, Child of Hawaii*. Honolulu: Topgallant Publishing, 1984.
A biographical novel focusing on a Japanese girl who grows up in a Hawaiian sugar-plantation community.

854. **Kawano, Roland. "Leaving Work." *RIKKA* 9.2 (1984): 21–26.
Portrait of a *nikkei* man who aspires to be a writer.

855. Kimura, Shuji. "Christmas Trees." *Tulean Dispatch Magazine* Jan. 1943: 6+.
A man recalls his life in America.

856. Kitagawa, Daisuke. *Issei and Nisei: The Internment Years*. New York: Seabury, 1967. Foreword Daniel K. Inouye. New York: Seabury, 1974.
Autobiography.
Rev. Martin E. Marty, *Christian Century* 3 Jan. 1968: 26; John Modell, *Pacific Historical Review* 39 (May 1970): 247–49; Roger W. Shugg, *Saturday Review* 13 Jan. 1968: 89.

857. **Kitagawa, Muriel. *This Is My Own: Letters to Wes and Other Writings on Japanese Canadians, 1941–1948*. Ed. Roy Miki. Vancouver: Talonbooks, 1985.
A posthumous collection of writings by a *nisei* Canadian.
Rev. George Yamada, *Amerasia Journal* 13.2 (1986–87): 222–24.

858. Kitano, Kimberly. "One Hundred Candles." *Hanai* [#161] 43–45.
An old gardener thinks about his past.

859. Kitano, Mary. "Snafued." *Rafu Shimpo* 20 Dec. 1949: 13.
A recently divorced man reconsiders his decision to divorce but discovers that his ex-wife has started a relationship with her lawyer.

860. Kiyooka, Chiyono Sugimoto. *But the Ships Are Sailing—Sailing—*. Tokyo: Hokuseido Press, 1959.
Autobiography. Also contains biographical information on Etsu Sugimoto, the author's mother.

861. ———. *Chiyo's Return*. Garden City, NY: Doubleday, 1935.
The American-born daughter of writer Etsu Inagaki Sugimoto relates her experiences in Japan.

862. **Kiyooka, Roy. "We Asian North Americanos: An Unhistorical 'Take' on Growing Up Yellow in a White World." *The Asian-Canadian and the Arts* [#96] 15–17.
Autobiographical essay.

863. Kochi, Paul S. *Imin No Aiwa (An Immigrant's Sorrowful Tale)*. Trans. Ben Kobashigawa. Los Angeles: privately printed, 1978.
Story of an Okinawan *issei* who enters the US illegally from Mexico.

Kochi, Shinsei. See Kochi, Tofu.

864. Kochi, Tofu [Shinsei Kochi]. "Vacation." *History of the Okinawans in North America* [#155].
Depicts the harsh life of *issei* farmers in the Imperial Valley.

865. **Kogawa, Joy. "Coaldale: Gem of the West." *RIKKA* 10.3 (1985): 1–7.
The narrator reminisces about her childhood in Coaldale, Canada, before her family was forced to leave their home during World War II.

866. ———. *Obasan*. Toronto: Lester & Orpen Dennys, 1981. Boston: Godine, 1982.
A novel about the evacuation of Japanese Canadians during World War II.
Rev. Diana Kiesners, *RIKKA* 8.2 (1981): 36–37; Michiko Lambertson, *Canadian Woman Studies* 4.2 (1982): 94–95; David Low, *Bridge* 8.3 (1983): 22+; Edith Milton, *New York Times Book Review* 5 Sept. 1982: 8+; B. A. St. Andrews, *Amerasia Journal* 13.2 (1986–87): 167–71; Hilda L. Thomas, *Canadian Literature* 96 (1983): 103–05; Edward M. White, *Los Angeles Times Book Review* 11 July 1982: 3; Suzi Wong, *East Wind* 2.1 (1983): 79–80.

867. Kokubun, Elaine. "An Absence of Fear." *Rafu Shimpo* 19 Dec. 1967: 21+.
An autobiographical account.

868. Komai, Chris. "He Knew." *Rafu Shimpo* 21 Dec. 1974: 6+.
Based on a true incident, this short story describes the final moments of a rebellious young Japanese American man's life and the pressures that contributed to his death.

869. ———. "Loose Ends." *Rafu Shimpo* 21 Dec. 1983: 15+.
A short story focusing on the friendship between two *sansei* men.

870. ———. "Open Casket." *Rafu Shimpo* 22 Dec. 1984: 12+.
Describes a death in a family.

871. Kondo, Carl. "Magic Girdle." *Rafu Shimpo* 20 Dec. 1949: 12.
An apparently mismatched couple realize that they need each other despite the gossip of others.

872. ———. "One Mind in Making." *Kashu Mainichi* 1 Jan. 1933: 2.
A socialist from Japan courts a superficial *nisei* woman.

873. ———. "Rain." *Reimei* ns 1.1 (1932): 19–20.
A Japanese man's fiancée leaves him for someone else.

874. Kono, Robert H. "Akiko's Acre of Love." *Pacific Citizen* 19–26 Dec. 1980: 28+.
Rpt. in *Ayumi* [#141] 199–205.
Through an interior monologue, an *issei* chronicles her life while waiting for her son and his family to visit her.

875. ———. "A Branch of the River." *Bridge* 6.3 (1978): 19+.
A fishing trip brings a young *sansei* closer to his grandfather.

876. ———. "The Exile." *Hokubei Mainichi* 1 Jan. 1980, supplement: 1–3.

877. ———. "The Stalwarts." *Pacific Citizen* 21–28 Dec. 1979: 51+.
In the face of impending war between Japan and the US, an *issei* instills in his two sons his idea that they must be loyal to America.

878. ———. "A String of Fish." *Hokubei Mainichi* 1 Jan. 1981, supplement: 1–2.

879. Konya, Tosh. "Looking Back." *Rafu Shimpo* 22 Dec. 1984: 15+.
An inmate of Manzanar recalls his early life in camp.

880. Korenaga, Mary. "Chiyono." *Gyo-Sho: A Magazine of Nisei Literature* [Mt. Vernon, IA: English Club of Cornell Coll., mid-1930s] 22–23.
Rpt. in *Hokubei Mainichi* 1 Jan. 1986, supplement: 3.
Describes the conflict and reconciliation between a woman and her sister-in-law.

881. ———. "In a Dream." *Kashu Mainichi* 1 Jan. 1933: 2.
An allegory about growing up.

882. Kubo, Keiko. "Matsuda's Wife." *Yoisho!* [#183] 1–7.
The marriage of an *issei* man to a black woman spurs the speculations of a rural community.

883. ———. "Motherhood." *Asian American Review* (1976): 50–53.
Rpt. in *Ayumi* [#141] 205–09.
A woman grapples with the possibility that she is infertile.

884. *Kubo, Mari Nakamura. "Advisor." *Hawaii Review* 2.2 (1974): 36–37.
Ghosts visit the narrator of this sketch.

885. ———. "The Eel-Wife." *Hawaii Review* 2.1 (1973): 61–65.
Rpt. in *Talk Story* [#104] 13–18.
A supernatural tale of a young Japanese woman whose soul is overtaken by the spirit of an eel.

886.   ———. "Kazashi's Revenge." *Seaweeds and Constructions: Anthology Hawaii*. Ed. Richard Hamasaki, Paul Oliveira, and Wayne Westlake. N.p.: Seaweeds and Constructions, 1979. 74–76.
A woman is frightened to death by the ghost of her husband's first wife.

887.   ———. "The Match." *Hawaii Review* 14 (1982–83): 76–77.
A woman believes that her lover is a demon.

888.   *Kubojiri, Clara. "A Cock's Tale." *Nisei: In Hawaii and the Pacific* 9 (Spring 1955): 8+.
Describes a confrontation between a rooster and a mongoose.

889.   ———. "The Little Sansei." *Nisei: In Hawaii and the Pacific* 8 (Spring 1954): 5+.
An *issei* has problems with his daughter-in-law.

890.   ———. "Yasuko Rebels." *Nisei: In Hawaii and the Pacific* 8 (June 1954): 10+.
Rpt. in *Kodomo No Tame Ni: For the Sake of the Children*. Honolulu: U of Hawaii P, 1978. 428–34.
A *nikkei* woman rejects an arranged marriage.

891.   Kubota, Sumio. "The Apple." *Fusion Too* [#158] 39–42.
An older *nisei* man ponders on the life and suicide of the Japanese author Mishima.

892.   Kubota, Warren S. "Kenzo, the Noble Mercenary." *Hokubei Mainichi* 5 Jan. 1980: 1–2.

893.   ———. "The Outside Jap" [excerpt]. *Yoisho!* [#183] 8–18.
A young *sansei* discusses with his older sister his problems with their father.

894.   ———. "The Witch." *Fusion '83* [#156] 93–99.
A grandfather tells his grandson that an old Japanese woman they see on the street is a witch.

895.   Kunitsugu, Katsumi. "The Halcyon Days." *Pacific Citizen* 18 Dec. 1953: B15–B16.
A chance encounter with a *nikkei* woman who was a junior high school classmate causes a Chicano man to reminisce about his youth.

897.   Kuroki, Ben. "Fighting Together." *Common Ground* 4.4 (1944): 44–52.
An autobiographical account of World War II.

898.   Kuroyanagi, Tetsuko. *Totto-chan: The Little Girl at the Window*. Trans. Dorothy Britton. Tokyo: Kodansha, 1982.
Autobiography.

899.   Kusunoki, Sharon M. "Rest in Peace, For the Error Shall Not Be Repeated." *Pacific Citizen* 21–28 Dec. 1984: C30–C31.
A survivor of the atomic bombing of Hiroshima loses his bitterness after being adopted by an American family.

900.   Kyogoku, Yurii. ". . . As a Hatter." *Pacific Citizen* 22 Dec. 1951: 63.
        A young girl encounters a mentally ill neighbor.

901.   Mainaga, Kay. "Night at the Bon Odori." *Fusion '83* [#156] 100–01.
        Meeting a Japanese American activist prompts a young woman to be-
        come more involved in the Japanese American community.

902.   *Manabe [Kobayashi], Jody. "In Search of Girls' Day." *Bamboo Ridge* 11
        (1981): 26–31.
        Rpt. in *The Best of* Bamboo Ridge [#103] 154–58.
        Reminiscences about dolls.

903.   ———. "The Shrine." *Bamboo Ridge* 5 (1979–80): 20–27.
        Short story.

904.   Masaoka, Jan. "I Forgot My Eyes Were Black." *Asian Women* [#84] 57–59.
        An essay on the dilemma of being an Asian woman.

905.   Masaoka, Mike, with Bill Hosokawa. *They Called Me Moses Masaoka: An
        American Saga*. New York: Morrow, 1987.
        Autobiography.

906.   *Masuchika, Glenn. "Nagasaki." *Hawaii Review* 18 (1985): 93–96.
        Describes a boy and his mother after the atomic bombing of Nagasaki.

907.   Masumoto, David Mas. "Cultural Delivery." *Pacific Citizen* 20–27 Dec.
        1985: A45–A46.
        The birth of his baby spurs the author to think about cultural differ-
        ences between himself and his wife.

908.   ———. *Distant Voices: A Sansei's Journey to Gila River Relocation Cen-
        ter*. Del Rey, CA: Inaka Countryside Publications, 1982.
        Describes the emotional journey back to the relocation camp that held
        the author's parents during World War II.

909.   ———. "Harvest Waters." *Fusion '83* [#156] 70–80.
        Rpt. in *Silent Strength* 17–37.
        Two Fresno farmers, one Japanese American and the other Armenian
        American, must deal with the problem of irrigating their land within a
        24-hour period.

910.   ———. "The Meeting." *Fusion Too* [#158] 15–19.
        Rpt. in *Silent Strength* 67–75.
        A *nikkei* exchange student meets relatives in Japan.

911.   ———. "September Rains." *Fusion Too* [#158] 14–15.
        The narrator describes how rain destroys his father's raisin crop.

912.   ———. "Shinimizu." *Rafu Shimpo* 20 Dec. 1986: 12–15.
        Describes the guilt aroused in four older *nisei* when their mother is in-
        jured in a fall.

913.   ———. *Silent Strength*. Del Rey, CA: New Currents International, 1984.
        A collection of short stories on the Japanese American family farm com-
        munity.

914.   ———. "Western Temple." *Pacific Citizen* 19–26 Dec. 1986: B32+.
        An *issei* man sets fire to a Japanese American community center.

915.   Matsui, Doug. "The Root of Evil." *Yardbird Reader* 5 (1976): 267–72.
        Rpt. in *Yardbird Lives!* [#164] 136–41.
        A man who loves to smoke marijuana has a conflict with an older
        neighbor.

916.   Matsui, Haru [Ayako Ishigaki]. *Restless Wave: An Autobiography*. New
        York: Modern Age, 1940.

917.   Matsumoto, Linda. "Turning Japanese." *Fusion-San* [#157] 23–28.
        A *sansei* learns to appreciate her parents as she becomes involved in the
        redress movement.

918.   Matsumoto, Toru. *The Seven Stars*. New York: Friendship Press, 1949.
        Describes the lives of seven classmates at a Christian school in Japan
        before, during, and after World War II.

919.   Matsumoto, Toru, and Marion Lerrigo. *A Brother Is a Stranger*. New York:
        John Day, 1946.
        An autobiographical novel focusing on the strained relationship be-
        tween the author and his brother.

920.   *Matsumura, Grace. "The Weeping Mango Tree." *Paradise of the Pacific*
        May 1946: 9.
        A group of children discover human bones under a mango tree.

921.   Matsunaga, Daigan, and Alicia Matsunaga. *Yuki: Temple Dog*. Beverly
        Hills, CA: Buddhist Books International, 1986.
        Told from the dog's point of view.

922.   Matsuno, Tamaki. "The Red Carp." *Ayumi* [#141] 25–26.
        After hearing that fresh carp blood has a miraculous healing power,
        an *issei* man catches a carp in the fountain of the city hall in order to give
        its blood to his ailing wife.

923.   *Matsuoka, Cynthia M. Y. "Grammy Is Patience." *Bamboo Ridge: The
        Hawaii Writers' Quarterly* 20 (1983): 19–20.
        A woman marvels at how her mother can handle three active grand-
        children without losing her patience.

924.   Matsuoka, H. Doug. "And Finally—Paradise." *Seaweeds and Construc-
        tions* 5 (1978): 67–79.
        Short story.

925.   ———. "Incident in Peking: Matsuoka's Testimony before the Select
        Committee Subcommittee Investigation for the Unethical Propagation
        of Imperialism." *Seaweeds and Constructions: Anthology Hawaii*. Ed.
        Richard Hamasaki, Paul Oliveira, and Wayne Westlake. N.p.: Seaweeds
        and Constructions, 1979. 12–25.
        A satire of American culture and anticommunism.

926.   Matsuoka, Yoko. *Daughter of the Pacific*. New York: Harper, 1952.
        Autobiography.

927.   Mayeda, Jean. "Obon Remembrance." *Hokubei Mainichi* 1 Jan. 1974: Supplement, 1.

928.   *Mikasa, Julienne K. "Measure of a Man." *Sandwich Isles U.S.A.* [#115] 24–26.
        An *issei* examines his life after learning that his wealthy sister from Japan will visit him.

929.   Mirikitani, Janice. "Assaults and Invasions." *Bamboo Ridge: The Hawaii Writers' Quarterly* 30 (1986): 46–47.
        A sketch about a battered wife and the US invasion of Grenada.

930.   ———. "Spoils of War." *Awake in the River.* San Francisco: Isthmus Press, 1978. N. pag.
        Making love to a Caucasian prompts a woman to think about her tragic Japanese American past.

931.   ———. "The Survivor." *Amerasia Journal* 7.1 (1980): 121–27.
        A woman sitting in her office thinks about a possible promotion and is reminded of her mother's life.

932.   ———. "The Woman and the Hawk." *Ayumi* [#141] 217–21.
        Compares a hawk's swooping to kill its prey with a woman's warped sense of loss after her abusive husband dies.

933.   Mishima, Sumie Seo. *My Narrow Isle: The Story of a Modern Woman in Japan.* New York: John Day, 1941.
        An autobiography of a Japanese woman who attends college in America.

934.   Mitogawa, Mitsuo. "The Grey Cemetery." *Ayumi* [#141] 30–33.
        A discussion about the purchase of a cemetery plot leads an *issei* to think of his experiences in the US.

935.   Miyadi, Al T. "It Came upon a Midnight Clear." *Pacific Citizen* 23 Dec. 1950: 5+.
        A fictional account of the immediate aftermath of a nuclear attack on an American city.

936.   ———. "You Lucky." *Rafu Shimpo* 20 Dec. 1949: 22–23.
        After winning a large sum at a backroom gambling den, a man is warned by the Chinese American janitor of the establishment not to return.

937.   Miyakawa, Edward. *Tule Lake.* Waldport, OR: House by the Sea, 1979.
        A novel based on historical research about the Japanese Americans incarcerated in Tule Lake during World War II.
        Rev. Yuri Kageyama, *Amerasia Journal* 7.2 (1980): 152–54; Neil Nakadate, *MELUS* 8.2 (1981): 100–04.

938.   *Miyamoto, Kazuo. *Hawaii: End of the Rainbow.* Rutland, VT: Bridgeway Press, Charles E. Tuttle, 1964.
        Excerpt entitled "Escape from Waipunalei" in *Talk Story* [#120] 44–59.
        A historical novel about Japanese immigrants in Hawaii.

939.   ———. *A Nisei Discovers Japan*. Tokyo: Japan Times Press, 1957.
        Travelogue.

940.   ———. *One Man's Journey: A Spiritual Autobiography*. [Honolulu?]:
        Buddhist Study Center, Honpa Hongwanji Mission of Hawaii, 1981.

941.   Miyasaki, Gail. "Obachan." *Asian Women* [#84] 16–17.
        A biographical sketch of the author's grandmother.

942.   *Miyasato, Bill. "Confession." *Bamboo Ridge* 19 (1983): 16–19.
        A man reveals his thoughts at the end of a homosexual relationship.

943.   ———. "Double Eyes." *Bamboo Ridge* 13 (1981–82): 21–24.
        A young boy cuts his eyelids to make his eyes look larger.

944.   ———. "To Be Home." *Bamboo Ridge* 11 (1981): 32–37.
        Short story.

945.   Miyatake, Martha. "The Book Burning." *Hokubei Mainichi* 1 Jan. 1985:
        1–2.

946.   Miyazaki, Yoshimi. "Annie's Other Eye." *Hokubei Mainichi* 1 Jan. 1981,
        supplement: 2.

947.   Miyoshi, Tami. *The Cherry Dance*. Los Angeles: Holloway House, 1969.

948.   Morey, Den. "Bird's-Eye View." *Pacific Citizen* 24 Dec. 1949: 50+.
        A *sansei* boy sympathizes with his grandfather who is banished from
        the dinner table when a white guest visits.

949.   ———. "Growing Up." *Pacific Citizen* 21 Dec. 1956: A19–A21.
        A boy learns that Santa Claus does not exist.

950.   ———. "Midori." *Pacific Citizen* 20 Dec. 1957: B12–B14.
        A *nisei* woman suspects her husband of having an affair with a youn-
        ger friend.

951.   ———. "Remember I'm Your Father." *Pacific Citizen* 18 Dec. 1953:
        B17–B19.
        Examines a *nisei*'s relationship with her childlike father.

952.   ———. "Uncle Tad." *Pacific Citizen* 17 Dec. 1954: A11.
        A white farmer wants to buy a tombstone for his hired hand, an *issei*
        man.

953.   Mori, Chiye. "Tanya." *Kashu Mainichi* 8 May 1932: 2.
        A Russian immigrant recounts how she gave birth to an illegitimate
        child.

954.   Mori, Kyoko. "The First Cicada." *Apalachee Quarterly* 18 (1982): 19–24.
        On her 75th birthday, a widow thinks about the dead members of her
        family.

955.   ———. "Pink Trumpets." *Sun Dog* 6.2 (1985): 12–20.
        During a race, a girl is haunted by memories of her dead mother.

956.   Mori, Toshio. "An American Story." *Pacific Citizen* 20 Dec. 1947: 41+.
        A young *nisei* meets the family of his former roommate.

957.   ———. "Between You and Me." *Iconograph* Mar. 1941: n. pag.
         Depicts the spread of gossip about a domestic quarrel within a Japanese American community.

958.   ———. "The Chauvinist." *Amerasia Journal* 3.2 (1976): 74–81.
         Rpt. in *"The Chauvinist" and Other Stories* 17–24.
         An old man's interior monologue.

959.   ———. *"The Chauvinist" and Other Stories*. Introd. Hisaye Yamamoto.
         Los Angeles: Asian American Studies Center, Univ. of California, 1979.
         Rev. Cheng Lok Chua, *Studies in Short Fiction* 18 (1981): 470–71; Garrett Kaoru Hongo, *Amerasia Journal* 7.2 (1980): 147–49; Linda Ching Sledge, *MELUS* 7.1 (1980): 86–90.

960.   ———. "The Chessmen." *Clipper* 2.2 (1941): 7–10.
         Rpt. in *Yokohama, California* 1985: 97–107; *Counterpoint* [#113] 480–83.

961.   ———. "The Fruit Pickers." *Fusion '83* [#156] 12–14.
         An *issei* laborer, while picking fruit, sings of his pride for his son who is serving in the US Army.

962.   ———. "Grandpa and the Promised Land." *Pacific Citizen* 25 Dec. 1948: 10+.
         An *issei* woman relates to her grandchildren her early experiences with prejudice, her multicultural discoveries, and her initial friendships in America.

963.   ———. "He Who Has the Laughing Face." *New Directions in Prose and Poetry* 1938: n. pag.
         Rpt. in *Yokohama, California* 1985: 121–26.

964.   ———. "Homecoming." *Pacific Citizen* 19 Dec. 1952: 52+.
         Rpt. in *Aion* 1.2 (1971): 22–29; *Ayumi* [#141] 137–44.
         An *issei* visits her wounded son in a California hospital during World War II.

965.   ———. "Join Me in Laughter." *Pacific Citizen* 23 Dec. 1950: 33+.
         Describes an *issei* woman's encounters with kind and mean-spirited people after being released from Topaz concentration camp.

966.   ———. "Lil' Yokohama." *Common Ground* 1.2 (1941): 54–56.
         Rpt. in *Yokohama, California* 1985: 71–76.
         A sketch of a Japanese American community.

967.   ———. "My Countryman." *Pacific Citizen* 21 Dec. 1946: 17+.
         Describes a Mexican migrant worker.

968.   ———. "One Happy Family." *Trek* June 1943: 12–13.
         A child learns that his father was taken away by the FBI after the Pearl Harbor attack.

969.   ———. "1, 2, 3, 4, Who Are We For?" *Clipper* 1.5 (1940): 19–21.
         Rpt. in *"The Chauvinist" and Other Stories* 117–21.
         A Chinese American and a Japanese American discuss personal problems and international politics.

970. ———. "Operator! Operator!" *Amerasia Journal* 4.1 (1977): 151–56.
Rpt. in *"The Chauvinist" and Other Stories* 51–56.
An old man looks in vain for work.

971. ———. "The Remembered Days." *Pacific Citizen* 24 Dec. 1949: 25+.
An *issei* chronicles her train trip to Topaz concentration camp and the subsequent news that one of her sons has been killed in combat.

972. ———. "Say It with Flowers." *Writer's Forum* Mar. 1943.
Rpt. in *Yokohama, California* 1985: 54–64; *Asian-American Heritage* [#177] 88–97.
About a man who cares more about people than about profit.

973. ———. "Tomorrow Is Coming, Children." *Trek* Feb. 1943: 13–16.
Rpt. in *Hokubei Mainichi* 1 Jan. 1977, supplement: 1+; *Yokohama, California* 1985: 15–21; *Greenfield Review* 6.1–2 (1977): 1–5.
An *issei* woman describes her early life in America.

974. ———. "The Travelers." *All Aboard* [#81] 49–55.
Rpt. in *"The Chauvinist" and Other Stories* 127–32.
A *nisei* soldier meets a group of relocating *nisei* at a train station.

975. ———. "The Trees." *Trek* Dec. 1942: 23–24.
Rpt. in *Yokohama, California* 1985: 136–39.
A sketch depicting the lack of effective communication between two men.

976. ———. *Woman from Hiroshima*. San Francisco: Isthmus Press, 1979.
A Japanese immigrant tells her grandchildren about her life in America, from her arrival to her confinement in an American concentration camp.

977. ———. "Year of Opportunity." *Pacific Citizen* 22 Dec. 1951: 9+.
An *issei* woman tells her grandchildren about her life in America.

978. ———. *Yokohama, California*. Introd. William Saroyan. Caldwell, ID: Caxton, 1949. Introd. Lawson Fusao Inada. Seattle: U of Washington P, 1985.
"The Eggs of the World" is rpt. in *Speaking for Ourselves* [#110] 174–77 and *Asian-American Authors* [#125] 95–99. "Slant-Eyed Americans" is rpt. in *American Letter* [#125] 318–21. "The Woman Who Makes Swell Doughnuts" is rpt. in *AIIIEEEEE!* [#100] 1983: 124–26.
Short stories focusing on the fictional town of Yokohama, California.
Rev. Joseph Henry Jackson, *San Francisco Chronicle* 3 Mar. 1949: 16; Eddie Shimano, *Common Ground* 9.4 (1949): 110.

979. Morimitsu, Arthur T. "The Barber's Wife." *Tulean Dispatch Magazine* Feb. 1983: 3+.
A young man recalls an adolescent infatuation.

980. Morimitsu, George. "Shipment." *Common Ground* 3.2 (1943): 89–90.
Describes new recruits in the armed forces.

981. Morioka, Lois. *The Long Road from White River*. N.p.: New Writer's Press, 1983.
A love story between a Japanese American man and a Caucasian American woman during World War II.

982. Morita, Nancy Anne. "The Kimono." *Hokubei Mainichi* 1 Jan. 1976: Supplement, 1–2.

983. Murakami, Satoko. "I Am Alive." *Common Ground* 2.3 (1942): 15–18.
The author expresses her faith in democratic values.

984. *Murayama, Milton. *All I Asking for Is My Body.* 1959. San Francisco: Supa Press, 1975. Excerpts entitled "I'll Crack Your Head *Kotsun*" in *Arizona Quarterly* 15.2 (1959): 137–49; *The Spell of Hawaii.* Ed. A. Grove Day and Carl Stroven. New York: Meredith, 1968. 323–35.
Describes generational conflict between *issei* and *nisei* in Hawaii.

985. Mushi. "A Chapter from Utopia." *Aion* 1.1 (1970): 53–54.
An essay about sexual experiences.

986. Nagai, Kafu. "The Road through the Pasture." Trans. Take Beekman and Allan Beekman. *Pacific Citizen* 24–31 Dec. 1965: B20.
The story of a Japanese immigrant who goes insane.

987. *Nagai, Masato. "Chapter 13 from *Island Household.*" *Bamboo Ridge: The Hawaii Writers' Quarterly* 11 (1981): 43–47.

988. *Nagata, Alan. "Da Well." *Hawaii Review* 14 (1982–83): 44–46.
Written in pidgin English, this short story describes a cane-field worker who becomes mentally ill.

989. Nagata, C. M. "Little Grandma." *Hokubei Mainichi* 1 Jan. 1975: Supplement, 1+.

990. Nagata, Setsuko. "The Old Man on Crutches." *Ayumi* [#141] 38–40.
The author recalls an old *issei* poet whom she met while working as a waitress in the Tanforan assembly center.

991. Nakadate, Kakuya. "Local Lad Back from South Pacific: An Item in the *Southeast San Diego News* of November 22, 1945." *Echoes from Gold Mountain* 1978: 43–47.
Describes a *nikkei* soldier's experiences while on a US ship in the South Pacific during World War II.

992. Nakae, Tomeo [Okui]. *Recollections: An Autobiography of the Wife of a Japanese Immigrant.* Trans. Masako Nakae. Ed. Howard Nakae. N.p.: privately printed, [1982].

993. Nakagawa, Al. "Once upon a Hype." *Echoes from Gold Mountain* 1978: 32–34.
A series of scenes from the life of a Japanese American drug addict.

994. Nakamura, Ayako. "Fallen Leaves." *Rafu Shimpo* 20 Dec. 1961: 15+.
A biographical account of the author's parents.

995. ———. "Maturity of Number One." *Rafu Shimpo* 19 Dec. 1967: 14+.
Describes the author's son.

996. ———. "Noriko." *Rafu Shimpo* 20 Dec. 1972: 17+.
Describes a future daughter-in-law.

997. ———. "Parent's Day." *Rafu Shimpo* 19 Dec. 1964: 26+.
The author recounts a visit to her son's school.

998.   ———. "She Danced at the World's Fair." *Rafu Shimpo* 20 Dec. 1963: 23+.
          Memories of dancing at a New York summer festival lead to a description of Washington, DC.

999.   ———. "The Wedding." *Rafu Shimpo* 19 Dec. 1973: 13.
          A dramatic production serves as a controlling metaphor for the author's description of her son's wedding.

1000.   ———. "Weekend at the Waldorf." *Rafu Shimpo* 20 Dec. 1965: 25+.
          Describes a hectic Buddhist convention in New York.

1001.   ———. "Yassa, Yassa." *Rafu Shimpo* 20 Dec. 1975: 9.
          Memories of a visiting Japanese dance troupe lead the author to assert her relationship with Japanese culture.

1002.   Nakamura, J. V. "The Eurasian's Tale." *AsiAm* May 1987: 66–69.
          A Eurasian describes his adventure in Japan.

1003.   Nakamura, Jobo. "A Day in Asakusa." *Rafu Shimpo* 19 Dec. 1959: 13.
          An *issei* who returns to live in Japan is swindled upon his arrival.

1004.   ———. "For Tomorrow Is Another Day." *Pacific Citizen* 22 Dec. 1945: 14–15.
          A young *nisei* spending Christmas Eve alone remembers his camp experiences but is cheered when another *nisei* takes him to a dance.

1005.   ———. "I'll Always Remember. . . . " *Tulean Dispatch Magazine* Dec. 1942: 7+.
          A man remembers how he romanced his wife.

1006.   ———. "In the Beginning. . . . " *Rafu Shimpo* 20 Dec. 1957: 11.
          A Japanese woman is forced into marriage with a Japanese man who has recently returned from America.

1007.   ———. "Let Me Walk in the Fields" *Pacific Citizen* 20 Dec. 1947: 31.
          A *nisei* student studying science in Chicago reminisces about his past.

1008.   ———. "On Borrowed Time." *The Pen* [#160] 61–62.
          A man writes of his life prior to internment.

1009.   ———. "A Saturday Morning in Chicago." *Pacific Citizen* 21 Dec. 1946: 24.
          A description of a walk in Chicago develops into a discussion of the integration of *nisei* into American society.

1010.   ———. "A Trip to the Country." *Rafu Shimpo* 20 Dec. 1951: 23.
          A trip through the country sparks memories of childhood in a young *nisei* man.

1011.   *Nakamura, Peter. "Makana Pali." *Mana: A South Pacific Journal of Language and Literature* 6.1 (1981): 27–40.
          Short story.

1012.   Nakamura, Shingo. "Autobiography." *Ayumi* [#141] 43–45.
          The author recounts how he first learned of jobs in America and prepared for his trip to the US.

1013.   *Nakano, Dennis. "Tsukenokoshi's Bride." *Bamboo Ridge: The Hawaii Writers' Quarterly* 11 (1981): 59–82.

1014.   **Nakano, Takeo Ujo, with Leatrice Nakano. *Within the Barbed Wire Fence: A Japanese Man's Account of His Internment in Canada.* Toronto: U of Toronto P, 1980. Seattle: U of Washington P, 1981.
        Autobiography.
        Rev. Rita Takahashi Cates, *Amerasia Journal* 10.2 (1983): 93–96; Roy Miki, *Asianadian* 3.3 (1981): 24–28.

1015.   Nakashima, Naoto. "Kanaka." Trans. Take Beekman and Allan Beekman. *Pacific Citizen* 20–27 Dec. 1968: C9+.
        A wake turns raucous.

1016.   Nakashima, Ted. "Concentration Camp: U.S. Style." *New Republic* 15 June 1942. Rpt. in *American Letter* [#128] 322–23.
        Autobiographical essay.

1017.   Nakashima, Teresa. "The Peace Murder." *Hokubei Mainichi* 1 Jan. 1974: Supplement, 1–2.

1018.   ———. "The Wait." *Hokubei Mainichi* 1 Jan. 1975: Supplement, 1–2.

1019.   Nakata, Carla Michie. "The One That Got Away." *Fusion '83* [#156] 50–54.
        A black-humored account of a young woman's thoughts and memories during a suicide attempt.

1020.   Nakata, I. S. "The Tamarind Tree." *Fusion-San* [#157] 33–37.
        A Japanese American boy befriends an old Chinese bachelor after stealing tamarinds from his yard.

1021.   Nash, Alice. "An American Christmas." *Pacific Citizen* 20–27 Dec. 1985: B66.
        Describes an elderly *issei* woman living in New York City.

1022.   ———. "Making Osushi." *Pacific Citizen* 20–27 Dec. 1985: B9+.
        A grandmother teaches two of her grandchildren how to make sushi.

1023.   Nishiyama, Sen. "Kuma's Return." *Kashu Mainichi* 17 Apr. 1932: 2.
        Describes a disturbance experienced by a family of fishermen.

1024.   Noda, Barbara. "Thanksgiving Day." *Lesbian Fiction: An Anthology.* Ed. Elly Bulkin. Watertown, MA: Persephone Press, 1981. 61–62.
        Describes a grandfather's burial.

1025.   Noguchi, Rei. "Benny." *Rafu Shimpo* 19 Dec. 1970: 10+.
        A sketch of a *sansei* farm worker and his family.

1026.   ———. "A Prayer for Emil." *Rafu Shimpo* 19 Dec. 1970: 10+.
        A *nikkei* nursery worker tries to comfort a coworker whose abusive father has just died.

1027.   ———. "The Sangha." *Rafu Shimpo* 18 Dec. 1971: 18+.
        A Buddhist minister tries to help a Mexican American locate his father.

1028.   ———. "Sushi." *Rafu Shimpo* 19 Dec. 1967: 7+.
A girl learns from her elderly neighbor of the Japanese American internment during World War II.

1029.   Noguchi, Yone. *The American Diary of a Japanese Girl*. New York: Frederick A. Stokes, 1901.

1030.   ———. *The American Letters of a Japanese Parlor-Maid*. Tokyo: Fuzanbo Publishing, 1905.
Epistolary novel.

1031.   ———. *The Story of Yone Noguchi, Told by Himself*. Philadelphia: George W. Jacobs, 1915.

1032.   ———. *Yone Noguchi: Collected English Letters*. Ed. Ikuko Atsumi. Tokyo: Yone Noguchi Soc., 1975.

1033.   *Nunes, Shiho S. "Excerpts from *Growing Up with Ghosts*. *Hawaii Review* 14 (1982–83): 92–96.
A series of ghost stories that take place in Hawaii and Japan.

1034.   *Nunes, Susan. ". . . And Mud Lane Shall Be Known as Piopio." *Bamboo Ridge: The Hawaii Writers' Quarterly* 7 (1980): 2–4.
Rpt. in *"A Small Obligation"* 67–69.
Short story.

1035.   ———. "The Confession." *Hapa* 2 (Spring 1982): 66–72.
Rpt. in *"A Small Obligation"* 31–37; *The Best of* Bamboo Ridge [#103] 214–20.
A story about religious dogmatism gone awry.

1036.   ———. "The Grandmother." *Hawaii Review* 8 (1978): 18–21.
Rpt. in *"A Small Obligation"* 26–29; *The Best of* Bamboo Ridge [#103] 221–24.
A girl is both frightened and fascinated by her friend's grandmother.

1037.   ———. "The Immigrant." *Bamboo Ridge: The Hawaii Writers' Quarterly* 3 (1979): 22–26.
Rpt. in *"A Small Obligation"* 9–12.
Short story.

1038.   ———. "The Ministers." *Bamboo Ridge: The Hawaii Writers' Quarterly* 9 (1980): 10–18.
Rpt. in *"A Small Obligation"* 70–76.
Short story.

1039.   ———. "Morning." *Hawaii Review* 11 (1981): 34–38.
Rpt. in *"A Small Obligation"* 45–50.
A short story about a suicide.

1040.   ———. "A Small Obligation." *Hawaii Review* 13 (1982): 71–79.
Rpt. in *"A Small Obligation"* 78–87; *Passages to the Dream Shore* [#170] 147–56.
A woman describes her mother and grandmother.

1041. ———. *"A Small Obligation" and Other Stories*. Spec. issue of *Bamboo Ridge: The Hawaii Writers' Quarterly* 16 (1982).

1042. ———. "What Would You Do if I Sang Out of Tune?" *Hapa* 3 (1983): 110–31.
      Short story.

1043. ———. "Winterpear: 1951." *Bamboo Ridge: The Hawaii Writers' Quarterly* 7 (1980): 5–8.
      Rpt. in *"A Small Obligation"* 38–41.
      Short story.

1044. Oba, Minako. "The Three Crabs." *This Kind of Woman: Ten Stories by Japanese Women Writers, 1960–76*. Ed. Yukiko Tanaka and Elizabeth Hanson. New York: Perigee-Putnam's, 1982. 89–113.

1045. Obasan [pseud.]. "Ideograms with Eights." *Reimei* ns 1.2 (1932): 17–19.
      A young white woman is interested in things Japanese.

1046. *Ochiai, Kiyo. "Mizu No Oto." *Bamboo Ridge: The Hawaii Writers' Quarterly* 9 (1980): 6–9.
      Short story.

1047. Oda, Edward. "The Family Reunion." *Dwell among Our People* [#109] 18–20.
      Reveals the exploitation that results from the stereotype of the docile Asian American.

1048. *Oda, Pat. "Papa." *Nisei: In Hawaii and the Pacific* 5 (Spring 1951): 7+.
      An autobiographical piece focusing on the author's father.

1049. *Ogai, Seiko. "Battlefront Madonna." *Paradise of the Pacific* Dec. 1949: 45.
      A *nisei* veteran recalls how an Italian woman helped him and his friends during World War II.

1050. ———. "The Easter Bunny's Visit." *Paradise of the Pacific* 63 (Mar. 1951): 35+.
      A Japanese girl spends Easter in Waikiki.

1051. ———. "The Kapiolani Candy Man." *Paradise of the Pacific* May 1949: 15+.
      A child recalls a popular candy vendor.

1052. ———. "Love among the Pineapples." *Nisei: In Hawaii and the Pacific* 10 (Summer 1956): 8+.
      The author recounts a friend's summer romance at a pineapple cannery.

1053. ———. "The Other Angel." *Nisei: In Hawaii and the Pacific* 6 (holiday issue 1952): 1+.
      A *nikkei* Sunday-school teacher discovers that one of her students has been hit by the student's drunken father.

1054. ———. "Upon the Sea." *Paradise of the Pacific* Jan. 1949: 28+.
      A comic sketch about a girl who misunderstands the lyrics of a song.

1055. *Ogawa, Vivian M. "The Scarlet Mirror." *Ka Alele O Kula (The Kula Messenger)* 8 (1937): 47–49.
A tragic love story.

1056. O'Hara, Dan. "There Are Such People." *Tulean Dispatch Magazine* 1.11 (n.d.): 19–27.
Chronicles a bachelor's final day in internment camp and his relationships with two women.

1057. Ohara, Thalia. "Voyage to Hawaii." *Fusion '83* [#156] 27–29.
An *issei* recounts his departure from Japan, his work on a Hawaiian plantation, and his eventual success as a businessman.

1058. *Ohme, Leslie. "Letter to Japan." *Paradise of the Pacific* Feb. 1956: 22–23.
Describes a woman's struggle to keep a relative from taking away her son.

1059. *Ohta, Emily N. "It Came to Pass." *Ka Alele O Kula (The Kula Messenger)* 8 (1937): 53+.
An ironic story about arranged marriages.

1060. Ohta, Koji. [Untitled.] *Rising Waters* 1975: n. pag.
A *sansei* remembers a friend while attending his funeral.

1061. Oka, Shigeki. "Am I a Traitor?" *Ayumi* [#141] 50–52.
The author describes his antifascist activities during World War II.

1062. Okada, Fred. "Rice instead of Potato." *Common Ground* 8.4 (1948): 68–71.
Describes a Chinese restaurant in the Nevada desert.

1063. Okada, John. *No-No Boy.* Rutland, VT: Charles E. Tuttle, 1957. Introd. Lawson Fusao Inada. Afterword Frank Chin. Seattle: U of Washington P, 1979.
Excerpts in *Asian-American Heritage* [#177] 267–82; *AIIIEEEEE!* [#100] 1983: 130–40; *Counterpoint* [#113] 498–501.
Delineates a Japanese American draft resister's struggle of adjustment after World War II.
Rev. Gordon Hirabayashi, *Pacific Affairs* 5 (1981): 176–77; Peter Nazareth, *RIKKA* 8.2 (1981): 42–46.

1064. Okamoto, Frances. "On a Night like This." *Tulean Dispatch Magazine* Nov. 1942: 5+.
A short story about a young man suspected of murder.

1065. ———. "What Makes Peter Run." *Tulean Dispatch Magazine* Mar. 1943: 10+.
A boy believes that the ghost of an elderly friend visits him.

1066. Okano, Gary. "The Hustler." *Hokubei Mainichi* 1 Jan. 1974, supplement: 1–2.

1067. Okazaki, David. "A Christmas Undelivered." *Hokubei Mainichi* 1 Jan. 1976, supplement: 1–2.

1068. ———. "Holiday Flight." *Hokubei Mainichi* 1 Jan. 1975, supplement: 2.

1069.   Okazaki, Ginko. "The Earth of Salinas (An Excerpt)." *Ayumi* [#141] 57–60.
Explores the problems of a rural Japanese American family.

1070.   Okazaki, Joan. ". . . We Must Cultivate Our Garden." *Hokubei Mainichi*
1 Jan. 1977, supplement: 1+.

1071.   Okazaki, Lois. "The Mistress of Go." *Hokubei Mainichi* 1 Jan 1977, supplement: 4.

1072.   Oki, Kazuichi. "Desert Indian (Hopi Tribe)." *Ayumi* [#141] 64–66.
Records the customs of the Hopi and describes a visit with the Oraibi
people.

1073.   Okimoto, Daniel. *American in Disguise*. New York: Walter-Weatherhill,
1971.
Excerpt entitled "Prisoners" in *Asian American Heritage* [#177] 185–96.
Autobiography.
Rev. Donald Teruo Hata, *Journal of Ethnic Studies* 1.1 (1973): 74–75;
David K. Willis, *Christian Science Monitor* 15 May 1971: 11.

1074.   Okubo, Miné. *Citizen 13660*. New York: Columbia UP, 1946. New York:
AMS, 1968. New York: Arno, 1978. Pref. author. Seattle: U of Washing-
ton P, 1983.
A collection of drawings and thoughts about World War II relocation
camps.
Rev. *Common Ground* 7.2 (1947): 107.

1075.   *Okuda, Michio. "Oh Frankie!" *Hawaiian Digest* 3 (Apr. 1948): 47–48.
Describes a dispute between a brother and sister.

1076.   ———. "The Singing Cat of Abe-San." *Aloha* 3.17 (1949): 10–12.
A son, tired of his dull existence, decides to play a trick on his father.

1077.   Okumura, Nancy. "Everybody Has a First Time." *Hokubei Mainichi* 1 Jan.
1974, supplement: 4.

1078.   *Okumura, Takie. *Seventy Years of Divine Blessing*. Kyoto: Naigai Publishing, 1940.
Autobiography.

1079.   ———. *Thirty Years of Christian Mission Work among Japanese in Hawaii*. Honolulu: privately printed, 1917.
Autobiography.

1080.   Ono, Ernest. "Services for Sale—At Bargain Prices." *Rafu Shimpo* 20 Dec.
1958: 27–28.
Describes a day in the life of a hard-working English teacher.

1081.   ———. "The Toss of the Coin." *Rafu Shimpo* 20 Dec. 1957: 13+.
An *issei* remembers how coin tosses played eventful roles in the life of
his son, who was killed in the Korean War.

1082.   Osaka, Mary R. "Downtown." *Hokubei Mainichi* 1 Jan. 1979, supplement:
1–2.

1083.   Osato, Sono. *Distant Dances*. New York: Knopf, 1980.
Autobiography.

1084.   Oshima, Kon. "The Referee." *Ayumi* [#141] 145–51.
    A *nisei* boxer encounters discrimination.

1085.   Osho [Junsuke Takaya]. "An Awakening." Trans. Mei Takaya Nakano and Seizo Oka. *Pacific Citizen* 21–28 Dec. 1979: 50+.
    A *nisei* girl matures when her father debates whether to send his children to Japan.

1086.   O'Suga, Riley [Hiroshi Sugasawara]. "Her Name Is Woman." *Tulean Dispatch Magazine* Jan. 1943: 3+.
    The chronicle of a young couple's adventures while taking a walk in the windy countryside.

1087.   ———. "Nisei America: Entrails of a Thought." *Tulean Dispatch Magazine* Mar. 1943: 6+.
    An essay that comments on America's ethnic diversity.

1088.   ———. "Sloop Nakano." *Tulean Dispatch Magazine* Nov. 1942: 5+.
    Portrait of a gentle-spirited artist.

1089.   Ota, Alan. "Hershey Bar Kids in the Chocolate City." *Asian American Review* 1 (1976): 96–101.
    A sketch of a Chinese American man.

1090.   Ota, Shelley Ayame Nishimura. *Upon Their Shoulders*. New York: Exposition Press, 1951.
    Chronicles the experiences of a Japanese man who immigrates to Hawaii.

1091.   Otani, Andrew N. *Hope Shines in the White Cloud: An Issei's Story*. Minneapolis: Minnisei Printing, [1973?].

1092.   Otani, Kosho K. *The Successor: My Life*. Beverly Hills, CA: Buddhist Books International, 1985.
    The autobiography of the 25th Supreme Primate of the Otani sect of Jodo Shinshu Buddhism.

1093.   Oyama, Joe. "The Legacy of a Cemetery." *Ayumi* [#141] 152–55.
    Describes the author's return to Los Angeles.

1094.   ———. "My Family Roots." *Pacific Citizen* 22–29 Dec. 1978: 49.
    An account of the author's family.

1095.   ———. "1918 Cordelia, California (from a Child's Perspective)." *Fusion-San* [#157] 18–19.
    A drunk tries to enter a Japanese American home by breaking a window.

1096.   Oyama, Mary. "After Pearl Harbor—Los Angeles." *Common Ground* 2.3 (1942): 12–13.
    Describes how people in Los Angeles reacted to the bombing of Pearl Harbor.

1097.   ———. "Coming of Age." *Gyo-Sho: A Magazine of Nisei Literature* [Mt. Vernon, IA: English Club of Cornell Coll., mid-1930s] 7–10.
    Rpt. in *Hokubei Mainichi* 1 Jan. 1986, supplement: 3.
    Describes a woman's first experience at voting.

1098.   ———. "A Nisei Report from Home." *Common Ground* 6.2 (1946): 26–28.
        Autobiographical sketch.

1099.   ———. "This Isn't Japan." *Common Ground* 3.1 (1942): 32–34.
        Autobiographical account.

1100.   Oyama, Richard. "Basket Man." *Fusion-San* [#157] 73–74.
        Describes a railroad worker whose job is to ignite dynamite in mountain cliffs.

1101.   Ozawa, Norman. "Autumn Maple." *Hokubei Mainichi* 1 Jan. 1975, supplement: 1–2.

1102.   Ozawa, Norman [under pseud. Vernyn Ronnam]. "For Those like Her and Me as Well." *Hokubei Mainichi* 6 Jan. 1979: 1–2.

1103.   *Planas, Alvin. "This Particular Sound." *Hanai* [#161] 55–65.
        Describes a guitar player.

1104.   Roberts, Chiori E. T. "All Time Yet." *Hokubei Mainichi* 1 Jan. 1974, supplement: 1.

1105.   Rokumin [Jippo Yogi]. "The Linnet." *History of the Okinawans in North America* [#155].
        Describes the isolated lives of Okinawan immigrants who live in boarding houses.

1106.   *Saikawa, Yuko. "Evening Breeze." *Bamboo Ridge* 2 (1979): 34–39.
        Excerpt from an unpublished novel that describes the beginning of a relationship between an English professor and a woman who has recently returned to Hawaii from the mainland.

1107.   Saiki, B. "Well It's Grand." *The Pen* [#160] 54.
        A man recalls the events that landed him in jail.

1108.   Saiki, Jessica. *"Once, a Lotus Garden" and Other Stories.* St. Paul: New Rivers Press, 1987.

1109.   *Saiki, Patsy Sumie. "Communion." *Bamboo Ridge* 6 (1980): 7–17.
        Rpt. in *The Best of* Bamboo Ridge [#103] 240–49; *Passages to the Dream Shore* [#170] 165–73.
        Focuses on a comatose man and his wife.

1110.   ———. "Just Wait and See." *Bamboo Ridge* 1 (1978): 47–55.
        A young boy retreats into an imaginary world in order to escape the misery of his life.

1111.   ———. *Sachie: A Daughter of Hawaii.* Honolulu: Kisaku, 1977.
        An account of Hawaiian life seen through the eyes of a Japanese American girl.
        Rev. Judy Yung, *Bridge* 7.3 (1980): 46–47.

1112.   ———. "The Unwilling Bride." *Talk Story* [#120] 60–63.
        Short story.

1113.   Saito, Jiro. "The Red Tricycle." *Pacific Citizen* 20–27 Dec. 1985: A25.
         Depicts the evacuation of a rural Japanese American family and the
         sympathetic action of one soldier.

1114.   Sakai, Katsuma. "The Biography of Shige Kiino" [an excerpt]. *Ayumi*
         [#141] 70–71.
         Describes the difficult life of Shige Kiino, an *issei* woman.

1115.   Sakai, Sueko. *Chop Suey Collection of Facts and Fantasies*. New York: Van-
         tage, 1973.
         A collection of short stories, anecdotes, and poems.

1116.   *Sakamoto, Michael R. "The Night of the Kepalo." *Bamboo Ridge* 27
         (1985): 29–42.
         A short story about sexual jealousy.

1117.   Sasaki, Ruth Aiko. "The Loom." *Hokubei Mainichi* 3 Sept. 1983.
         Rpt. in *Rafu Shimpo* 21 Dec. 1983: 13+; *Pacific Citizen* 23–30 Dec.
         1983: A1+.
         Chronicles the lives of a *nisei* woman and her four daughters.

1118.   Sasaki, Sasabune. "A Letter." *Ayumi* [#141] 75–76.
         An anonymous letter of support becomes a focal point for the *issei* men
         interned in a special camp for leaders of the Japanese American com-
         munity.

1119.   Sasaki, Shuichi. "Looking Up Old Friends." Trans. Yasuo Sasaki and Seizo
         Oka. *Pacific Citizen* 23–30 Dec. 1983: C1+.
         An excerpt from "Amerika Seikatsu" ("A Life in America"), an auto-
         biographical account.

1120.   Sasaki, Yasuo. "Razzberries in Blue." *Kashu Mainichi* 21 Aug. 1932: 2.
         Rpt. in *Fusion '83* [#156] 7–10.
         Two men recount the success of a friend in the jazz world and the bro-
         ken romance that inspired the musician to write the work that made him
         famous.

1121.   ———. "Young Atheists." *Kashu Mainichi* 3 Apr. 1932: 2.
         The death of a philosophical friend affects a man.

1122.   ———. "War and Youth." *Reimei* ns 1.2 (1932): 27–30.
         Autobiographical essays discussing the literature of World War I.

1123.   Sawabe, Richard. "A Day." *Pacific Citizen* 22–29 Dec. 1972: B9–B10.
         An account of a young man's unpleasant internment experiences.

1124.   Sawada, George. "A Letter to Dad." *Rafu Shimpo* 19 Dec. 1970: 4+.

1125.   Sawada, Noriko. "Memoir of a Japanese Daughter." *Ms.* Apr. 1980: 68+.
         The author describes her strained relationship with her mother, which
         resulted in part from her mother's harsh life.

1126.   ———. "Papa Takes a Bride." *Harpers* Dec. 1980: 58+.
         Chronicles an *issei*'s attempt to secure a picture bride.

1127.   Schraubi, Globularius [pseud.]. "Of Rice and Men: Shah House Murder
         Case." *Trek* Feb. 1943: 21–24.
         A comic detective story.

1128. Seko, Sachi. "The Patriarch." *Pacific Citizen* 24–31 Dec. 1976: 81+.
Describes the author's strong-willed and disciplinary grandfather.

1129. Seto, Thelma. "The Inheritance." *Bridge* 7.3 (1980): 7–8.
Depicts the strained relationship between an old Japanese American farmer and his book-loving son.

1130. Shibata, Welly. "An American." *Reimei* ns 1.1 (1932): 22.
Rpt. in *Kashu Mainichi* 30 Oct. 1932: 2; *Fusion '83* [#156] 11.
A *nisei* who plans to run away from home because of his father's authoritarian behavior is stunned to hear that his father has been crippled in a car accident.

1131. *Shigenaga, Christi. "Dear Valerie." *Hawaii Review* 9 (1979): 108–11.
Diary entries addressed to a woman dying of cancer.

1132. Shimabukuro, Mort. "Philadelphia Meeting." *The Pen* [#160] 63–64.
Two young *nisei* men who have relocated from camp meet in Philadelphia.

1133. Shimasaki, Paul. "Triple X's at the Trail's End." *Quilt* 2 (1981): 201–06.
A story about a Chinese cowboy in Texas.

1134. Shimazu, Sharon. "Within a Bootcamp Childhood." *Rafu Shimpo* 22 Dec. 1984: 8+.
A comic tale about growing up under a samurai father.

1135. **Shiomi, Rick. "Akemi." *Asianadian* 3.2 (1980): 5–9.
A Japanese Canadian man tries to seduce a visitor from Japan.

1136. ———. "U. B. C. Co-Ed Kidnapped." *Asianadian* 3.1 (1980): 16–19; 3.2 (1980): 26–29.
Satirizes both the detective-fiction genre and the stereotypes of Asians.

1137. *Shirota, Jon. *Lucky Come Hawaii*. New York: Bantam, 1965.
Describes Okinawans and Japanese in Hawaii during World War II.

1138. ———. *Pineapple White*. Los Angeles: Ohara Publications, 1972.
Describes the experiences of a Hawaiian Japanese American on the mainland.

1139. Sone, Monica. *Nisei Daughter*. Boston: Little, 1953. Introd. S. Frank Miyamoto. Seattle: U of Washington P, 1979.
Excerpt entitled "Pearl Harbor Echoes in Seattle" in *Northwest Review* 17.2–3 (1977): 243–58.
The author describes her childhood on the Seattle waterfront, her evacuation and camp experience, and her life after being released from camp.
Rev. Joseph Henry Jackson, *San Francisco Chronicle* 20 Jan. 1953: 17; Takashi Oka, *Christian Science Monitor* 26 Feb. 1953: 11; Georgianne Sampson, *New York Herald Tribune Book Review* 1 Feb. 1953: 4; Mitsuye Yamada, *MELUS* 7.3 (1980): 92.

1140. Sueda, Annie. "Welcome Back, Yoko-chan!" *Hokubei Mainichi* 1 Jan. 1981, supplement: 3.

Suematsu, Toshiaki Fumio. See Toshi.

1141.   Sugano, Douglas. "Inheritance." *Rafu Shimpo* 20 Dec. 1980: 13+.

Sugasawara, Hiroshi. See O'Suga, Riley.

1142.   Sugimoto, Etsu Inagaki. *A Daughter of the Narikin*. Garden City, NY:
Doubleday, 1932. Rutland, VT: Charles E. Tuttle, 1968.
A shy girl is forced into marriage by her aristocratic stepmother.
Rev. Isidor Schneider, *Books* 23 Oct. 1932: 11; *Christian Science Mon-
itor* 31 Dec. 1932: 13; *New York Times Book Review* 23 Oct. 1932: 18.

1143.   ———. *A Daughter of the Nohfu*. Garden City, NY: Doubleday, 1935.
Depicts generational conflicts in a rural Japanese family.
Rev. F. H. Britten, *Books* 24 Nov. 1935: 8; *Christian Science Monitor*
8 Jan. 1936: 12; Harold G. Henderson, *Saturday Review of Literature* 7
Dec. 1935: 7; Alfred Kazin, *New York Times Book Review* 1 Dec. 1935:
9+; *Time* 23 Dec. 1935: 52.

1144.   ———. *A Daughter of the Samurai*. Garden City, NY: Doubleday, 1925.
This autobiographical novel describes how a woman raised in a tradi-
tional samurai household and destined to become a Buddhist priestess
comes to America to marry.
Rev. Miriam Beard, *New York Herald Tribune Books* 22 Nov. 1925: 10;
New York Times Book Review 10 Jan. 1926: 2.

1145.   ———. *Grandmother O Kyo*. New York: Doubleday, 1940.
Contrasts the character of different generations in pre–World War II
Japan.
Rev. *Booklist* 1 Jan. 1940: 384; Jessica Powers, *Commonweal* 7 Jan. 1940:
154; Bradford Smith, *Books* 12 May 1940: 3; *New York Times* 12 May
1940: 7.

1146.   Suyahara, Roku. "Stepping with Suzuko." *Kashu Mainichi* 16 Oct. 1932:
2.
Chronicles a man's relationship with a woman of expensive tastes.

1147.   Suyeda, Richard. "The Colonist." *Rafu Shimpo* 18 Dec. 1971: 25+.
Describes a *sansei* man's search for identity.

1148.   ———. "Omoide." *Rafu Shimpo* 20 Dec. 1972: 14.
Depicts a *sansei* guitar player who travels throughout the US and
Europe.

1149.   ———. "On All Cause." *Rafu Shimpo* 19 Dec. 1973: 16.
Follows a group of people who leave a detention center.

1150.   Suzaki, Ruth M. "How Does Your Garden Grow." *Amerasia Journal* 9.2
(1982): 120–29.
A *nisei*'s garden serves as a metaphor for his relationship with his wife,
an unconventional *nisei* woman who has recently been released from
prison.

1151.   Suzukawa, Jan. "In the Night Season." *Quilt* 2 (1981): 214–20.
A waitress wishes for a better life.

1152.   *Tachiyama, Gary. [Untitled.] *Bamboo Ridge* 1 (1978): 14.
        Autobiographical recollections of childhood.

1153.   Tagasaki, Kazue. "A Nisei's Life with Father." *Pacific Citizen* 25 Dec. 1948:
        44+.
        Reminiscences about youth.

1154.   Taira, Haruko. "Farewell Okinawa! Be Strong and True." *History of the
        Okinawans in North America* [#155].
        Autobiographical essay.

1155.   Tajima, Kinjiro. "Camp Disturbance." Trans. Take Beekman and Allan
        Beekman. *Pacific Citizen* 22–29 Dec. 1967: B13+.
        A tale of adultery and death among Japanese immigrants in Hawaii.

1156.   Tajima, Ted. "Christmas—Civilized, Organized, Christianized." *Rafu
        Shimpo* 19 Dec. 1966: 21–22.
        Describes a family's activities before Christmas.

1157.   ———. "Christmas List—1936." *Rafu Shimpo* 19 Dec. 1964: 11+.
        A nine-year-old boy purchases Christmas gifts for his family.

1158.   ———. "The 50-Cent Gift." *Rafu Shimpo* 20 Dec. 1969: 20+.
        Describes how a young soldier and his wife exchange inexpensive but
        meaningful gifts during their first Christmas as husband and wife.

1159.   ———. "The Guns Were Silent." *Rafu Shimpo* 20 Dec. 1965: 11+.
        A German soldier and an American soldier come to the aid of a French
        woman and her child on Christmas.

1160.   ———. "Home for Christmas." *Rafu Shimpo* 21 Dec. 1974: 22.
        The author recounts a visit to a neighborhood in Cleveland where he
        and his wife settled after their release from an internment camp.

1161.   ———. "I Don't See No Star." *Rafu Shimpo* 19 Dec. 1959: 29–30.
        The author juxtaposes images of a modern Christmas with the birth
        of Christ.

1162.   ———. "O Tannenbaum, O Tannenbaum." *Rafu Shimpo* 20 Dec. 1961:
        17+.
        Describes a man's experience of working in a Christmas-tree lot.

1163.   ———. "S. C. R. I. P." *Rafu Shimpo* 10 Dec. 1970: 33+.
        A group of boys discover that Santa Claus does not exist.

1164.   ———. "A Table for Moderns." *Rafu Shimpo* 20 Dec. 1962: 19.

1165.   ———. "You Who Are 25." *Rafu Shimpo* 19 Dec. 1967: 11+.
        The author speculates on what the Japanese Americans born in con-
        centration camps are doing.

1166.   Tajiri, Larry. "Ghost Rancho." *Kashu Mainichi* 9 Oct. 1932: 2.
        A group of people encounter a strange man in a ghost town.

1167.   ———. "The Waters Swirl." *Kashu Mainichi* 10 July 1932: 2.
        A sketch about two *nikkei* living in an artist's colony.

1168. Takata, Timothy David. *The Last Exam*. New York: Libra Publishers, 1977.
A novella about taking the bar exam.

Takaya, Junsuke. See Osho.

1169. Takaya, Shikako. "From My Bed." Trans. Mei Takaya Nakano and Seizo Oka. *Pacific Citizen* 22–29 Dec. 1978: 52–53.
Records an *issei* woman's thoughts while recovering from severe burns.

1170. Takei, George, and Robert Asprin. *Mirror Friend, Mirror Foe*. Chicago: Playboy, 1979.
A science fiction novel about killer robots.

1171. Taketa, Margie Kōike. "Sumi-E." *Chicago Review* 29.4 (1978): 101–05.
A woman whose grandfather has committed suicide in Japan discourages her brother from imitating traditional Japanese behavior.

1172. Taketa, Tom. "Okaa-san." *Hokubei Mainichi* 1 Jan. 1980, supplement: 1–2.

1173. Takeuchi, Annie. "Grandmother's Wisdom." *Hokubei Mainichi* 1 Jan. 1977, supplement: 4.

1174. ———. "A New Year's Carol." *Hokubei Mainichi* 1 Jan. 1979, supplement: 1–2.

1175. Tamagawa, Kathleen Eldridge. *Holy Prayers in a Horse's Ear*. New York: Ray Long and Richard R. Smith, 1932.
The author recounts her conflicts as the child of a Japanese father who wishes to be Westernized and an Irish mother who wishes to live like the Japanese.

1176. Tana, Daisho. "Japanese Nisei Getting Strong." *Ayumi* [#141] 82.
Comments on the *nisei*'s right to confront claims that they are not "American."

1177. Tanabe, Frank S. "In the Still of the Night." *Tulean Dispatch Magazine* Feb. 1943: 6+.
A short story about a man who is visited by the spirit of his dead fiancée.

1178. Tanaka, Ron. "Greg." *Journal of Ethnic Studies* 4.1 (1976): 53–74.
Describes a *nisei* architect's relationships with his distant wife and his identity-seeking son.

1179. Taniguchi, Alice. "I Am Nickey the Cat." *Hokubei Mainichi* 1 Jan. 1974, supplement: 2.

1180. Tao, Yoshie. "No More Dreams for Mr. Kushino." *Hokubei Mainichi* 1 Jan. 1984: 1.
Rpt. in *Fusion Too* [#158] 33–35.
At the funeral of an *issei* migratory worker, the narrator remembers the man and wonders about his life in America.

1181. Tasaki, Hanama. *Long the Imperial Way*. 1949. Westport, CT: Greenwood, 1970.
An antiwar novel by a Hawaiian-born Japanese American.

1182. Tashima, Eugene. "The Meeting." *Fusion Too* [#158] 24–25.
An *issei* sits silently at a meeting regarding an urban redevelopment that will destroy his home.

1183. ———. "Musings of a Wayward Samurai." *Fusion '83* [#156] 87–88.
A map becomes a metaphor for the varying concerns of *issei*, *nisei*, and *sansei*.

1184. Tatsukawa, Steve. "Waiting for Good Snow." *Rafu Shimpo* 20 Dec. 1977: 11+.
A *sansei* man waits to buy cocaine.

1185. Tatsuno, Sheridan. "Hara-kiri at 5 O'clock." *Hokubei Mainichi* 1 Jan. 1979, supplement: 1–3.

1186. ———. "The Medicine Man's Lament." *Yoisho!* [#183] 46–53.
A *sansei* hitchhiking through Maine receives rides from a Caucasian lumberjack and from an elderly Native American medicine man who draws parallels between Native American culture and Japanese American culture.

1187. ———. "The Mochi-Man." *Bridge* 8.4 (1983): 19–22.
Rpt. in *Hokubei Mainichi* 1 Jan. 1984: 2.
A sketch of a *nisei* who has pretensions of being a magician, only to be humiliated when he performs before his community.

1188. ———. "Sake and Whispers." *Fusion '83* [#156] 40–46.
An *issei* recounts to her daughter how she was lured away from Japan and forced into prostitution in San Francisco.

1189. ———. "Shadows of the Cloud (An Excerpt)." *Echoes from Gold Mountain* 1979: 86–94.
A young man who travels to Hiroshima remembers the atomic bombing that killed his mother.

1190. ———. "Sundown in Topaz." *Echoes from Gold Mountain* 1982: 52–60.
Conflicts erupt when loyalty oaths are administered at the Topaz concentration camp.

1191. *Terada, Wini. "Intermediate School Hapai." *Bamboo Ridge* 5 (1979–80): 28–45.
Rpt. in *The Best of* Bamboo Ridge [#103] 250–66.
Written in pidgin dialect, the story describes the relationship between a brother and sister.

1192. Togashi, John. "The Graveyard." *Rising Waters* 1975: n. pag.
A young man escapes to a Los Angeles graveyard to think.

1193. ———. "Hagemasu—Encouragement." *Yoisho!* [#183] 56–61.
A young Japanese American boy runs away from the Amache concentration camp and meets a Native American woman who explains to him how her parents died when the Kiowa were forcibly moved.

1194. Tokuda, Tama. "Matsutake." *Pacific Citizen* 21–28 Dec. 1984: C28–C29.
Describes four *nisei*'s search for *matsutake* mushrooms, a Japanese delicacy, in the mountains near Seattle.

1195. Toshi [Toshiaki Fumio Suematsu]. "Born of the Pacific, Book I: A Letter to Hisae." *Bamboo Ridge: The Hawaii Writers' Quarterly* 2 (1979): 2–12. Rpt. in *The Best of Bamboo Ridge* [#103] 267–85.
Discusses identity among Japanese Americans.

1196. Tsuchiyama, Ray K. "Even Marv's German Auntie Hates Me." *Journal of Ethnic Studies* 4.1 (1976): 82–84.
A white woman who marries a Japanese American examines the problems she faces with her husband's family.

1197. ———. "Law and Oda." *Journal of Ethnic Studies* 4.1 (1976): 75–81. Rpt. in *Ayumi* [#141] 241–46.
A Hawaiian *sansei* has problems coping with the legacy of his father's life.

1198. Uba, Gregory Mark. "Naruse Gazing into the Pool." *Fusion-San* [#157] 76–79.
An old man's hostile feelings toward a carp parallel his antagonistic feelings toward his son-in-law.

1199. Uchida, Yoshiko. *Desert Exile: The Uprooting of a Japanese American Family.* Seattle: U of Washington P, 1982.
The story of a family's internment experience.
Rev. Rita Takahashi Cates, *Amerasia Journal* 10.2 (1983): 93–96.

1200. ———. *Picture Bride: A Novel.* Flagstaff, AZ: Northland Press, 1987.
About a woman who is disillusioned by her husband and culturally estranged from her daughter.

1201. ———. "Something to Be Remembered By." *The Hawk's Well* [#119] 107–14.
An old man who returns to Japan after spending 40 years in America wants to leave a memento.

1202. *Uda, Lowell. "Crabs." *Talk Story* [#104] 19–32.
Chronicles a doctor's sexual neurosis and eventual insanity.

1203. ———. "A Hawaiian Tale and a Maori Tale." *Hawaii Review* 2.1 (1973): 72–74.
The two tales are "The Woman Who Loved to Eat Squid" and "Haukiwahos' Face."

1204. ———. "Hina and the Moon." *Hawaii Review* 2.2 (1974): 38–43.
A tale explaining the sweet potato's origin.

1205. ———. "Kapa." *Sandwich Isles, U.S.A.* [#115] 55–58.
A retelling of the Hawaiian legend explaining the development of *Kapa* material.

1206. Uehara, Michael. "The Intrusion of Uncle Shig." *AsiaWeek* 1 Feb. 1987.
Short story.

1207. Uehara, Yachiyo. "Moving Day." *Fusion-San* [#157] 53–55.
A woman recalls experiences in the apartment she is about to move out of.

1208. ———. "One Small Woman." *Fusion-San* [#157] 55–60.
      A *nisei* reminisces about her mother.

1209. ———. "One with the Angels." *Hokubei Mainichi* 1 Jan. 1984: 2.

1210. ———. "Perfect Strangers." *Hokubei Mainichi* 1 Jan. 1981: Supplement, 3.

1211. ———. "The Seed That Grew." *Hokubei Mainichi* 1 Jan. 1983: Supplement, 1.

1212. Uno, Ernest. "Be Careful, Go, and Do Return. . . ." *Hokubei Mainichi* 1 Jan. 1976: Supplement, 2.

1213. Wada, Sachi. "Journey at Christmas." *Pacific Citizen* 17 Dec. 1954: A14.
      Chronicles the life and death of a young soldier from the perspective of the moon and a tree.

1214. *Wakayama, Mary. "1895: The Honeymoon Hotel." *Bamboo Ridge: The Hawaii Writers' Quarterly* 27 (1985): 3–10.
      A short story about a picture bride.

1215. ———. "Go to Home." *Bamboo Ridge* 13 (1981–82): 13–16.
      Rpt. in *The Best of* Bamboo Ridge [#103] 286–89.
      A man asks his wife's corpse for forgiveness because he could not be with her when she died.

1216. ———. "Watching Fire." *Bamboo Ridge* 17 (1982–83): 20–27.
      Rpt. in *Passages to the Dream Shore* [#170] 183–90.
      Describes a blaze in a Hawaiian sugar plantation.

1217. Wakiji, George. "Just Memories. . . ." *Rafu Shimpo* 20 Dec. 1960: 20.
      The author reminisces about the traditions of his childhood: Japanese school, rice pounding, Japanese fencing, and prefectural picnics.

1218. Watanabe, Colin. "Symposium." *Asian American Review* 2.1 (1975): 105–07.
      An account of discovering an old Asian man lying prone on a San Francisco street.

1219. Watanabe, Philip. "Great Nisei Novel." *Rafu Shimpo* 20 Dec. 1949: 12.
      Two *nisei* men discuss various plot lines for a novel that one of them is planning to write.

1220. *Watanabe, Sylvia. "Colors." *Pacific Citizen* 20–27 Dec. 1985: B17–B19.
      A *sansei* returns to the Hawaiian village in which she was raised and confronts difficulties with her institutionalized father, her rambunctious grandmother, and her practical aunt.

1221. ———. "The Prayer Lady." *Greenfield Review* 13.1–2 (1985): 44–48.
      Rpt. in *Bamboo Ridge* 25 (1985): 21–25; *The Stories We Hold Secret* [#89] 252–58; *The Best of* Bamboo Ridge [#103] 290–94.
      Describes an old woman who has a reputation for healing by touch.

1222. ———. "The Sea Birds." *Bamboo Ridge* 24 (1984): 26–31.
      Rpt. in *Passages to the Dream Shore* [#170] 191–96.
      Juxtaposed scenes of a Japanese American woman caring for an elderly relative and of the woman's husband jogging through their neighborhood.

1223.　———. "A Spell of Kono Weather." *Bamboo Ridge* 30 (1986): 18–24.
A young woman tries to commit suicide after her face is disfigured in a car accident.

1224.　———. "A Summer Waltz." *Bamboo Ridge* 19 (1983): 2–4.
An eccentric bartender wants to dance with two eight-year-old girls.

1225.　Watkins, Yoko Kawashima. *So Far from the Bamboo Grove.* New York: Lothrop, 1985.
An autobiographical novel about a Japanese woman who grows up in Korea.

1226.　Yakata, Larry. "L. A. 1967." *Rafu Shimpo* 20 Dec. 1975: 13.
An autobiographical sketch about the death of the author's grandmother.

1227.　*Yamachika, Takeo [Ted]. "An Old Debt." *Nisei: In Hawaii and the Pacific* 3 (May 1949): 16–17.
Rpt. in *Pacific Citizen* 17 Dec. 1954: B23.
A son repays his father's debt to his employer.

1228.　———. "The Party." *Nisei: In Hawaii and the Pacific* 4 (Spring 1950): 21+.
Rpt. in *Pacific Citizen* 18 Dec. 1953: B24.
The siblings of a *nisei* soldier try to prevent their mother from discovering that their brother has been sent to the European front.

1229.　———. "Shine, Mister?" *Nisei: In Hawaii and the Pacific* 4 (Summer 1950): 10.
A *nisei* man observes a timid shoe-shine boy.

1230.　———. "The Story of Peepeekoko and Its Folly (The Town without Traffic Problems)." *Nisei: In Hawaii and the Pacific* 3 (Summer 1949): 11+.
A satire on the desire for material wealth.

1231.　———. "Two Friends." *Nisei: In Hawaii and the Pacific* 2 (Spring 1948): 10.
Describes the friendship between two *issei* men.

1232.　*Yamada, Holly. "Circle of Lot." *Literary Arts Hawaii* 85 (Summer 1987): 17.

1233.　———. "Fixing Random." *Hawaii Review* 16 (1984): 42–46.
A short story about a woman's romantic relationships.

1234.　Yamada, Jim. "The Dance They Saved for John." *Trek* Feb. 1943: 29–32.
A *nisei* college student fantasizes while at a dance.

1235.　———. "Gaudeamus Igitur. . . ." *Trek* June 1943: 20–24.
A short story about an *issei* man who attends his son's university graduation.

1236.　*Yamada, Joanne Y. "A Day." *Bamboo Ridge* 17 (1982–83): 7–18.
A snobbish woman is annoyed by a visit from her unsophisticated neighbor.

1237.   Yamada, Mitsu. "Random Whirligig." *The Pen* [#160] 65–66.
        The author describes the changing tone of letters she receives from
        friends before and after internment.

1238.   Yamamoto [DeSoto], Hisaye. "An Abandoned Pot of Rice." *Rafu Shimpo*
        22 Dec. 1984: 6+.
        Describes life before World War II.

1239.   ———. "Appointment in Japan." *Rafu Shimpo* 21 Dec. 1954: 12.
        A sketch of a young man who pursues a religious life.

1240.   ———. "Bettina." *Rafu Shimpo* 21 Dec. 1955: 6+.
        Describes an unmarried pregnant woman.

1241.   ———. "The Brown House." *Harper's Bazaar* Oct. 1951: 166+.
        Rpt. in *Asian-American Authors* [#125] 114–22; *Yardbird Reader* 3
        [#179] 205–11; *Seventeen Syllables* 56–66.
        Describes the conflicts between an *issei* woman and her husband, who
        gambles.

1242.   ———. "Christmas Eve on South Boyle." *Rafu Shimpo* 20 Dec. 1957: 9+.
        Describes the South Boyle neighborhood of Los Angeles and a partic-
        ular midnight mass that the narrator attends.

1243.   ———. "A Day in Little Tokyo." *Amerasia Journal* 13.2 (1986–87): 21–28.
        Describes *nisei* life in Los Angeles before World War II.

1244.   ———. "Dry Snakeskin." *Rafu Shimpo* 22 Dec. 1952: 15.
        Explains the origins of folk remedies.

1245.   ———. "Eju-kei-shung! Eju-kei-shung!" *Rafu Shimpo* 20 Dec. 1980: 11+.
        Vignettes of grammar school.

1246.   ———. "The Enormous Piano." *Rafu Shimpo* 20 Dec. 1977: 6+.
        The author reminisces about her childhood in Southern California.

1247.   ———. "Epithalamium." *Carleton Miscellany* 1.4 (1960): 56–67.
        A Japanese American woman secretly marries an Italian-American
        alcoholic.

1248.   ———. "The Eskimo Connection." *Rafu Shimpo* 21 Dec. 1983: 9+.
        A short story about the relationship between a *nisei* woman writer and
        an incarcerated Eskimo man who corresponds with her.

1249.   ———. "A Fire in Fontana." *Rafu Shimpo* 21 Dec. 1985: 8+.
        The death of a black family in a fire intensifies the narrator's social con-
        sciousness against racism.

1250.   ———. "Gang Aft a-Gley." *Rafu Shimpo* 21 Dec. 1953: 13–14.
        A woman is overwhelmed by having to care for a toddler and two young
        children.

1251.   ———. "Having Babies." *Rafu Shimpo* 20 Dec. 1962: 21.
        Autobiographical account.

1252.   ———. "The High-Heeled Shoes." *Partisan Review* Oct. 1948: 1079–85.
        Episodes about the subtle and overt sexual abuse faced by women.

1253.　———. "In Search of a Happy Ending." *Pacific Citizen* 22 Dec. 1951: 17+.

A *nisei* who serves in the Japanese army against his will during World War II struggles to regain American citizenship afterwards.

1254.　———. "Ingurishi Tsuransureishan." *Rafu Shimpo* 20 Dec. 1958: 9.

Describes the problems of speaking English with a Japanese accent.

1255.　———. "Kichi Harada." *Pacific Citizen* 20 Dec. 1957: B11.

Describes an *issei* woman who lives in a Catholic shelter in New York City.

1256.　———. "Las Vegas Charley." *Arizona Quarterly* 17 (1961): 303–22.

Rpt. in *Asian-American Heritage* [#177] 97–121; *The Third Woman* [#112] 470–84.

A story about an *issei* man in Las Vegas.

1257.　———. "The Legend of Miss Sasagawara." *Kenyon Review* 12.1 (1950): 99–115.

Rpt. in *Speaking for Ourselves* [#110] 162–73; *Amerasia Journal* 3.2 (1976): 10–22; *The Ethnic American Woman* [#88] 199–208; *Ayumi* [#141] 161–71; *Seventeen Syllables* 35–55.

Describes the mysterious actions of an aloof *nisei* woman in an internment camp.

1258.　———. "Life among the Oilfields." *Rafu Shimpo* 21 Dec. 1979: 13+.

Rpt. in *Seventeen Syllables* 67–81.

A callous white couple injures a Japanese American child in a car accident and refuses to compensate.

1259.　———. "The Losing of a Language." *Rafu Shimpo* 20 Dec. 1963: 7.

The author describes how she lost her command of the Japanese language.

1260.　———. "A Man from Hiroshima." *Rafu Shimpo* 20 Dec. 1956: 9.

Describes an *issei* man who lives in a New York City mission.

1261.　———. "Miyoko O'Brien (Or, Everybody's Turning Japanese)." *Pacific Citizen* 20–27 Dec. 1985: A46.

An essay on interracial marriage.

1262.　———. "Morning Rain." *Pacific Citizen* 19 Dec. 1952: 46+.

Rpt. in *Greenfield Review* 6.1–2 (1977): 77–79.

A *nisei* discovers her father's loss of hearing.

1263.　———. "My Father Can Beat Muhammad Ali." *Echoes* 4 (1986): 14–15.

A *nisei* wants to prove his athletic prowess to his two sons.

1264.　———. "The Nature of Things." *Rafu Shimpo* 20 Dec. 1965: 7+.

A comic description of the problems encountered by the narrator and her family after buying a home unconnected to the city's sewer lines.

1265.　———. "Nip in the Bud." *Rafu Shimpo* 20 Dec. 1961: 9–10.

A mother has problems with a son who misuses money.

1266.　————. "The Other Cheek." *Rafu Shimpo* 19 Dec. 1959: 9.
The author recounts how her pacifist beliefs affect her young daughter.

1267.　————. "Pleasure of Plain Rice." *Rafu Shimpo* 20 Dec. 1960: 9+.
Rpt. in *Southwest: A Contemporary Anthology*. Albuquerque, NM:
Red Earth Press, 1977. 295–301.
Describes a *nisei* woman's experiences while working in the home of
a wealthy widow.

1268.　————. "Seventeen Syllables." *Partisan Review* Nov. 1949: 1122–34.
Rpt. in *The American Equation* [#149] 79–92; *Ethnic American Short
Stories* [#150] 89–104; abridged version in *In Question*. New York: Harcourt, 1975. 116–27; *Counterpoint* [#113] 490–95; abridged version in
Ideas. Ed. Philip Mcfarland et al. Boston: Houghton, 1978. 277–86;
abridged version in *New Voices 4 (in Literature, Language, and Compo-
sition)*. Ed. Jay Cline et al. Lexington: Ginn, 1978. 79–90; *The Third
Woman* [#112] 485–95; abridged version in *Our World Today*. Ed. Hans
P. Guth and Patricia Strandness Schnider. Lexington: Heath, 1981.
99–106; *Exploring Literature (through Reading and Writing)*. Ed. Bernard A. Drabeck et al. Boston: Houghton, 1982. 250–60; *Between
Mothers and Daughters: Stories across a Generation*. Ed. Susan Koppelman. Old Westbury, NY: Feminist Press, 1985. 161–76; *Seventeen Syllables* 1–18.
A *nisei* girl on the verge of womanhood witnesses conflict between her
father, a farmer, and her mother, a poet.

1269.　————. *Seventeen Syllables: Five Stories of Japanese American Life*. Ed.
Robert Rolf and Norimitsu Ayuzawa. Tokyo: Kirihara Shoten, 1985.
"Seventeen Syllables," "The Legend of Miss Sasagawara," "Yoneko's
Earthquake," "The Brown House," and "Life among the Oilfields."

1270.　————. "Sidney, the Flying Turtle." *Rafu Shimpo* 18 Dec. 1967: 15+.
An essay concerning the various pets of the narrator's family.

1271.　————. "A Slight Case of Mistaken Identity." *Rafu Shimpo* 19 Dec. 1964:
6.
Recounts three instances when the author was thought to be another
type of person because of her appearance.

1272.　————. "The Streaming Tears." *Rafu Shimpo* 20 Dec. 1951: 22+.
A short story about an *issei*'s encounter with a remorseful man who
claims to be one of the pilots who flew the plane that dropped the atomic
bomb on Hiroshima.

1273.　————. "La tante de ma plume." *Rafu Shimpo* 21 Dec. 1982: 11+.
A sketch of an *issei* woman.

1274.　————. "Tomato Surprise." *Rafu Shimpo* 19 Dec. 1966: 26+.
An essay on culinary problems and varieties.

1275.　————. "Underground Lady." *Pacific Citizen* 19–26 Dec. 1986: A15+.
A short story about a *nisei* woman's encounter with a homeless woman.

1276.   ———. "Wilshire Bus." *Pacific Citizen* 23 Dec. 1950: 17+.
    While taking a bus to visit her hospitalized husband, a Japanese American woman witnesses a drunken Caucasian man harass a Chinese couple.

1277.   ———. "Writing." *Rafu Shimpo* 20 Dec. 1968: 14+.
    Rpt. in *Amerasia Journal* 3.2 (1976): 126–33.
    Autobiographical essay.

1278.   ———. "Yellow Leaves." *Rafu Shimpo* 20 Dec. 1986: 36+.
    An essay about aging.

1279.   ———. "Yoneko's Earthquake." *Furioso* 6.1 (1951): 5–16.
    Rpt. in *Best American Short Stories of 1952*. Ed. Martha Foley. Boston: Houghton, 1952; *AIIIEEEEE!* [#100] 1983: 178–90; *West Coast Fiction* [#124] 346–57; *Seventeen Syllables* 19–34.
    A tragic story about domestic upheavals in a Japanese American family.

1280.   *Yamanaka, Cedric. "What the Ironwood Whispered." *Hawaii Review* 18 (1985): 1–26.
    Rpt. in *Passages to the Dream Shore* [#170] 197–220.
    A high school senior encounters an unusual friend.

1281.   Yamasaki, Tosuke. "On Riding Rods." *Reimei* ns 1.1 (1932): 15–18.
    Rpt. in *Hokubei Mainichi* 1 Jan. 1985, supplement: 3.
    A portrait of life among hoboes.

1282.   Yamashita, Karen. "The Bath." *Amerasia Journal* 3.1 (1975): 137–52.
    A young Japanese American woman travels in Japan.

1283.   ——— [K. T. Yamashita]. "Tucano." *Rafu Shimpo* 20 Dec. 1975: 11+.
    A tale of a Japanese man's fantasy upon arriving in the jungle of Brazil where he is to farm.

1284.   ———. "The Dentist and the Dental Hygienist." *AsiAm* Apr. 1987: 66–70.
    The hygienist delivers extensive lectures to her captive patients.

1285.   ———. "In Brasil the Earth Is Red." *Rafu Shimpo* 18 Dec. 1976: 18+.
    Describes the problems faced by Japanese immigrants to Brazil.

1286.   Yamato, Kiku. "*Masako*: A Short Novel in Four Parts." Trans. Hoshina Airan. *Reimei* ns 1.2 (1932): 7–15.
    Scenes from the life of a young wealthy Japanese woman in the early 20th century.

1287.   ———. "*Masako*: Part Two." Trans. Hoshina Airan. *Reimei* ns 1.3 (1933): 24–28.
    A wealthy young Japanese woman plans to marry.

1288.   Yamauchi, Wakako. "And the Soul Shall Dance." *Rafu Shimpo* 19 Dec. 1966: 9+.
    Rpt. in *AIIIEEEEE!* [#100] 1983: 193–200; *Solo: Women on Woman Alone*. Ed. Linda Hamalian and Leo Hamalian. New York: Dell, 1977. 232–39.
    Describes a Japanese American girl's perceptions of her troubled neighbors.

1289.   ———. "The Big Lick." *Rafu Shimpo* 19 Dec. 1959: 20+.
          The author recounts how a shy acquaintance develops self-confidence.

1290.   ———. "The Boatmen on Toneh River." *Amerasia Journal* 2.2 (1974): 203–07.
          Rpt. in *Counterpoint* [#113] 531–33; *Structure and Meaning: An Introduction to Literature.* Ed. Anthony Dube et al. Boston: Houghton, 1983. 368–72.
          A dying *nisei* woman remembers her parents as she thinks about her daughter.

1291.   ———. "Chartered Lives." *Rafu Shimpo* 21 Dec. 1982: 14+.
          A recently divorced *nisei* becomes involved in her employer's troubled marriage.

1292.   ———. "The Coward." *Rafu Shimpo* 20 Dec. 1977: 7+.
          A middle-aged *nisei* woman sorts out the various feelings produced by her relationship with an artist.

1293.   ———. "Don't Step on the Line." *Rafu Shimpo* 18 Dec. 1967: 19+.
          A young woman who believes she has magical powers sets out to prove them.

1294.   ———. "The Handkerchief." *Rafu Shimpo* 20 Dec. 1961: 13–14.
          Rpt. in *Amerasia Journal* 4.1 (1977): 143–50.
          Recounts how a young boy deals with his mother's absence.

1295.   ———. "Hang Loose." *Rafu Shimpo* 20 Dec. 1969: 15+.
          An autobiographical sketch of the author's youth.

1296.   ———. "Hundred and Second Dalmation." *Rafu Shimpo* 20 Dec. 1963: 23+.
          Personal sketch.

1297.   ———. "In Heaven and Earth." *Rafu Shimpo* 21 Dec. 1968: 24+.
          Rpt. in *Greenfield Review* 6.1–2 (1977): 90–98; *Ayumi* [#141] 172–77.
          Describes how a *nikkei* drifter affects a rural Japanese American family.

1298.   ———. "A Journey of Reminiscence." *Rafu Shimpo* 19 Dec. 1964: 21+.
          A mosaic serves as an analogy for a trip through the cities in which the author was raised.

1299.   ———. "Makapuu Bay." *Bamboo Ridge* 3 (1979): 2–11.
          A story about a divorcée.

1300.   ———. "Maybe." *Rafu Shimpo* 22 Dec. 1984: 28+.
          Describes life in a sweatshop.

1301.   ———. "Me and Puerto Vallarta." *Rafu Shimpo* 19 Dec. 1970: 9+.
          Describes the author's experiences during a painting seminar in Puerto Vallarta.

1302.   ———. "My Sister's Family." *Rafu Shimpo* 19 Dec. 1971: 16+.
          Autobiographical sketch.

1303.   ———. "Otoko." *Rafu Shimpo* 20 Dec. 1980: 9+.

1304. ———. "Poston Revisited." *Rafu Shimpo* 20 Dec. 1965: 13–14.
The author recalls her internment experiences.

1305. ———. "The Sensei." *Yardbird Reader* 3 [#179] 245–54.
A *nisei* couple encounter an unfortunate *issei* man who was a respected Buddhist priest during World War II but who now gambles his earnings away in Las Vegas.

1306. ———. "Shirley Temple Hotcha-cha." *Rafu Shimpo* 20 Dec. 1979: 7+.
A Japanese American woman who is sent to Japan in her youth returns to America after the war only to see the destruction of her marriage.

1307. ———. "Something Better for Miwa." *Rafu Shimpo* 20 Dec. 1958: 23–24.
An *issei* couple in a loveless marriage center their hopes on their only daughter.

1308. ———. "Songs My Mother Taught Me." *Amerasia Journal* 3.2 (1976): 63–73.
Describes an *issei* woman's unwanted pregnancy.

1309. ———. "That Was All." *Amerasia Journal* 7.1 (1980): 115–20.
Rpt. in *Rafu Shimpo* 21 Dec. 1983: 7+.
A woman remembers her infatuation with her father's friend, an older *issei* farmer.

1310. ———. "A Way To Go." *Rafu Shimpo* 20 Dec. 1963: 17+.
Describes the relationship between a young *nisei* and an older white woman who work in a factory.

1311. ———. "Whisper at School." *Rafu Shimpo* 20 Dec. 1960: 26.
The author recalls a frightening experience.

1312. Yashima, Taro [Jun Atsushi Iwamatsu]. *Horizon Is Calling*. New York: Holt, 1947.
An autobiography with drawings describing Japanese antifascists in the early days of the Sino-Japanese War.

1313. ———. *The New Sun*. New York: Holt, 1943.
Drawings and observations on the author's anti-fascist activities in Japan.

1314. Yasuda, Mitsu. "Mr. Matsuo." *Pacific Citizen* 19 Dec. 1952: 36+.
An *issei* man wishes to become an American citizen.

1315. Yazawa, Jennifer Y. "Bon-San." *Fusion-San* [#157] 68.
Describes a girl's impressions of a Buddhist priest.

Yogi, Jippo. See Rokumin.

1316. Yoshida, Gerri Igarashi. "The First Day of School." *Fusion-San* [#157] 29–30.
A *sansei* girl is taunted by her classmates.

1317. ———. "My Father." *Fusion '83* [#156] 58–60.
The author declares pride in her Japanese American heritage.

1318.   *Yoshida, Jim, with Bill Hosokawa. *The Two Worlds of Jim Yoshida.* New York: Morrow, 1972.
An autobiography of a Japanese American caught in Japan during World War II.
Rev. John W. Conner, *English Journal* 61 (Dec. 1972): 1384; Forrest E. LaViolette, *Pacific Affairs* 47 (1974): 257–58.

1319.   *Yoshimori, Alice. "I Had to Write It, Emma." *Paradise of the Pacific* July 1946: 10–11.
A letter asking Caucasians to respect speakers of pidgin English.

1320.   *Yoshioka, Clarence K. "Ah Leong's New Year Gift." *Hawaii Quill Magazine* 3 (Apr. 1930): 10–13.
A hardworking man wishes to return to China.

Poetry

1321.   Abe, Ryan. *Golden Sunrises—A Narrative in Haiku.* San Mateo, CA: Farris Press, 1973.

Adachi, Jeffrey. *Yancha!* See #686.

1323.   Ai. *Conversations: For Robert Lowell.* St. Paul: printed at the Toothpaste Press for Bookslinger, 1981.

1324.   ———. *Cruelty.* Boston: Houghton, 1973.

1325.   ———. *Cruelty/Killing Floor.* Foreword Carolyn Forché. New York: Thunder's Mouth Press, 1987.

1326.   ———. *Killing Floor.* Boston: Houghton, 1979.
Rev. Yuri Kageyama, *Contact II* 7.38–40 (1986): 12–14.

1327.   ———. *Sin: Poems.* Boston: Houghton, 1986.

1328.   Akiyoshi, Dennis. *Poetry.* Los Angeles: International Publication, 1984.

Chock, Eric. See Chinese American section.

1329.   Foster, Sesshu. *Angry Days.* Los Angeles: West End Press, 1987.

1330.   Fujita, Jun. *Tanka: Poems in Exile.* Chicago: Covici-McGee, 1923.

1331.   Furuta, Soichi. *To Breathe.* Westbury, NY: Edition Heliodor, 1980.
Rev. Yuri Kageyama, *Contact II* 7.38–40 (1986): 12–14.

1332.   Hartman, Yuki. *Hot Footsteps.* New York: Telephone Books, 1976.
Rev. Yuri Kageyama, *Contact II* 7.38–40 (1986): 12–14.

1333.   ———. *A One of Me.* Genesis, NY: Grasp Press, 1970.

1334.   ———. *Ping.* New York: Kulchar Foundation, 1984.
Rev. Oliver Conant, *Contact II* 7.38–40 (1986): 62–63.

1335.   ———. *Red Rice: Poems.* Putnam Valley, NY: Swollen Magpie, 1980.
Rev. Yuri Kageyama, *Contact II* 7.38–40 (1986): 12–14.

1336.   Hartmann, [Carl] Sadakichi. *"Drifting Flowers of the Sea" and Other Poems to Elizabeth Blanche Walsh.* N.p.: n.p., 1904. [Manifold copy.]

1337.   ———. *Japanese Rhythms, Tanka, Haik(ai) and Other Forms Translated, Adapted or Imitated by Sadakichi Hartmann.* . . . N.p.: n.p., 1926.

1338.   ———. *My Rubaiyat.* St. Louis: Mangan Printing, 1913. New York: G. Bruno, 1916.

1339.   ———. *Naked Ghosts: Four Poems.* South Pasadena, CA: Fantasia, 1925.

1340.   ———. *Tanka and Haiku: 14 Japanese Rhythms.* New York: G. Bruno, 1915.

1341.   Hongo, Garrett Kaoru. *The River of Heaven.* New York: Knopf, 1988.

1342.   ———. *Yellow Light.* Middletown: Wesleyan UP, 1982.
        Poems about the search for origins.
        Rev. Fred Wei-han Houn, *East Wind* 2.2 (1983): 65–67; Deborah Lee, *Contact II* 7.38–40 (1986): 60–61; George Uba, *Journal of Ethnic Studies* 12.4 (1985): 123–25.

1343.   *Honma, Dean. *Night Dive.* Honolulu: Petronium Press, 1985.
        Chapbook.

1344.   Ikeda, Patricia Y. *House of Wood, House of Salt.* Cleveland: Cleveland State UP, 1978.
        Rev. David Brewster, *Contact II* 7.38–40 (1986): 19.

1345.   Imura, Ernest Sakayuki. *Sunrise-Sunset: A Continuous Cycle of Living.* New York: Vantage, 1976.

1346.   Inada, Lawson F. *Before the War: Poems as They Happened.* New York: Morrow, 1971.
        Rev. *Choice* 8 (1971): 1014; Bill Katz, *Library Journal* 1 Jan. 1971: 82.

1347.   Kagawa, Bunichi. *Hidden Flame.* Stanford: Half Moon Press, 1930.

1348.   *Kakugawa, Frances. *Sand Grains.* San Antonio: Naylor, 1970.

1349.   ———. *Golden Spike.* San Antonio: Naylor, 1976.

1350.   ———. *Path of Butterflies.* San Antonio: Naylor, 1976.

1351.   ———. *Winter Ginger Blossom.* San Antonio: Naylor, 1971.

1352.   Kaneko, Lonny. *Coming Home from Camp.* Waldron Island, WA: Brooding Heron Press, 1986.

1353.   **Kiyooka, Roy. *The Fontainebleau Dream Machine: 18 Frames from a Book of Rhetoric.* Toronto: Coach House, 1977.

1354.   ———. *Kyoto Airs.* Vancouver: Periwinkle Press, 1964.

1355.   ———. *Nevertheless These Eyes.* Toronto: Coach House, 1967.
        Rev. Roy Mac Skimming, *Canadian Literature* 37 (1968): 88–89.

1356.   ———. *Stoned Gloves.* Toronto: Coach House, 1971.

1357.   ———. *Transcanada Letters.* Vancouver: Talonbooks, 1975.
        Rev. Lonny Kaneko, *Contact II* 7.38–40 (1986): 15–17.

1358.   ———. *Wheels.* Toronto: Coach House, 1982.

1359. **Kogawa, Joy. *A Choice of Dreams*. Toronto: McClelland & Stewart, 1974.
About half of the poems describe scenes the poet witnessed on a trip to Japan; most of the rest are about Canada.
Rev. Eric Thompson, *Canadian Literature* 63 (1975): 112.

1360. ———. *Jericho Road*. Toronto: McClelland & Stewart, 1977.
Rev. Al Purdy, *Canadian Literature* 76 (1978): 126–27.

1361. ———. *The Splintered Moon*. Fredericton, NB: Fiddlehead Poetry Books, 1968.
Rev. Peter Stevens, *Canadian Literature* 36 (1968): 84.

1362. ———. *Woman in the Woods*. Tucson, AZ: Mosaic Press, 1985.

1363. Kudaka, Geraldine. *Numerous Avalanches at the Point of Intersection*. Greenfield Center, NY: Greenfield Review Press, 1979.
Rev. Jesse Hiraoka, *Contact II* 7.38–40 (1986): 63–64.

1364. *Matsueda, Pat. *The Fishcatcher*. Honolulu: Petronium Press, 1985.
Chapbook.
Rev. Craig Howes, *Literary Arts Hawaii* 78–79 (Spring 1986): 4–5.

1365. Mirikitani, Janice. *Awake in the River*. San Francisco: Isthmus Press, 1978.
Rev. Fred Wei-han Houn, *East Wind* 2.2 (1983): 65–67; Connie Young Yu, *Contact II* 7.38–40 (1986): 11.

1366. ———. *Shedding Silence*. Berkeley: Celestial Arts Publishing, 1987.
Poetry and prose poems.
Rev. Patricia Holt, *San Francisco Sunday Examiner and Chronicle* 5 July 1987, rev. sec.: 1+.

1367. Mitsui, James [Masao]. *After the Long Train*. Minneapolis: Bieler Press, 1985.
Rev. Tina Koyama, *Contact II* 7.38–40 (1986): 59–60.

1368. ———. *Crossing the Phantom River*. Port Townsend, WA: Graywolf Press, 1978.

1369. ———. *Journal of the Sun*. Port Townsend, WA: Copper Canyon Press, 1974.

1370. Nishizaki, Robert Kiyoshi. *Mongolian Blue: The Collected Poems of Robert Kiyoshi Nishizaki, 1963–1978*. Manhattan Beach, CA: Middle Walter Press, 1978.

1371. Nixon, Lucille M., and Tomoe Tana, eds. and trans. *Sounds from the Unknown: A Collection of Japanese American Tanka*. Denver: A. Swallow, 1963.

1372. Noda, Barbara. *Strawberries*. Berkeley: Shameless Hussy Press, 1979.
Rev. Tina Koyama, *Contact II* 7.38–40 (1986): 18.

1373. Noguchi, Yone. *From the Eastern Sea*. London: Elkin Mathews; Tokyo: Fuzanbo Publishing, 1903.

1374. ———. *The Ganges Calls Me: Book of Poems*. Tokyo: Kyobunkwan, 1938.

1375. ———. *Japanese Hokkus*. Boston: Four Seas, 1920.

1376. ———. *Noguchi's Song unto Brother Americans*. Oakland, CA, 1897.

1377. ———. *The Pilgrimage*. Kamakura, Japan: Valley Press, 1909.

1378. ———. *Seen and Unseen; or Monologues of a Homeless Snail*. New York: Orientalia; San Francisco: G. Burgess & P. Garnett, 1897.

1379. ———. *The Selected Poems of Yone Noguchi*. Boston: Four Seas, 1921.

1380. ———. *The Summer Cloud: Prose Poems*. Tokyo: Shunyodo, 1906.

1381. ———. *These Scattered Flowers of My Poetry Are Presented to You with My Compliments*. Oakland: privately printed, n.d.

1382. ———. *The Voice of the Valley*. San Francisco: W. Doxey, 1897.

1383. Oka, Francis Naohiko. *Poems: Memorial Edition*. San Francisco: City Lights, 1970.

1384. Sakaki, Nanao. *Bellyfulls*. Eugene, OR: Toad Press, 1966.

1385. ———. *Real Play: Poetry and Drama*. San Juan Pueblo, NM: Tooth of Time Books, 1983.
       A collection of poems written by feet with sand and rainwater.

1386. Sasaki, Yasuo. *Ascension*. Pasadena: Balconet Press, 1968.

1387. ———. *Village Scene/Village Herd*. Cincinnati and Berkeley: Balconet Press, 1986.
       Rev. Russell Leong, *Amerasia Journal* 13.2 (1986–87): 243–45.

1388. **Shikatani, Gerry. *Barking of Dog*. Toronto: Missing Link Press, 1973.

1389. ———. *Haliburton*. Toronto: Missing Link Press, 1975.

1390. ———. *Ship Sands Island*. Toronto: Ganglia Press, 1978.

1391. ———. *A Sparrow's Food*. Toronto: Coach House, 1985.
       Rev. Christopher Wiseman, *Canadian Literature* 105 (1985): 188–89.

1392. Tanaka, Ronald. *The Shino Suite*. Greenfield Center, NY: Greenfield Review Press, 1981.
       Rev. Lori Higa, *Contact II* 7.38–40 (1986): 17–18; Fred Wei-han Houn, *East Wind* 2.2 (1983): 65–67.

1393. Tsuda, Margaret. *Cry Love Aloud*. New York: Poetica Press, 1972.

1394. ———. *Urban River*. Newark, NJ: Discovery Books, 1976.

1395. Yamada, Mitsuye. *"Camp Notes" and Other Poems*. Berkeley: Shameless Hussy Press, 1976.
       Rev. Tina Koyama, *Contact II* 7.38–40 (1986): 9.

1396. ———. *Desert Run*. New York: Kitchen Table Press, forthcoming.

1397. Yasuda, Kenneth [under pseud. Shosun]. *A Pepper-Pod: Classic Japanese Poems together with Original Haiku*. Foreword John Gould Fletcher. New York: Knopf, 1947.

Drama

1398.   Amano, Alfred. *The Wolf at the Door: A Fantasy. Reimei* ns 1.2 (1932): 22–24.
        Describes a poor family.

1399.   *Amano, Lynette. *Ashes. Kumu Kahua Plays* [#97] 3–46.

1400.   Becker, Elaine. *The Best of Both Worlds* [act 1]. *Hanai* [#161] 46–54.
        Explores the difference between two Eurasian sisters.

1401.   Gotanda, Philip Kan. *The Dream of Kitamura. West Coast Plays* 15–16 (1983): 191–223.
        A mythical tale of guilt and deceit.

1402.   ———. "Excerpt from the play *Fish Head Soup." Echoes* 4 (1986): 13.
        A man describes a strange dream to his brother.

1403.   Hartmann, [Carl] Sadakichi. Buddha, Confucius, Christ: *Three Prophetic Plays*. Ed. Harry Lawton and George Knox. New York: Herder, 1971.

1404.   ———. *Buddha (Written 1891–1895): A Drama in Twelve Scenes*. New York: privately printed, 1897.

1405.   ———. *Christ; A Dramatic Poem in Three Acts*. [Boston]: privately printed, 1893.

1406.   ———. *Confucius: A Drama in Three Acts (Written 1894–1916, 1920–1922)*. Los Angeles: privately printed, 1923.

1407.   ———. *Moses: A Drama in Six Episodes. . . .* N.p.: n.p., 1934.

1408.   ———. *A Tragedy in a New York Flat: A Dramatic Episode in Two Scenes*. [New York]: privately printed, 1896.

1409.   Higa, Lori. "[Excerpt from] *Calamity Jane Meets Sushi Mama and the B.V.D. Kid: Or, . . . Lady Murasaki Rides the Wild Wild West." Rising Waters* 1976: n. pag.

1410.   Iko, Momoko. *The Gold Watch* [act 1]. *AIIIEEEEE!* [#100] 1983: 89–114.
        Describes the interaction of *issei, nisei,* and *kibei* during World War II.

1411.   *Inouye, Bessie Toishigawa. *Reunion. Kumu Kahua Plays* [#97] 47–61.

1412.   Kondo, Carl. *A Dame Did It to Me. Rafu Shimpo* 20 Dec. 1951: 24–25.

1413.   *Kubojiri, Clara. *Country Pie. Talk Story* [#120] 6–21.

1414.   Mori, Toshio. *Time Out at Al's. Pacific Citizen* 22 Dec. 1945: 19–20.
        Characters representing the spectrum of America's multicultural society gather at a café.

1415.   *Murayama, Milton. *Yoshitsune. Hawaii Review* 10 (1980): 59–73; *Hapa* 1 (1981): 39–48.
        Excerpts from a 13-scene play about a Japanese military genius.

1416.   *Nakano, Dennis. *Lucky You Live Hawaii. Bamboo Ridge* 10 (1981): 32–43.

1417.   Nakasako, Spencer. *Metal Pail Blues*. *Hanai* [#161] 31–42.
         A *sansei* woman learns that her mentally disturbed father has died in
         an accident.

Sakaki, Nanao. *Real Play: Poetry and Drama*. See #1385.

1419.   *Sakamoto, Edward. *In the Alley*. *Talk Story* [#104] 157–67. Expanded
         version in *Kumu Kahua Plays* [#97] 123–42.

1420.   Sasaki, Yasuo. *Suyetsumuhana: A Dialogue Irrelevantly Devised from
         Lady Murasaki's Novel, Written 1050 A.D.* *Reimei* ns 1.3 (1933): 19–20.
         A dialogue between a princess and her lover.

1421.   **Shiomi, R. A. *Yellow Fever*. *West Coast Plays* 13–14 (1982): 1–44.
         Follows the adventures of a Japanese Canadian detective.

1422.   *Tamayose, Tremaine. *Big Boys Don't Cry*. *Bamboo Ridge* 10 (1981):
         21–28.

1423.   ———. *Onolulu*. *Bamboo Ridge* 10 (1981): 29–31.

1424.   *Tsujimoto, Joseph. *The Last Samurai*. *Hawaii Review* 8 (1978): 94–121.
         A film script based on the life of Japanese novelist Yukio Mishima.

1425.   *Yamada, Joanne Y. "Excerpt from *Shizue's World.*" *Bamboo Ridge* 25
         (1985): 38–63.
         Centers on an 80-year-old woman and her family.

1426.   Yamauchi, Wakako. *And the Soul Shall Dance*. *West Coast Plays* 11–12
         (1982): 117–64.
         Based on a short story with the same title.

Filipino American Literature

For an explanation of the variant spellings *Pilipino* and *Filipino*, see *Amerasia Journal* 13.1 (1986–87): viii–ix.

Prose

1427. Ancheta, Shirley. "Bananas." *Rising Waters* 1975: n. pag.
A father describes life in the Philippines.

1428. Bacho, Peter. "A Manong's Heart." *Turning Shadows into Light* [#175] 39–42.
A sketch of a Filipino boxer.

1429. Baltasar, Silveria S. *Your House Is My House*. Manila: Regal, 1966.
A novel of Filipino experiences in America.

1430. Bernad, Miguel A. *"The Lights of Broadway" and Other Essays: Reflections of a Filipino Traveller*. 1st ser. Quezon City, Philippines: New Day Publishers, 1980.

1431. Brainard, Cecilia Manguerra. "The Black Man in the Forest." *Amerasia Journal* 12.1 (1985–86): 101–05.
Set in the Philippines during the Spanish-American War, the short story registers the response of a Filipino general to the death of a black soldier.

1432. Buaken, Manuel J. *I Have Lived with the American People*. Caldwell, ID: Caxton Printers, 1948.
An autobiographical account of the author's experiences of economic and social discrimination in California.

1433. Bulosan, Carlos. *America Is in the Heart: A Personal History*. 1943. Introd. Carey McWilliams. Seattle: U of Washington P, 1973.
Excerpts in *AIIIEEEEE!* [#100] 1983: 4–10; *Asian-American Heritage* [#177] 250–55; *American Letter* [#128] 195–99; *Counterpoint* [#113] 485–88. Excerpt entitled "Why Had I Left Home?" in *The Well of Time* [#135] 10–28.
An autobiographical novel that covers the life of a worker in the Philippines and in America.
Rev. *Booklist* 15 Mar. 1946: 225; Max Cissen, *New Republic* 25 Mar. 1946: 421; *Common Ground* 6.4 (1946): 111; John J. Espey, *New York Herald Tribune Weekly Book Review* 10 Mar. 1944: 3; *Foreign Affairs* 25 (1946): 165; *Kirkus* 15 Feb. 1946: 84; William S. Lynch, *Saturday Review of Literature* 9 Mar. 1946: 7; John Monaghan, *Commonwealth* 24 May 1946: 119; John Norcross, *Chicago Sun-Times Bookweek* 10 Mar. 1946: 4; Helene Scherff Taylor, *Library Journal* 1 Mar. 1946: 343; *United States Quarterly Booklist* 2.2 (1946): 96; *Wisconsin Library Journal* 42.3 (1946): 45.

1434. ———. "The Americano from Luzon." *Amerasia Journal* 6.1 (1979): 87–93.
A farm worker decides to start a newspaper.

1435. ———. "Amorous Ghost." *Mademoiselle* Oct. 1946: 186+.
A ghost keeps falling in love with young girls.

1436. ———. "Andong, the Great Lover." *Arizona Quarterly* 3.1 (1947): 60–68.
A man proposes to many women during a famine.

1437. ———. "As Long as the Grass Shall Grow." *Common Ground* 9.4 (1949):
38–43; *Philippines Free Press* 9 Dec. 1950; *Pathways to Philippine Literature in English* [#167] 1958: 135–43; *If You Want to Know What We Are*
45–52; *Philippine Short Stories 1941–1955* [#181] 2: 764–71.
Personal reminiscence of a white teacher's attempt to start a class among
young Filipino migrant workers.

1438. ———. "Be American." *Amerasia Journal* 4.1 (1977): 157–63.
Rpt. in *If You Want to Know What We Are* 53–58.
Describes the hardship endured by a Filipino immigrant before he finally becomes an American citizen.

1439. ———. *Carlos Bulosan: An Introduction with Selections.* Ed. Epifanio
San Juan, Jr. Manila: National Book Store, 1983.

1440. ———. "The Champion Hog Stealer." *Arizona Quarterly* 2.2 (1946):
17–23.
A short story about two men who have made hog stealing into a respectable profession.

1441. ———. "The Courtship of Uncle Ponso." *Arizona Quarterly* 2.4 (1946):
20–25.
Ponso tries to marry the richest girl.

1442. ———. "The End of the War." *New Yorker* 2 Sept. 1944: 21–23.
Rpt. in *Amerasia Journal* 6.1 (1979): 69–74.
Soldiers vie with one another to tell an auspicious dream, revealing their
common desire for World War II to end.

1443. ———. "Father Goes to Church." *Town and Country* Sept. 1943: 99+.
A satire on greed.

1444. ———. "Freedom from Want." *Saturday Evening Post* 6 Mar. 1943:
12–13.
Describes the sorry plight of farm workers in America.

1445. ———. "The Gift of My Father." *New Yorker* 23 Oct. 1943: 66+.
A man gives his house away as a wedding gift.

1446. ———. "Homecoming." *Amerasia Journal* 6.1 (1979): 75–81.
Rpt. in *If You Want to Know What We Are* 64–70; *Amerasia Journal*
13.1 (1986–87): 125–30.
A man who has failed miserably in America encounters worse poverty
when he returns to his home in the Philippines.

1447. ———. "How My Stories Were Written." *Solidarity* Sept. 1971: 28–31.
Rpt. in *If You Want to Know What We Are* 21–26.
Autobiographical essay.

1448.   ———. "I Am Not a Laughing Man." *Writer* May 1946: 143–46.
Rpt. in *Amerasia Journal* 6.1 (1979): 121–25.
An autobiographical essay about unpleasant experiences in America.

1449.   ———. "I Would Remember." *Amerasia Journal* 6.1 (1979): 95–99.
Rpt. in *If You Want to Know What We Are* 59–63.
Describes various encounters with tragic or violent deaths.

1450.   ———. *If You Want to Know What We Are: A Carlos Bulosan Reader*.
Ed. E. San Juan, Jr. Introd. Leigh Bristol-Kagan. Minneapolis: West End
Press, 1983.
Rev. Roger J. Bresnahan, *Minnesota Review* 23 (Fall 1984): 180–83; Fred
Wei-han Houn, *Amerasia Journal* 13.1 (1986–87): 187–88; Juanita Tamayo
Lott, *Contact II* 7.38–40 (1986): 100+.

1451.   ———. "Labor and Capital: The Coming Catastrophe." *Commonwealth
Times* 15 June 1937.
Rpt. in *Amerasia Journal* 6.1 (1979): 133–34; *If You Want to Know
What We Are* 13–14.
Essay.

1452.   ———. *The Laughter of My Father*. New York: Harcourt, 1944.
"The Song of My Father" is rpt. in *Love in Philippine Story and Verse*
[#139] 22–27.
A collection of short stories.
Rev. *Booklist* 1 May 1944: 300; Florence H. Bullock, *New York Herald
Tribune Weekly Book Review* 23 Apr. 1944: 4; *Christian Century* 19 Apr.
1944: 498; *Common Ground* 4.4 (1944): 110; Leo Kennedy, *Chicago Sun
Book Week* 30 Apr. 1944: 3; *Kirkus* 1 Mar. 1944: 103; Clara S. Littledale,
Saturday Review of Literature 9 Mar. 1946: 7; *New Republic* 1 May 1944:
614; Thomas Sugra, *New York Times Book Review* 30 Apr. 1944: 7; *Wis-
consin Library Journal* 40 (1944): 84.

1453.   ———. "The Laughter of My Father." *New Yorker* 19 Dec. 1944: 24–25.
A comic short story about a man suspected of dishonoring a bride.

1454.   ———. "A Letter." *Poetry* Feb. 1936: 292–93.
An autobiographical sketch.

1455.   ———. "Letter in Exile." *Amerasia Journal* 13.1 (1986–87): 131–33.

1456.   ———. "Letter to a Filipino Woman." *New Republic* 8 Nov. 1943:
645–46.
Describes the social function of literature.

1457.   ———. "Life and Death of a Filipino in the U.S.A." *East Wind* 1.2 (1982):
42–44.
A version of "I Would Remember."

1458.   ———. "The Lovely Angel." *Arizona Quarterly* 4.2 (1948): 140–47.
A fanciful story about an angel who helps a farmer regain his land.

1459.   ———. "Man against the World." *Commonwealth Times* 28 Aug. 1940.
Rpt. in *Amerasia Journal* 6.1 (1979): 135–38.
Attacks corporate wealth.

1460.   ———. "The Marriage of My Father." *New Yorker* 25 Sept. 1943: 38–41.
A comic story about a couple who go through two wedding ceremonies, in a *presidencia* and in church.

1461.   ———. "My Brother Osong's Career in Politics." *New Yorker* 22 July 1944: 18–20.
Rpt. in *Best American Short Stories of 1945*. Ed. Martha Foley. Boston: Houghton, 1945. 30–37.
A satire on politicians.

1462.   ———. "My Brother's Short Stay." *Harper's Bazaar* Mar. 1944: 106+.
A man tries to procure a rich wife for his son.

1463.   ———. "My Cousin Vincente's Homecoming." *University of Kansas City Review* 12.4 (1946): 293–96.

1464.   ———. "My Education." *Amerasia Journal* 6.1 (1979): 113–19.
Rpt. in *If You Want to Know What We Are* 15–20.
Autobiographical essay.

1465.   ———. "My Family Goes to the Army." *Town and Country* June 1944: 63+.

1466.   ———. "My Father and the White Horse." *Scholastic* [Dayton, OH] 17 Feb. 1947: 21+.
Satire.

1467.   ———. "My Father Goes to Court." *New Yorker* 13 Nov. 1943: 47+.
Rpt. in *Philippines Free Press* 26 Jan. 1947; *Philippine Short Stories 1941–1955* [#181] 1: 283–88.
Describes a conflict between a rich and a poor family.

1468.   ———. "My First Day in America." *Town and Country* Dec. 1944: 84.
Rpt. in *Turning Shadows into Light* [#175] 83–84.
Describes the experiences of innocent Filipinos abroad.

1469.   ———. "My Uncle Runs for President." *Town and Country* Mar. 1944: 83+.

1470.   ———. *The Philippines Is in the Heart*. Introd. E. San Juan, Jr. Quezon City, Philippines: New Day Publishers, 1975.
A collection of retold Philippine folktales.

1471.   ———. "The Power of the People." *Alive Magazine* 10 Sept. 1977.

1472.   ———. *The Power of the People*. Afterword E. San Juan, Jr. Ontario: Tabloid Books, 1977. Manila: National Book Store, 1986.
Political novella.

1473.   ———. "A Rich Man in the Family." *Arizona Quarterly* 2.1 (1946): 76–82.
A satire about a family that tries to please a rich relative.

1474.   ———. "The Romance of Magno Rubio." *Amerasia Journal* 6.1 (1979): 33–50.
A tragicomic story about an ugly Filipino man who falls in love with a beautiful white woman.

1475. ———. "Selected Letters of Carlos Bulosan." *Amerasia Journal* 6.1 (1979): 143–54.

1476. ———. "Silence." *Amerasia Journal* 6.1 (1979): 57–60.
Describes a lonely man's fantasy.

1477. ———. "Sometimes It's Not Funny." *This Week* [Sunday magazine of *Manila Chronicle*] 15 Feb. 1948.
Rpt. in *Amerasia Journal* 6.1 (1979): 51–56; *Philippine Short Stories 1941–1955* [#181] 1: 325–30.
A man languishes for a woman who has accepted two marriage proposals from his friends.

1478. ———. *Sound of Falling Light: Letters in Exile.* Ed. Dolores S. Feria. Quezon City: Dilliman Review, Univ. of the Philippines, 1960.
Depicts the writer's inner life.

1479. ———. "The Springtime of My Father." *Western Review* 11.1 (1946): 23+.
The father falls in love with a newcomer to a Philippine village.

1480. ———. "The Story of a Letter." *New Masses* 30 Apr. 1946: 11–13.
Rpt. in *Philippine Short Stories 1941–1955* [#181] 1: 236–41; *If You Want to Know What We Are* 39–44.
For years a Filipino family is unable to read a letter from a son because it is written in English.

1481. ———. "Terrorism Rides the Philippines." *Amerasia Journal* 6.1 (1979): 139–41.
An essay first printed in the 1952 yearbook of the ILWU Local 37 (Seattle).

1482. ———. "The Thief." *Amerasia Journal* 6.1 (1979): 83–85.
Describes a Filipino Robin Hood who steals in order to help destitute students.

1483. ———. "The Time of Our Lives." *Amerasia Journal* 6.1 (1979): 127–32.
An autobiographical essay about the author's interaction with other writers.

1484. ———. "To a God of Stone." *Commonwealth Times* 15 Nov. 1939.
Rpt. in *Amerasia Journal* 6.1 (1979): 61–67.
A short story about a destitute man who struggles to write.

1485. ———. "A Virgin for Cousin Pedro." *Interim* 2.2 (1946): 43–48.

1486. Carunungan, Celso Al. "Hideout for a Hero." *Colliers* 19 Aug. 1955: 56+.
A Filipino family gives shelter to an American soldier.

1487. ———. "Liberation." *Catholic World* June 1954: 186–88.
A true story of the author's experiences during the Japanese siege of Manila in 1945.

1488. ———. *Like a Big Brave Man: A Novel.* New York: Farrar, 1960
A Filipino boy's family saves an American soldier, who then gives the boy a plane ticket to the US.

1489. ———. "My Father's First Son." *Sign* 34 (Nov. 1954): 40+.

1490. ———. *"Return to Gomora" and Other Stories*. Manila: Alberto S. Florentino, 1963.

1491. ———. "The Samurai Sword and the Music Box." *Southwest Review* 39 (Summer 1954): 196–203.
       Describes the interaction between Filipino women and Japanese officers during World War II.

1492. ———. *To Die a Thousand Deaths: A Novel on the Life and Times of Lorenzo Ruiz*. Manila: Social Studies Publications, 1980.

Casper, Linda T. See Ty-Casper, Linda.

1493. Castro, Fernando. *Big White American*. New York: Vantage, 1969.
       Novel.

1494. Castro, Luisa. "Trilliums and Rhododendrons." *Asian American Review* 2.1 (1975): 170–81.
       A woman who has been abused as a child reminisces about her experiences.

1495. Casuga, Albert B., ed. *Summer Suns: A Book of Poems and Short Stories by Albert B. Casuga and Cirilo F. Bautista*. Introd. Ricaredo Demetillo. Manila: n.p., 1962.

1496. Dionisio, J. C. "A Summer in an Alaskan Salmon Cannery." *Philippine Magazine*.
       Rpt. in *Asian-American Authors* [#125] 1976: 154–60.
       Portrays Filipino workers.

1497. Echaore, Susan Domingo. "There Are No Plows or Carabao in America." *Echoes from Gold Mountain* 1979: 78–85.
       During a conversation with his nurse, a Filipino bachelor recalls his youth in the Philippines.

1498. Enrado, Patricia. *House of Images*. Quezon City, Philippines: New Day Publishers, 1983.
       A novel about Zamboanga during the Japanese occupation.

1499. ———. "Picture Bride." *Bridge* 10.1 (1985): 44–48.
       Short story.

1500. ———. *"The White Horse of Alih" and Other Stories*. Quezon City, Philippines: New Day Publishers, 1985.

1501. *Felipe, Virgilio Menor. "Chapter I. 'Once in the First Times' from *What You Like Know? An Oral Biography of Bonipasyo*." *Bamboo Ridge: The Hawaii Writers' Quarterly* 11 (1981): 48–58.
       Rpt. in *The Best of* Bamboo Ridge [#103] 122–30.
       A young boy describes a raid by Spaniards.

1502. ———. "Hawaii: Plantation of Destiny." *Manna-Mana*. Ed. Leonard Lueras. Honolulu: privately printed, 1973. 3–20. Excerpt in *Talk Story* [#120] 26–31.
       A biographical story about a Filipino American immigrant.

1503. ———. "Some Brown People I Know." *Hawaii Pono Journal* 1 (Nov. 1970): 13–16.
   Describes the lives of immigrant Filipino laborers.

1504. Feria, Benny F. *Filipino Son*. Boston: Meador Press, 1954.
   Autobiography.

1505. Flowers, Ruby Reyes. "Ruby's Discovery." *The Ethnic American Woman* [#88] 292–96.
   An autobiographical account about a woman who clings to her Filipino heritage despite her American birth and upbringing.

1506. *Fruto, Ligaya Victorio. *One Rainbow for the Duration*. Honolulu: Rainbow Publications, 1976.
   Nine months of correspondence between a Filipino and an American soldier fighting in the Philippines during World War II.

1507. ———. *"Yesterday" and Other Stories*. Quezon City, Philippines: Vibal Printing, 1969.
   A collection of short stories.

García Villa, José. See Villa, José García.

1509. *Gersaba, George. "Short." *Hawaii Review* 7 (1977): 23–33.
   Rpt. in *Talk Story* [#104] 39–54.
   Describes an American platoon in Vietnam.

Gill, Lakshmi. See South Asian American section.

1510. Gonzalez, N[estor] V[icente] M[adali]. "Among the Wounded." *Asiaweek Literary Review* 1 Nov. 1985: 62.
   An essay exploring why there are few Asian Nobel Prize–winners in literature.

1511. ———. *The Bamboo Dancers*. Manila: Benipayo, 1957. Denver: Alan Swallow, 1964.
   A novel told from the point of view of a cosmopolitan but alienated Filipino.

1512. ———. "The Blue Skull and the Dark Palms." *Sunday Times Magazine* [Philippines] 12 Feb. 1950.
   Rpt. in *Hopkins Review* 3.4 (1950): 3–11; *"Children of the Ash-Covered Loam"* 110–32; *Philippine Contemporary Literature*. Ed. Asuncion David-Maramba. Manila: Bookmark, 1962. 40–50; *The Development of Philippine Literature in English* [#106] 211–17; *Mindoro and Beyond: Twenty-One Stories*. 112–22; *Philippine Short Stories 1941–1955* [#181] 2: 617–26; *Short Story International* Feb. 1984: 52–62.
   A story told from a female schoolteacher's point of view.

1513. ———. "The Bread of Salt." *Sunday Times Magazine* [Manila] (1958).
   Rpt. in *Look, Stranger, on This Island Now* 3–22; *Selected Stories* 119–38; *Asian PEN Anthology* [#129] 108–15; *Mindoro and Beyond: Twenty-One Stories* 155–63; *Short Story International* June 1979: 91–100.
   A fourteen-year-old Filipino violinist aspires to win the love of a wealthy Spanish girl.

1514.   ——. "Buntot-Pagi." *Manila Tribune* 19 Oct. 1986: 17–20.

1515.   ——. "The Calendar Christ." *PEN Short Stories.* Ed. Francisco Arcellana. Manila: Philippine Chapter, Int. PEN, 1962. 92–96.
       Rpt. in *Sinag-lahi.* Ed. M. L. Santoramana. Manila: Writers Union of the Philippines, 1975. 105–08.
       A teacher describes a student who resembles Christ.

1516.   ——. "Children of the Ash-Covered Loam." *This Week* [Sunday magazine of *Manila Chronicle*] 14, 21 Dec. 1951.
       Rpt. in *"Children of the Ash-Covered Loam"* 5–34; *Carlos Palanca Memorial Awards for Literature Prize Stories: 1950–1955.* Ed. Kerima Polotan. Manila: La Tondena, 1957. 49–69; *Selected Stories* 11–40; *Readings in Philippine Arts and Letters.* Ed. Comm. on the Humanities. Manila: Ken, 1965; *The Development of Philippine Literature in English* [#106] 201–09; *Mindoro and Beyond: Twenty-One Stories* 49–61; *Philippine Short Stories 1941–1955* [#181] 2: 882–95.
       A story depicting folk rituals and beliefs in a Filipino village where human beings, animals, and vegetation all partake of the natural rhythm.

1517.   ——. *"Children of the Ash-Covered Loam" and Other Stories.* Introd. Francisco Arcellana. Illus. Malang. Manila: Benipayo, 1954. Manila: Bookmark, 1977.

1518.   ——. "Come and Go." *Philippines Free Press* 1954.
       Rpt. in *Look, Stranger, on This Island Now* 64–84; *Selected Stories* 98–118.

1519.   ——. "Far Horizons." *Philippine Magazine* Nov. 1935: 544+.
       Rpt. in *Seven Hills Away* 13–17; *Philippine Short Stories 1925–1940* [#180] 270–74; *Mindoro and Beyond: Twenty-One Stories* 23–26.

1520.   ——. "The Happiest Boy in the World." *Philippine Magazine* Mar. 1940: 102–03.
       Rpt. in *Seven Hills Away* 72–76; *The Wonder World of Reading.* 2 vols. Ed. Basilisa J. Manhit and Damiana L. Eugenio. Manila: Macaraig, 1964. 2: 95–99.
       Rpt. in *Mindoro and Beyond: Twenty-One Stories* 43–46.
       Registers a father's hope for his son's education.

1521.   ——. "Hunger in Barok." *Philippine Magazine* Jan. 1939: 20–21.
       Rpt. in *Seven Hills Away* 30–35; *Philippine Short Stories 1925–1940* [#180] 420–25; *Insight: A Study of the Short Story.* Ed. Joseph V. Landy. Manila: Jesuit Educational Assn., 1975. 202–07; *Mindoro and Beyond: Twenty-One Stories* 27–31.
       Describes the interaction between a landlord and a tenant farmer during a drought.

1522.   ——. "The Island of the Sitting Hen." *Weekend (Philippines Daily Express Magazine)* 15 Aug. 1982: 28–29.
       Autobiographical story.

1523.   ———. "A Land of Plenty." *Weekend (Philippines Daily Express Magazine)* 25 Dec. 1983: 20–26.
After a sojourn in the city, a mother returns to the village where her family once lived.

1524.   ———. "Life and Death in a Mindoro Kaingin." *Philippine Magazine* Jan. 1934: 7–8.
Rpt. in *Seven Hills Away* 7–12; *Philippine Short Stories 1925–1940* [#180] 229–33.
Spirits haunt the Kagulangan, a stretch of forest on the west side of the Barok River.

1525.   ———. "The Listener." *Weekend (Philippines Daily Express Magazine)* 24 Oct. 1982: 28–29.
Autobiographical essay.

1526.   ———. "The Lives of Great Men." *Philippines Free Press* 30 May 1964: 20+.
Rpt. in *Mindoro and Beyond: Twenty-One Stories* 217–24.
A man revisits a childhood haunt and notes the changes that have taken place.

1527.   ———. *Look, Stranger, on This Island Now*. Manila: Benipayo Press, 1963.
A collection of 10 stories.

1528.   ———. "Lupo and the River." *Diliman Review* [Philippines] 1.1 (1953): 28–71.
Rpt. in *"Children of the Ash-Covered Loam"* 35–109; *Carlos Palanca Memorial Awards for Literature Prize Stories: 1950–1955*. Ed. Kerima Polotan. Manila: La Tondena, 1957. 101–51; *Modern Philippine Short Stories*. Ed. Leonard Casper. Albuquerque: U of New Mexico P, 1962. 113–53; *Mindoro and Beyond: Twenty-One Stories* 62–93; *Short Story International* Oct. 1982: 91–125.
A story about a doomed wedding match, told from a nine-year-old boy's point of view.

1529.   ———. "The Man with the Two-Armed Guitar." *Orient/West* 9.1 (1964): 64–66.
Essay.

1530.   ———. *Mindoro and Beyond: Twenty-One Stories*. Quezon City: U of the Philippines P, 1979.
Rev. Gertudes Ang, *Philippine Quarterly of Culture and Society* 8 (1980): 191–93; V. A. Makarenko, *Contemporary Foreign Literature* Oct. 1981: 86–88.

1531.   ———. "The Morning Star." *This Week* [Sunday Magazine of *Manila Chronicle*] 1 Jan. 1950.
Rpt. in *Life and Letters: Stanford Short Stories 1950*. Ed. Wallace Stegner. Stanford: Stanford UP, 1950. 77–85; *"Children of the Ash-Covered Loam"* 133–49; *Pathways to Philippine Literature in English* [#16] 151–60; *Span*. Ed. Lionel Wigmore. Melbourne: Cheshire, 1958. 208–15;

Selected Stories 41–57; *Asian-American Authors* [#125] 143–50; *Mindoro and Beyond: Twenty-One Stories* 104–11; *Philippine Short Stories 1941–1955* [#181] 2: 577–84; *Short Story International* Apr. 1982: 97–105.
An old man and a mute sailor witness the birth and death of an infant.

1532. ———. "Moving On: A Filipino in the World." *Foreign Values and Southeast Asian Scholarship.* Ed. Joseph Fischer. Berkeley: Center for South and Southeast Asia Studies, Univ. of California, 1972. 123–57.
The author describes his own artistic development.

1533. ———. "On the Eve." *Solidarity.*
Rpt. in *Mindoro and Beyond: Twenty-One Stories* 3–22.

1534. ———. "On the Ferry." *Literary Review* 3.4 (1960): 478–85.
Rpt. in *Look, Stranger, on This Island Now* 139–56; *Modern Short Stories from Many Lands.* Ed. Clarence R. Decker and Charles Angoff. New York: Manyland Books, 1963. 217–26; *Mindoro and Beyond: Twenty-One Stories* 193–200.
A bankrupt father lies about his son to the passengers on a ferry.

1535. ———. "Owl in the Moon." *Philippine Magazine* Jan. 1937: 16+.
Rpt. in *Seven Hills Away* 23–29.

1536. ———. "Pare Lucio and the Law." *Philippine Magazine* Aug. 1938: 378–79.
Rpt. in *Seven Hills Away* 40–46.

1537. ———. "Pioneer." *Philippine Magazine* Aug. 1934: 337+.
Rpt. *Seven Hills Away* 3–6; *Philippine Short Stories 1925–40* [#180] 262–65; *Asian-Pacific Literature.* Ed. James Harstad and Cheryl A. Harstad. Honolulu: Dept. of Education, State of Hawaii, 1981. 135–39.
A young man sets off to a wilderness in Mindoro to look for his pioneer father and becomes a pioneer himself.

1538. ———. "The Sea Beyond." *Sunday Times Magazine* [Philippines] 1954.
Rpt. in *"Children of the Ash-Covered Loam"* 192–209; *Selected Stories* 80–97; *New Writing from the Philippines* [#98] 217–25; *Mindoro and Beyond: Twenty-One Stories* 123–30; *Short Story International* 31 (1982): 96–105.
Describes a rough sea voyage with a dying man on board.

1539. ———. *A Season of Grace.* 1956. Manila: Benipayo Press, 1963. Manila: Bookmark, 1975.
A novel about the *kaingin* ("rice fields") peasants in the Philippines.
Rev. Miguel Bernad, *Philippines Studies* 5 (1957): 340.

1540. ———. "Secrets." *Acacia* 2.3 (1985): 4–5.

1541. ———. *Selected Stories.* Denver: Alan Swallow, 1964.

1542. ———. "Serenade." *Philippines Free Press* 24 Oct. 1964: 18+.
Rpt. in *Mindoro and Beyond: Twenty-One Stories* 133–51.
A story in which commercial, aesthetic, and human values are interwoven.

1543.   ———. "Seven Hills Away." *Philippine Magazine* Mar. 1939: 115–16. Rpt. in *Seven Hills Away* 58–71.

1544.   ———. *Seven Hills Away.* Denver: Alan Swallow; Manila: Halcon House, 1947.

A collection of twelve short stories depicting folk life in the Philippines.

1545.   ———. "The Tomato Game." *Asia Philippines Leader* 16 June 1972.

Rpt. in *The Well of Time* [#135] 40–46; *Mindoro and Beyond: Twenty-One Stories* 211–16; *Filipino Magazine* 1.1 (1986): 31–33.

An old Filipino immigrant who desires to marry pays for the passages of a Filipina and her "son."

1546.   ———. "The University Experience with Philippine Letters." *Solidarity* 2.6 (1967): 94–99.

Essay.

1547.   ———. "A Warm Hand." *Sewanee Review* 58.1 (1950): 118–29.

Rpt. in *Stanford Short Stories 1950.* Ed. Wallace Stegner. Stanford: Stanford UP, 1950. 33–43; *Philippine Writing.* Ed. T. D. Agcaoili. Manila: Archipelago, 1953. 108–16; *"Children of the Ash-Covered Loam"* 150–71; *Selected Stories* 58–79; *Pathways to Philippine Literature in English* [#16] 161–71; *Modern Philippine Short Stories.* Ed. Leonard Casper. Albuquerque: U of New Mexico P, 1962. 154–65; *Mentor Book of Modern Asian Literature.* Ed. Dorothy Blair. New York: New American Library, 1969. 365–74; *Mindoro and Beyond: Twenty-One Stories* 94–103.

During a stormy night a maid taking shelter in an old couple's house thinks that she is touched by a warm hand.

1548.   ———. "Where's My Baby Now?" *Sunday Times Magazine* [Philippines] 28 May 1950.

Rpt. in *Hopkins Review* 4.3 (1951): 20–27; *"Children of the Ash-Covered Loam"* 172–91; *Modern Philippine Short Stories.* Ed. Leonard Casper. Albuquerque: U of New Mexico P, 1962. 102–12; *Philippine Short Stories 1941–1955* [#181] 2: 688–96.

A story about a passive husband who loves to watch children's games and a wife who aspires to be a feminist.

1549.   ———. "The Whispering Woman." *KATHA: An Anthology of Philippine Writing in English.* Ed. J. C. Tuvera. Manila: Benipayo Press, 1955. 64–72.

Rpt. in *Look, Stranger, on This Island Now* 23–36; *Mindoro and Beyond: Twenty-One Stories* 164–70.

A lonely bachelor reflects on his landlady and her daughter.

1550.   ———. *The Winds of April.* Manila: U of the Philippines P, 1941.

An autobiographical novel set in Mindoro.

1551.   ———. "The Wireless Tower." *This Week* [Sunday magazine of *Manila Chronicle*] 1963.

Rpt. in *Look, Stranger, on This Island Now* 37–53; *Selected Stories* 139–55; *The Development of Philippine Literature in English* [#106] 278–83; *Mindoro and Beyond: Twenty-One Stories* 201–08.

A 15-year-old boy climbs a tower to check whether lightning has indeed split a rod, as rumored.

1552.   ———. "Work on the Mountain." *Solidarity* [Manila] July-Aug. 1967:
94–98.
Essay.

1553.   Gonzalez, Narita Manuel. "Apo Bakit." *This Week* [Sunday magazine of
Manila Chronicle] 3 Feb. 1952: 16–18.
The title means "old grandmother."

1554.   ———. "The Birthday." *Sunday Times Magazine* [Philippines] 18 Apr.
1948.

1555.   ———. "The Day Begins." *Evening News Magazine* [Philippines] 17
Mar. 1951: 8–9.

1556.   ———. "Death of a Child." *Evening News Magazine* [Philippines] 26
Mar. 1949.

1557.   ———. "Fair Hope." *Evening News Magazine* [Philippines] 23 Sept.
1950.

1558.   Guzman, Conte. "When There's a Will." *Echoes from Gold Mountain*
1982: 79–90.
An elderly Filipino believes that he will inherit the money of his
nephew.

1559.   Hagedorn, Jessica. "The Blossoming of Bongbong." *Bridge* 8.3 (1983):
19+.
A short story about a man who is becoming insane.

1560.   ———. "Bump City." *Yardbird Reader* 4 (1975): 90–93.
A prose poem about an encounter in a nightclub.

1561.   ———. *Dangerous Music: The Poetry and Prose of Jessica Hagedorn*. San
Francisco: Momo's Press, 1975.

1562.   ———. "From the Novel *Mango Tango*." *Y'Bird Magazine* 1.1 (1977):
58–65.
Describes intermarriages and sexual intrigues.

1563.   ———. *Pet Food and Tropical Apparitions*. San Francisco: Momo's Press,
1981.
Poetry and prose.
Rev. Lori Higa, *Contact II* 7.38–40 (1986): 23–24; Mary MacKey, *Review* 8 Aug. 1982: 5.

1564.   Ignacio, Art. "City-Slickers, the Pigs and Uncle Tommy." *Asian American Review* 2.1 (1975): 66–81.
Describes the experience of killing pigs and the attendant reflections.

1565.   Lim, Paulino, Jr. "Father in the Sun." *Amerasia Journal* 12.2 (1985–86):
78–83.
Rpt. in *"Passion Summer."*
A family gathering triggers thoughts on absent fathers.

1566. ———. "Homecoming." *Asiaweek* [Hong Kong] 26 Jan. 1986: 52–55. Rpt. in *"Passion Summer."*
A man returns to visit the Philippines after living in the US for many years.

1567. ———. *"Passion Summer" and Other Stories.* Quezon City, Philippines: New Day Publishers, 1988.
Twelve stories.

Lim, Paul Stephen. See Chinese American section.

1568. Lopez, Agustin. *Taming of a Dream.* Pompano Beach, FL: Exposition Press of Florida, 1987.
On the adventures of a Filipino immigrant.

1569. Magwili, Dom. "I Rode with Frank Chin." *Echoes from Gold Mountain* 1982: 47–51.
A true story about how the author and the Chinese American writer counter racist slurs in a restaurant.

Manuel, Narita. See Gonzalez, Narita Manuel.

1570. Mella, Cesar T. *"A Priest to the World" and Other Prose Works.* Quezon City, Philippines: New Day Publishers, 1984.
Autobiographical stories.

1571. *Morales, Rodney. "Daybreak over Haleakala." *Bamboo Ridge* 29 (1985): 12–29.
Rpt. in *The Best of* Bamboo Ridge [#103] 195–213.
Describes an adventure on a deserted island.

1572. Morano, Salvador. "Old Place." *Echoes from Gold Mountain* 1978: 26–28.
A Filipino man returns to America to visit his impoverished relatives.

1573. Morantte, P. C. *God Is in the Heart: Poetical and Symbolical Essays.* Foreword Bienvenido N. Santos. Quezon City, Philippines: New Day Publishers, 1982.

1574. Nicanor, Precioso M. *Martyrs Never Die.* New York: Pre-Mar Publishing, 1968.
A novel based on conditions experienced by Filipinos before World War II.

1575. Nitamayo. "Going to the Country." *Liwanag* [#95] 203–05.
Describes family excursions in Watsonville.

1576. ———. "Pilipino Partytime." *Liwanag* [#95] 201–02.
Describes food obsession at Filipino parties.

1577. Peñaranda, Oscar F. "The Believers." *Liwanag* [#95] 119–20.
Villagers pray for rain during a drought.

1578. ———. "Dark Fiesta." *AIIIEEEEE!* [#100] 1983. 142–49.
Describes a school boy's unnerving experience.

1579. ———. "Musings." *Liwanag* [#95] 110–14.
Describes a meeting between ex-lovers.

1580.   ———. "The Price." *Asian-American Authors* [#125] 173–84.
        Rpt. in *Liwanag* [#95] 123–29.
        A visionary tries to turn barren land into flowering fields.

1581.   ———. "The Visitor." *Bamboo Ridge: The Hawaii Writers' Quarterly* 13
        (1981–82): 51–57.
        A version of "Musings."

1582.   *Planas, Alvin. "This Particular Sound." *Hanai* [#161] 55–65.
        A story about a guitar player.

1583.   *Quiocho, Cynthia. "My Grandparents in Hawaii." *Sandwich Isles U.S.A.*
        [#115] 21–22.
        The author reminisces about her grandparents.

1584.   Ramos, Maximo D. "Entry November 9." *Love in Philippine Story and
        Verse* [#139] 52–61.
        A diary entry describing how a love affair ended because of a misun-
        derstanding.

1585.   ———. "Home for Christmas." *Philippine Review* Dec. 1944.
        Rpt. in *Philippine Short Stories 1941–1955* [#181] 1: 150–59.
        Describes a difficult journey to Lala by three men and their families
        during World War II.

1586.   ———. "Homestead." *Pillars* [Philippines] Oct. 1944.
        Rpt. in *Philippine Short Stories 1941–1955* [#181] 1: 141–49.
        A Filipino couple who have moved to the country during World
        War II are haunted by various beasts of prey.

1587.   ———. "Patricia of the Green Hills." *Philippine Cross-Section: An An-
        thology of Filipino Short Stories in English.* 4th ed. Ed. Maximo D. Ramos
        and Florentino B. Valeros. Quezon City, Philippines: Alegar-Phoenix
        Publishing House, 1977. 85–92.
        An orphan girl is much more drawn to the jungle than to school.

1588.   ———. "Story for Summer." *Philippines Free Press* 27 Sept. 1947.
        Rpt. in *Philippine Short Stories 1941–1955* [#181] 1: 297–303.

1589.   Rómulo, Carlos P. *I Walked with Heroes.* New York: Holt, 1961.
        Rev. Miguel A. Bernad, *Philippine Studies* 9.3 (1961): 551.

1590.   ———. *Mother America: A Living Story of Democracy.* Garden City, NY:
        Doubleday, 1943.

1591.   ———. *My Brother Americans.* Garden City, NY: Doubleday, 1945.

1592.   Roque-Lutz, Marichelle, and Roger Bomba Arienda. *Free within Prison
        Walls.* Quezon City, Philippines: New Day Publishers, 1983.
        An account of a convict who becomes a Christian.

1593.   Rosca, Ninotchka. *"Bitter Country" and Other Stories.* Introd. Bienvenido
        Lumbera. Quezon City, Philippines: Malaya Books, 1970.

1593a. ———. "Diabolus of Sphere." *Philippine Free Press* 12 Dec. 1964: 53+.
        About a religious prostitute.

1594. ———. "The Man Who Made the Grade." *Bridge* 8.2 (1982–83): 44–47.
Describes an immigration officer.

1595. ———. *The Monsoon Collection*. St. Lucia, NY: U of Queensland P,
1983.
A collection of short stories.
Rev. Leonard Casper, *Solidarity* [Manila] 5 (1984): 77–79.

1596. ———. "The Neighborhood." *Manila Review* 9 (1976): 3–19.
Rpt. in *Hawaii Review* 10 (1980): 5–12.
Violence and death erupt in a neighborhood when a widow's son elopes
with a carpenter's daughter.

1597. Santa Elena, Antonio E. *The Bridge and I*. Los Angeles: Ted Villaganas,
1986.
Describes the experiences of a tolltaker on the Golden Gate Bridge.

1598. Santos, Bienvenido N. "Accept the Homage." *This Week* [Sunday Magazine of *Manila Chronicle*] 16 Sept. 1951.
Rpt. in *You Lovely People* 175–85; *Philippine Short Stories 1941–1955*
[#181] 2: 872–81.
Centers on a debate between Filipinos who want to stay in the Philippines and those who want to leave for the US.

1599. ———. " . . . And Men Decay." *Graphic* 11 July 1940.
Rpt. in *Brother, My Brother* 1–11; *Philippine Short Stories 1925–1940*
[#180] 506–14.
A man who returns home after being away for seven years discovers that
everyone he used to know has aged.

1600. ———. *Brother, My Brother*. Introd. Leonard Casper. Manila: Benipayo
Publishers, 1960. Manila: Bookmark, 1976.
"The Common Theme" is rpt. in *Modern Philippine Short Stories*. Ed.
Leonard Casper. Albuquerque: U of New Mexico P, 1962. 79–89.
A collection of short stories about people in the Philippines.

1602. ———. *The Day the Dancers Came: Selected Prose Works*. 1967. Ma-
nila: Bookmark, 1979.
"The Contender" is rpt. in *Scent of Apples* 129–39. "The Day the
Dancers Came" is rpt. in *Speaking for Ourselves* [#110] 195–207; *Coun-
terpoint* [#113] 502–08; *Scent of Apples* 113–28. "Quicker with Arrows"
is rpt. in *Scent of Apples* 140–67. "Footnote to a Laundry List" is rpt. in
Scent of Apples 168–78.
A collection that includes a play, a novel excerpt, and short stories.

1603. ———. "The Door." *Sunday Post Magazine* 2 June 1946.
Rpt. in *Love in Philippine Story and Verse* [#139] 73–87; *Philippine
Short Stories 1941–1955* [#181] 1: 252–63; *Scent of Apples* 86–97.
A short story about a Filipino immigrant whose Caucasian wife has fre-
quent affairs with other men.

1604. ———. *Dwell in the Wilderness: Selected Short Stories (1931–1941)*. Introd. Doreen G. Fernandez. Foreword Leonor Aureus-Briscoe. Quezon City, Philippines: New Day Publishers, 1985.
Rev. Cecilia Manguerra Brainard, *Amerasia Journal* 13.1 (1986–87): 182–83; Roger Bresnahan, *Asiaweek* 28 June 1985: 56.

1605. ———. "The Enchanted Plant." *Asian PEN Anthology* [#129] 134–43.
Rpt. in *The Day the Dancers Came* 1–21.
A story about a Filipino couple living in Japan.

1606. ———. "Even Purple Hearts." *Sunday Times Magazine* [Philippines] 6 Jan. 1952.
Rpt. in *The Carlos Palanca Memorial Awards for Literature: Prize Stories 1950–55*. Ed. Kerima Polotan. Manila: La Tondena, 1957. 70–84; *Philippine Short Stories 1941–1955* [#181] 2: 925–34.
Describes a Filipino veteran in Washington.

1607. ———. "Far from the City." *Philippine Magazine* Aug. 1933.
Rpt. in *Brother, My Brother* 36–46; *Philippine Short Stories 1925–1940* [#180] 199–207.
Describes various mysterious and intriguing events that occur in a rural village.

1608. ———. "The Filipino as Exile." *Greenfield Review* 6.1–2 (1977): 47–55.
Autobiographical account.

1609. ———. "The House That I Built." *Philippine Magazine* Feb. 1939.
Rpt. in *Brother, My Brother* 75–84; *Philippine Short Stories 1925–1940* [#180] 426–33.
A ruthless landlord wants to destroy a house built by two newlyweds in order to build a summer house.

1610. ———. "Immigration Blues." *New Letters* June 1977: 3–20.
Rpt. in *Short Story International* Dec. 1979: 89–106; *Scent of Apples* 3–20.
A woman tries to immigrate to the US by means of marriage.

1611. ———. *The Man Who (Thought He) Looked like Robert Taylor*. Quezon City, Philippines: New Day Publishers, 1983.
A novel about a Filipino immigrant in Chicago who is deserted by one woman after another.

1612. ———. "Meeting in San Francisco." *American Voice* 2 (Spring 1986): 12–23.
A journalist meets a woman who begs for the homeless.

1613. ———. *The Praying Man*. Quezon City, Philippines: New Day Publishers, 1982.
A novel about a Filipino who achieves prominence through personal connections and corrupt practices. The title puns on pray/prey.

1614. ———. "The Prisoners." *Evening News Saturday Magazine* [Philippines] 22 Dec. 1951.
Rpt. in *You Lovely People* 20–29; *Philippine Short Stories 1941–1955* [#181] 2: 916–24.
Describes an encounter between a Filipino expatriate and some German prisoners in Kansas during World War II.

1615.   ———. "Scent of Apples." *This Week* [Sunday Magazine of *Manila Chronicle*] 14 Nov. 1948.
         Rpt. in *You Lovely People* 137–46; *Scent of Apples* 21–29; *Asian-American Authors* [#125] 162–71; *Philippine Short Stories 1941–1955* [#181] 1: 451–59.
         A visiting lecturer from the Philippines encounters a nostalgic old-timer in Michigan.

1616.   ———. *Scent of Apples: A Collection of Short Stories.* Introd. Leonard Casper. Seattle: U of Washington P, 1979.
         A collection of short stories about various Filipino Americans' continued attachment to the homeland. Eleven of the seventeen stories in this collection originally appeared in *You Lovely People.*
         Rev. Cheng Lok Chua, *Studies in Short Fiction* 17 (1980): 507–08; Hisaye Yamamoto, *MELUS* 7.2 (1980): 92–93; Wakako Yamauchi, *Amerasia Journal* 8.2 (1981): 196–98.

1617.   ———. "The Transfer." *Kislap-Graphic* (1959).
         Rpt. in *Midland: Twenty-Five Years of Fiction and Poetry Selected from the Writing Workshops of the State University of Iowa.* Ed. Paul Engle with Henri Coulette and Donald Justice. New York: Random, 1961. 250–60.
         A church committee attempts to remove a priest who is too old to serve efficiently.

1618.   ———. "Transience." *Philippine Magazine* Feb. 1931.
         Rpt. in *Dwell in the Wilderness* 1–4.
         Describes a widow's short-lived grief.

1619.   ———. *Villa Magdalena.* Manila: Erewhon, 1965. Quezon City, Philippines: New Day Publishers, 1986. Excerpts entitled "Moonlight Laundry" in *Philippine Studies* 13.1 (1965): 100–08; "Without Heir" in *Literature East and West* 9 (1965): 75–78.
         Set in the Philippines, this novel of a wealthy landed family spans three generations.

1620.   ———. *The Volcano.* Quezon City, Philippines: Phoenix Publishing House, 1965. Introd. Tomas N. Santos. Quezon City, Philippines: New Day Publishers, 1986.
         Set in the Philippines during World War II, the novel describes interaction between American, Spanish, and Filipino characters.

1621.   ———. *What the Hell for You Left Your Heart in San Francisco.* Quezon City, Philippines: New Day Publishers, 1987.
         A novel describing a new breed of Filipino immigrants in America.

1622.   ———. *You Lovely People.* Introd. N. V. M. Gonzalez. Manila: Benipayo Press, 1955. Manila: Bookmark, 1976.
         "And Beyond, More Walls," "The Door," "For These Ruins," "The Hurt Men," "Letter: The Faraway Summer," "Lonely in the Autumn Evening," "Manila House," "Nightclub," "Of Other Deaths," "A Peculiar Rustling," and "Scent of Apples" are rpt. in *Scent of Apples.*

1623.   Santos, Tomas. "Changing Neighborhood." *Greenfield Review* 6.1–2
(1977): 30–38.
A couple keeps moving to avoid living among Filipino immigrants.

1624.   ———. "Fish." *Amerasia Journal* 3.2 (1976): 95–105.
A Filipino family witnesses the doomed affections between a traditional
woman and a westernized Filipino American.

1625.   ———. "Generosity, Good Fortune." *Manila Review* 4.3 (1978): 3–17.
A young Filipino learns about class differences when he falls in love.

1626.   ———. "Lantern." *Ohio Journal* 7.1 (1982): 10–13.
A Vietnamese deaf-mute struggles with the idea of suicide.

1627.   ———. "Playing Tennis in Argentina." *North American Review* 264.1
(1979): 46–49.
Describes an aging tennis coach.

1628.   Sikat, Dorian [pseud.]. *To Where Streets Are Made of Gold: The Story
of a Filipino Immigrant.* Smithtown, NY: Exposition Press, 1982.
Describes a Filipino immigrant's disillusionment in America.

1629.   Syquia, Serafin. "The Alaskan Trip." *Liwanag* [#95] 180–81.
An essay about Filipino workers and their union.

1630.   Tabios, Presco. "Scarecrow." *Asian American Review* (1976): 24–27.
Focuses on a drug dealer and a prostitute.

1631.   ———. "Something I Forgot to Tell You." *Yoisho!* [#183] 41–45.
A father never tells his son about the mother who died at childbirth.

1632.   Tagami, Jeff. "Gemeline." *Rising Waters* 1976: n. pag.
Describes a recent Filipino immigrant's interaction with her relatives
in America.

1633.   Tagatac, Sam. "I Came to Tell You Something." *Liwanag* [#95] 197–200.
A seducer rekindles passion in a couple.

1634.   ———. "The New Anak." *AIIIEEEEE!* [#100] 1983: 151–68.
A prose poem depicting flashes of memories.

1635.   ———. "Tomato Boxes." *Aion* 1.2 (1971): 55–56.
A sketch of three frustrated men.

1636.   Tiempo-Torrevillas, Rowena. *"Upon the Willows" and Other Stories.*
Quezon City, Philippines: New Day Publishers, 1980.

1637.   Ty-Casper, Linda. "Application for a Small Life." *Nantucket Review* 4
(Summer 1979): 39–45.
Rpt. in *Short Story International* June 1986: 98–104.
A writer registers the joys and sorrows in her life.

1638.   ———. *Awaiting Trespass.* New York: Readers International, 1985.
The mourners at a funeral contemplate the state of the Philippines un-
der martial law.
Rev. Roger J. Bresnahan, *Asiaweek* [Hong Kong] 16 Feb. 1986: 59.

1639. ———. "Blind Stones." *Solidarity* [Manila] Jan.-Feb. 1975: 3–6.
Rpt. in *Descant* 23.1 (1978): 4–7.

1640. ———. "The Charred Gods." *Literary Apprentice* 1961–63: 44–52.

1641. ———. "The Convert." *New Mexico Quarterly* 35.1 (1965): 29–38.
A woman is caught between religiously dogmatic relatives.

1642. ———. "Dead Well." *Asia Magazine* [Hong Kong] June 1963: 12–13.

1643. ———. *Dread Empire*. Hong Kong: Heinemann, 1980.
This novel about politics and corruption focuses on a tyrannous landlord who believes he is infallible.

1644. ———. "Fellow Passengers." *Greensboro Review* 36 (Summer 1984):
81–90.
Portrays two elderly priests.

1645. ———. *Fortress in the Plaza*. Quezon City, Philippines: New Day Pub-
lishers, 1985.
Describes the stress undergone by people during political turmoil.
Rev. Ruth Imperial, *Amerasia Journal* 13.1 (1986–87): 191.

1646. ———. "Gently Unbending." *Four Quarters* 26.2 (1977): 28–38.
A girl tries to deal with a rivalry between her mother and her aunt.

1647. ———. "Germinal." *Solidarity* [Manila] Mar. 1970: 27–37.
Describes a fastidious woman who supports her poor relatives.

1648. ———. "Hazards of Distance." *Manila Review* Mar. 1977: 12–25.

1649. ———. *Hazards of Distance*. Quezon City, Philippines: New Day Publishers, 1981.
A novella about family members who redefine their relationships.

1650. ———. "In Time of Moulting Doves." *Sunday Times Magazine* [Philip-
pines] 1956: 38–40.

1651. ———. "Light from the Cavern." *Philippines Free Press* Feb. 1969.

1652. ———. "The Longer Ritual." *Antioch Review* 18 (Summer 1958):
229–35.
A boy awaits the death of his estranged father.

1653. ———. "Losses of Sunday." *Solidarity* [Manila] 3.96 (1983): 74–80.
Follows the experiences of an American soldier in the Philippine-
American War.

1654. ———. "Mulch." *Prairie Schooner* 51.3 (1977): 239–45.
Describes a woman's experiences with a difficult neighbor.

1655. ———. "The Outside Heart." *Asia Magazine* [Hong Kong] 3 Nov. 1968:
PH2+.

1656. ———. *The Peninsulars*. Manila: Bookmark, 1964.
A novel about political intrigue among the Spanish colonial rulers of
the Philippines.

1657.   ———. "Salted Land." *Philippines Free Press* June 1963: 20+.

1658.   ———. "The Secret Runner." *Solidarity* [Manila] Oct. 1972: 71–78.
A man experiences a moral dilemma in occupied Manila.

1659.   ———. *"The Secret Runner" and Other Stories*. Manila: A. S. Florentino, 1974.

1660.   ———. "Small Lives." *Cuyahoga Review* Fall 1985–Winter 1986: 101–11.
A woman moves into an apartment and is drawn into the lives of two elderly neighbors.

1661.   ———. "Sometimes My Body Remembers Singing." *Nantucket Review* Fall 1979: 30–33.
A mother struggles to discipline and to express love to her young daughter.

1662.   ———. "A Swarm of Sun." *Mr. and Ms.* [Philippines] Nov. 1980: 24–27.

1663.   ———. *Ten Thousand Seeds*. Quezon City, Philippines: Ateneo de Manila UP, 1987.

1664.   ———. *The Three-Cornered Sun*. Quezon City, Philippines: New Day Publishers, 1979. Portions of this book appear earlier as "The Three-Cornered Sun." *TriQuarterly* Fall 1974: 129–41, and as "Two Stories." *Solidarity* [Manila] Sept. 1968: 74–84.
A novel about the Philippine Revolution of 1896.
Rev. Ninotchka Rosca, *Journal of Asian Studies* 40 (1981): 859–60.

1665.   ———. *"The Transparent Sun" and Other Stories*. Manila: A. S. Florentino, 1963.
"The Transparent Sun" is rpt. in *New Mexico Quarterly* 37.3 (1967): 281–88.

1666.   ———. "Triptych for a Ruined Altar." *University of Windsor Review* 12.1 (1976): 21–29.
Told from three perspectives, this story focuses on a terminally ill woman.

1667.   ———. "Two." *Manila Review* 1 (Jan. 1975): 5–17.
Portrays two elderly sisters, one physically crippled and the other emotionally crippled.

1668.   ———. "Unleavened Flesh." *Southwest Review* 46 (Summer 1961): 217–20.
A proud man seeks to receive his pension.

1669.   ———. "A Wake for Childbearers." *Hawaii Review* 11 (1981): 39–48.
Describes the thoughts of a mother and a daughter just before the daughter goes into labor.

1670.   ———. "Wine of Beeswings." *Nation* [Philippines] Dec. 1968: 26+.

1671.   ———. *Wings of Stone*. London: Readers International, 1986.
Follows the experiences of a Filipino who returns to the Philippines after living in the US for a number of years.

1672. Villa, José García. "Daughter of Rizal." *Clay* 3 (Spring 1932): 24–27.

1673. ———. "Death of a Child." *New Tide* Oct.-Nov. 1934: 23–24.
        The story of a poor family. *New Tide* was a bimonthly journal that published short stories and poetry.

1674. ———. "The Fence." *Philippines Free Press* 24 Dec. 1927.
        Rpt. in *Prairie Schooner* 6 (Summer 1932): 203–09; *Best American Short Stories of 1933*. Ed. Edward J. O'Brien. Boston: Houghton, 1933. 314–20; *Philippine Short Stories 1925–1940* [#180] 43–49.
        Two women build a bamboo fence between their houses after one of them has an affair with the other's husband.

1675. ———. "Footnote to Youth." *Frontier* 12 (Jan. 1932): 125+.
        Rpt. in *Pathways to Philippine Literature in English* [#16] 31–35; *Philippine Short Stories 1925–1940* [#180] 120–26.
        A father reflects on the dreams of youth as his sons ask permission to marry.

1676. ———. *Footnote to Youth: Tales of the Philippines and Others.* Introd. Edward J. O'Brien. New York: Scribner's, 1933.

1677. ———. "Given Woman." *Scribner's* Dec. 1931: 650–52.
        A woman lives with a man who eventually leaves her.

1678. ———. "Kamya." *New Mexico Quarterly* 2.2 (1932): 112–18.
        A tragic love story.

1679. ———. "Like My Boy." *Clay* 3 (Spring 1932): 48–51.

1680. ———. "Little Tales." *Clay* 3 (Spring 1932): 54–56.

1681. ———. "Malakas." *New Mexico Quarterly* 1.2 (1931): 167–76.
        A tale of love and sacrifice.

1682. ———. "The Man Who Looked like Rizal." *Frontier* 12.4 (1932): 330–36.
        Examines the development of a magnanimous man.

1683. ———. "Resurrection." *Clay* 2 (Winter 1931): 39–42.
        Portrait of a man who fears that his wife will give birth to a stillborn baby.

1684. ———. *Selected Stories.* Manila: Alberto S. Florentino, 1962.

1685. ———. "The Son of Rizal." *Prairie Schooner* 6.1 (1932): 1–9.
        A man befriends another man who claims to be the son of a Philippine national hero.

1686. ———. "A Story for My Country." *Prairie Schooner* 7.2 (1933): 83–86.
        Describes family tensions.

1687. ———. "Untitled Story." *Clay* 1 (Autumn 1931): 17–26.
        Rpt. in *Graphic* 9 Sept. 1931; *Best American Short Stories of 1932*. Ed. Edward J. O'Brien. New York: Dodd, 1932. 253–63; *The American Equation* [#149] 52–63; *Philippine Short Stories 1925–1940* [#180] 172–80.
        A son who is sent to America describes his hardship and romance.

1688. ———. "Valse Triste." *Clay* 3 (Spring 1932): 33–36.

1689. ———. "Walk at Midnight." *Clay* 2 (Winter 1931): 49–52.
Focuses on a sensitive youth's relationship with friends and family.

1690. ———. "White Interlude." *Clay* 2 (Winter 1931): 25–31.
A companion story to "Walk at Midnight."

1691. ———. "Young Writer in a New Country." *New Mexico Quarterly* 2.3
(1932): 220–22.
A prose poem contrasting the Philippines and America.

1692. Villanueva, Marianne. "Ginseng." *StoryQuarterly* 20 (1985): 13–18.
Describes the rapid physical decline of a Filipino immigrant after his
wife has died.

1693. Viray, Manuel A. "Broken Glass." *Sunday Times Magazine* [Philippines]
2 May 1948.
Rpt. in *Philippine Short Stories 1941–1955* [#181] 1: 347–54; *Solidarity* Sept.-Oct. 1967: 57–61.
Reflections of World War II.

1694. ———. "Bureaucrat's Morning." *Philippine Cross-Section: An Anthology of Filipino Short Stories in English.* 4th ed. Ed. Maximo D. Ramos
and Florentino B. Valeros. Quezon City, Philippines: Alemar-Phoenix
Publishing House, 1977. 147–56.
Describes office politics for promotion.

1695. ———. "Green Twigs." *This Week* [Sunday magazine of *Manila Chronicle*] 24 Dec. 1950.
Rpt. in *Philippine Short Stories 1941–1955* [#181] 2: 772–82.
Describes the inner thoughts of a newlywed staying at his parents'
home.

1696. ———. "Receding Darkness." *Evening News Saturday Magazine* [Philip-
pines] 27 Mar. 1948.
Rpt. in *Philippine Short Stories 1941–1955* [#181] 1: 341–46.
Describes the meeting of two ex-lovers.

1696a. ———. "Shawl from Kashmir and Other Stories." *Solidarity* [Manila]
Sept.-Oct. 1967: 51–71.
The other stories are "Broken Glass," "Dark Eyes," and "Portrait of a
Great Man."

1696b. ———. "The Short Stories of Manuel A. Viray." *Solidarity* [Manila] Nov.-
Dec. 1967: 39–74.
The stories are "Verdict," "Lapse," "One Man's Death . . . ," "To Pre-
pare a Face," "The Beleaguered," and "Formation."

1697. Zarco, Cyn. "Zelda and the Safecracker." *Quilt* 5 (1986): 181–82.
Describes a woman's intense longing for a man.

Poetry

1698. Angeles, Carlos A. *A Stun of Jewels*. Introd. Leonard Casper. Manila: Alberto S. Florentino, 1963.
Rev. Morli Dharam, *Manila Times* 6 June 1964: 11-A+; F. P. Makabenta, *Chronicle Magazine* [Manila] 5 Sept. 1964: 20–21; Monina A. Mercado, *Philippines Herald* 15 Apr. 1964: 5.

1699. Bergonio, Gemma. *"Mirror at Dawn" and Other Poems*. City of Industry, CA: Ted A. Villagonas, L. A. C. Publishing, 1985.

1700. Bulosan, Carlos. *Dark People*. Los Angeles: Wagon and Star, 1944.

1701. ———. *Letters from America*. Prairie City, IL: J. A. Decker, 1942.

1702. Caigoy, Faustino. *Bitter Sweet Chocolate Meat*. Los Angeles: Inner City Cultural Center, 1974.
A mosaic of poetry and art.

1703. Concepción, Marcelo de Gracia. *Azucena*. New York: Putnam's, 1925.

1704. ———. *Bamboo Flute*. Manila: Community Book, 1932.

De Gracia Concepción, Marcelo. See Concepción, Marcelo de Gracia.

Doveglion. See Villa, José García.

1704a. Feria, Benny F. *Never Tomorrow*. New York: Exposition Press, [1947].

García Villa, José. See Villa, José García.

**Gill, Lakshmi. See South Asian American section.

1705. Hagedorn, Jessica. *Dangerous Music: The Poetry and Prose of Jessica Hagedorn*. San Francisco: Momo's Press, 1975.

1706. ———. "The Death of Anna May Wong." *Four Young Women: Poems by Jessica Tarahata Hagedorn, Alice Karle, Barbara Szerlip, and Carol Tinker*. Ed. and introd. Kenneth Rexroth. New York: McGraw, 1973. 3–43.
Nineteen poems.

1707. ———. *Pet Food and Tropical Apparitions*. San Francisco: Momo's Press, 1981.
Poetry and prose.
Rev. Lori Higa, *Contact II* 7.38–40 (1986): 23–24; Mary MacKey, *Review* 8 Aug. 1982: 5.

1708. Mariano, Bayani Lingat. *Selected Poems*. Healdsburg, CA: Ya-Ka-Ama Indian Education and Development, [1977].

1709. Reyes, Myrna Peña. *The River Singing Stone*. Eugene, OR: Pacific House Books, 1984. Omaha, NE: Buttonhole Press, forthcoming.
Rev. Peter Bacho, *Contact II* 7.38–40 (1986): 57.

1710. Robles, Al[fred A.]. *Kayaomunggi vision of a Wandering Carabao*. San Francisco: Isthmus Foundation, 1983.

1711. San Juan, E[pifanio], Jr. *"The Ashes of Pedro Abad Santos" and Other Poems*. Mansfield Depot, CT: Philippines Research Center, 1985.
Limited edition.

1712.   ———. *"The Exorcism" and Other Poems*. Manila: Panitkan Publications, 1967.

1713.   ———. *Godkissing Carrion: Selected Poems 1954–64*. Cambridge, MA: Concord Press, 1964.

1714.   ———. *We Who Are about to Die*. Manila: [privately printed?], 1987. Discourses, meditation, plays.

1715.   Santos, Bienvenido. *Distances: In Time—Selected Poems*. Quezon City, Philippines: Ateneo de Manila UP, 1983.
         Rev. Cecilia Manguerra Brainard, *Amerasia Journal* 13.1 (1986–87): 182–83.

1716.   ———. *The Wounded Stag*. Introd. Manuel A. Viray. Manila: Capitol Publishing House, 1956.

1716a.   Tagami, Jeff. *October Light*. San Francisco: Kearny Street Workshop, 1987.

1717.   Villa, José García. *Appassionata: Poems in Praise of Love*. New York: King & Cowen, 1979.

1718.   ———. *Have Come, Am Here*. New York: Viking, 1942.

1719.   ———. *Makata 3: Poems in Praise of Love: The Best Love Poems of José García Villa*. Manila: Alberto S. Florentino, 1973.

1720.   ———. *Many Voices: Selected Poems by José García Villa*. Manila: Philippine Book Guild, 1939.

1721.   ———. *Poems 55 (The Best of José García-Villa as Chosen by Himself)*. Manila: Alberto S. Florentino, 1962.

1722.   ———. *Poems by Doveglion* [pseud.]. Manila: Philippine Writers' League, [1941].

1723.   ———. *Selected Poems and New*. New York: McDowell, Oblensky, 1958.

1724.   ———. *Seven Poems*. Cambridge, MA: Wake, 1948.

1725.   ———. *Volume Two*. New York: New Directions, 1949.

1726.   Viray, Manuel A. *After This Exile*. Introd. Richard Eberhart. Introd. Leonard Casper. Afterword Bienvenido N. Santos. Quezon City, Philippines: Phoenix Publishing House, 1965.

1727.   ———. *Morning Song*. Quezon City, Philippines: New Day Publishers, forthcoming.

1728.   ———. *Where Blood with Light Collides*. Manila: privately printed, 1975.

1729.   Zarco, Cyn. "Souvenirz." *Jambalaya: Four Poets*. Ed. Steve Cannon. New York: Reed Cannon & Johnson, n.d. 1–23.
         Thirty-one poems.

Drama

1730.　Florentino, Alberto S. *The World Is an Apple. Philippine Contemporary Literature in English and Pilipino* [#108] 234–42.
　　　One-act play.

1731.　Hagedorn, Jessica Tarahata. *Chiquita Banana. Third World Women* [#174] 118–27.
　　　One-act play.

Lim, Paul Stephen. See Chinese American section.

San Juan, E[pifanio], Jr. See #1714.

1733.　Santos, Bienvenido N. *The Bishop's Pets. Philippines Free Press* [Manila] 10 Sept. 1966.
　　　One-act play.

1734.　———. *The Long Way Home. The Day the Dancers Came* [#1602] 167–95.
　　　One-act play.

Korean American Literature

Prose

1735. Cha, Theresa Hak Kyung. *Dictee*. New York: Tanam Press, 1982.
A collage of prose and poetry interweaving the lives of several women.
Rev. Lori Higa, *Contact II* 7.38–40 (1986): 24–25.

1736. Fenkl, Heinz. "In the House of the Japanese Colonel." *Bridge* 8.4 (1983): 41–46.
An excerpt from *Into the Western Land*, a novel in progress.

Hahn, Gloria. See Kim Ronyoung.

1737. *Hyun, Peter. *Man Sei! The Making of a Korean American*. Honolulu: U of Hawaii P, 1986.
Describes the childhood and adolescence of the author in Japanese-occupied Korea, his exile in Shanghai, and his immigration to Hawaii.

1738. ———. "The Tale of Chuyong's Lament as Told by Peter Hyun." *Korean Culture* 1.2 (1980): 40–41.
A retelling of a myth about a cuckold.

1739. ———. "Zen, American Style." *Yardbird Reader* 5 (1976): 73–75.
Essay.

1740. Kang, Younghill. *East Goes West: The Making of an Oriental Yankee*. New York: Scribner's, 1937.
Excerpt in *Asian-American Heritage* [#177] 217–50.
Autobiographical novel.
Rev. *New Republic* 8 Dec. 1937: 153–54; *New Yorker* 18 Sept. 1937: 74.

1741. ———. *The Grass Roof*. New York: Scribner's, 1931.
An autobiographical novel.
Rev. Lady Hosie, *Saturday Review of Literature* 4 Apr. 1931: 707.

1742. ———. "Oriental Yankee." *Common Ground* 1 (Winter 1941): 59–63.
Autobiographical essay.

1743. Kennel, Nancy Lee. "Mirrors." *Gathering Ground* [#105] 43–44.
Describes the sufferings of three generations of Korean women.

1744. Kilburn, Kumi. "No Dogs and Chinese Allowed." *The Ethnic American Woman* [#88] 171–74.
An autobiographical account about a Korean American woman who reclaims her Korean name.

1745. *Kim, Ahn [Andrew]. "A Homeward Journey." *75th Anniversary of Korean Immigration to Hawaii 1903–1978* [#136] 22–27.
A third-generation Korean American describes his journey to Korea.

1746. Kim, Elizabeth M. "Detours down Highway 99." *Quilt* 2 (1981): 103–10.
A woman encounters a handicapped old man during a Greyhound bus ride.

1747.   ———. "Experience Preferred." *Express* [Berkeley, CA] 21 Nov. 1980: 1+.
Describes the painful experiences of looking for a job and a place to
live in Berkeley.

1748.   *Kim, Jonathan. "Girls. Are They Worth It?" *Bamboo Ridge* 3 (1979):
44–49.
Short story.

1749.   Kim, Kichung. "America, America." Forthcoming in *San Jose Studies*
(Spring 1988).
Describes the breakup of a Korean family after immigrating to Hawaii.

1750.   ———. "A Homecoming." *Bridge* 2.6 (1973): 27–31.
Describes the impressions of a Korean American in Korea.

1751.   ———. "What's in a Name." *Career: A Teacher's Guide*. Ed. Adele
Meyer. New York: Asian Soc. of New York, 1986. 44–46.
A personal essay about cultural differences between Koreans and
Americans.

1752.   *Kim, Leigh. "Da Kine." *Echoes from Gold Mountain* 1982: 95–106.
Describes a Korean American's humiliation in Hawaii.

1753.   *Kim, Richard. "Picture Love." *75th Anniversary of Korean Immigration
to Hawaii, 1903–1978* [#136] 47.
An elderly widower recalls his excitement when traveling to meet his
picture bride from Korea.

1754.   Kim, Richard E. *The Innocent*. Boston: Houghton, 1968. New York: Ballantine, 1969.
A political novel about a military coup.

1755.   ———. *Lost Names: Scenes from a Korean Boyhood*. New York: Praeger, 1970.
"Crossing" is rpt. in *Asian-American Heritage* [#177] 31–48. "An Empire for Rubber Balls" is rpt. in *Asian-American Heritage* [#177] 62–88.
A collection of short stories; the title refers to the Japanese practice of
forcing Koreans to change their personal names from Korean to Japanese.

1756.   ———. *The Martyred*. New York: Braziller, 1964; Pocket, 1965.
An existential novel describing the reactions of various men to the
deaths of 14 Christian ministers captured by communists during the Korean War.
Rev. Chad Walsh, *New York Times Book Review* 16 Feb. 1964: 1+.

1757.   Kim Ronyoung [Gloria Hahn]. *Clay Walls*. New York: Permanent Press,
1986.
A novel, told from three characters' points of view, about a Korean cou-
ple who emigrate to Los Angeles before World War II.
Rev. Amy Engeler, *New York Times Book Review* 11 Jan. 1987: 18;
Kichung Kim, *San Francisco Sunday Examiner and Chronicle* 2 Aug.
1987, review sec.: 1+; S. E. Solberg, *Korean Culture* 7.4 (1986): 30–35;
Eun Sik Yang, *Los Angeles Times Book Review* 26 Apr. 1987: 1+.

1758.   Kim Yong Ik. "A Book-Writing Venture." *Writer* 78 (Oct. 1965): 28–30.
         An autobiographical essay depicting the pains and joys of writing a book in a second language.

1759.   ———. "From Here You Can See the Moon." *Texas Quarterly* 11.2 (1968): 201–08.
         Rpt. in *Korean Culture* 1.3 (1980): 22–27; *Short Story International* Apr. 1982: 73–82.
         An immigrant who has spent 10 years in the US describes his return to Korea and his reunion with his father.

1760.   ———. "The Gold Watch." *Stories* 5 (May-June 1983): 19–33.
         Rpt. in *Short Story International* Feb. 1985: 91–104.
         Follows a professor's encounters with a beggar in the period between the end of World War II and the beginning of the Korean War.

1761.   ———. "Gourd Dance Song." *Confrontation* 27–28 (1984): 44–51.
         Rpt. in *Short Story International* Dec. 1986: 67–78.
         Recounts two village boys' secret admiration for a young female singer.

1762.   ———. *Love in Winter.* Seoul: Korea UP, 1963. Garden City, NY: Doubleday, 1969.
         "After Seventeen Years" is rpt. in *Short Story International* Dec. 1980: 57–60. "From Below the Bridge" is rpt. in *Short Story International* Feb. 1986: 49–61. "The Seed Money" is rpt. in *Short Story International* Aug. 1982: 45–62. "The Sunny Side after the Harvest" is rpt. in *Short Story International* Feb. 1983: 75–80. "The Taste of Salt" is rpt. in *Short Story International* Apr. 1984: 99–110. "They Won't Crack It Open" is rpt. in *Asian-American Heritage* [#177] 49–62.
         A collection of 13 short stories set in postwar Korea.

1763.   ———. "The Snake Man." *TriQuarterly* 58 (Fall 1983): 133–51.
         Rpt. in *Short Story International* June 1986: 78–97.
         A man cuckolded by the king seeks revenge by impregnating the queen.

1764.   ———. "Spring Day, Great Fortune." *Sewanee Review* 86 (1978): 496–512.
         Rpt. in *Short Story International* Dec. 1983: 93–109.
         Describes a family in Korea.

1765.   ———. "Translation President." *Hudson Review* 33.2 (1980): 233–44.
         Describes a translator's experience with a Korean prostitute.

1766.   ———. "Village Wine." *Atlantic Monthly* May 1976: 70–73.
         Rpt. in *Short Story International* June 1987: 71–77.
         An American soldier seeks refuge in the house of a Korean official during the Korean War.

1767.   ———. "The Wedding Shoes." *New Yorker* 1952.
         Rpt. in *Midland: Twenty-Five Years of Fiction and Poetry Selected from the Writing Workshops of the State University of Iowa.* Ed. Paul Engle with Henri Coulette and Donald Justice. New York: Random, 1961. 140–53.
         Explores the conflict between a butcher's son and his neighbor, a maker of wedding shoes.

1768.   *Lee, Tony. "Nowadays Not like Before." *Bamboo Ridge* 1 (Dec. 1978): 3–11.
        Rpt. in *The Best of* Bamboo Ridge [#103] 167–74.
        A series of sketches based on experiences and observations at Bamboo Ridge, a fishing area on Oahu.

1769.   New Il-Han. *When I Was a Boy in Korea.* Boston: Lothrop, 1928.

1770.   Pahk, Induk. *The Cock Still Crows.* New York: Vantage, 1977.
        Describes how the high school headed by the author in Korea branches out into a junior college.

1771.   ———. *The Hour of the Tiger.* New York: Harper, 1965.
        Describes how the author struggles to build a vocational high school in Korea.

1772.   ———. *September Monkey.* New York: Harper, 1954.
        Christian autobiography. The title alludes to the author's birthday in September during the Year of the Monkey.

1773.   *Pak, Ty. "A Fire." *Bamboo Ridge* 7 (1980): 28–36.
        Rpt. in *Asian and Pacific Literature* 1 (1982): 443–50; *Guilt Payment* 97–104.
        A man whose house in Korea was burned when he was a child commits suicide by causing a fire.

1774.   ———. "The Foe." *Hawaii Review* 15 (Spring 1984): 25–28.
        A short story about the Vietnam War.

1775.   ———. "The Gardener." *Bamboo Ridge* 21 (1983): 49–64.
        A story about a gardener whose "legal" daughter is actually unrelated to him.

1776.   ———. *Guilt Payment.* Spec. issue of *Bamboo Ridge* 18 (1983).
        Collection of short stories.

1777.   ———. "Guilt Payment." *Guilt Payment* 5–18.
        Rpt. in *The Best of* Bamboo Ridge [#103] 225–39.

1778.   ———. "Steady Hands." *Bamboo Ridge* 13 (1982): 27–34.
        Rpt. in *Guilt Payment* 77–84.
        A Korean American surgeon discovers that he fathered a son while in Vietnam.

1779.   *Pang, Morris. "A Korean Immigrant." *Social Process in Hawaii* 13 (1949): 19–24.
        A son chronicles his father's life.

1780.   Park, No-Yong. *Chinaman's Chance: An Autobiography.* Boston: Meador Publishing, 1940.
        Set in China, Europe, and America.

1781.   *Song, Cathy. "Beginnings (for Bok Pil)." *Hawaii Review* 6 (Spring 1976): 55–65.
        Juxtaposed descriptions of the narrator's abortion in a modern hospital and her grandmother's unsuccessful attempt to abort a child.

1782.   *Yoon, Esther. "Vanishing Point." *Hawaii Review* 16 (Fall 1984): 61–63.
         Describes the death of an elderly Korean American woman.

Poetry

1783.   Kim, Chungmi. *Chungmi (Selected Poems)*. Anaheim: Korean Pioneer
         Press, 1982.
             Rev. Diana Chang, *Contact II* 7.38–40 (1986): 97–98; Barbara Con-
         stance Jones, *Korean Culture* 3.3 (1982): 25–27; Elaine H. Kim, *Contact
         II* 7.38–40 (1986): 21–23.

1784.   Kim, Willyce. *Eating Artichokes*. Oakland: Women's Press Collective,
         1972.

1785.   ———. *Under the Rolling Sky*. N.p.: Maude Gonne Press, 1976.

1786.   Ko, Sung-Won [also, Won Ko; Ko Won]. *With Birds of Paradise*. Los An-
         geles: Azalea Press, 1984.

1787.   ———. *The Turn of Zero*. New York: Cross-Cultural Communications,
         1974.

1788.   *Song, Cathy. *Picture Bride*. Foreword Richard Hugo. New Haven: Yale
         UP, 1983.
             Rev. Marjorie Sinclair Edel, *Hawaii Literary Arts Council Newsletter*
         June-July 1983: n. pag.; Shirley Lim, *MELUS* 10.3 (1983): 95–99; Stephen
         H. Sumida, *Contact II* 7.38–40 (1986): 52–55.

Drama

1789.   Binari [Korean-American Cultural Troupe]. *When the Green Mountain
         Stirs Our Hearts Again: A Madang-Gut (An Epic Drama)*. New York: pri-
         vately printed, 1985.
             Political allegory.

South Asian American Literature

Prose

1790. **Ahmad, Iqbal. "The Clown." *Toronto South Asian Review* 5.2 (1986): 18–23.
A professor remembers his son who was martyred in India's fight for independence.

1791. ———. "The Kumbh Fair." *Fiddlehead* 80 (1969): 44–52.
A student tries to rescue a kidnapped prostitute.

1792. Alexander, Meena. "House of Mirrors." *Toronto South Asian Review* 5.2 (1986): 14–17.

1792a. ———. "From *Tales of the Emperor.*" *Chelsea* 46 (1987): 255–65.

1793. **Annand, Alan Mark. "Able Baker One." *Antigonish Review* 18 (Summer 1974): 59–66.

1794. ———. "A Bagful of Holes." *Antigonish Review* 30 (Summer 1977): 11–14.
Describes a boy's reaction to the drowning of kittens.

1795. ———. "Rosie Was a Good Old Dog." *Fiddlehead* 106 (1975): 31–37.
Describes an eccentric family.

1796. **Bannerji, Himani. "Going Home." *RIKKA* 7.1 (1980): 23–26.
An expatriate whose wife is dying in a Western hospital recalls her wish to return to India.

1797. **Batliwalla, Bapai. "Decisions." *Toronto South Asian Review* 4.3 (1986): 58–63.
Describes a woman's problems in trying to emigrate from India to Canada.

1798. **Bissoondath, Neil. *Digging up the Mountains.* Toronto: Macmillan of Canada, 1985. New York: Viking, 1986.
A collection of short stories.

1799. ———. "Insecurity." *Toronto South Asian Review* 5.1 (1986): 163–69.
A businessman tries to take his money out of a Carribbean country.

1800. ———. "Things Best Forgotten." *Literary Review* 29.4 (1986): 402–11.
Reminiscences about a father.

1801. Burney, Shehla. "Two Contraptions of Reality: Theatre in the Street." *Toronto South Asian Review* 5.2 (1986): 55–60.
The narrator imagines two stories upon viewing two pictures.

1802. **Chahal, Amarjit. "A Lady and Her Car." *Toronto South Asian Review* 2.1 (1983): 60+.
Short story.

1803. Chandra, G. S. Sharat. "Bhat's Return." *Missouri Short Fiction.* Ed. Conger Beasley. Kansas City: BookMark Press, 1985. 1–8.
Describes an American-educated Indian's return to India.

1804. ———. "The Elephant Stop." *Overland* [Melbourne, Austral.] 66 (1977): 2–3.
Rpt. in *Short Story International* Aug. 1980: 103–07.
Describes a maharaja's royal elephant.

1805. ———. "The Holy Wristwatch." *London Magazine* 22.3 (1982): 56–60.
Rpt. in *Short Story International* Dec. 1984: 99–103.
A laborer receives a wristwatch from a famous yogi.

1806. ———. "Iyer's Hotel." *Stories* 14 (1986): 40–48.
Describes an Indian vegetarian hotel that is haunted by English ghosts.

1807. ———. "Jamal the Constable." *Winter's Tales 21*. Ed. A. D. Maclean. London: Macmillan, 1975. 42–56.
Rpt. in *Writing Fiction: A Guide to Narrative Craft*. Ed. Janet Burroway. Boston: Little, 1982; *Short Story International* Aug. 1978: 81–94.
Portrays an Indian police constable.

1808. ———. "Maya." *Swallow's Tail* [Tallahassee, FL] 1 (1983): 6–12.
Rpt. in *Short Story International* Apr. 1986: 68–75.
Describes a double wedding.

1809. ———. "Reincarnation." *These and Other Lands*. [Ed.] Heartlands Fiction Collective. Loose Creek, MO: Westphalia Press, 1986. 123–33.
An Indian guru attempts to be reborn.

1810. ———. "Saree of the Gods." *Female* [Singapore] (1979).
Rpt. in *Short Story International* Apr. 1981: 43–50; *The Shock of Being Foreign*. Yarmouth, ME: Intercultural Press, 1986.
Describes an expatriate Indian woman's tribulations in America.

1811. ———. "Selves." *Stories* 9 (1984): 29–34.
Describes an Indian dentist's cultural adaptation.

1812. ———. "This Time Goat, Next Time Man." *Stories* 4 (Mar.-Apr. 1983): 1–13.
Describes the rise of a poor Indian singer to political power.

Chauhan, Vijay Lakshmi. See Lakshmi [Chauhan], Vijay.

1813. **Cowasjee, Saros. *Goodbye to Elsa*. London: Bodley Head; Toronto: New Press, 1974. New Delhi: Orient Paperbacks, 1975.
A satirical novel chronicling the love life and withdrawal of an Anglo-Indian professor in western Canada.

1814. ———. *"Nude Therapy" and Other Stories*. New Delhi: Orient Paperbacks, 1978. Ottawa: Borealis Press, 1979.
Set in India and Canada.

1815. ———. *Stories and Sketches*. Calcutta: Writers Workshop, 1970.

1816. ———. *Suffer Little Children*. New Delhi: Allied Publishers, 1982.
Novel.

1817. **Dabydeen, Cyril. "Across the River." *Toronto South Asian Review* 1.2 (1982): 11–18.
Short story.

1818. ———. "At the Dawning." *RIKKA* 9.2 (1984): 14–17.
A boy is fascinated and frightened by British soldiers stationed in his village.

1819. ———. "At the Going Down of the Sun." *Wascana Review* 2 (1981): 67–75.

1820. ———. "At Your Peril." *Canadian Author and Bookman* 57.4 (1982): 15–18.

1821. ———. "The Committee." *Toronto South Asian Review* 2.3 (1984): 53+.
Short story.

1822. ———. "Everlasting Love." *Antigonish Review* 23 (Autumn 1975): 53–55.

1823. ———. "A Far Place Home." *RIKKA* 7.2 (1980): 25–28.
A schoolboy in a South American village daydreams about Canada.

1824. ———. "Funny Ghosts." *Quarry* [Kingston, ON] 30 (Spring 1981): 35–39.

1825. ———. *The Glass Forehead.* Cornwall, ON: Vesta, 1983.

1826. ———. "A Kind of Feeling." *Antigonish Review* 44 (Winter 1980): 83–90.

1827. ———. "A Mighty Vision from Punjabi." *Canadian Fiction Magazine* 36–37 (1980): 136–41.
A weightlifter who works on a sugarcane plantation fantasizes about becoming a Mr. Universe.

1828. ———. "A Plan Is a Plan." *Dalhousie Review* 62.4 (1982–83): 659–67.

1829. ———. "The Puja Man." *Toronto South Asian Review* 5.1 (1986): 182–90.
Describes the feelings of a man who is about to be deported from Canada.

1830. ———. "The Rink." *Fiddlehead* 143 (1985): 21–27.

1831. ———. "Something to Talk About." *Journal of South Asian Studies* 19.1 (1984): 137–40.

1832. ———. *Still Close to the Island.* Ottawa: Commoner's Publishing, 1980.
"Mammita's Garden Grove" is rpt. in *Literary Review* 29.4 (1986): 523–35.
A collection of short stories set in the West Indies and Canada.
Rev. Himani Bannerji, *Asianadian* 4.1 (1982?): 27–29; Frank Birbalsingh, *Toronto South Asian Review* 1.3 (1983): 101+.

1833. ———. *The Wizard Swami.* Calcutta: Writers Workshop, 1985.
A young man tries to join the All India League in Guyana by acquiring prestige as a Hindu priest.
Rev. Frank Birbalsingh, *Toronto South Asian Review* 4.3 (1986): 76–78.

1834. Da Silva, Ladis. "Portrait of a Hog." *Journal of South Asian Literature* 18.1 (1983): 131–43.
Describes the ways in which pigs have served human needs.

1835.   ———. "Zanzibar." *Journal of South Asian Literature* 18.1 (1983): 258–65.

An autobiographical essay about growing up in Zanzibar, an island off the east coast of Africa.

1836.   Da Silva, Marion. "Return to Goa." *Journal of South Asian Literature* 18.1 (1983): 272–74.

Essay.

1837.   Desani, G[ovindas] V[ishnoodas]. *All About Mr. Hatterr.* London: Francis Aldor, 1948; Saturn Press, 1950. Rev. ed. entitled *All About H. Hatterr.* New York: Farrar, 1951. Further rev. ed. New York: Farrar, 1970. Further rev. ed. [with new chapter]. Introd. Anthony Burgess. Harmondsworth, Eng.: Penguin, 1972. New Paltz, NY: McPherson, 1986.

A comic, philosophical novel about the education of an Anglo-Indian orphan.

1838.   ———. "A Passage to Midwest U.S.A.—Fly High to Chicago!" *University College Quarterly* 24 (May 1979): 24–32.

Describes a tour through Chicago.

Devajee, Ved. See Gool, Réshard.

1839.   **Dewji, Ismail M. "From a Wayfarer's Notebook." *Toronto South Asian Review* 2.1 (1983).

Describes Indians in Zanzibar and the east coast of Africa at the turn of the century.

1840.   Furtado, Raul de L. *Burnt Sienna*. Delhi: Delhi Book, 1961.

A collection of short stories.

1841.   ———. "Flight of the Heron." *Journal of South Asian Literature* 18.1 (1983): 172–75.

In the middle of a drought a family spots a heron, the harbinger of rain.

1842.   ———. "Port of Call." *Journal of South Asian Literature* 18.1 (1983): 105–09.

A short story set in Aden.

1843.   Gandhbir, Lalita. "Amba." *Toronto South Asian Review* 4.3 (1986): 44–52.

A girl learns the truth of her parentage.

1844.   Ghose, Zulfikar. *The Beautiful Empire*. London: Macmillan, 1975.

The second part of a three-part novel under the general title of *The Incredible Brazilian*.

Rev. Anne Barnes, *Times Literary Supplement* 16 Jan. 1976: 65; Bilqis Siddiqi Karachi, *World Literature Today* 51 (Winter 1977): 159.

1845.   ———. *Confessions of a Native-Alien*. London: Routledge, 1965.

Autobiography.

1846.   ———. *The Contradictions: A Novel by Zulfikar Ghose*. London: Macmillan; New York: St. Martin's, 1966.

Follows the experiences of a woman who marries a senior officer in the Indian civil service.

1847.   ———. *Crump's Terms: A Novel by Zulfikar Ghose*. London: Macmillan, 1976.
Depicts the interaction between a West London schoolteacher and his students through a mosaic of internal and external events.

1848.   ———. *A Different World*. London: Macmillan, 1978. Woodstock, NY: Overlook Press, 1984.
The third part of a three-part novel under the general title of *The Incredible Brazilian*.

1849.   ———. *Don Bueno*. New York: Holt, 1983.
Set in Brazil, the novel unravels a cycle of crimes committed by four generations of fathers and sons.

1850.   ———. *Figures of Enchantment*. New York: Harper, 1986.

1851.   ———. *The Incredible Brazilian: The Native*. London: Macmillan, 1972.
The first part of a three-part novel set in the Amazon jungle during a rubber boom in the nineteenth century.

1852.   ———. *The Murder of Aziz Khan: A Novel by Zulfikar Ghose*. London: Macmillan, 1967. New York: John Day, 1969.
Centers on the opposition between a Pakistani peasant landowner and a group of industrial entrepreneurs.

1853.   ———. *A New History of Torments*. New York: Holt, 1982.
A succession of calamities befalls a wealthy family in South America.

1853a. ———. "The Savage Mother of Desire." *Chelsea* 46 (1987): 279–90.

1854.   Ghose, Zulfikar, and B. S. Stanley. *Statement against Corpses: Short Stories by B. S. Stanley and Zulfikar Ghose*. London: Constable, 1964.

1855.   **Gill, Lakshmi. "An Excerpt from *Puja for Papa*." *Toronto South Asian Review* 1.3 (1983): 67+.
Autobiography.

1856.   ———. "Excerpt from *Puja for Papa*." *Toronto South Asian Review* 3.3 (1985): 1+.
Autobiography.

1857.   Gill, Stephen. *Immigrant: A Novel*. Cornwall, ON: Vesta, 1978.
Describes the disillusioning experiences of a recent Indian immigrant to Canada.
Rev. Cyril Dabydeen, *Asianadian* 2.1 (1979): 29; Lino Leitão, *Asian Tribune* 15 Aug. 1980: 4; Andrew E. West, *Canadian Book Review Annual* 1979: 138; W. F. Westcott, *Christian Monitor* 2 Nov. 1980: 6.

1858.   ———. *Life's Vagaries: Fourteen Short Stories*. Cornwall, ON: Vesta, 1974.
Rev. Arlee Barr, *Alive* 35; Robert Durrell, *Canadian India Times* 4 Mar. 1976: 5; Peggy Fletcher, *Canadian India Times* 4 Mar. 1976: 7; P. K. F., *Sarnia Observer* May 1975.

1859.   ———. *The Loyalist City.* Cornwall, ON: Vesta Publications, 1979.
A novel about life in Canada.
Rev. George Bonavia, *Books International Corner* June 1980; *Review
Journal* 2 (Dec. 1980): 84.

1860.   ———. *Sketches of India.* Cornwall, ON: Vesta Publications, 1980.
Essays.
Rev. *Books International Corner* Feb. 1981; Ron Santanna, *Canadian
India Times* 15 Sept. 1980: 7; W. F. Westcott, *Asian Tribune* 21 Feb. 1981:
6.

1861.   ———. *Why?* Cornwall, ON: Vesta, 1976.
Describes an Indian who leaves Canada to work as a schoolteacher in
Ethiopia.
Rev. Robert Durrell, *Nugget Focus* 13 Jan. 1978: 2; Manjula Parakot,
Canadian India Times 5 May 1977: 5; Philip Walsh, *Canadian Book Re-
view Annual* (1977): 145; *Sarnia Observer* 12 Feb. 1977: 4.

1862.   **Gool, Réshard [under pseud. Ved Devajee]. *Nemesis Casket.* Charlottetown, PE: Square Deal Publications, 1979.
Set in Canada, the novel seeks to "unravel North America in the way
that Durrell's *Alexandria Quartet* unravels Alexandria."

1863.   ———. "Operation Cordelia." *Toronto South Asian Review* 1.3 (1983):
35+.
Short story.

1864.   ———. *The Price of Admission.* 1973. Rev. and retitled as *Price.*
Charlottetown, PE: Square Deal Publications, 1976.
Set in the late 1940s, the novel shows how totalitarian rule affects life
in South Africa.

1865.   **Hosein, Clyde. "The Bookkeeper's Wife." *Toronto South Asian Review*
1.3 (1983): 72+.
Short story.

1866.   ———. *"The Killing of Nelson John" and Other Stories.* London: Lon-
don Magazine Editions, 1980.
"Morris, Bhaiya" is rpt. in *Toronto South Asian Review* 2.2 (1983):
80–90.
Set in the West Indies.
Rev. Frank Birbalsingh, *Toronto South Asian Review* 1.3 (1983): 103+.

1867.   ———. "The Man at the Gate of the House of Refuge." *Toronto South
Asian Review* 4.1 (1985): 7+.
Short story.

1868.   **Itwaru, Arnold. "The Attendant." *RIKKA* 6.1 (1979): 22–24.
A man who has been unemployed for three months finds a job in a
mental ward.

Jhabvala, Ruth Prawer. See Literature by Non-Asians section.

1869.   **Kachroo, Balkrishan. "Two Indian Middles." *Toronto South Asian Review* 3.3 (1985): 60–61.
Short story.

1870.   **Kalsey, Surjeet. "Confined by Threads." *Canadian Fiction Magazine* 19 (Spring 1976): 140–42.
Short story.

1871.   ———. "Mirage in the Cave." Trans. author. *Canadian Fiction Magazine* 36–37 (Fall 1980): 126–29.
Rpt. in *Toronto South Asian Review* 1.1 (1982): 37+.
A short story about a deserted wife.

1872.   **Kaur, Paramjit. "Shashi." *Toronto South Asian Review* 2.1 (1983): 70+.
Short story.

1873.   Khan, Ismith. *The Jumbie Bird.* New York: I. Obolensky, 1961.
Depicts the erosion of cultural heritage within a Pathan Indian family living in Trinidad.

1874.   ———. *Obeah Man.* London: Hutchinson, 1964.
Portrays the passionate relationships among four people during the carnival in Port of Spain.

1875.   ———. "The Red Bull." *Toronto South Asian Review* 5.1 (1986): 96–103.
A boy seeks acceptance from his father and from his peers.

1876.   **Ladoo, Harold Sonny. *No Pain like This Body.* Toronto: Anansi, 1972.
Portrays Indians in rural Trinidad.

1877.   ———. "The Quiet Peasant." *Impulse* [Toronto] 2 (Winter 1973): 11–17.
Describes the struggle of a poor peasant in the Caribbean.

1878.   ———. *Yesterdays.* Toronto: Anansi, 1974.
A Trinidad Indian wants to start a Hindu mission.

1879.   Lakshmi [Chauhan], Vijay. "Distances." *Journal of Indian Writing in English* [Special number on Indian writers abroad; Univ. of Gularga publication] July 1985: 48–55.
Describes the changing states of mind of a female immigrant.

1880.   ———. "Smokescreen." *Femina* [*Times of India Publication*, Bombay] Apr. 1984: 61+.
Describes befogged people.

1881.   ———. "Touchline." *Orbis* [Eng.]. Forthcoming.
Describes an expatriate's unsuccessful attempt at persuading her mother to move to the US.

1882.   **Leitão, Lino. *Collected Short Tales.* New York: Carlton, 1972.
"Jaffer's Chicken" is rpt. in *Short Story International* June 1986: 105–31.

1883.   ———. "The Colonial Bishop's Visit." *Toronto South Asian Review* 2.2 (1983): 52–54.
Rpt. in *Short Story International* Aug. 1987: 132–36.

1884.   ———. "The Curse." *Toronto South Asian Review* 1.1 (1982): 1+.
Short story.

1885.   ———. "Dirges." *Toronto South Asian Review* 5.2 (1986): 46–48.
A woman who is separated from her husband attends her mother-in-law's funeral.

1886. ———. "Dona Amalia Quadros." *African Writing Today* 1981.
Rpt. in *Short Story International* Dec. 1984: 127–40.
Describes a woman who excels in turning things to her advantage.

1887. ———. *Gift of the Holy Cross.* Yorkshire, Eng.: Peepal Tree Press, 1987.
Novel.

1888. ———. *Goan Tales.* Cornwall, ON: Vesta, 1977.
"The Son" is rpt. in *Journal of South Asian Literature* 18.1 (1983):
131–43; *Short Story International* Apr. 1985: 128–43.

1889. ———. *Six Tales.* Cornwall, ON: Vesta, 1981.
A collection of stories set in Goa and East Africa.
Rev. Peter Nazareth, *World Literature Today* 56.2 (1982): 405.

1890. Majmudar, Uma. "The Pleasures and Pains of the Indian-American Ethnic
Experience." *The Ethnic American Woman* [#88] 324–29.
An autobiographical account about the clash of cultural values ex-
perienced by an immigrant.

1891. Mehta, Ved [Parkash]. *Daddyji.* New York: Farrar, 1972.
The first volume of an autobiographical work. Portrays the author's
father.

1892. ———. *Delinquent Chacha.* New York: Harper, 1963.
Describes the adventures of an Indian in London. Material originally
published in *New Yorker.*

1893. ———. *Face to Face: An Autobiography.* Boston: Little, 1957. Bombay:
Jaico, 1963.
Describes the blind author's life in India and in America.

1894. ———. *A Family Affair: India under Three Prime Ministers.* New York:
Oxford UP, 1982.
Sequel to *The New India.*

1895. ———. *Fly and the Fly-Bottle: Encounters with British Intellectuals.* Boston: Little, 1962. London: Weidenfeld, 1963.
A journalistic account of the philosophy and historiography prevalent
in England, peppered with personal reflections.

1896. ———. *John Is Easy to Please: Encounters with the Written and the Spo-
ken Word.* New York: Farrar, 1962. London: Secker, 1971.
A collection of six pieces, originally published in *New Yorker,* on the
themes of tongue and pen.

1897. ———. *The Ledge between the Streams.* New York: Norton, 1984.
The fourth volume of an autobiographical work. Describes the author's
childhood.

1898. ———. *Mahatma Gandhi and His Apostles.* Delhi: Indian Book, 1977.
A biography that weaves factual details into an ironical narrative.
Rev. L. A. Gordon, *Nation* 2 July 1977: 26; Paul Johnson, *New York
Times Book Review* 6 Feb. 1977: 3; Eric Stokes, *Times Literary Supple-
ment* 5 Aug. 1977: 954.

1899. ———. *Mamaji.* New York: Oxford UP, 1979.
The second volume of an autobiographical work. Portrays the author's mother.

1900. ———. *The New India.* New York: Viking, 1978.
Recounts the political history of India from its independence in 1947.

1901. ———. *The New Theologian.* New York: Harper, 1965. London: Weidenfeld, 1966. Harmondsworth, Eng.: Penguin, 1968.
Describes the views of various theologians.

1902. ———. *The Photographs of Chachaji: The Making of a Documentary Film.* New York: Oxford UP, 1980.
On television.

1903. ———. *Portrait of India.* New York: Farrar, 1970. Delhi: Vikas, 1971.
Describes a country trying to modernize itself.

1904. ———. *Sound-Shadows of the New World.* New York: Norton, 1985.
The fifth volume of an autobiographical work. Describes the author's adolescent years in Arkansas.

1905. ———. *Three Stories of the Raj.* Berkeley: Scholar, [1986?].

1906. ———. *Vedi.* New York: Oxford UP, 1982.
The third volume of an autobiographical work. Describes the author's early education in an Indian orphanage for the blind.

1907. ———. *Walking the Indian Streets.* Boston: Little, 1960. Rev. ed. Introd. Ved Mehta. London: Weidenfeld, 1971.
Travel memoir.

1908. **Memon, Muhammad Umar. "The Worm and the Sunflower." *Toronto South Asian Review* 1.3 (1983): 17+.
Short story.

1909. **Mistry, Rohinton. "Lend Me Your Light." *Toronto South Asian Review* 2.3 (1984): 5+.
Short story.

1910. Mukherjee, Bharati. "Angela." *Mother Jones* Dec. 1984: 12–16.
Rpt. in *Best American Stories, 1985.* Ed. Gail Godwin. Boston: Houghton, 1985. 157–67; *Darkness* 7–20.
Miracles and accidents, sex and violence are superimposed in this tale told by an orphan.

1911. ———. *Darkness.* New York: Penguin, 1985.
A collection of short stories.
Rev. Peter Nazareth, *Canadian Literature* 110 (1986): 184–91; Uma Parameswaran, *Canadian Ethnic Studies* 18.3 (1986): 157–59; George Woodcock, *Canadian Literature* 107 (1985): 150–52.

1913. ———. "Debate on a Rainy Afternoon." *Massachusetts Review* 7 (Spring 1966): 257–70.
A frustrated schoolteacher in Calcutta interrupts a British Council debate on love and war.

1914.   ———. "Fathering." *Chelsea* 46 (1987): 274–78.

1915.   ———. "An Invisible Woman." *Saturday Night* [Toronto] Mar. 1981: 36–40.
An autobiographical essay about discrimination against Indians in Canada.

1916.   ———. "Isolated Incidents." *Saturday Night* [Toronto] Oct. 1980.
Rpt. in *Darkness* 77–93.
Centers on the reunion of two women who have pursued different careers.

1918.   ———. "The Lady from Lucknow." *Missouri Review* 8.3 (1985): 29–35.
Rpt. in *Darkness* 23–34.
On fatal and mundane passion.

1919.   ———. "The Middle-Man." *Playboy* Apr. 1986.
Rpt. in *Editor's Choice*. Vol. 4. Ed. George Murphy. New York: Bantam, 1987.
Short story.

1920.   ———. *"The Middleman" and Other Stories*. New York: Grove, 1988.
A collection of short stories.

1921.   ———. "Saints." *Three Penny Review* [Berkeley] 6.2 (1985): 14–15.
Rpt. in *Darkness* 145–58.
A child of divorced parents receives a book on a Hindu saint from his father after witnessing his mother's lover courting another woman.

1922.   ———. "Tamurlaine." *Canadian Forum* June–July 1985: 29–31.
Rpt. in *Darkness* 117–25.
Legal and illegal immigrant workers in a restaurant are surprised by a raid.

1923.   ———. "The Tenant." *Literary Review* 29.4 (1986): 481–92.
Rpt. in *Best American Stories: 1987*. Ed. Ann Beattie. Boston: Houghton, 1987. 178–92.
Describes a divorced woman's various sexual encounters.

1924.   ———. *The Tiger's Daughter*. Boston: Houghton, 1971. London: Chatto, 1973. New York: Penguin, 1987.
An Indian woman educated in the US returns to India after a seven-year absence.

1925.   ———. *Wife*. Boston: Houghton, 1975.
Describes a traditional Indian woman who is unable to adjust to her marriage and her life in the US.

1926.   ———. "A Wife's Story." *Mother Jones* Jan. 1986: 33–40.
Rpt. in *86: Best Canadian Stories*. Ed. David Helwig and Sandra Martin. N.p.: Oberon Press, 1986. 45–63.
An Indian woman in America reveals her changing consciousness.

1927.   ———. "The World according to Hsu." *Chatelaine* [Toronto] Oct. 1983: 84+.
    Rpt. in *Darkness* 37–56.
    Describes a couple's adventure in an island off the coast of Africa.

1928.   Mukherjee, Bharati, with Clark Blaise. *Days and Nights in Calcutta.* Garden City, NY: Doubleday, 1977.
    Travel memoir: a husband and wife chronicle a year spent in Bombay and Calcutta in 1973–74.
    Rev. Robert S. Anderson, *Canadian Literature* 76 (1978): 111–13; Uma Parameswaran, *Journal of Canadian Fiction* 24 (1979): 156–58.

1928a.   ———. *The Sorrow and the Terror: The Haunting Legacy of Air India 182.* New York: Penguin, 1987.
    Reconstruction of the terrorist bombing of Air India Flight #182, on 23 June 1985, and a second, related incident at Tokyo Airport.

1929.   Naim, C. M. "On Becoming American." *Toronto South Asian Review* 1.1 (1982): 48+.
    Essay.

1930.   **Namjoshi, Suniti. *The Conversations of Cow.* Illus. Sarah Baylis. London: Women's Press, 1985.
    Dialogue between a lesbian separatist and a brahmin lesbian cow.

1931.   ———. *Feminist Fables.* London: Sheba Feminist Publishers, 1981.
    A feminist rendition of traditional fables.

1932.   Naqvi, Tahira. "Summer Sojourn." *Bridge* 9.2 (1984): 32–35.
    A South Asian immigrant recounts her encounter with a cleaning woman at her parents' home in Pakistan.

1933.   Nazareth, Peter. "The Confessor." *Dhana* [Kampala] 4.2 (1974–75): 69–73.
    Rev. version in *Short Story International* Oct. 1981: 151–57.
    Describes a voyeur.

1934.   ———. "Departure." *OKIKE* [Nigeria] 10 (May 1976): 38–48.
    Rpt. in *Toronto South Asian Review* 1.2 (1982): 65+.
    Ch. 24 of *The General Is Up.*

1935.   ———. "Dom." *Ghala* [Nairobi] 9.1 (1972).
    Rpt. in *Goa Today* [Panjim, Goa] 5.10 (1972); *Yardbird Reader* 4 (1975): 42–47.
    A comic tale about a man whose love affairs always end miserably.

1936.   ———. "Eccentric Ferns." *Dhana* [Kampala] 2.1 (1972).
    Rpt. in *Short Story International* Apr. 1980: 127–32.
    Describes a nonconformist in a Catholic community.

1937.   ———. *The General Is Up: A Novel.* Calcutta: Writers Workshop, 1984.
    Depicts Goans in East Africa.

1938.   ———. "The Headmaster." *East Africa Journal* [Nairobi] 5 (Jan. 1968): 23–27.
    A conflict erupts between an authoritarian headmaster and a Dutch chaplain.

1939. ———. *In a Brown Mantle.* 1972. Nairobi: Kenya Literature Bureau, 1981.
　　　Excerpt in *Journal of South Asian Literature* 18.1 (1983): 40–56. Excerpt entitled "The Leader" in *Merely a Matter of Colour.* Ed. Arnold Kingston and E. A. Markham. Middlesex, Eng.: "Q" Books, 1973.
　　　A political novel about postindependence Africa.
　　　Rev. Lino Leitão, *Toronto South Asian Review* 1.1 (1982): 98+.

1940. ———. "The Institute." *Dhana* [Kampala] 4.1 (1974): 65–69.
　　　A controversy arises over the renaming of the Goan Inst. in Africa.

1941. ———. "Mama's Umbrella." *Pacific Quarterly Moana* [Hamilton, NZ] 3.2 (1978): 179–85.
　　　Rpt. in *Goa Today* [Panjim, Goa] 14.11 (1980).

1942. ———. "Moneyman." *Zuka* [Nairobi] 6 (Jan. 1972): 36–39.
　　　Describes a civil servant who practices usury.

1943. ———. "The Night the Ghost Reappeared: Another Fantasie." *Penpoint* [Kampala] 7 (Mar. 1960).

1944. ———. "Rosie's Theme." *Callaloo* 2 (Feb. 1978): 44–60.
　　　Rpt. in *Literary Review* 29.4 (1986): 496–506.
　　　An autobiographical essay about the diaspora of the Goans.
　　　Rev. Renato Rodrigues, *Toronto South Asian Review* 2.3 (1984): 88+.

1945. Obeyesekere, Ranjini. "Despair." *Hemisphere* [Austral.] Dec. 1974: 36–37.
　　　A despondent female doctor runs into a beggar woman whose child is about to die.

1946. ———. *"A Treasure in the Forest" and Other Stories.* 1969. Colombo: Lake House Publishers, 1974.

1947. **Ondaatje, Michael. *Coming through Slaughter.* Toronto: Anansi, 1976. New York: Norton, 1977.
　　　A novel about the jazz musician Buddy Bolden.
　　　Rev. Sam Solecki, *Canadian Forum* 56 (Dec. 1976–Jan. 1977): 46.

1948. ———. *In the Skin of a Lion.* New York: Knopf, 1987.
　　　Picaresque novel.

1949. ———. "Jaffna Afternoons." *Interchange: A Symposium on Regionalism, Internationalism, and Ethnicity in Literature.* Ed. Linda Spalding and Frank Stewart. Honolulu: Interarts, 1980: 31–33.
　　　Autobiographical story.

1950. ———. *Running in the Family.* Toronto: McClelland, 1982.
　　　Excerpts entitled "Monsoon Notebooks" in *Hawaii Review* 13 (1982): 80–83; *Literary Review* 29.4 (1986): 512–20.
　　　An autobiographical account of a visit to Sri Lanka.

1951. ———. "The Scratch." *Interchange: A Symposium on Regionalism, Internationalism, and Ethnicity in Literature.* Ed. Linda Spalding and Frank Stewart. Honolulu: Interarts, 1980: 27–29.
　　　Autobiographical essay.

1952. **Pandya, Sandy. "Practical Jokers." *Quarry* [Kingston, ON] 28.4 (1979): 16–19.
A joke leads to a homicide.

1953. **Parameswaran, Uma. "Panchali's Hour of Choice." *The First Writers Workshop Literary Reader.* Ed. P. Lal. Calcutta: Writers Workshop, 1972.

1954. Parthasarathy, R. *"The Mother's Call" and Other Stories.* Bombay: Bharatiya Vidya Bhavan, 1972.
Eleven short stories.

1955. Qazi, Javaid. "The Beast of Bengal." *Toronto South Asian Review* 4.2 (1985): 34+.
Rpt. in *Chelsea* 46 (1987): 266–73.
Short story.

1956. **Rajan, Balachandra. *The Dark Dancer.* New York: Simon, 1958. London: Heinemann, 1959. New Delhi: Arnold-Heinemann, 1975.
An Indian returns home from Cambridge Univ. during the nationalist movement of 1942.

1957. ———. *Too Long in the West.* London: Heinemann, 1961. New York: Atheneum, 1962.
Describes the ordeals of a woman who returns to India after being in America.

1958. Rama Rau, Santha. *The Adventuress: A Novel.* New York: Harper, 1970. London: Joseph, 1971.
After World War II, a young Filipino woman seeks to go to the US.

1959. ———. *Gifts of Passage: Autobiography.* London: Gollancz, 1961. New York: Harper, 1961.
Describes the customs and peculiarities of various peoples.

1960. ———. *Home to India.* New York: Harper, 1945.
Autobiographical narrative of someone who has spent ten years in Europe.
Rev. Isabelle Mallet, *New York Times* 3 June 1945: 4; Margaret Williamson, *Christian Science Monitor* 5 June 1945: 14.

1961. ———. *Remember the House.* New York: Harper, 1956. London: Gollancz, 1956.
Westernized life in Bombay is contrasted with traditional life in Malabar.

1962. ———. *View to the Southeast.* New York: Harper, 1957.
Travel memoir about Southeast Asia.
Rev. Percy Wood, *Chicago Sunday Tribune* 13 Oct. 1957: 3.

1963. Rao, Raja. *The Cat and Shakespeare: A Tale of India.* New York: Macmillan, 1964. Delhi: Hind Pocket Books, 1971.
A comedy about an office clerk in Kerala during World War II.

1964. ———. *Comrade Kirillov.* Delhi: Orient Paperbacks, 1976.

1965.   ———. *"The Cow of the Barricades" and Other Stories*. London: Oxford UP, 1947.
         A collection of short stories.

1966.   ———. *Kanthapura*. Introd. C. D. Narasimhaiah. London: Allen, 1938. Delhi: Oxford UP, 1974.
         Describes the effect of the nationalist movement of the 1930s on a village in Mysore.

1967.   ———. *The Policeman and the Rose*. Afterword C. D. Narasimhaiah. Delhi: Oxford UP, 1978.
         A collection of short stories.

1968.   ———. *The Serpent and the Rope*. London: Murray, 1960. New Delhi: Orient Paperbacks, 1963.
         A South Indian brahmin married to a French woman is ill at ease in Europe.

Rau, Santha Rama. See Rama Rau, Santha.

1969.   Rustomji, Roshni. "The Foreign Affair." *Toronto South Asian Review* 2.2 (1983): 3–10.
         Short story.

1970.   ———. "Jerbanoo." *Toronto South Asian Review* 4.2 (1985): 52+.
         Short story.

1971.   ———. "Rhodabeh." *Literary Review* 29.4 (1986): 527–37.
         Describes an invalid woman whose husbands die in succession.

1972.   **Sadhu. "Welcome Address." *Toronto South Asian Review* 2.1 (1983): 69+.
         Short story.

1973.   **Sadiq, Nazneen. "[Excerpt] From 'Smile, You Are in Pakistan.'" *Toronto South Asian Review* 2.2 (1983): 28–31.

1974.   **Selvon, Sam [also Samuel Selvon]. *A Brighter Sun: A Novel*. 1952. New York: Viking, 1953.
         Set in Trinidad, the novel describes the married life of a 16-year-old and his child bride.
         Rev. Edith Efron, *New York Times Book Review* 18 Jan. 1953: 50; Selden Rodman, *Saturday Review* 24 Jan. 1953: 21; *Times Literary Supplement* 11 Feb. 1972: 145.

1975.   ———. "Cane Is Bitter." *Toronto South Asian Review* 1.3 (1983): 1+.
         Short story.

1976.   ———. *The Housing Lark*. London: MacGibbon, 1965.
         Describes the rackets and sexual markets among West Indians in London.
         Rev. Peter Vansittart, *Spectator* 26 Mar. 1965: 410.

1977. ———. *I Hear Thunder.* New York: St. Martin's, 1963.
Describes an interracial couple in Trinidad.
Rev. Dion Reilly, *New York Times Book Review* 18 Aug. 1963: 33; Anthony West, *New Yorker* 7 Dec. 1963: 238–42.

1978. ———. *The Lonely Londoners.* 1956. New York: St. Martin's, 1958.
Describes West Indians in England.
Rev. Whitney Balliett, *New Yorker* 18 Jan. 1958: 99–100.

1979. ———. *Moses Ascending.* London: Davis-Poynter, 1975.
Sequel to *The Lonely Londoners.* Moses, an immigrant, aspires to be a landlord in London and gets embroiled in the smuggling racket of his Pakistani tenants.
Rev. Valentine Cunningham, *Times Literary Supplement* 29 Aug. 1975: 961; Peter Nazareth, *World Literature Today* 51.1 (1977): 150–51.

1980. ———. *Moses Migrating.* Harlow, Essex, Eng.: Longman, 1983.
Sequel to *The Lonely Londoners.*

1981. ———. *The Plains of Caroni.* London: MacGibbon, 1970. Toronto: Williams-Wallace, 1985.
A portion of the work appears as "The Harvester" in *Toronto South Asian Review* 5.1 (1986): 21–30.
Describes a peasant family in postindependence Trinidad.

1982. ———. *Those Who Eat the Cascadura.* London: Davis-Poynter, 1972.
Romantic fiction.
Rev. *Times Literary Supplement* 11 Feb. 1972: 145.

1983. ———. *Turn Again Tiger.* London: MacGibbon, 1958. New York: St. Martin's, 1959.
Sequel to *A Brighter Sun.*
Rev. Selden Rodman, *New York Times Book Review* 3 May 1959: 28.

1984. ———. *Ways of Sunlight.* New York: St. Martin's, 1957. London: Longman Drumbeat, 1979.
A collection of nineteen short stories. The first nine are about life in Trinidad and the rest are about West Indians living in London.
Rev. Rye Vervaet, *New York Times Book Review* 2 Nov. 1958: 40; Francis Wyndham, *Spectator* 28 Feb. 1958: 273.

1985. Seth, Vikram. *From Heaven Lake: Travels through Sinkiang and Tibet.* London: Chatto, 1983.
Travel memoir.
Rev. Jonathan Mirsky, *New Statesman* 7 Oct. 1983: 25.

1986. ———. *Mappings.* Calcutta: Writers Workshop, 1982.

1987. Shahane, Vasant A. *Doctor Fauste.* New Delhi: Arnold-Heinemann, 1987.
An Indian version of the Faustus legend.

1988. ———. *Prajapati: God of the People.* New Delhi: Arnold-Heinemann, 1984.
A novel in which four young men, representing the four castes of Hindu society, make a solemn vow of friendship at their graduation from college.
Rev. M. K. Naik, *Indian Book Chronicle* 1 July 1984: 227–29.

1989.   **Sharma, Hari Prakash. "Coming Back." *Toronto South Asian Review* 1.3 (1983): 82+.
Short story.

1990.   **Singh, Hardev. "Hanuman." *Toronto South Asian Review* 2.1 (1983): 86+.
Short story.

1991.   **Sugunasiri, Suwanda. "Fellow Travelers." Trans. from Sinhala by author. *Toronto South Asian Review* 1.1 (1982): 63+.
A short story about an abused domestic servant in Sri Lanka.

1992.   ———. "The Ingrate." Trans. from Sinhala by author. *Journal of South Asian Literature* 2.4 (1966): 25–30.
Describes a daughter's reaction to an ailing mother.

1993.   **Vassanji, M. G. "A Matter of Detail." *Asianadian* 4.4 (1983): 3–6.
A religious Indian immigrant is troubled by his feelings of sexual desire for white women.

1994.   ———. "Waiting for the Goddess." *Toronto South Asian Review* 1.2 (1982): 78+.
A woman in an East African town is denounced as a whore for spending time with a white man.

1995.   Walji, Perviz. "Thoughts of a Winter's Night." *Toronto South Asian Review* 3.1 (1984): 6+.
Short story.

1996.   Walke, John. "Blossoms in the Dust." *Bridge* 8.4 (1983): 5–10.
Working on an essay assignment, a student daydreams about Calcutta.

Poetry

1997.   Alexander, Meena. *The Bird's Bright Ring: A Long Poem*. Calcutta: Writers Workshop, 1976.

1998.   ———. *House of a Thousand Doors*. Washington: Three Continents Press, 1987.

1999.   ———. *I Root My Name*. Calcutta: United Writers, 1977.

2000.   ———. *Stone Roots*. New Delhi: Arnold-Heinemann, 1980.

2001.   ———. *Without Place*. Calcutta: Writers Workshop, 1977.

2002.   **Bannerji, Himani. *A Separate Sky: A Book of Poems*. Toronto: Domestic Bliss Press, 1982.
Rev. Sabi M. Jailail, *Asianadian* 4.4 (1982): 22–25.

2003.   **Bhaggiyadatta, Krisantha Sri. *Domestic Bliss*. Toronto: Domestic Bliss Press, 1982.

2004.   Chandra, G. S. Sharat. *Aliens*. Safford, AZ: Scattershot Press, 1986.

2005.   ———. *April in Nanjangud*. London: London Magazine, 1971.

2006.   ———. *"Bharat Natyam Dancer" and Other Poems*. Calcutta: Writers Workshop, 1968.

2007.   ———. *The Ghost of Meaning*. Lewiston, ID: Confluence Press, 1983.

2008.   ———. *Heirloom*. Delhi: Oxford UP, 1982.

2009.   ———. *Offsprings of Servagna*. Calcutta: Writers Workshop, 1975.

2010.   ———. *Once or Twice*. Sutton, Surrey: Hippopotamus Press, 1975.

2011.   ———. *Will This Forest*. Milwaukee, WI: Morgan Press, 1969.
        Surreal poems.

2012.   **Crusz, Rienzi. *Elephant and Ice*. Erin, ON: Porcupine's Quill, 1980.

2013.   ———. *Flesh and Thorn*. Illus. Virgil Burnett. Stratford, ON: Pasdeloup Press, 1974.

2014.   ———. *Singing against the Wind*. Erin, ON: Porcupine's Quill, 1985.
        Rev. Michael Estok, *Toronto South Asian Review* 4.2 (1985): 94+.

2015.   ———. *A Time for Loving*. Introd. Réshard Gool. Toronto: TSAR, 1986.

2016.   **Dabydeen, Cyril. *Distances*. Fredericton, NB: Fiddlehead Poetry Books, 1977.

2017.   ———. *Elephants Make Good Stepladders: Poems*. London, ON: Third Eye, 1982.

2018.   ———. *Goatsong*. Oaksville, ON: Mosaic Press/Valley Editions, 1977.

2019.   ———. *Heart's Frame*. Cornwall, ON: Vesta, 1979.
        Rev. Lakshmi Gill, *Asianadian* 2.3 (1979): 27.

2020.   ———. *Islands Lovelier than a Vision*. Yorkshire, Eng.: Peepal Tree Press, 1986.

2021.   ———. *Poems in Recession*. Georgetown, Guyana: Sadeek Press, 1972.

2022.   ———. *They Call This Planet Earth*. Ottawa: Borealis Press, 1979.

2023.   *Da Silva, Marion. *Faces of Life*. Toronto: Mission Press, 1982.

2024.   **Day, Stacey B. *Poems and Etudes*. Montreal: Cultural and Educational Productions, 1968.

2025.   ———. *Ten Poems and a Letter from America for Mr. Sinha*. Montreal: Cultural and Educational Productions, [1971].

2026.   Furtado, R[aul] de L. *"The Oleanders" and Other Poems*. Calcutta: Writers Workshop, 1968.

2027.   Ghose, Zulfikar. *Jets from Orange: Poems by Zulfikar Ghose*. London: Macmillan, 1967.

2028.   ———. *The Loss of India*. London: Routledge, 1964.

2029.   ———. *A Memory of Asia: New and Selected Poems*. Austin, TX: Curbstone Publishing, 1984.
        Rev. Shirley Lim, *CRNLE* 1 (1986): 22–25.

2030.   ———. *The Violent West: Poems by Zulfikar Ghose*. London: Macmillan, 1972.

2031.   **Gill, Darshan. *Man and the Mirror*. Surrey, BC: Indo-Canadian Publishers, 1976.

2032.   **Gill, Lakshmi. *During Rain, I Plant Chrysanthemums*. Toronto: Ryerson Press, 1966.

2033.   ———. *First Clearing (An Immigrant's Tour of Life): Poems*. Manila: Estaniel Press, 1972.

2034.   ———. *Mind Walls*. Fredericton, NB: Fiddlehead Poetry Books, 1970.

2035.   ———. *Novena to St. Jude Thaddeus*. Fredericton, NB: Fiddlehead Poetry Books, 1979.
         Rev. Carol Matsui, *Asianadian* 3.1 (1980): 28–29.

2036.   **Gill, Stephen M. *Moans and Waves*. Cornwall, ON: Vesta, 1982.

2037.   ———. *Reflections: A Collection of Poems*. Cornwall, ON: Rytes, 1972; Vesta, 1973.

2038.   ———. *Reflections and Wounds*. Cornwall, ON: Vesta, 1978.
         Rev. Rajesh Shukla, *Christian Monitor* 2 Oct. 1981: 6–8; Frank M. Tierney, *Canadian India Times* 15 Nov. 1973: 5.

2039.   ———. *Wounds: A Collection of Poems*. Cornwall, ON: Vesta, 1974.
         Rev. *Canadian India Times* 19 Sept. 1974: 5; Linda Annesley Pyke, *Quill & Quire* June 1974: 12.

2040.   **Gool, Réshard. *"In Medusa's Eye" and Other Poems*. Introd. Ronald Baker. Charlottetown, PE: Square Deal Publications, 1972. Rev. ed. Charlottetown, PE: Square Deal Publications, 1979.

2041.   **Hardev. *Doodles and Scribbles*. London, ON: Shabd Publications, 1978.

2042.   **Itwaru, Arnold. *Shattered Songs: A Journey from Somewhere to Somewhere*. Toronto: Aya Press, 1982.
         Rev. F. Ivor Case, *Toronto South Asian Review* 2.1 (1983): 100+.

2043.   **Kalsey, Surjeet. *Speaking to the Winds*. London, ON: Third Eye Publications, 1982.
         Translation.

2045.   **Namjoshi, Suniti. *The Authentic Lie*. Fredericton, NB: Fiddlehead Poetry Books, 1982.
         Rev. Ian Sowton, *Canadian Literature* 97 (1983): 124–26.

2046.   ———. *Cyclone in Pakistan*. Calcutta: Writers Workshop, 1971.

2047.   ———. *From the Bedside Book of Nightmares*. Fredericton, NB: Fiddlehead Poetry Books/Goose Lane, 1984.
         Rev. Lorraine M. York, *Canadian Literature* 105 (1985): 191–92.

2048.   ———. *The Jackass and the Lady*. Calcutta: Writers Workshop, 1980.

2049.   ———. *More Poems*. Calcutta: Writers Workshop, 1970.

2050.   ———. *Poems*. Calcutta: Writers Workshop, 1967.

2051.   **Ondaatje, Michael. *The Collected Works of Billy the Kid*. Toronto: Anansi; New York: Norton, 1970.
       Poetry and prose.

2052.   ———. *The Concessions*. Blyth, ON: M. Ondaatje, 1982.

2053.   ———. *The Dainty Monsters*. Toronto: Coach House, 1967.

2054.   ———. *Elimination Dance*. Ilderton, ON: Nairn Coldstream, 1978.

2055.   ———. *The Man with Seven Toes*. 1969. Toronto: Coach House, 1971.

2056.   ———. *"Rat Jelly" and Other Poems*. Toronto: Coach House, 1973. Rev. ed. *"Rat Jelly" and Other Poems, 1963–78*. London: Marion Boyars, 1980.

2057.   ———. *Secular Love: Poems*. New York: Norton, 1985.

2058.   ———. *There's a Trick with a Knife I'm Learning to Do: Poems, 1963–1978*. Toronto: McClelland; New York: Norton, 1979.

2059.   ———. *Tin Roof*. Lantzville, BC: Island Writing Series, 1982.

2060.   **Padmanab, S. *Ages of Birds*. Calcutta: Writers Workshop, 1976.

2061.   ———. *A Separate Life*. Calcutta: Writers Workshop, 1974.

2062.   ———. *Songs of the Slave: A Collection of Poems*. Cornwall, ON: Vesta, 1977.

2063.   **Parameswaran, Uma. *Cyclic Hope, Cyclic Pain*. Calcutta: Writers Workshop, 1973.

2064.   ———. *Trishanku*. Toronto: TSAR; Madras: East-West Press, 1988.

2065.   Rajan, Balachandra. *"Monsoon" and Other Poems*. Cambridge: n.p., 1943.

2066.   **Rajan, Tilottama. *Myth in a Metal Mirror*. Calcutta: Writers Workshop, 1967.

2067.   Ramanujan, A. K. *Relations*. London: Oxford UP, 1971.

2068.   ———. *Selected Poems*. Delhi: Oxford UP, 1976.

2069.   ———. *The Striders*. London: Oxford UP, 1967.

2070.   **Rampuri, Jeewan, and Robert Sward. *Cheers for Muktananda*. Victoria, BC: Soft Press, 1976.

2071.   **Rasha, Mittar. *Murmurs*. Cornwall, ON: Vesta, 1979.

2072.   **Ravi, Ravinder. *Restless Soul*. Surrey, BC: Indo Canada Publishers, 1978.

2073.   ———. *Wind Song*. Surrey, BC: Indo Canada Publishers, 1980.

2074.   Seth, Vikram. *The Golden Gate: A Novel in Verse.* New York: Random, 1986.
        Rev. Martin Amis, *Observer* 22 June 1986: 23; Raymond Mungo, *New York Times Book Review* 11 May 1986: 11.

2075.   ———. *The Humble Administrator's Garden.* Manchester: Carcanet, 1985.
        Rev. Bruce King, *Sewanee Review* 94 (1986): 44–46.

2076.   Sharma, P. D. *The New Caribbean Man.* Hayward, CA: Carib House, 1981.

2077.   **Singh, Nirmala. *The Shiva Dance.* Cornwall, ON: Vesta, 1979.

2078.   **Weerasinghe, Asoka. *Exile.* Cornwall, ON: Vesta, 1978.

2079.   ———. *Home Again Lanka.* Ottawa: Commoner's, 1981.

2080.   ———. *Hot Tea and Cinnamon Buns.* Cornwall, ON: Vesta, 1980.

2081.   ———. *Poems for Jeannie.* Cornwall, ON: Vesta, 1976.

2082.   ———. *Poems in November.* Ottawa: Commoner's, 1977.

2083.   ———. *Selected Poems (1958–83).* Cornwall, ON: Vesta, 1983.

Drama

2084.   Alexander, Meena. *In the Middle Earth. Enact* [New Delhi] 125–26 (May-June 1977): n. pag.
        A one-act play about a woman building a wall.

2085.   **Cota, Alba. *A Better Way. Toronto South Asian Review* 3.1 (1984): 29+.

2086.   **Cowasjee, Saros. *The Last of the Maharajas.* Calcutta: Writers Workshop, 1980.
        Screenplay based on Mulk Raj Anand's novel *Private Life of an Indian Prince.*

2087.   Desani, G[ovindas] V[ishnoodas]. *Hali: A Poetic Play.* Foreword T. S. Eliot and E. M. Forster. London: Saturn, 1950. Calcutta: Writers Workshop, 1969.
        A beautiful man is envied by gods and mortals.

2088.   **Gill, Tarlochan Singh. *Ashok.* Toronto: Asia Publications, 1983.
        Translated from Punjabi.

2089.   Nazareth, Peter. *Brave New Cosmos. Origin East Africa.* Ed. David Cook. London: Heinemann, 1965. 167–78.
        Rpt. in *Goa Today* [Panjim, Goa] 7.5 (1972).

2090.   ———. *Two Radio Plays.* Kampala: East African Literature Bureau, 1976.
        The two plays are *The Hospital* and *X.*

2091.   **Parameswaran, Uma. *Rootless but Green Are the Boulevard Trees. Toronto South Asian Review* 4.1 (1985): 62–103.

2092.   Rama Rau, Santha. *A Passage to India*. Introd. Vasant A. Shahane. London: Edward Arnold, 1960. New York: Harcourt, 1961. Delhi: Oxford UP, 1976.
         A dramatic version of E. M. Forster's novel.

2093.   **Rode, Ajmer. *One Girl, One Dream*. *Toronto South Asian Review* 2.1 (1983): 89+.
         Translated from Punjabi.

Vietnamese and Other Southeast Asian American Literature

Prose

2094. Công-Huyền-Tôn-Nữ Nha-Trang. "Memories of a Huế Girlhood." *Vietnam Forum* 3 (1984): 147–54.
Childhood reminiscences.

2095. Doãn Quốc Sỹ. "The Rat." Trans. Võ Đình. *Vietnam Forum* 1 (1983): 17–23.
A political allegory.

2096. Hà Thúc Sinh [Phạm Vĩnh Xuân]. "Welcome to Trang Lon, Re-education Camp." *Vietnam Forum* 6 (1985): 260–70.
Prologue and ch. 1 of *Schools of Blood and Tears* (a memoir of communist reeducation camps), adapted by Huỳnh Sanh Thông from the Vietnamese *Dai-hoc Mau*. San Jose, CA: Nhan-Van, 1985.

2097. *Ho, Mary. "The Incorrigible Daughter." *Bamboo Ridge: The Hawaii Writer's Quarterly* 17 (1982–83): 30–33.
A sketch of a Laotian refugee in Hawaii who has difficulties with English and with a daughter who keeps running away with men.

2098. Law-Yone, Wendy. *The Coffin Tree.* New York: Knopf, 1983. Boston: Beacon, 1987.
A novel concerning a young Burmese woman who almost loses her mind upon immigrating from Burma to America.

2099. Lê Tất Điều. "Ocean Light." Trans. Võ-Đình Mai [Võ Đình] *Vietnam Forum* 9 (1987): 138–48.
Describes an incident aboard a ship that has rescued some boat people.

2100. Linh Bảo [Võ thị Diệu Viên]. "Kites and Kites." Trans. Huỳnh Sanh Thông. *Vietnam Forum* 3 (1984): 155–56.
An allegorical sketch about Vietnamese who have left their native land.

2101. Minh Đức Hoài Trinh. [pseud.]. "Karma" Trans. Cao Thị Nhủ Quỳnh and John C. Schafer. *Vietnam Forum* 8 (1986): 234–39.
A short story about a woman impregnated by a pirate.

2102. ———. *This Side, the Other Side (Bên Ni Bên Tê).* Montrose, CA: Occidental Press, 1985.
Novel.

2103. Nguyễn Mộng Giác. [pseud.]. "Return to the Circus." Trans. Huỳnh Sahn Thông. *Vietnam Forum* 4 (1984): 106–10.
A violinist becomes a circus clown.

2104. ———. "Suicides." Trans. Huỳnh Sanh Thông. *Vietnam Forum* 7 (1986): 239–75.
Recounts several incidents of actual and attempted suicide that occur after the Vietnam War.

2105. Nguyễn Ngọc Ngạn. "The Two Ducks." Trans. Stephen O. Lesser and Huỳnh Sanh Thông. *Vietnam Forum* 5 (1985): 164–73.
A prisoner tries in vain to save the two ducks he has been raising at a reeducation camp.

2106. ———. *The Will of Heaven*. New York: Dutton, 1982.
Autobiography.

2107. Nguyễn, Rose. "My Name Is River." *Gió Đông: Eastwind/From the Vietnamese Students of UCLA*. Ed. Trần Quang Tri. Los Angeles: n.p., n.d.
Rpt. in *Pacific Ties* Nov.-Dec. 1986: 8+.
A biographical story about a Vietnamese couple who rebel against French colonization in the 1930s.

2108. ———. "Only Butterflies are Free." *Gió Đông: Eastwind/From the Vietnamese Students of UCLA*. Ed. Trần Quang Tri. Los Angeles: n.p., n.d.
Rpt. in *Pacific Ties* Nov.-Dec. 1986: 9+.
A story about boat people.

2109. Nguyễn Tú An [pseud.]. "Death of a Stranger." *Pacific Ties* Nov.-Dec. 1986: 8.
Describes the struggle and exploitation of immigrants.

2110. Nhật Tiến [Bùi Nhật Tiến]. "In the Footsteps of a Water Buffalo." Trans. Huỳnh Sanh Thông. *Vietnam Forum* 8 (1986): 218–28.
Describes farming conditions under the communist government.

2111. Tran Van Dinh. *Blue Dragon, White Tiger: A Tet Story*. Philadelphia: TriAm Press, 1983.
A novel concerning a young Vietnamese man's return to Vietnam after living in the US.
Rev. Heinz Fenkl, *Bridge* 9.2 (1984): 37–38.

2112. ———. "Death in the Land of Skyscraper." *Bridge* 8.1 (1982): 22.
Describes the immigrants' sense of loss upon coming to America.

2113. ———. *No Passenger on the River*. New York: Vantage, 1965.
A novel set in Vietnam.

2114. Trùng Dương [Nguyễn Thị Thái]. "Sleep Well, Mother." *Vietnam Forum* 1 (1983): 99–104.
Reflections upon a mother's death.

2115. Truong Nhu Tang, with David Chanoff and Doan Van Toai. *A Vietcong Memoir*. San Diego: Harcourt, 1985.
Autobiography.

2116. Tuong Nang Tien [pseud.]. "Communism and Guigoz-Canism." *Vietnam Forum* 7 (1986): 228–37.
A satirical piece on Communism.

2117. **Võ Kỳ Điền. "Brother Ten." Trans. Huỳnh Sanh Thông. *Vietnam Forum* 9 (1987): 252–61.
A story about a communist cadre put in charge of education in a province of South Vietnam after 1975.

2118.   Võ Phiến [Đoàn Thế Nhởn]. "A Spring of Quiet and Peace." Trans. Huỳnh Sanh Thông. *Vietnam Forum* 1 (1983): 93–98.
    A prose poem about being uprooted.

Poetry

Vietnam Forum regularly publishes poems by Vietnamese immigrants.

2119.   Bùi-Tiến-Khôi [Huy-Lực]. *America, My First Feelings: Poems*. Houston: privately printed, 1981.

2120.   Du Tử Lê. *Thơ Tình (Love Poem)*. Orange County, CA: Tu sach van hoc Nhan chung Hoa Ky, 1984.
    In Vietnamese and English.

2121.   Larson, Wendy Wilder, and Trần Thị Nga. *Shallow Graves: Two Women and Vietnam*. New York: Random, 1986.

2122.   Nguyễn Long. *Thỏ con đừờng Máu & Nước Mắt: The Road of Blood & Tears*. Santa Ana, CA: privately printed, 1981.

Nhất Hạnh, [Thích]. See Thích Nhất-Hạnh.

2123.   Thích Nhất-Hạnh [also Nhất Hạnh]. *The Cry of Vietnam*. Trans. author with Helen Coutant. Drawings by Võ Đinh. Santa Barbara, CA: Unicorn Press, 1968.

2124.   ———. *The Viet Nam*. Santa Barbara, CA: Unicorn Press, 1967.

2125.   ———. *Zen Poems*. Trans. Teo Savory. Greensboro, NC: Unicorn Press, 1976.

Literature for Children and Young Adults: Selected Books

2126.   Arguilla, Manuel, and Lyd Arguilla. *Stories of Juan Tamad*. Illus. Elizaldo Navarro. Manila: Alberto S. Florentino, 1965.

2127.   Aruego, José. *Juan and the Asuangs: A Tale of Philippine Ghosts and Spirits*. Illus. author. New York: Scribner's, 1970.
        A boy rescues the animals in his village from the *Asuang*s, or jungle spirits.

2128.   ———. *The King and His Friends*. Illus. author. New York: Scribner's, 1969.
        For grades 1–3. The king tries to stop a unicorn stampede.

2129.   ———. *Look What I Can Do*. Illus. author. New York: Scribner's, 1971.
        For preschool–grade 2. Two carabaos learn that imitation can lead to trouble.

2130.   ———. *Pilyo the Piranha*. Illus. author. New York: Macmillan, 1971.
        For preschool–kindergarten. A piranha wants to eat a man who is sleeping.

2131.   ———. *Symbiosis: A Book of Unusual Friendships*. Illus. author. New York: Scribner's, 1970.
        For grades 1–3. Describes mutual exchanges between completely different animals.

2132.   Aruego, José, and Ariane Aruego. *A Crocodile's Tale: A Philippine Folk Story*. New York: Scribner's, 1972. New York: Scholastic, 1975.
        For preschool–kindergarten.

2133.   Bagai, Leona B. *East Indians and Pakistanis in America*. Minneapolis: Lerner Publishers, 1972.
        Nonfiction.

2134.   Chang, Diana. *An Animal Named Year: The Story of the Chinese New Year Retold by Diana Chang*. Illus. Helen Chu. Oakland: Four Treasure Press, 1980.

2135.   Chang, Isabelle. *Tales from Old China: A Collection of Chinese Folktales, Fairy Tales, and Fables*. Illus. Tony Chen. New York: Random, 1969.
        A collection of Chinese folk and fairy tales.

2136.   Chang, Kathleen. *The Iron Moonhunter*. Illus. author. San Francisco: Children's Book Press, 1977.
        Based on a legend about Chinese American railroad builders. In English and Chinese.
        Rev. Judy Yung, *Bridge* 6.1 (1978): 63–64.

2137.   Chen, Tony [Anthony Chen]. *Run, Zebra, Run*. Illus. author. New York: Lothrop, 1972.
        For grades 1–4. Poetry book about wildlife.

2138.   Chen, Tony, and Suzanne Noguere. *Little Koala*. Illus. Tony Chen. New York: Holt, 1979.
For kindergarten–grade 2. Depicts animals in Australia.

2139.   Chen, Yuan-tsung. *The Dragon's Village*. New York: Pantheon, 1980.
For grades 8–up.

2140.   Fuentes, Vilma M. *The Fairy of Masara*. Quezon City, Philippines: New Day Publishers, 1984.
A greedy farmer is transformed into a crocodile.

2141.   ———. *Kimod & the Swan Maiden*. Quezon City, Philippines: New Day Publishers, 1984.
Kimod marries the swan maiden through trickery.

2142.   ———. *Manggob & His Golden Top*. Quezon City, Philippines: New Day Publishers, 1985.
A story of a child warrior.

2143.   ———. *The Monkey & the Crocodile*. Quezon City, Philippines: New Day Publishers, 1984.
A story about a cruel monkey trickster.

2144.   **Gill, Stephen. *Simon and the Snow King*. Cornwall, ON: Vesta, 1982.

2145.   Hernandez, Tomas. *Under the Coconut Tree*. Honolulu: General Assistance Center for the Pacific, Coll. of Education, Educational Foundations, Univ. of Hawaii, 1976.
The story of a young immigrant from the Philippines who encounters prejudice.

Houston, Jeanne Wakatsuki, and James Houston. *Farewell to Manzanar*. See #779.

2146.   Huynh Quang Nhuong. *The Land I Lost: Adventures of a Boy in Vietnam*. Illus. Võ-Đình Mai. New York: Harper, 1982.
For grades 7–up. Reminiscences of the author's youth in Vietnam.

2147.   Ignacio, Melissa Macagba. *The Philippines: Roots of My Heritage (A Journey of Discovery by a Pilipina American Teenager)*. San Jose, CA: Pilipino Development Assn., 1977.
Autobiography.

2148.   Joe, Jeanne. *Ying-Ying: Pieces of a Childhood*. Illus. Faustino Caigoy. San Francisco: East/West Publishing, 1982.
For grades 4–6.

Kaneko, Hisakazu. *Manjiro: The Man Who Discovered America*. See #834.

2149.   Kang, Younghill. *Happy Grove*. Illus. Leroy Baldridge. New York: Scribner's, 1933.

2150.   Kim Yong Ik. *Blue in the Seed*. Illus. Artur Marokvia. Boston: Little, 1964.

2151.   ———. *The Dividing Gourd*. Illus. Sidonie Coryn. New York: Knopf, 1962.
A novel about a Korean fisherwoman.

2152. ———. *The Happy Days*. Illus. Artur Marokvia. Boston: Little, 1960. Published in England as *The Days of Happiness*. London: Hutchinson, 1962.
For grades 5–9. Set in Korea.

2153. ———. *The Moons of Korea*. Seoul: Korean Information Service, 1959. Nonfiction.

2154. ———. *The Shoes from Yang San Valley*. Illus. Park Minja. Garden City, NY: Doubleday, 1970.
A pair of silk brocade shoes reminds a boy in wartorn Korea of a happy past.

2155. *Kodani, Arthur. *Inside Story (One Point of View)*. Honolulu: General Assistance Center for the Pacific, Coll. of Education, Educational Foundations, Univ. of Hawaii, 1976.

2156. Kogawa, Joy. *Naomi's Road*. Illus. Matt Gould. Toronto: New Canadian; London: Oxford UP, 1986.
Novel for young adults about a Japanese Canadian girl's experience during World War II.

2157. Lee, Virginia [Chin-lan]. *The Magic Moth*. Illus. Richard Cuffari. New York: Seabury, 1972.
For grades 2–5. Describes how a family copes with the loss of a child.

2158. Lim, Genny. *Wings for Lai Ho*. San Francisco: East/West, 1982.
A bilingual children's book.

2159. **Lim, John. *At Grandmother's House*. Illus. author. Montreal: Tundra Books, 1977.
Set in Singapore.

2160. ———. *Merchants of the Mysterious East*. Illus. author. Montreal: Tundra Books, 1981.
Set in Singapore.

2161. **Lim, Sing. *West Coast Chinese Boy*. Montreal: Tundra Books, 1979.

2162. Lin, Adet. *"The Milky Way," and Other Chinese Folktales*. Illus. Enrico Arno. New York: Harcourt, 1962.
Contains a dozen folktales.

2163. **Ling, Frieda, and Mee-Shan Lau. *The Maiden of Wu Long*. Toronto: Kids Can Press, 1978.
For grades 1–4.

2164. Lord, Bette Bao. *In the Year of the Boar and Jackie Robinson*. New York: Harper, 1984.
A Chinese child who came to Brooklyn in 1947 learns to enjoy baseball.

2165. Louie, Ai-Ling. *Yeh-Shen: A Cinderella Story from China Retold by Ai-Ling Louie*. Illus. Ed Young. New York: Philomel, 1982.

2166. McCunn, Ruthanne Lum. *Pie-Biter*. Illus. You-shan Tang. San Francisco: Design Enterprises of San Francisco, 1984.
Biographical novel for young people.

2167.　Mitsunaga, Spencer S., and Earle Kunio Mitsunaga. *The Young Castaways*. New York: Vantage, 1967.

2168.　Mizumura, Kazue. *Flower, Moon, Snow: A Book of Haiku*. Illus. author. New York: Crowell, 1977.

2169.　———. *If I Built a Village*. Illus. author. New York: Crowell, 1971. For preschool–grade 3.

2170.　———. *If I Were a Cricket*. Illus. author. New York: Crowell, 1973.

2171.　———. *If I Were a Mother*. Illus. author. New York: Crowell, 1968.

2172.　Namioka, Lensey. *The Samurai and the Long-Nosed Devils*. New York: McKay, 1976. For grades 7–10. An adventure tale set in Japan.

2173.　———. *Valley of the Broken Cherry Trees*. New York: Delacorte, 1980. Fiction for young adults.

2174.　———. *Village of the Vampire Cat*. New York: Delacorte, 1981. For grades 7–up. Set in medieval Japan.

2175.　———. *White Serpent Castle*. New York: McKay, 1976. For grades 7–10. Sequel to *The Samurai and the Long-Nosed Devils*.

2176.　———. *Who's Hu*. New York: Vanguard, 1980. For grades 4–up.

2177.　Paek, Min. *Aekyung's Dream*. Illus. author. San Francisco: Children's Book Press, 1978. Describes a Korean girl who has immigrated recently to America.

2178.　Pahk, Induk, comp. *The Wisdom of the Dragon: Asian Proverbs*. Illus. Gloria Kim. New York: Harper, 1970.

2179.　Ramos, Maximo D. *Boyhood in Monsoon Country*. Manila: Regal Publishing, 1976. Set in the Philippines.

2180.　Robles, Al[fred A.]. *Looking for Ifugao Mountain*. Illus. Jim Dong. San Francisco: Children's Book Press, 1977. A Filipino American child seeks his ancestral past. In English and Pilipino. Rev. Judy Yung, *Bridge* 6.1 (1978): 63–64.

2181.　Sagara, Peter, with R. E. Simon, Jr. *Written on Film*. Chicago: Children's Press, 1970. Autobiography of a photographer.

2182.　Say, Allen. *Dr. Smith's Safari*. Illus. author. New York: Harper, 1972. For grades 1–3. Describes a doctor's interaction with animals.

2183.　———. *The Feast of Lanterns*. New York: Harper, 1976. For grades 3–4. Set in Japan.

2184. ———. *The Ink-Keeper's Apprentice*. New York: Harper, 1979.
For grades 6–up. A teenager in postwar Tokyo is asked by his Korean father whether he would like to go to America.

**Sui Sin Far [Edith Maud Eaton]. *Mrs. Spring Fragrance*. See #530.

2185. **Takashima, Shizuye. *A Child in Prison Camp*. Illus. author. 1971. New York: Morrow, 1974.
For grades 7–9. Describes the author's experiences during World War II in a Canadian prison camp where Japanese Canadians were confined.
Rev. Bruce Iwasaki, *Amerasia Journal* 1.4 (1972): 57–59.

2186. Telemaque, Eleanor Wong. *It's Crazy to Stay Chinese in Minnesota*. New York: Nelson, 1978.
For grades 6–up. Describes the pressure on teenagers to assimilate into white society.
Rev. Judy Yung, *Bridge* 7.2 (1979): 38–39.

2187. ———. *Tai-Wang*. New York: Marek, 1982.

2188. Trần, Khánh Tuyết, ed. *Children of Vietnam: A Storybook for Children*. Berkeley: Indochina Resource Center, 1976.
Prose and poetry. Contains poems by Vietnamese children.

2189. ———. *The Little Weaver of Thai-Yen Village*. Illus. Nancy Hom. Trans. N. H. Jenkins and author. San Francisco: Children's Book Press, 1977.
Centers on a Vietnamese girl who is adopted by an American family.
Rev. Judy Yung, *Bridge* 6.1 (1978): 63–64.

2190. Trần Văn Diên. *The Childhood Memories of Vietnam*. Illus. Kim Bang. El Toro, CA: Bilingual Publishing, 1981.

2191. Uba, Gregory. *Is a Mountain Just a Rock?* Berkeley: Mina Press, 1984.

2192. Uchida, Yoshiko. *The Best Bad Thing*. New York: Atheneum, 1983.

2193. ———. *The Birthday Visitor*. Illus. Charles Robinson. New York: Scribner's, 1975.
For grades 2–4. Set in the US.

2194. ———. *"The Dancing Kettle," and Other Japanese Folk Tales*. Illus. Richard C. Jones. New York: Harcourt, 1949.
For grades 4–6.

2195. ———. *The Forever Christmas Tree*. Illus. Kazue Mizumura. New York: Scribner's, 1963.

2196. ———. *The Full Circle*. Illus. author. New York: Friendship Press, 1957.

2197. ———. *The Happiest Ending*. New York: Atheneum, 1985.
For grades 6–8.

2198. ———. *Hisako's Mysteries*. Illus. Susan Bennett. New York: Scribner's, 1969.
For grades 4–6. Set in modern Japan.

2199. ———. *In-Between Miya*. New York: Scribner's, 1967.
For grades 4–7. Set in Japan.

2200. ———. *A Jar of Dreams*. New York: Atheneum, 1981.
A young girl grows up in a closely knit Japanese American family during a time of great prejudice.

2201. ———. *Journey Home*. Illus. Charles Robinson. New York: Atheneum, 1978.
For grades 5–9. Sequel to *Journey to Topaz*.
Rev. *Bridge* 7.2 (1979): 44.

2202. ———. *Journey to Topaz: A Story of the Japanese American Evacuation*. Illus. Donald Carrick. New York: Scribner's, 1971.
After the attack on Pearl Harbor, an 11-year-old Japanese American girl and her family are forced into a camp in Utah.

2203. ———. *The Magic Listening Cap: More Folk Tales from Japan*. Illus. author. New York: Harcourt, 1955.
For grades 4–6.

2204. ———. *Makoto, the Smallest Boy: A Story of Japan*. Illus. Akihito Shirakawa. New York: Crowell, 1970.

2205. ———. *Mik and the Prowler*. Illus. William M. Hutchinson. New York: Harcourt, 1960.
For preschool–grade 3.

2206. ———. *New Friends for Susan*. Illus. Henry Sugimoto. New York: Scribner's, 1951.
For grades 2–4. Set in California.

2207. ———. *The Promised Year*. Illus. William M. Hutchinson. New York: Harcourt, 1959.
For grades 4–6.

2208. ———. *Rokubei and the Thousand Rice Bowls*. Illus. Kazue Mizumura. New York: Scribner's, 1962.

2209. ———. *The Rooster Who Understood Japanese*. New York: Scribner's, 1976.

2210. ———. *Samurai of Gold Hill*. Illus. Ati Forberg. New York: Scribner's, 1972.
For grades 4–6. Seeking a new life in 19th-century California with his samurai father, a young Japanese finds it difficult to adjust to the idea of being a farmer and not a samurai.

2211. ———. *"The Sea of Gold," and Other Tales from Japan*. Introd. Marcia Brown. Illus. Marianne Yamaguchi. New York: Scribner's, 1965. Boston: Gregg, 1980.

2212. ———. *Sumi and the Goat and the Tokyo Express*. Illus. Kazue Mizumura. New York: Scribner's, 1969.

2213. ———. *Sumi's Prize*. Illus. Kazue Mizumura. New York: Scribner's, 1964.
For preschool–grade 3.

2214. ———. *Sumi's Special Happening*. Illus. Kazue Mizumura. New York: Scribner's, 1966.

2215.   ———. *Tabi: Journey through Time. Stories of the Japanese in America.* El Cerrito, CA: Sycamore Congregational Church, 1980.

2216.   ———. *Takao and Grandfather's Sword.* Illus. William M. Hutchinson. New York: Harcourt, 1958.

2217.   ———. *The Two Foolish Cats.* Illus. Margot Zemach. New York: McEldery-Macmillan, 1987.

2218.   Villa, José García. *Mir-i-Nisa.* Illus. Larry Alcala. Manila: Alberto S. Florentino, 1966.
           A tale of the Philippine South Seas. Mir-i-Nisa, a beautiful woman loved by many men, chooses to marry an honest one.

Watkins, Yoko Kawashima. *So Far from the Bamboo Grove.* See #1225.

Wong, Jade Snow. *Fifth Chinese Daughter.* See #562.

2219.   Wong, Kat. *Don't Put the Vinegar in the Copper.* Illus. Stephanie Lowe. San Francisco: Children's Book Press, 1978.
           Describes the language barrier between a daughter and a mother. In English and Chinese.

2220.   Yagawa, Sumiko. *The Crane Wife.* Trans. Katherine Paterson. Illus. Suekichi Akaba. New York: Morrow, 1981.

2221.   Yashima, Taro [Jun Atsushi Iwamatsu]. *Crow Boy.* Illus. author. New York: Viking, 1955. New York: Penguin, 1976.
           For grades 1–up. A Japanese boy is shunned by his classmates.

2222.   ———. *Plenty to Watch.* Illus. author. New York: Viking, 1954.
           For preschool–grade 1. Depicts a Japanese village.

2223.   ———. *Seashore Story.* Illus. author. New York: Viking, 1967.
           For grades 1–3. A Japanese Rip Van Winkle story.

2224.   ———. *Umbrella.* Illus. author. New York: Viking, 1958.
           For preschool–grade 2. Describes a Japanese American girl in New York.

2225.   ———. *The Village Tree.* Illus. author. New York: Viking, 1953.
           For grade 1.

2226.   Yashima, Taro, and Mitsu Yashima [Tomoe Iwamatsu]. *Momo's Kitten.* New York: Viking, 1961.
           For preschool–grade 2. A Japanese American girl finds a stray kitten under a bush.

2227.   Yep, Laurence. *Child of the Owl.* New York: Harper, 1977.
           For grades 7–up. A young Chinese girl is sent to live with her grandmother in Chinatown.
           Rev. Sharon Wong, *Bridge* 6.1 (1978): 64–65.

2228.   ———. *Dragon of the Lost Sea.* New York: Harper, 1982.
           Novel for young adults.

2229.   ———. *Dragon Steel.* New York: Harper, 1985.
           Novel for young adults.

2230.   ———. *Dragonwings.* New York: Harper, 1975.
For grades 7–up. A historical fantasy created from a newspaper account about a 19th-century Chinese in America who invents a biplane.
Rev. Louie Ai-ling, *Bridge* 5.1 (1977): 46–47.

2231.   ———. *The Green Darkness.* New York: Harper, 1980.
Novel for young adults.

2232.   ———. *Kind Hearts and Gentle Monsters.* New York: Harper, 1982.
For grades 6–up. Two teenagers help each other to change and grow up.

2233.   ———. *Liar, Liar.* New York: Morrow, 1983.

2234.   ———. *The Mark Twain Murders.* New York: Four Winds Press, 1982.
For grades 6–up. A mystery about young Mark Twain.

2235.   ———. *Mountain Light.* New York: Harper, 1985.
For grades 7–up. Sequel to *The Serpent's Children.* Set in both China and America.

2236.   ———. *Sea Glass.* New York: Harper, 1979.
For grades 7–up. Describes a Chinese American boy whose father wants him to excel in sports.

2237.   ———. *The Serpent's Children.* New York: Harper, 1984.
For grades 7–up. A young girl tries to protect her family from bandits, famine, and domestic conflict.

2238.   ———. *Sweetwater.* Illus. Julia Noonan. New York: Avon, 1973.
Novel for young adults.

2239.   ———. *The Tom Sawyer Fires.* New York: Morrow, 1984.
For grades 6–up. An adventure tale involving young Mark Twain.

Secondary Sources

General Criticism

Books, Theses, and Dissertations

2240. Baker, Houston A., Jr., ed. *Three American Literatures: Essays in Chicano, Native American, and Asian American Literature for Teachers of American Literature*. Introd. Walter J. Ong. New York: MLA, 1982.
    Rev. George Uba, *Amerasia Journal* 12.2 (1985–86): 117–19.

2241. Chock, Eric, and Jody Manabe, eds. *Writers of Hawaii: A Focus on Our Literary Heritage*. Honolulu: Hawaii Comm. for the Humanities and the Hawaii Foundation for the Arts, 1981.
    A collection of papers presented at the conference "Writers of Hawaii: A Focus on Our Literary Heritage," Honolulu, Oct. 1980.

2242. Kim, Elaine H. *Asian American Literature: An Introduction to the Writings and Their Social Context*. Philadelphia: Temple UP, 1982.
    Covers Chinese American, Japanese American, Pilipino American, and Korean American literature.
    Rev. Forrest Gok, *East/West* 22 Dec. 1982: 10; Amy Ling, *MELUS* 10.3 (1983): 89–92; Stephen H. Sumida, *Amerasia Journal* 11.1 (1984): 105–09; George Uba, *Journal of Ethnic Studies* 13.2 (1985): 139–41.

2243. ———. "A Survey of Asian-American Literature: Social Perspectives." Diss. Univ. of California, Berkeley, 1976.

2244. Niiya, Brian T. "With Understanding but without Bitterness: A Survey of Asian American Autobiography." MA thesis, Univ. of California, Los Angeles, 1988.

2245. Simms, Norman. *Silence and Invisibility: A Study of the Literatures of the Pacific, Australia, and New Zealand*. Washington: Three Continents Press, 1986.
    Discusses Shirley Lim and Peter Nazareth.

2246. Stauffer, Robert. "The American Spirit in the Writings of Americans of Foreign Birth." Diss. Boston Univ., 1922.

2247. Sumida, Stephen. "Our Whole Voice: The Pastoral and the Heroic in Hawaii's Literature." Diss. Univ. of Washington, 1982.

2248. Wunsch, Marie Ann. "Walls of Jade: Images of Men, Women and Family in Second Generation Asian-American Fiction and Autobiography." Diss. Univ. of Hawaii, 1977.
    Discusses works published from the 1940s to the 1960s.

2249.   Zyla, Wolodymyr T., and Wendell M. Aycock, eds. *Ethnic Literatures since 1776: The Many Voices of America*. Vol. 9 of Proc. of Comparative Literature Symposium, Texas Tech Univ., 27–31 Jan. 1976. 2 pts. Lubbock: Texas Tech Press, 1978.
         Contains essays on Chinese American and Japanese American literature.

Articles

2250.   Chai, Alice Yun. "Toward a Holistic Paradigm for Asian American Women's Studies: A Synthesis of Feminist Scholarship and Women of Color's Feminist Politics." *Women's Studies International Forum* 8.1 (1985): 59–66.

2251.   Chan, Anthony B. "Born Again Asians: The Making of a New Literature." *Journal of Ethnic Studies* 11.4 (1984): 57–73.
         On Asian Canadian literature.

2252.   Chin, Frank, et al. "AIIIEEEEE! An Introduction to Asian-American Writing." *Yardbird Reader* 2 (1973): 21–46.

2253.   Chin, Frank, and Shawn Hsu Wong. "Introduction to *Yardbird Reader #3*." *Yardbird Reader* 3 [#179] vi–x.
         Discusses several Asian American authors.

2254.   Chock, Eric. "On Local Literature." *Writers of Hawaii* [#2241] 1–2.
         Rpt. in *Bamboo Ridge* 15 (1982): 3–7; *The Best of* Bamboo Ridge [#103] 6–9.

2255.   ———. "Poets in the Schools Playing Pretend Games: Creativity on the Big Island." *Literary Arts Hawaii* 78–79 (Spring 1986): 13.

2256.   Chun-Hoon, Lowell. "Teaching the Asian-American Experience: Alternative to the Neglect and Racism in Textbooks." *Amerasia Journal* 3.1 (1975): 40–58.

2257.   Dasenbrock, Reed Way. "Intelligibility and Meaningfulness in Multicultural Literature in English." *PMLA* 102 (1987): 10–19.
         Argues that ready intelligibility should not be made the sole criterion in the evaluation of multicultural texts, such as Kingston's *The Woman Warrior*.

2258.   Hata, Don, and Nadine Hata. "I Wonder Where the Yellow Went? Omissions and Distortions of Asian Americans in California Education." *Integrated Education* [Northwestern Univ.] May-June 1974: 17–21.

2259.   Hershinow, Sheldon. "Coming of Age? The Literature of Contemporary Hawaii." *Bamboo Ridge* 13 (1981–82): 5–10.

2260.   Hiraoka, Jesse. "A Sense of Place." *Journal of Ethnic Studies* 4.4 (1977): 72–84.
         Discusses Asian American authors and their sense of place.

2261. Hongo, Garrett Kaoru. "In the Bamboo Grove: Some Notes on the Poetic Line." *The Line in Postmodern Poetry*. Ed. Henry Sayre and Robert Frank. Urbana: U of Illinois P, 1988. 83–96.

2262. Houn, Fred Wei-han. "Asian American Art: Tradition and Information." *Asianadian* 5.1 (1983): 21–24.

2263. ———. "Revolutionary Asian American Art: Tradition and Change, Inheritance and Innovation, Not Imitation!" *East Wind* 5.1 (1986): 4–8.

2264. Iwasaki, Bruce. "High Tone." *Amerasia Journal* 3.2 (1976): 118–25.
   A longer version appears as the introduction to the Literature section in *Counterpoint* [#113] 453–63.
   Argues for the necessity of Asian American literature.

2265. ———. "Response and Change for the Asian in America: A Survey of Asian American Literature." *Roots* [#173] 89–99.

2266. Iwataki, Miya. "Asian American Art and Culture: A Melody of Resistance." *East Wind* 4.1 (1985): 11–15.

2267. Kageyama, Yuri. "The Empty Library." *Hokubei Mainichi* 1 Jan. 1985, supplement: 1.
   Discusses the perception that Asian American culture does not exist.

2268. Kiang, Peter. "Transformation: The Challenge Facing the Asian American Artist in the '80's." *East Wind* 4.1 (1985): 31–33.

2269. Kim, Elaine H. "Asian American Literature and the Importance of Social Context." *ADE Bulletin* 80 (1985): 34–41.

2270. ———. "Asian American Writers: A Bibliographical Review." *American Studies International* 22.2 (1984): 41–78.

2271. Lau, Alan Chong, and Laureen Mar, eds. "Asian American: North and South." *Contact II* 7.38–40 (1986): 1+.
   Poetry review.

2272. Leong, Charles L. "Asian American Writers." *Hokubei Mainichi* 23 Oct. 1982: 2; 26 Oct. 1982: 2; 29 Oct. 1982: 1; 30 Oct. 1982: 1.
   Rpt. in *Asian Week* 28 Oct. 1982: 18; 4 Nov. 1982: 7+.
   Contains the text of a speech given by Russell Leong at "Third World Writers Symposium," Sacramento, CA, 1981.

2273. Leong, Russell. "Asian American Literature: Towards the Next Generation." *Amerasia Journal* 9.2 (1982): 79–80.

2274. ———. "On Native Ground: Asian American Writers in Califia." *Amerasia Journal* 7.1 (1980): 111–14.
   Discusses "Visions of California," a conference on Asian American writers held in Venice, CA, 15 Nov. 1979, and "Caught in the Act of Living," a reading by Pacific Asian American Women Writers—West that took place in Amerasia Bookstore, Los Angeles, 8 Mar. 1980.

2275. Lew, Walter. "A New Decade of Singular Poetry." *Bridge* 8.4 (1983): 11–12.
   Discusses poetry by Asian Americans.

2276. Lim, Happy. "Literature, Art and Practical Struggle." *East Wind* 4.1 (1985): 18–19.

2277. Lim, Shirley. "Exotics and Existentials: The Course of Asian American Writing." *Homegrown* 11 (Winter 1984): 26–31.
Discusses the work of Monica Sone, Virginia Lee, and Diana Chang, among others.

2278. ———. "Reconstructing Asian American Poetry: A Case for Ethnopoetics." Forthcoming in *MELUS* 13.

2279. ———. "Twelve Asian American Writers in Search of Self-Definition." *MELUS* forthcoming.
Rpt. in *Redefining American Literary History*. Ed. A. LaVonne Ruoff et al. New York: MLA, forthcoming.

Ling, Amy. See #23.

2281. Ling, Amy. "I'm Here: An Asian American Woman's Response." *New Literary History* 19.1 (1987): 151–60.
A response to Ellen Messer-Davidow's "The Philosophical Bases of Feminist Literary Criticisms."

2282. Lum, Darrell H. Y. "Bamboo Ridge." *East West Photo Journal* [Honolulu] 1.2 (1980): 32.

2283. ———. "Hawaii's Literature and Lunch." *East Wind* 5.1 (1986): 32–33.
A slightly different version rpt. as "Local Literature and Lunch" in *The Best of* Bamboo Ridge [#103] 3–5.
Points out that many Hawaiian authors see themselves as "local" rather than as "Asian American" writers.

2284. ———. "Pacific Island Writers and Their Readers." *Pacific Islands Communication Journal* [Honolulu] 13.1 (1984): 61–65.
Describes the significance of Hawaiian literature and the goals of Bamboo Ridge Press.

2285. ———. "Some Characteristics of Local Short Stories." *Literary Arts Hawaii* 74 (June 1984): 16.

2286. Murayama, Milton. "Problems of Writing in Dialect and Mixed Languages." *Bamboo Ridge* 5 (1979–80): 8–10.

2287. Newman, Katharine. "An Ethnic Literary Scholar Views American Literature." *MELUS* 7.1 (1980): 3–19.

2288. ———. "Hawaiian-American Literature Today." *MELUS* 6.2 (1979): 46–47.

2289. Oyama, David. "Introduction: Asian-American Theatre, On the Road to Xanadu." *Bridge* 5.2 (1977): 4–6.

2290. Oyama, Richard. "Five Asian American Poets: A Response." *East Wind* 4.1 (1985): 44–45.
A response to Fred Wei-han Houn's review "Five Asian American Poets."

2291. Ramsdell, Daniel B. "Asia Askew: U. S. Best-Sellers on Asia, 1931–1980." *Bulletin of Concerned Asian Scholars* 15.4 (1983): 2–25.

2292. Santos, Bienvenido. "Touching Other Asians." *Asiaweek* [Hong Kong] 2 Aug. 1985: 56.
Discusses Asian American authors.

2293. Sledge, Linda Ching. "Teaching Asian American Literature." *ADE Bulletin* 80 (1985): 42–45.

2294. Sumida, Stephen H. "First Generations in Asian American Literature: As Viewed in Some Second Generation Works." *Issues in Asian and Pacific American Education*. Ed. Nobuya Tsuchida. Minneapolis: Asian/Pacific American Learning Resource Center, Univ. of Minnesota, 1986. 64–70.

2295. ———. "Localism in Asian American Literature and Cultures of Hawaii and the West Coast." *Hawaii Literary Arts Council Newsletter* 71 (Aug.-Sept. 1983): n. pag.
Rev. version forthcoming in *Seattle Review*.

2296. ———. "Waiting for the Big Fish: Recent Research in the Asian American Literature of Hawaii." *The Best of* Bamboo Ridge [#103] 302–21.

2297. Tanaka, Ronald. "Culture, Communication and the Asian Movement in Perspective." *Journal of Ethnic Studies* 4.1 (1976): 37–49.

2298. ———. "Towards a Systems Analysis of Ethnic Minority Literature." *Journal of Ethnic Studies* 6.1 (1978): 49–61.

2299. Wong, Shawn H. "Longtime Californ'." *CALAFIA* [#162] lv–lxx.

2300. Wong-Chu, Jim. "Ten Years of Asian Canadian Literary Arts in Vancouver." *Asianadian* 5.3 (1984): 23–24.

2301. Yamada, Mitsuye. "Asian American Women and Feminism." *This Bridge Called My Back* [#143] 71–75.

2301a. ———. "Invisibility Is an Unnatural Disaster: Reflections of an Asian American Woman." *This Bridge Called My Back* [#143] 35–40.

Commentary

2302. Chin, Frank. "Where I'm Coming From." *Bridge* 4.3 (1976): 28–29.
A Chinese American playwright's reflections on US literature.

2303. Kunitaki, Miko. "PAAWWW: Caught in the Act of Living." *Pacific Citizen* 3 Oct. 1980: 2.
Profile of Pacific Asian American Women Writers West.

2304. Nee, Dale Yu. "See Culture Is Made, Not Born . . . Asian American Writers' Conference." *Bridge* 3.6 (1975): 42–48.
Describes a conference held in the Oakland Museum.

2305. Noda, Barbara, Kitty Tsui, [and Z. Wong]. "Coming Out: We Are Here in the Asian Community." *Bridge* 7.1 (1979): 22–24.
Discusses lesbianism.

2306. Oyama, David. "Asian American Poetry—A Culture Discovering Itself." *Bridge* 4.4 (1976): 5.

2307. Smith, Susan. "The Creativity of Asian-Americans." *Los Angeles Times* 5 July 1980, pt. 2: 10.
Focuses on Pacific Asian American Women Writers West (PAAWWW).

2308. Tong, Ben. "Alan Watts Was Sure One Strange Kinda Chinaman." *Quilt* 1 (1981): 29–33.
Decries the distortion and misappropriation of Third World cultures by whites.

2309. Wong, Shawn H. "A Funny Thing Happened while I Was Screaming AIIIEEEEE!" *The Portrayal of Asian Americans in Children's Books*. Spec. double issue of *Interracial Books for Children Bulletin* 7.2–3 (1976): 33.
Recounts the publishing history of *AIIIEEEEE!* [#100].

2310. Yep, Laurence. "The Ethnic Writer as Alien." *Interracial Books for Children Bulletin* 10.5 (1979): 10–11.

Chinese American Literature

Books, Theses, and Dissertations

2311. Albrecht, Lisa Diane. "The Woman Writer Empowered: A Study of the Meanings of Experience of Ten Published Feminist Women Writers." Diss. State Univ. of New York, Buffalo, 1984.
Fay Chiang is one of the ten writers discussed.

2312. Chan, Joanna Wan-Ying. "The Four Seas Players: Toward an Alternative Form of Chinese Theatre: A Case Study of a Community Theatre in Chinatown, New York City." Diss. Teachers Coll., Columbia Univ., 1977.

2313. Chu, Limin. *The Images of China and the Chinese in the* Overland Monthly, *1868–1875, 1883–1935.* San Francisco: R and E Research Assoc., 1974.

2314. *Conflict and Change: The Visionary Role of Literature.* Papers presented at a symposium on Maxine Hong Kingston and Marsha Norman, Davenport, IA, 16–19 Mar. 1987. Davenport, IA: Visiting Artist Series, 1987.

2315. Fenn, William Purviance. *Ah Sin and His Brethren in American Literature.* Peiping: Coll. of Chinese Studies, 1933.
Studies the attitude toward Chinese in American literature.

2316. Foster, John Burt. "China and the Chinese in American Literature, 1850–1950." Diss. Univ. of Illinois, 1952.
Includes discussion of the portrayal of Chinese immigrants.

2317. Gardner, John Berdan. "The Image of the Chinese in the U.S., 1885–1915." Diss. Univ. of Pennsylvania, 1961.

2318. Han, Hsiao-min. "Roots and Buds: The Literature of Chinese Americans." Diss. Brigham Young Univ., 1980.

2319. Hsiao, Ruth Yu. "The Stages of Development in American Ethnic Literature: Jewish and Chinese American Literature." Diss. Tufts Univ., 1986.

2320. Li, Xiaolin. "Images of Early (1848–1945) Chinese in Literary Works Written by Chinese American Authors." MA thesis, Univ. of California, Los Angeles, 1983.
A Marxist approach to Chinese American literature.

2321. Wu, William F. *The Yellow Peril: Chinese Americans in American Fiction 1850–1940.* Hamden, CT: Archon, 1982.
Shows how writers perpetuate the Yellow Peril fear through the images they project of Chinese Americans.

Articles

2322. Arreola, Daniel D. "Chinatown in Literature: A Novel Look at Landscape." *China Geographer* 4 (Spring 1976): 49–69.
Discusses Lin Yutang and some non-Asian writers.

2323. Blinde, Patricia Lin. "The Icicle in the Desert: Perspective and Form in the Works of Two Chinese-American Women Writers." *MELUS* 6.3 (1979): 51–71.
Discusses Maxine Hong Kingston and Jade Snow Wong.

2324. Brewster, Anne. "Singaporean and Malaysian Women Poets, Local and Expatriate." *The Writer's Sense of the Contemporary: Papers in Southeast Asian and Australian Literature.* Ed. Bruce Bennett, Ee Tiang Hong, and Ron Shepherd. Nedlands, Austral.: Centre for Studies in Australian Lit., Univ. of Western Australia; printed Perth, Austral.: Vanguard, 1982. 46–50.
Discusses the poetry of Shirley Lim and May Wong.

2325. Brodhead, Michael J. "'But—He's a Chinaman!' Charlie Chan and the Literary Image of the Chinese-American." *Halcyon* 1984: 55–72.
Defends Earl Derr Biggers against the charge of racist portrayal.

2326. Carroll, Noel. "A Select View of Earthlings: Ping Chong (United States)." *Drama Review* 27 (Spring 1983): 72–81.

2327. Chan, Jeffery Paul. "Resources for Chinese American Literary Traditions." *The Chinese American Experience: Papers for the Second National Conference on Chinese American Studies (1980).* San Francisco: Chinese Historical Soc. of America and the Chinese Culture Foundation of San Francisco, 1984. 241–44.

2328. Chan, Jeffery Paul, et al. "An Introduction to Chinese-American and Japanese-American Literature." *Three American Literatures* [#2240] 197–228.
A reprint of the introduction to *AIIIEEEEE!* [#100], with a postscript.

2329. ———. "Resources for Chinese and Japanese American Literary Traditions." *Amerasia Journal* 8.1 (1981): 19–31.

2330. Chan Wing-Tsit. "Lin Yutang, Critic and Interpreter." *College English* 8.4 (1947): 163–69.

2331. Cheung, King-Kok. "'Don't Tell': Imposed Silences in *The Color Purple* and *The Woman Warrior.*" *PMLA* 103 (1988): 162–74.

2332. Chin, Frank. "From the Chinaman *Year of the Dragon* to the Fake *Year of the Dragon.*" *Quilt* 5 (1986): 58–71.
Describes the political organization of Chinatown to expose the distortions in Michael Cimino's movie *Year of the Dragon.*

2333. ———. "This Is Not an Autobiography." *Genre* 18.2 (1985): 109–30.
Describes the heroic tradition of Chinese Americans.

2334. Chua, C[heng] Lok. "Frank Chin." *Critical Survey of Drama: Supplement.* Ed. Frank N. Magill. Englewood Cliffs, NJ: Salem Press, 1987. 45–51.

2335. ———. "Golden Mountain: Chinese Versions of the American Dream in Lin Yutang, Louis Chu, and Maxine Hong Kingston." *Ethnic Groups* 4.1–2 (1982): 33–59.

2336.   ———. "Two Chinese Versions of the American Dream: The Golden Mountain in Lin Yutang and Maxine Hong Kingston." *MELUS* 8.4 (1981): 61–70.

2337.   Chung, Sue Fawn. "From Fu Manchu, Evil Genius, to James Lee Wong, Popular Hero: A Study of the Chinese American in Popular Periodical Fiction from 1920 to 1940." *Journal of Popular Culture* 10.3 (1976): 534–47.

2338.   Chun-Hoon, Lowell. "Jade Snow Wong and the Fate of Chinese-American Identity." *Amerasia Journal* 1.1 (1971): 52–63.
         Rpt. in *Asian Americans: Psychological Perspectives*. 2 vols. Ed. Stanley Sue and Nathaniel N. Wagner. Palo Alto: Science and Behavior Books, 1973. 1: 125–35.

2339.   Demetrakopoulos, Stephanie A. "The Metaphysics of Matrilinearism in Women's Autobiography: Studies of Mead's *Blackberry Winter*, Hellman's *Pentimento*, Angelou's *I Know Why the Caged Bird Sings*, and Kingston's *The Woman Warrior*." *Women's Autobiography: Essays in Criticism*. Ed. Estelle C. Jelinek. Bloomington: Indiana UP, 1980. 180–205.

2340.   Dong, Lorraine, and Marlon K. Hom. "Defiance or Perpetuation: An Analysis of Characters in *Mrs. Spring Fragrance*." *Chinese America: History and Perspectives*. Ed. Him Mark Lai, Ruthanne Lum McCunn, and Judy Yung. San Francisco: Chinese Historical Soc. of America, 1987. 139–68.

2341.   Eakin, Paul John. "Self-Invention in Autobiography: The Moment of Language." *Fictions in Autobiography: Studies in the Art of Self-Invention*. Princeton: Princeton UP, 1985. 181–278.
         Discusses Maxine Hong Kingston's *The Woman Warrior*.

2342.   Fischer, Michael M. J. "Ethnicity and the Post-Modern Arts of Memory." *Writing Culture: The Poetics and Politics of Ethnography*. Ed. James Clifford and George E. Marcus. Berkeley: U of California P, 1986. 194–233.
         Discusses the works of Jeffery Paul Chan, Frank Chin, Maxine Hong Kingston, and Shawn Hsu Wong.

2343.   Gong, Ted. "Approaching Cultural Change through Literature: From Chinese to Chinese American." *Amerasia Journal* 7.1 (1980): 73–86.
         Discusses Louis Chu, Frank Chin, and Monfoon Leong.

2344.   Holaday, Woon-Ping Chin. "From Ezra Pound to Maxine Hong Kingston: Expressions of Chinese Thought in American Literature." *MELUS* 5.2 (1978): 15–24.

2345.   Hom, Marlon. "A Case of Mutual Exclusion: Portrayals by Immigrant and American Born Chinese of Each Other in Literature." *Amerasia Journal* 11.2 (1984): 29–45.
         Discusses works written in both English and Chinese.

2346.   ———, trans. "Chinatown Literature during the Last Ten Years (1939–1949) by Wenquan." *Amerasia Journal* 9.1 (1982): 75–100.

2347. ———. "Some Cantonese Folksongs on the American Experience." *Western Folklore* 42.2 (1983): 126–39.

2348. Houn, Fred Wei-han. "The Revolutionary Writings of H. T. Tsiang." *East Wind* 6.1 (1987): 39–40.

2349. ———. "Songs from Gold Mountain: Chinese American Folk Literature, A Fierce Tradition." *East Wind* 4.1 (1985): 9.

2350. Hsu, Vivian. "Maxine Hong Kingston as Psycho-Autobiographer and Ethnographer." *International Journal of Women's Studies* 6.5 (1983): 429–42.

2351. Hyde, Stuart W. "The Chinese Stereotype in American Melodrama." *California Historical Society Quarterly* 34.4 (1955): 357–67.

2352. Johnson, Sally H. "Anger and Reconciliation in the Work of Maxine Hong Kingston." *Conflict and Change* [#2314] 34–46.

2353. Juhasz, Suzanne. "Maxine Hong Kingston: Narrative Technique and Female Identity." *Contemporary American Women Writers: Narrative Strategies*. Ed. Catherine Rainwater and William J. Scheick. Lexington: U of Kentucky P, 1985. 173–89.

2354. ———. "Towards a Theory of Form in Feminist Autobiography: Kate Millett's *Fear of Flying* and *Sita*; Maxine Hong Kingston's *The Woman Warrior*." *International Journal of Women's Studies* 2.1 (1979): 62–75.
Rpt. in *Women's Autobiography: Essays in Criticism*. Ed. Estelle C. Jelinek. Bloomington: Indiana UP, 1980. 221–37.

2355. Keim, Margaret Laten. "The Chinese as Portrayed in the Works of Bret Harte: A Study of Race Relations." *Sociology and Social Research* 25 (1941): 441–50.

2356. Kim, Elaine H. "Frank Chin: The Chinatown Cowboy and His Backtalk." *Midwest Quarterly* 20.1 (1978): 78–91.

2357. ———. "The Portrayal of Chinese in Anglo-American Literature." *The Chinese American Experience: Papers from the Second National Conference on Chinese American Studies (1980)*. San Francisco: Chinese Historical Soc. of America and Chinese Culture Foundation of San Francisco, 1984. 244–55.

2358. ———. "Visions and Fierce Dreams: A Commentary on the Works of Maxine Hong Kingston." *Amerasia Journal* 8.2 (1981): 145–61.

2359. Kingston, Maxine Hong. "Cultural Misreadings by American Reviewers." *Asian and Western Writers in Dialogue: New Cultural Identities*. Ed. Guy Amirthanayagam. London: Macmillan, 1982. 55–65.

2360. Lai, Chuen-Yan David. "Heritage Reruns: A 'Prison' for Chinese Immigrants." *Asianadian* 2.4 (1980): 16–19.
Discusses poetry and prose written by Chinese immigrants on the walls of a Canadian immigration center.

2361. Lau, Joseph S. M. "The Albatross Exorcised: The Rime of Frank Chin." *Tamkang Review* 12.1 (1981): 93–105.

Ling, Amy. See #23.

2362.   Ling, Amy. "Edith Eaton: Pioneer Chinamerican Writer and Feminist." *American Literary Realism, 1870–1910* 16.2 (1983): 287–98.

2363.   ———. "A Perspective on Chinamerican Literature." *MELUS* 8.2 (1981): 76–81.

2364.   ———. "A Rumble in the Silence: *Crossings* by Chuang Hua." *MELUS* 9.3 (1982): 29–37.

2365.   ———. "Thematic Threads in Maxine Hong Kingston's *The Woman Warrior.*" *Tamkang Review* 14 (1983–84): 155–64.

2366.   ———. "Winnifred Eaton: Ethnic Chameleon and Popular Success." *MELUS* 11.3 (1984): 5–15.

2367.   ———. "Writer in the Hyphenated Condition: Diana Chang." *MELUS* 7.4 (1980): 69–83.

2368.   ———. "Writers with a Cause: Sui Sin Far and Han Suyin." *Women's Studies International Forum* 9.4 (1986): 411–19.

2369.   Medwick, Lucille. "The Chinese Poet in New York." *New York Quarterly* 4 (1970): 95–115.
        Discusses the influence of cultural heritage on various Chinese American poets, including Diana Chang, Bonita Lei, Shih Shun Liu, Wing Tek Lum, Yuan-Ming Sung, and Walasse Ting.

2370.   Miller, Lucien, and Hui-chuan Chang. "Fiction and Autobiography: Spatial Form in *The Golden Cangue* and *The Woman Warrior.*" *Tamkang Review* 15.1–4 (1984–85): 75–96.

2371.   Miller, Margaret. "Threads of Identity in Maxine Hong Kingston's *The Woman Warrior.*" *Biography* 6.1 (1983): 13–32.

2372.   Ng, Franklin. "Maxine Hong Kingston: History as Myth." *Writers of Hawaii* [#2241] 50–53.

2373.   Pao, Patti. "Male Stereotypification in Maxine Hong Kingston's *China Men.*" *Critical Perspectives of Third World America* 1.1 (1983): 267–74.

2374.   Rabine, Leslie W. "No Lost Paradise: Social Gender and Symbolic Gender in the Writings of Maxine Hong Kingston." *Signs* 12.3 (1987): 471–92.

2375.   Rodecape, Lois. "Celestial Drama in the Golden Hills: The Chinese Theatre in California, 1849–1869." *California Historical Society Quarterly* 23.2 (1944): 97–116.

2376.   Rubenstein, Roberta. "Bridging Two Cultures: Maxine Hong Kingston." *Boundaries of the Self: Gender, Culture, Fiction.* Urbana: U of Illinois P, 1987. 164–89.

2377.   Sledge, Linda Ching. "Maxine Hong Kingston's *China Men*: The Family Historian as Epic Poet." *MELUS* 7.4 (1980): 3–22.

2378.   Solberg, S. E. "Sui Sin Far/Edith Eaton: First Chinese-American Fictionalist." *MELUS* 8.1 (1981): 27–40.

2379. Spoehr, Luther W. "Sambo and the Heathen Chinese: California's Racial Stereotypes in the Late 1870's." *Pacific Historical Review* 2nd ser. 42 (1973): 185–204.

2380. Tachibana, Judy M. "Outwitting the Whites: One Image of the Chinese in California Fiction and Poetry, 1849–1924." *Southern California Quarterly* 61.4 (1979): 379–89.

2381. Thompson, Phyllis Hoge. "This Is the Story I Heard: A Conversation with Maxine Hong Kingston and Earll Kingston." *Biography* 6.1 (1983): 1–12.

2382. Wand, David Hsin Fu. "The Chinese-American Literary Scene: A Galaxy of Poets and a Lone Playwright." *Ethnic Literatures since 1776: The Many Voices of America*. Ed. Wolodymyr T. Zyla and Wendell M. Aycock. Lubbock: Texas Tech, 1978. 121–46.
   Discusses Mei Berssenbrugge, Diana Chang, Frank Chin, Stephen S. N. Liu, Wing Tek Lum, and David Rafael Wang.

2383. ———. "The Use of Native Imagery by Chinese Poets Writing in English." *Language and Style* 6 (1973): 72–80.

2384. Wang, Ling-chi. "The Yee Version of Poems from the Chinese Immigration Station." *Asian American Review* (1976): 117–26.

2385. Whitmer, Marlin. "Stories of Stress/Stress in the Community." *Conflict and Change* [#2314] 47–59.
   Maxine Hong Kingston's *The Woman Warrior* is among the works discussed.

2386. Wong, Nellie. "Asian American Women, Feminism and Creativity." *Conditions Seven* 3.1 (1981): 177–84.

2387. Wong, Sau-ling Cynthia. "Necessity and Extravagance in Maxine Hong Kingston's *The Woman Warrior*: Inquiry into the Nature of Art and Its Relevance to the Ethnic Experience." Forthcoming in *MELUS*.

2388. ———. "Tales of Postwar Chinatown: Short Stories of *The Bud*, 1947–1948." Forthcoming in *Amerasia Journal*.

2389. Wong, Yen Lu. "Chinese-American Theatre." *Drama Review* 20.2 (1976): 13–18.
   Discusses Frank Chin's *The Year of the Dragon*.

2390. Yin, Kathleen Loh Swee, and Kristoffer F. Paulson. "The Divided Voice of Chinese-American Narration: Jade Snow Wong's *Fifth Chinese Daughter*." *MELUS* 9.1 (1982): 53–59.

2391. Yu, Connie Young. "Rediscovered Voices: Chinese Immigrants and Angel Island." *Amerasia Journal* 4.2 (1977): 123–39.

Interviews, Profiles, and Commentary

2392. Allen, Henry. "Warrior's Luck." *Washington Post* 26 June 1980: D-1+.
   Maxine Hong Kingston.

2393. Beck, Melinda, with Susan Agrest. "Mailer's Violent Pen Pal." *Newsweek* 3 Aug. 1981: 28.
Jack Henry Abbott.

2394. Braun, Joan Catherine. "'Yellow Daughters' Culture." *Plexus* [Oakland, CA] Oct. 1980: 8.
Comments on Unbound Feet, a collective of Chinese American women writers.

2395. Brownmiller, Susan. "Susan Brownmiller Talks with Maxine Hong Kingston, Author of *The Woman Warrior*." *Mademoiselle* Mar. 1977: 148+.

2396. C. F. L. *Land of Sunshine* 13.5 (1900): 336.
Profile of Shi Sin Far.

2397. Castagnozzi, Mary. "Maxine Hong Kingston Discusses Her Writing." *East/West* May 1981: 7.

2398. Cheung, King-Kok. "Food for All Her Living." *Critical Perspectives of Third World America* 1.1 (1983): 129–34.
A response to Frank Chin's "Food for All His Dead."

2399. ———. "*The Woman Warrior*: Counteracting Stress with Visions." *Conflict and Change* [#2314] 15–22.

2400. Chin, Frank. "Afterward." *MELUS* 3.2 (1976): 13–17.

2401. ———. "Backtalk." *News of the American Place Theater* 3 (May 1972). Rpt. in *Counterpoint* [#113] 556–57.
Introductory notes to *The Chickencoop Chinaman*.

2402. ———. "Don't Pen Us Up in Chinatown." *New York Times* 8 Oct. 1972, sec. 2: 1+.

2403. ———. "Interview with Roland Winters: The Last Charlie Chan of the Movies." *Combined Asian Resources Project Report* 30 Mar. 1971. Rpt. in *Amerasia Journal* 2 (1973): 1–19.

2404. ———. "*Kung Fu* is Unfair to Chinese." *New York Times* 24 Mar. 1974, sec. 2: 19.

2405. ———. "Letter to Y'Bird: February 3, 1977 — Frisco." *Y'Bird Magazine* 1.1 (1977): 42–45.
Argues that Asian American writers are a "dying people."

2406. ———. "Our Life Is War." *Weekly* [Seattle] 4 May 1983: 28+.

2407. ———. "Yellow Seattle." *Weekly* [Seattle] 1 Feb. 1978: 8–11.
Contrasts the stereotypical and the real Asian American.

2408. Ching, Frank, and Frank Chin. "Who Is Afraid of Frank Chin, or Is It Ching?" *Bridge* 2.2 (1972): 29–34.
Exchange of letters between Frank Chin and Frank Ching, manager-editor of *Bridge*. Chin and Ching disagree over the issue of Asian American sensibility.

2409. Christon, Lawrence. "Playwright Balances Life's Improbabilities." *Los Angeles Times* 12 Feb. 1986, sec. 6: 1+.
       Profile of David Henry Hwang.

2410. Chun-Hoon, Lowell. "Remarks on Maxine Hong Kingston." *Writers of Hawaii* [#2241] 43–49.

2411. Cowan, Peter. "Oakland Born Author Appreciates Heritage." *Tribune* [Oakland] 27 Dec. 1979: C1.
       Shawn Wong.

2412. Creamer, Beverly. "Maxine Kingston: A Time for Applause." *Honolulu Advertiser* 5 June 1980.

2413. DeRieux, Robin. "Cal Closeup/Yuan-Tsung Chen." *Berkeleyan* 25 Sept. 1985: 3.

2414. Dong, Stella. "Convict Author Free at Last with New Book—Thanks to Mailer, *NYRB* and Random Editor." *Publishers Weekly* 12 June 1981: 39–40.
       Jack Henry Abbott.

2415. "Edith Eaton Dead: Author of Chinese Stoires under the Name of Sui Sin Far." *New York Times* 9 Apr. 1914: 11.
       An obituary that obscures Eaton's Chinese ancestry.

2416. Flippo, Chet. "The Lionized and the Dead." *New York* 10 Aug. 1981: 31–34.
       Jack Henry Abbott.

2417. "The Ghosts of Yesterday's China Are Captured by a Woman Who Has Never Been There." *People* 7 Feb. 1977: 81+.
       Interview with Maxine Hong Kingston.

2418. Goddard, John. "Fred Wah." *Books in Canada* Oct. 1986: 40+.

2419. Gok, Forrest. "Ruthanne Lum McCunn: A Commitment to Historical Truth." *East Wind* 5.1 (1986): 26–27.

2420. Horton, Karen. "Honolulu Interview: Maxine Hong Kingston." *Honolulu* 14.5 (1979): 49+.

2421. Islas, Arturo. Interview with Maxine Hong Kingston. *Women Writers of the West Coast Speaking of Their Lives and Careers.* Ed. Marilyn Yalom. Santa Barbara, CA: Capra Press, 1983. 11–19.

2422. Kingston, Maxine Hong. "Reservatons about China." *Ms.* Oct. 1978: 67–68.
       Personal reflections on misogyny in China.

2423. ———. "Talk Story: No Writer Is an Island except in Hawaii." *Los Angeles Times* 4 June 1978: 3.
       Reflections on the Ethnic American Writers' Conference in Honolulu.

2424. LaGory, Michael. "Interview with Maxine Hong Kingston, July 27, 1984." *Literary Arts Hawaii* 75 (Aug. 1984): 4–5.

2425. Lenhart, Maria. "Combining American Know-How with a Chinese Legacy: Jade Snow Wong Blends Two Diverse Cultures as Author, Potter, Mother." *Christian Science Monitor* 31 Mar. 1981: 23+.
Interview.

2426. Lim, Edilberto G. "Arthur Sze. A New Mexican Poet Who Refuses to Be Categorized." *East/West* 13 Nov. 1986: 6–7.

2427. Mahon, Denise. "Amerasian Author Draws on Both Cultures in Producing Her Books." *East/West* 7 Mar. 1984: 9.
Profile of Ruthanne Lum McCunn.

2428. McCarthy, Richard M. "Chen Jo-hsi: Memories and Notes." *Two Writers and the Cultural Revolution.* Ed. George Kao. Hong Kong: Chinese UP, 1980. 129–30.

2429. Moody, Fred. "Shawn Wong: Out from the Shadows." *Pacific* [Sunday magazine of *Seattle Times*] 19 Jan. 1986: 4+.

2430. Nazareth, Peter. "An Interview with Chinese Author Hualing Nieh." *World Literature Today* 55.1 (1981): 10–18.

2431. Nee, Victor G., and Brett de Bary Nee. "Frank Chin, 32: Novelist, Playwright, and Essayist." *Longtime Californ': A Documentary Study of an American Chinatown.* New York: Pantheon, 1972. 377–89.

2432. Nemy, Enid. "It's Nice to Be Rich and Famous." *San Francisco Sunday Examiner and Chronicle* 3 Jan. 1982, rev. sec: 5+.
Interview with Bette Bao Lord.

2433. New York Chinatown History Project. "Tribute to a Chinese American Writer: Louis Chu (1915–1970)." *East Wind* 5.1 (1986): 39–41.

2434. Pfaff, Timothy. "Talk with Mrs. Kingston." *New York Times Book Review* 15 June 1980: 1+.

2435. ———. "Whispers of a Literary Explorer." *Horizon* July 1980: 58–63.
Maxine Hong Kingston.

2436. Price, John A. "Lin Yutang." *Wilson Library Bulletin* 11.5 (1937): 298.

2437. Robertson, Nan. "Ghosts of Girlhood Lift Obscure Book to Peak of Acclaim." *New York Times* 12 Feb. 1977: 26.
Maxine Hong Kingston.

2438. See, Lisa. "C. Y. Lee." *Publishers Weekly* 14 Aug. 1987: 84–85.
Profile.

2439. Solberg, S. E. "Sui, the Storyteller: Sui Sin Far (Edith Eaton), 1867–1914." *Turning Shadows into Light* [#175] 85–87.

2440. Stein, Ruthe. "Inside Look at Growing Up as an Outsider." *San Francisco Chronicle* 21 Sept. 1983: 39.
Profile of Ruthanne Lum McCunn.

2441. Vangelder, Robert. "An Interview with Doctor Lin Yutang." *New York Times Book Review* 4 May 1941: 2+.

2442. Vespa, Mary. "A Lifelong Con Springs Himself with a Book." *People* 20 July 1981: 62+.
Jack Henry Abbott.

2443. Warga, Wayne. "Bette Bao Lord Bridges 2 Cultures." *Los Angeles Times* 17 Dec. 1981, pt. 5: 14–15.

2444. "With Four Successful Plays to His Credit, David Henry Hwang Is Scaling the Great Wall of Fame." *People Weekly* 9 Jan. 1984: 88.

2445. Wong, Eddie. "An Interview with Genny Lim." *East Wind* 1.2 (1982): 48–50.

2446. Wong, Nellie. "What's a Nice Secretary like You . . . Doing in Politics like This?" *Big Mama Rag* [Denver] Dec. 1982: 4+.
Reprint of a paper on feminism presented at the Fourth Annual National Women's Studies Assn. Conference, Humboldt State Univ., Arcata, CA, 16–20 June 1982.

2447. ———. "A Woman's View: Hawaii's Ethnic American Writers' Conference." *Bridge* 6.3 (1978): 15+.

2448. Worthy, Edmund H. "Yung Wing in America." *Pacific Historical Review* 34.3 (1965): 265–87.
Analyzes what a Chinese student learned in America, as revealed in his diary and personal letters.

2449. Yim, Susan. "Frank Chin, Chinaman." *Honolulu Star Bulletin* 23 Nov. 1979: D1. [Profile.]

2450. Yung, Judy. "America through Chinese American Eyes." *Bridge* 5.1 (1977): 44–46.
Profile of Laurence Yep.

Japanese American Literature

Books, Theses, and Dissertations

2451.   Fujita, Gayle Kimi. "The 'Ceremonial Self' in Japanese American Literature." Diss. Brown Univ., 1986.

2452.   *The Life and Times of Sadakichi Hartmann, 1867–1944.* Riverside, CA: Rubidoux Printing, 1970.
Program and catalog for an exhibition presented and cosponsored by the Univ. Library and the Riverside Press-Enterprises Co. at the Univ. of California, Riverside, 1–31 May 1970.

2453.   Yogi, Stan. "Legacies Revealed: Uncovering Buried Plots in the Stories of Hisaye Yamamoto and Wakako Yamauchi." MA thesis, Univ. of California, Berkeley, 1988.

Articles

Chan, Jeffery Paul, et al. See #2328–29.

2454.   Chock, Eric. "Directions in Local Japanese Poetry." *Bamboo Ridge* 9 (1980–81): 57–66.

2455.   Crawford, John F. "Notes toward a New Multicultural Criticism: Three Works by Women of Color." *A Gift of Tongues: Critical Challenges in Contemporary American Poetry.* Athens: U of Georgia P, 1987. 155–95.
Discusses Janice Mirikitani's *Awake in the River.*

2456.   Crow, Charles. "Home and Transcendence in Los Angeles Fiction." *Los Angeles in Fiction.* Ed. David Fine. Albuquerque: U of New Mexico P, 1984. 189–205.
Discusses Hisaye Yamamoto's "Yoneko's Earthquake."

2457.   ———. "The *Issei* Father in the Fiction of Hisaye Yamamoto." *Opening Up Literary Criticism: Essays on American Prose and Poetry.* Ed. Leo Truchlar. Salzburg: Verlag Wolfgang Neugebauer, 1986. 34–40.

2458.   Fujita, Gayle Kimi. "'To attend the sound of stone': The Sensibility of Silence in *Obasan.*" *MELUS* 12 (1986).

2459.   Gottlieb, Erika. "The Riddle of Concentric Worlds in *Obasan.*" *Canadian Literature* 109 (1986): 34–53.

2460.   Haslam, Gerald W. "The Exotics: Yone Noguchi, Shiesei Tsuneishi, and Sadakichi Hartmann." *CLA Journal* 19.3 (1976): 362–73.

2461.   Inada, Lawson Fusao. "Of Place and Displacement: The Range of Japanese American Literature." *Three American Literatures* [#2240] 254–65.
Discusses Toshio Mori and John Okada.

2462.   ———. "The Vision of America in John Okada's *No-No Boy.*" *Ethnic Literatures since 1776: The Many Voices of America* [#2249] 275–87.

2463.   McDonald, Dorothy Ritsuko. "After Imprisonment: Ichiro's Search for Redemption in *No-No Boy.*" *MELUS* 6.3 (1979): 19–26.

2464.   McDonald, Dorothy Ritsuko, and Katharine Newman. "Relocation and Dislocation: The Writings of Hisaye Yamamoto and Wakako Yamauchi." *MELUS* 7.3 (1980): 21–38.

2465.   Okamura, Raymond Y. "*Farewell to Manzanar*: A Case of Subliminal Racism." *Amerasia Journal* 3.2 (1976): 143–47.

2466.   Suzuki, Peter T. "Wartime *Tanka*: Issei and Kibei Contributions to a Literature East and West." *Literature East and West* 21 (1977): 242–54.

2467.   Tanaka, Ronald. "The Circle of Ethnicity." *Journal of Ethnic Studies* 8.3 (1980): 1–65.
         Continues the discussion of the metaphysical foundations of a *sansei* poetics.

2468.   ———. "The Circle of Ethnicity, Part II." *Journal of Ethnic Studies* 8.4 (1981): 37–94.

2469.   ———. "On the Metaphysical Foundations of a *sansei* Poetics: Ethnicity and Social Science." *Journal of Ethnic Studies* 7.2 (1979): 1–36.

2470.   ———. "Shido: Or, The Way of Poetry." *Journal of Ethnic Studies* 9.4 (1982): 1–63.
         Concludes the author's series on the metaphysical foundations of *sansei* poetics.

2471.   Wilson, Rob. "The Languages of Confinement and Liberation in Milton Murayama's *All I Asking for Is My Body.*" *Writers of Hawaii* [#2241] 62–65.

2472.   Wong, Shawn H., and Connie Young Yu. "'State of the City,' from *Trek* (1942)." *Bulletin of Concerned Asian Scholars* 4.3 (1972): 49–55.
         Contains a long excerpt from Taro Katayama's "Falderol."

2473.   Yamamoto [DeSoto], Hisaye. " . . . I Still Carry It Around." *RIKKA* 3.4 (1976): 11–19.
         A study of the Japanese American literary force.

2474.   ———. "Japanese in American Literature." *Rafu Shimpo* 20 Dec. 1971: 13+.

2475.   Yamane, Kazuo. "Introduction to Yoshio Abe's *The Man of Dual Nationality.*" *Journal of Ethnic Studies* 12.4 (1985): 87.

2476.   Yamauchi, Wakako. "The Poetry of the Issei on the Relocation Experience." *CALAFIA* [#162] lxxi–lxxviii.

2477.   Zabilski, Carol. "Dr. Kyō Koike, 1878–1947: Physician, Poet, Photographer." *Pacific Northwest Quarterly* 68.2 (1977): 73–79.

Interviews, Profiles, and Commentary

2478.   Arkatov, Janice. "The Soul and the Playwright Shall Dance." *Los Angeles Times* 8 Feb. 1986: V-3.
         A profile of Wakako Yamauchi.

2479. Blauvelt, William. "An Interview with Poet and Activist Janice Mirikitani: 'I want to be able to sing, to capture the electricity, to talk about the real sweat and pain of struggle and make it beautiful.'" *International Examiner* 4 July 1984: 6–7.

2480. Boswell, Peyton. "Peyton Boswell Comments; King of Bohemia." *Art Digest* 19.5 (1944): 3.
      On Sadakichi Hartmann.

2481. Chin, Frank. "In Search of John Okada: The First Asian American Playwright Looks for the Origins of the First Asian American Novelist." *Weekly* [Seattle] 30 June 1976: 10–11.
      Rpt. in slightly different form as afterword to *No-No Boy* [#1063] 253–60.

2482. ———. "The Last Organized Resistance: The Heart Mountain Fair Play Committee." *Rafu Shimpo* 19 Dec. 1981: 5+.

2483. ———. "Whites Can't Relate to John Okada's *No-No Boy*." *Pacific Citizen* 23–30 Dec. 1977: 55–56.

2484. DeCasseres, Benjamin. "Portrait on Galvanized Iron." *Sadakichi Hartmann Newsletter* 4.3 (1974): n. pag.
      Profile of Sadakichi Hartmann.

2485. Din, Grant. "Soft Silver Interwoven with Quick Fire." *East Wind* 3.1 (1984): 8–9.
      A conversation with the poet Toyo Suyemoto.

2486. Elderman, Michael J. "Sadakichi Hartmann and Stephane Mallarmé." *Sadakichi Hartmann Newsletter* 1.1 (1969): 3–4.

2487. Endo, Ellen. "Is Anyone out There Really Listening? An Interview with Lawson Inada, Poet." *Rafu Shimpo* 21 Dec. 1974: 16.

2488. "An Evening with Author Milton Murayama." *San Francisco Center for Japanese-American Studies Newsletter* Jan. 1976.

2489. "Face to Face." *Asianadian* 2.1 (1979): 22–25.
      Joy Kogawa.

2490. "Face to Face with Shizuye Takashima." *Asianadian* 1.3 (1978): 26–30.

2491. "Farewell to Manzanar: How a Young Woman's Experience Became a Book." *Rafu Shimpo* 19 Dec. 1973: 4+.
      Interview with Jeanne Wakatsuki Houston.

2492. Fitzgerald, Michael. "Stockton Fertile Ground for Playwright." *Stockton Record* 19 Mar. 1987: D1–8.
      Profile of Philip Gotanda.

2493. Hamilton, Charles F. "The Roycroft Period: Hartmann, Hubbard, and East Aurora." *Sadakichi Hartmann Newsletter* 2.1 (1971): 1–5.

2494. ———. "The Roycroft Period: Little Known Karl Kipp Got Hartmann Boost." *Sadakichi Hartmann Newsletter* 4.1 (1973): 1–2.

2495. Hansen, Helga. "Requiem (In Memory of Sadakichi Hartmann)." *Art Digest* 19.6 (1944): 24.

2496. Hartmann, Sadakichi. "A Tuesday Evening at Stephane Mallarmé's." *Sadakichi Hartmann Newsletter* 3.2 (1972): 4–5.

2497. Hill, Richard. "The First Hippie." *Swank International* 16.2 (1969): 16–18. On Sadakichi Hartmann.

2498. ———. "The Life and Times of Sadakichi Hartmann." *Florida Accent* 10 Nov. 1968: 8–10.

2499. Hirahara, Naomi. "A Farmer's Voice." *Rafu Shimpo* 20 Dec. 1986: 16–19. A profile of David Mas Masumoto.

2500. Hiura, Arnold. "Comments on Milton Murayama." *Writers of Hawaii* [#2241] 65–67.

2501. ———. "Profile: Larry Lindsey Kimura." *Hawaii Herald* 17 June 1983: 7+.

2502. Horikoshi, Peter. "Interview with Toshio Mori." *Counterpoint* [#113] 472–79.

2503. Horr, Alexander S. "Sadakichi Hartmann as a Photographic Writer." *Photo-Beacon* Oct. 1904: 307–09.

2504. Hosokawa, Bill. "Saiki Book Sketches a Childhood in Rural Hawaii." *Pacific Citizen* 4 Sept. 1987: 5. Profile of Jessica Saiki.

2505. Hotta, G. Haruko. "Nothing but Our Voices. . ." *East Wind* 4.1 (1985): 22–23. Discusses *issei* and *nisei* creativity in concentration camps.

2506. Houston, James D. "Writing a Non-Fiction Novel about the Internment of Japanese-Americans during World War II." *Solidarity* [Manila] 9.5 (1975): 66–72. On *Farewell to Manzanar.*

2507. Hull, Roger P., ed. "Along Timberline: An Unpublished Hartmann Nature Essay." *Sadakichi Hartmann Newsletter* 5.3 (1975): 4–7. Draft of an essay by Hartmann.

2508. ———. "Nature Writings of Sadakichi Hartmann." *Sadakichi Hartmann Newsletter* 5.3 (1975): 1–4.

2509. Inada, Lawson Fusao. "Tribute to Toshio." *Ayumi* [#141] 189–90. Discusses Toshio Mori.

2510. Katayama, Taro. "Literature as I Think It Should Be." *Reimei* ns 1.1 (1932): 3–4. Rpt. in *Kashu Mainichi* 24 Sept. 1932: 2.

2511. Klausner, Oscar. "Sadakichi in Detroit: The Recollections of Oscar Klausner." *Sadakichi Hartmann Newsletter* 3.2 (1972): 1–3.

2512.   Knox, George, ed. "Aspirations of a Playwright." *Sadakichi Hartmann Newsletter* 5.1 (1974): 6–8; 5.2 (1974–75): 2+.
        Essay by Hartmann.

2513.   ———. "Lost in Limbo: Some Nineteenth Century Critics." *Sadakichi Hartmann Newsletter* 4.1 (1973): 5–7.

2514.   ———, ed. "Sadakichi Discusses Eugene O'Neill." *Sadakichi Hartmann Newsletter* 4.3 (1974): 4–7.
        Essay by Hartmann.

2515.   ———. "The Whitman-Hartmann Controversy: Part I: First Meeting with Whitman." *Sadakichi Hartmann Newsletter* 1.2 (1970): 2–3.

2516.   ———. "The Whitman-Hartmann Controversy: Part II: Launching of a Whitman Society." *Sadakichi Hartmann Newsletter* 1.3 (1970): 5–7.

2517.   ———. "The Whitman-Hartmann Controversy: Part III: God Helps All Wanderers." *Sadakichi Hartmann Newsletter* 1.4 (1970): 7–9.

2518.   ———. "The Whitman-Hartmann Controversy: Part IV: The Controversy Erupts." *Sadakichi Hartmann Newsletter* 2.2 (1971): 8–12.

2519.   ———. "The Whitman-Hartmann Controversy: Part V: Fellowship and Some Fellows." *Sadakichi Hartmann Newsletter* 3.3 (1972): 3–8.

2520.   Kuniyoshi, Yasuo. "The Artist and the War." *Common Ground* 4.3 (1944): 33–35.
        Comments on the artist's role in World War II.

2520a. Kuroki, Ben. *Ben Kuroki's Story.* Berkeley: Pacific Coast Comm. on American Principles and Fair Play, 1944.
        An address by Sergeant Ben Kuroki at the Commonwealth Club, San Francisco, 4 Feb. 1944.

2521.   Lawton, Harry. "The Ezra Pound Correspondence: Letter to a Member of the Lost Legion." *Sadakichi Hartmann Newsletter* 1.4 (1970): 1–3.
        Examines the letters and postcards written by Pound to Hartmann between 1924 and 1940.

2522.   ———. "The Lost Bohemian." *Fortnight* 19.4 (1956): 31.
        On Sadakichi Hartmann.

2523.   Lee, Teri. "An Interview with Janice Mirikitani." *Asian American Review* (1976): 34–44.

2524.   Leong, Russell. "Toshio Mori: An Interview." *Amerasia Journal* 7.1 (1980): 89–108.

2525.   Lipton, Lawrence. "The Life and Times of Sadakichi Hartmann." *Los Angeles Free Press* 4 Feb. 1972, sect. 2: 2.

2526.   Matsushita, M. "Garrett Hongo." *Tozai Times* [Los Angeles] Jan. 1987: 10–11.

2527.   Moffet, Penelope. "Verses Chronicle Tales of Asian-Americans." *Los Angeles Times* 9 Mar. 1987, pt. 5: 1+.
        Profile of Garrett Kaoru Hongo.

2528. "The Most Mysterious Personality in American Letters." *Current Opinion* Aug. 1916: 124–25.
Sadakichi Hartmann.

2529. Muramoto, Gail. "An Evening with Senator Daniel Inouye." *Bridge* 4.2 (1976): 44–45.

2530. Murayama, Tamotsu. "An Issei Poet Who Composed in English." *Pacific Citizen* 22 Dec. 1961: A11.
On Isen Kanno.

2531. Nakao, Annie. "Nisei Author's Gift to Children." *San Francisco Examiner* 29 Sept. 1985: S1+.
Profile of Yoshiko Uchida.

2532. Nash, Philip Tajitsu. "Philip Kan Gotanda: Portrait of the Artist as a Youhen." *Bridge* 10.1 (1985): 4–7.

2533. "Nisei Writer Fosters Japanese American Identity." *Hokubei Mainichi* 4 Nov. 1981: 4.
Profile of Yoshiko Uchida.

2534. Ota, Saburo. "Carl Sadakichi Hartmann and Japan: I. Hartmann's Japanese Ancestry." *Sadakichi Hartmann Newsletter* 3.1 (1972): 1–3.

2535. ———. "Carl Sadakichi Hartmann and Japan: II. A Bridge to the East." *Sadakichi Hartmann Newsletter* 4.1 (1973): 3–4.

2536. ———. "Carl Sadakichi Hartmann and Japan: III. Conclusion." *Sadakichi Hartmann Newsletter* 4.2 (1973): 1–3.

2537. Oyama, Richard. "Martha Miyatake Wins Prestigious PEN Award for Unpublished Fiction." *Hokubei Mainichi* 6 Sept. 1984: 1.

2538. "Questions & Answers." *Writers of Hawaii* [#2241] 67–69.
Milton Murayama.

2539. Sasaki, Yasuo. "Reimei—an Awakened Dream." *Hokubei Mainichi* 1 Jan. 1986: 1.
Describes the genesis of *Reimei*, a Japanese American literary magazine.

2540. Schwab, Arnold. "James Gibbons Huneker's 'An Early Estimate of Sadakichi Hartmann.'" *Sadakichi Hartmann Newsletter* 1.4 (1970): 4–6.

2541. Sodetani, Naomi. "Janice Mirikitani: Words from the Third World." *East Wind* 4.1 (1985): 28–30.

2542. Suyemoto, Toyo. "Writing of Poetry." *Amerasia Journal* 10.1 (1983): 73–76.
Self-portrait.

2543. Tokutomi, Kiyoshi. "Haiku by a Nisei." *Hokubei Mainichi* 1 Jan. 1974, supplement: 2–3.
On Akira Tao.

2544. ———. "Shirota Thinking of Writing a Novel Based on Vietnam War." *Hokubei Mainichi* 1 Jan. 1973, supplement: 3.
On Jon Shirota.

2545. Tuerk, Richard. "The Making of an Art Critic: Sadakichi Lunches with a Famous Lady." *Sadakichi Hartmann Newsletter* 3.1 (1972): 6+.

2546. Van Doren, Carl. "A Hero with His Prose." *Roving Critic*. New York: Knopf, 1923. 219–20.
        Sadakichi Hartmann.

2547. Wada, Yori. "Keynote Address at 'Coming of Age in the Thirties: The Nisei and the Japanese Immigrant Press,' Los Angeles, September 15, 1985." *Fusion-San* [#157] 1–17.
        Rpt. as "Growing Up in Central California" in *Amerasia Journal* 13.2 (1986–87): 3–20.

2548. Wakayama Group. "Why Are There So Few Sansei Writers?" *Bridge* 2.1 (1972): 17–21.

2549. Wakayama, Mary. "A Talk with Joy Kogawa." *Literary Arts Hawaii* 76–77 (Spring 1985): 6–7.

2550. Wayne, Joyce. "*Obasan*: Drama of Nisei Nightmare." *RIKKA* 8.2 (1981): 22–23.
        Profile of Joy Kogawa.

2551. Wong, Mina, and Satish Dhar. "Face to Face with Rick Shiomi." *Asianadian* 5.3 (1984): 10–13.

2552. Wong, William, and Joyce Mende Wong. "Interview with Gary Sone: Once a Japanese Houseboy." *Yardbird Reader* 3 [#179] 62–77.
        Also interviews Monica Sone.

2553. Yamada, Joyce. "Early 20th Century Japanese Writers in America: The Cultural Nomads." *AAMPLITUDE* [Washington] 1.2 (1986): 10–11.

2554. Yamamoto, J. K. "Hongo Offers a Poet's View of JA Experience." *Pacific Citizen* 20 Feb. 1987: 1+.
        Profile of Garrett Kaoru Hongo.

2555. Yim, Susan. "In a Hailstorm of Words." *Honolulu Star-Bulletin* 20 Sept. 1984, evening ed.: D1+.
        Interview with Joy Kogawa.

Filipino American Literature

For an explanation of the variant spellings *Pilipino* and *Filipino*, see *Amerasia Journal* 13.1 (1986–87): viii–ix.

Books, Theses, and Dissertations

2556. Agcaoili, T. D., ed. *Philippine Writing*. Manila: Archipelago, 1953.

2557. Alegre, Edilberto N., and Doreen G. Fernandez, eds. *The Writer and His Milieu: An Oral History of First Generation Writers in English*. Manila: De la Salle UP, 1984.
     Includes an interview with Bienvenido N. Santos.

2558. ———. *Writers and Their Milieu: An Oral History of Second Generation Writers in English*. Manila: De la Salle UP, 1987.
     Includes interviews with Carlos Angeles, N. V. M. Gonzalez, and Manuel A. Viray.

2559. Barrios, Mary Angela. "A Grammatical and Rhetorical Study of the Style of N. V. M. Gonzalez." Diss. Ateneo de Manila Univ. [Quezon City, Philippines], 1981.

2560. Bernad, Miguel A. *Bamboo and the Greenwood Tree: Essays on Filipino Literature in English*. Introd. Alfred Stirling. Manila: Bookmark, 1961.

2561. ———. *Philippine Literature: A Twofold Renaissance*. Manila: Bookmark, 1963.

2562. ———. *Tradition and Discontinuity: Essays on Philippine History and Culture*. Manila: National Book Store, 1983.

2563. Bresnahan, Roger J., ed. *Literature and Society: Cross-Cultural Perspectives*. Manila: Philippine-American Educational Foundation and American Studies Assn. of the Philippines, 1977.

2564. Casper, Leonard. *Firewalkers: Literary Concelebrations, 1964–1984*. Quezon City, Philippines: New Day Publishers, 1987.
     Discusses N. V. M. Gonzalez, Ninotchka Rosca, E. San Juan, Jr., Bienvenido N. Santos, and Manuel A. Viray.

2565. ———. *The Wayward Horizon: Essays on Modern Philippine Literature*. Manila: Community Publishers, 1961.

2566. ———. *The Wounded Diamond: Studies in Modern Philippine Literature*. Manila: Bookmark, 1964.

2567. Casuga, Albert B., ed. *Philippine Poetry from José García Villa to Jose Lacaba*. Manila: De la Salle Coll., 1971.

2568. Cruz, Isagani R. *Beyond Futility: The Filipino as Critic*. Quezon City, Philippines: New Day Publishers, 1984.

2569. ———, ed. *A Short History of Theater in the Philippines*. Manila: Bureau of Printing, 1971.

2570.   Evangelista, Susan, ed. *Carlos Bulosan and His Poetry: A Biography and Anthology.* Seattle: U of Washington P, 1985.
Rev. Maurice Kenny, *Contact II* 7.38–40 (1986): 25.

2571.   ———. "Carlos Bulosan and the Beginnings of Third World Consciousness." Diss. Univ. of the Philippines, 1981.

2572.   Florentino, Alberto S., ed. *Literature at the Crossroads: 3 Symposia on the Filipino Novel, Filipino Poetry, the Filipino Theater.* Manila: Alberto S. Florentino, 1965.

2573.   ———. *Midcentury Guide to Philippine Literature in English.* Manila: Filipiniana Publishers, 1963.

2574.   Galdon, Joseph A., ed. *Essays in Literature.* Quezon City, Philippines: Ateneo de Manila UP, 1977.

2575.   ———, ed. *Essays on the Philippine Novel in English.* Quezon City, Philippines: Ateneo de Manila UP, 1979.

2576.   ———, ed. *Philippine Fiction: Essays from Philippine Studies, 1953–1972.* Quezon City, Philippines: Ateneo UP, 1972.

2577.   Hosillos, Lucila. *Originality as Vengeance in Philippine Literature.* Quezon City, Philippines: New Day Publishers, 1984.

2578.   ———. *Philippine-American Literary Relations 1898–1941.* Quezon City: U of the Philippines P, 1969.

2579.   Lopez, Salvador P. *Literature and Society: Essays on Life and Letters.* Manila: Univ. Book Supply, 1940.

2580.   Lumbera, Bienvenido. *Revaluation: Essays of Philippine Literature, Cinema and Popular Culture.* N.p.: Index Press, 1984.

2581.   Majid [bin Nabi Baksh], Abdul. *The Filipino Novel in English.* Spec. issue of *Philippine Social Sciences and Humanities Review* [Quezon City, Philippines] 35.1–2 (1970).

2582.   Manuud, Antonio G., ed. *Brown Heritage: Essays on Philippine Cultural Tradition and Literature.* Quezon City, Philippines: Ateneo de Manila UP, 1967.

2583.   Maramba, Asuncion David. *Outline History of Philippine Literature in English from the Beginnings to 1972.* Manila: National Book Store, 1981.

2584.   Menez, Herminia. *Folkloric Communication among Filipinos in California.* New York: Arno, 1980.

2585.   Mojares, Resil B. *Origins and Rise of the Filipino Novel.* Quezon City: U of the Philippines P, 1983.

2586.   Morantte, P. C. *Remembering Carlos Bulosan (His Heart Affair with America).* Introd. N. V. M. Gonzalez. Quezon City, Philippines: New Day Publishers, 1984.
Personal reminiscences.
Rev. Fred Wei-han Houn, *Amerasia Journal* 13.1 (1986–87): 187–88.

2587.   Nudas, Alfeo G. *Telic Contemplation: A Study of Grace in Seven Philippine Writers.* Quezon City: U of the Philippines P, 1979.

2588.   San Juan, E[pifanio], Jr. *Carlos Bulosan and the Imagination of the Class Struggle.* Quezon City: U of the Philippines P, 1972. New York: Orion Press, 1975.

2590.   ———, ed. *Introduction to Modern Pilipino Literature.* New York: Twayne, 1974.

2591.   ———, ed. *Makibaka! Revolutionary Writing from the Philippines.* Mansfield Depot, CT: Philippines Research Center, 1979.

2592.   ———. *Only by Struggle: Literature and Revolution in the Philippines.* Mansfield Depot, CT: Philippines Research Center, 1980.

2593.   ———. *A Preface to Pilipino Literature.* Quezon City, Philippines: Alemar-Phoenix Publishers, 1971.

2594.   ———. *The Radical Tradition in Philippine Literature.* Quezon City: U of the Philippines P, 1960. Quezon City, Philippines: Manlapaz Publishing, 1971.
        Ch. 4 discusses Carlos Bulosan.

2595.   ———. *Toward a People's Literature: Essays in the Dialectics of Praxis and Contradiction in Philippine Writing.* Quezon City: U of the Philippines P, 1984.

2596.   Univ. of the Philippines Library. *José García Villa: A Bio-Bibliography.* Quezon City: Univ. of the Philippines Library, 1973.

2597.   Valeros, Margarita. "An Appreciative Study of the Life and Works of Carlos Bulosan." MA thesis, National Teachers Coll., 1955.

2598.   Yabes, Leopoldo Y., ed. *Filipino Essays in English: A Historico-Critical Anthology in Two Volumes, 1910–1954.* Quezon City: Univ. of the Philippines, 1954.

Articles

2599.   Abad, Gémino H. "Two Poems by Carlos A. Angeles: An Experiment in Poetics." *Asian Studies* 10.3 (1972): 344–60.
        Rpt. in *In Another Light: Poems and Essays.* Quezon City: U of the Philippines P, 1976. 195–218.
        The two poems are "From the Rooftop" and "The Summer Trees."

2600.   Abad, Gémino H., and Edna Z. Manlapaz. "Rereading Past Writ: Toward a History of Filipino Poetry from English, 1905 to the Mid-50s." *Philippine Studies* 34 (1986): 374–87.

2601.   Arcellana, Francisco. "Bienvenido N. Santos." *Brown Heritage* [#2582] 714–21.

2602.   Bernad, Miguel A. "Philippine Literature: A Twofold Renaissance." *Thought* 37 (Autumn 1962): 427–48.

2603.   Bresnahan, Roger J. "The Midwestern Fiction of Bienvenido N. Santos." *Society for the Study of Midwestern Literature Newsletter* 13.2 (1983): 28–37.

2604.   Bulosan, Carlos. "Filipino Writers in a Changing World." *Books Abroad* July 1942: 252–54.
        Introduces various Filipino writers.

2605.   Casper, Leonard. "The Critical Mass in E. San Juan." *Solidarity* [Manila] 102 (1985): 132–38.

2606.   ———. "José García Villa." *Critical Survey of Poetry* 7 (1984): 2976–84.

2607.   ———. "N. V. M. Gonzalez." *Critiques and New Writing from the Philippines*. Syracuse: Syracuse UP, 1962. 42–45.
        Rpt. in *Critical Survey of Long Fiction*. Ed. Frank Magill. La Canada, CA: Salem Press, 1983. 3: 1139–44.

2609.   ———. "The Opposing Thumb: Recent Philippine Literature in English." *Pacific Affairs* 56 (1983): 301–09.
        Discusses N. V. M. Gonzalez, Paul Stephen Lim, and Linda Ty-Casper.

2610.   ———. "Paperboat Novels: The Later Bienvenido Santos." *Amerasia Journal* 13.1 (1986–87): 163–70.

2611.   ———. "Truth in Fiction and History." *Pilipinas* 6 (1986): 53–56.

2612.   Cheung, King-Kok. "Bienvenido Santos: Filipino Old-Timers in Literature." *Markham Review* 15 (1986): 49–53.

2613.   Daroy, P. B. "Carlos Bulosan: The Politics of Literature." *St. Louis Quarterly* [St. Louis Univ., Bagio City, Philippines] 6.2 (1968): 193–206.

2614.   De Jesus, Edilberto, Jr. "On This Soil, in This Climate: Growth in the Novels of N. V. M. Gonzalez." *Brown Heritage* [#2582] 739–64.

2615.   Demetillo, Ricaredo. "The Authentic Voice of Poetry." *The Authentic Voice of Poetry*. Quezon City: Office of Research Coordination, Univ. of the Philippines, 1962. 256–70.
        Discusses the poems in *Six Filipino Poets*, ed. Leonard Casper.

2616.   ———. "José García Villa vs. Salvador P. Lopez." *The Authentic Voice of Poetry*. Quezon City: Office of Research Coordination, Univ. of the Philippines, 1962. 294–321.

2617.   Edwardson, Jean. "Disaster and Survival in the Poetry of Carlos Angeles." *Collegian New Review* [Univ. of the Philippines] 1.5 (1954): 7–9.

2618.   Foronda, Marcelino A., Jr. "Recent Ilokano Fiction in Hawaii." *Bulletin of the American Historical Collection* 6.4 (1978): 8–30.

2619.   Galdon, Joseph A. "Romance and Realism: The Philippine Novel in English." *Essays on the Philippine Novel in English* [#2575] 1–24.

2620.   Gonzalez, N. V. M. "The Artist in Southeast Asia." *Books Abroad* Autumn 1956: 387–91.
        Rpt. in *Literary Apprentice* 20.2 (1956): 77–83.

2621.   ———. "The Difficulties with Filipiniana." *Brown Heritage* [#2582] 539–45.
Discusses the state of literary criticism in the Philippines and in America.

2622.   ———. "Drumming for the Captain." *World Literature in English* 15.2 (1976): 415–27.
Discusses the anonymity and cultural colonialism suffered by Filipino writers.

2623.   ———. "The Filipino and the Novel." *Fiction in Several Languages*. Ed. Henri Peyre. Boston: Beacon, 1968. 19–29.

2624.   ———. "Holding the Rainbow." *Manila Review* 1.3 (1975): 59–69.
An essay on Third World literature.

2625.   ———. "Imagination and the Literature of Emerging Nations." *Solidarity* [Manila] 9.5 (1975): 31–40.
Rpt. in *Literature East and West* 17 (1973): 371–87.

2626.   ———. "Imaginative Writing in the Philippines." *Philippine Writing* [#2556] 321–28.

2627.   ———. "In the Workshop of Time and Tide." Supp. to *The Well of Time* [#135].
Rpt. in *Mindoro and Beyond* [#1530] 231–56.
Surveys the development of modern Filipino literature.

2628.   ———. "The Lonely Heresy: An Update." *Pilipinas* 3.2 (1982): 26–29.
A review article on Philippine criticism.

2628a.   ———. "The Needle under the Rock." *Manila Review* 6 (1976): 32–41.
Carlos Bulosan, Bienvenido N. Santos, and José García Villa are among the writers discussed.

2629.   ———. "Philippine Letters Today." *Books Abroad* Winter 1955: 26–30.

2630.   ———. "Rizal and the Poetic Myth." *Literature and Society*. Manila: Alberto S. Florentino, 1964. 32–54.

2631.   ———. "A Story Yet to Be Told." *Quadrant No. 68* 14.6 (Nov.-Dec. 1970): 111–15.
Attributes the untapped and unrecognized native Philippine imagination to inadequate cultural leadership.

2632.   ———. "Whistling up the Wind: Myth and Creativity." *Philippine Studies* 31 (1983): 216–26.
Discusses Filipino myths and their regenerative power.

2633.   Grow, L. M. "Modern Philippine Literature in English: Current Trends and the Tradition." *World Literature Written in English* 15.2 (1976): 392–97.

2634.   Guzman, Richard P. "'As in Myth, the Signs Were All Over': The Fiction of N. V. M. Gonzalez." *Virginia Quarterly Review* 60 (Winter 1984): 102–18.

2635. Hernandez, Jose M. "Filipino Writing in English." *Manila Times Magazine* 4 Feb. 1948.

2636. Hufana, A. G. "Transvaluation in N. V. M. Gonzalez's *Mindoro and Beyond: Twenty-One Stories.*" *Likhaan* 1 (Dec. 1979): 145–50.

2637. Lumbera, Bienvenido. "Desolate Loneliness within the Premises of Guilt." *Philippine Studies* 13 (1965): 850–59.
    Rpt. as "Desolate Loneliness in Casper's *Peninsulars*" in *Revaluation* [#2580] 227–40.

2638. Menez, Herminia Q. "Agyu and the Skyworld: The Philippine Folk Epic and Multicultural Education." *Amerasia Journal* 13.1 (1986–87): 135–49.

2639. ———. "The Performance of Folk Narrative in Filipino Communities in California." *Western Folklore* 36.1 (1977): 57–70.

2641. Morales, Alfredo T. "The Filipino Quality of Living as Reflected in N. V. M. Gonzalez' *The Bamboo Dancers.*" *WeekEnd* 15 Aug. 1982: 25–26.

2642. Reyes, Soledad S. "Death-in-Life in Santos's *Villa Magdalena.*" *Essays on the Philippine Novel in English* [#2575] 125–49.

2643. Rómulo, Carlos P. "The Future of Filipino Literature." *Diliman Review* [Philippines] 11 (Jan. 1963): 3–16.

2644. San Juan, E[pifanio], Jr. "Art against Imperialism." *Journal of Contemporary Asia* 4 (1974): 297–307.
    Rpt. in *The Weapons of Criticism*. Ed. Norman Rudich. Palo Alto: Ramparts Press, 1975. 147–60.

2645. ———. "Carlos Bulosan: An Introduction." *Asian and Pacific Quarterly of Cultural and Social Affairs* 10.2 (1978): 43–48.

2646. ———. "Cultural Resurgence in Philippine Literature." *Literature East and West* 9 (Winter 1965): 16–23.

2647. ———. "Eros Committed: Bulosan's 'Love' Fiction." *Researcher* [Univ. of Pangasinan, Philippines] 3 (1971).

2648. ———. "Literature and Revolution in the Third World." *Social Praxis* 6 (1979): 19–34.

2649. ———. "Overthrowing U.S. Hegemony: Dialectics of U.S.–Philippines Literary Relations." *Minnesota Review* Spring 1986: 61–82.

2650. ———. "The Pilipino American Writer: A Struggle on Two Fronts." *Bridge* 6.1 (1977): 48–51.
    An introduction to Carlos Bulosan's unpublished novel *The Cry and the Dedication*.

2651. ———. "Translation and Philippine Poetics." *East-West Review* 2 (Spring-Summer 1966): 279–90.

2652. Santos, Bienvenido. "The Filipino Novel in English." *Brown Heritage* [#2582] 634–47.

2653. ———. "The Personal Saga of a 'Straggler' in Philippine Literature." *World Literature Written in English* 15.2 (1976): 398–405.
  "Stragglers" in this article refer to "Filipino writers in English who were already publishing before the 40's."

2654. Santos, Tomas N. "The Filipino Writer in America—Old and New." *World Literature Written in English* 15.2 (1976): 406–14.

2655. States, Mark. "Third World American Dream: Unionist and Socialist Politics in the Art of Hughes and Bulosan." *Critical Perspectives of Third World America* 1.1 (1983): 91–115.

2656. Syquia, Serafin Malay. "Politics and Poetry." *Liwanag* [#95] 178.

2657. Tiempo, Edith L. "Carlos A. Angeles: The Landscape as Reflexion." *Manila Review* 6 (Mar. 1976): 58–61.

2658. Tinio, Rolando S. "Period of Awareness: The Poets." *Brown Heritage* [#2582] 618–33.
  Discusses Carlos Angeles, N. V. M. Gonzalez, Epifanio San Juan, and José García Villa.

2659. ———. "Villa's Values: Or, The Poet You Cannot Always Make Out, or Succeed in Liking Once You Are Able To." *Brown Heritage* [#2582] 722–38.

2660. Ty-Casper, Linda. "Literature: A Flesh Made of Fugitive Suns." *Philippine Studies* 28 (1980): 59–73.

2661. ———. "Philippine Literature in English." *Solidarity* [Manila] 100 (1984): 41–45.

2662. Viray, Manuel A. "Certain Influences in Filipino Writing." *Pacific Spectator* 6 (Summer 1952): 292–99.

2663. ———. "Philippine Writing Today." *Literary Review* 3 (Summer 1960): 465–77.

2664. Zuraek, Maria Elnora C. "N. V. M. Gonzalez's *A Season of Grace*." *Essays on the Philippine Novel in English* [#2575] 109–24.

Interviews, Profiles, and Commentary

2666. Bresnahan, Roger J. "Slashing Vision, Burning Hope." *Asiaweek* [Hong Kong] 11 Dec. 1982.
  Profile of N. V. M. Gonzalez.

2667. Chow, Christopher. "A Brother Reflects: An Interview with Aurelio Bulosan." *Amerasia Journal* 6.1 (1979): 155–66.
  Reflections on Carlos Bulosan.

2668. Dawson, Diane. "Hayward Author Tells Stories of a Rural Filipino Island." *Daily Review* 27 Mar. 1980: 25.
  N. V. M. Gonzalez.

2669. Feria, Dolores Stephens. "High Adventure in N. V. M. Gonzalez Country." *Philippine Panorama* 8 May 1983: 32+.

2670. Houn, Fred Wei-han. "The Brown Power Poet: Serafin Malay Syquia (1943–1973)." *East Wind* 5.1 (1986): 34–38.

2671. Mensalvas, Chris. "Reporting for Carlos Bulosan." *Daily People's World* 28 Dec. 1956.

2672. Morantte, P. C. "Two Filipinos in America." *Books Abroad* 18.4 (1944): 323–27.
   Profiles of Carlos Bulosan and José García Villa.

2673. "Return of a Native Son." *Asiaweek* [Hong Kong] 5 Jan. 1986: 56.
   Profile of Paulino Lim, Jr.

2674. Reyes, Soledad S. "Response: Reyes on San Juan." *New Philippine Review* 1.2 (1984): 36–37.

2675. San Juan, E[pifanio], Jr. "Carlos Bulosan: The Poetics and Necessity of Revolution." *Researcher* [Univ. of Pangasinan, Philippines] 2 (1969): 113.

2676. ———. "The Filipino Worker in the U.S.: An Introduction to Carlos Bulosan." *East Wind* 1.2 (1982): 45–47.

2677. ———. "In the Belly of the Monster: The Filipino Revolt in the U.S." *Praxis* 3 (Winter-Spring 1976–77): 60–66.

2678. ———. "Towards a People's Literature: San Juan on San Juan." *New Philippine Review* 1.2 (1984): 34–35.

2679. Santos, Alfonso P. "As I Knew Them." *Literary Apprentice* [Manila] Oct. 1956: 95–101.
   On Carlos Bulosan and Marcelo de Gracia Concepción.

2680. Syquia, Lou, and Ernestine Tayabas. "Sayaw of Words, Kanta of Spirit." *East Wind* 4.1 (1985): 37–38.
   Introduces a Filipino American writing group.

2681. Torres, Manzel de la Cruz. "A Weekend with N. V. M. Gonzalez." *Filipino-American Panorama* Dec. 1983: 29.

2682. Valderrama, N. G. "Allos." *This Week* [Sunday magazine of *Manila Chronicle*] 21 Mar. 1948.
   Carlos Bulosan.

2683. Walbridge, Earle F. "Carlos Bulosan." *Wilson Library Journal* Apr. 1946: 570.

2684. Yabes, Leopoldo. "The Dream of Carlos Bulosan." *Evening News Saturday Magazine* 25 Jan. 1947.

2685. ———. "More on Carlos Bulosan." *Sunday Post Magazine* 16 Mar. 1947.

Korean American Literature

Articles

2686. Galloway, David D. "The Love Stance: Richard E. Kim's *The Martyred*." *Critique* 7 (1964–65): 163–71.

2687. Kim, Elaine H. "Searching for a Door to America: Younghill Kang." *Asian American Review* 1976: 102–16.
        Rpt. in *Korea Journal* July 1977: 38–47.

2688. Stephens, Michael. "Korea: Theresa Hak Kyung Cha." *The Dramaturgy of Style: Voice in Short Fiction*. Crosscurrents Modern Critiques Third Series. Carbondale: Southern Illinois UP, 1986. 184–210.

2689. Wolf, Susan. "Theresa Cha: Recalling Telling ReTelling." *AfterImage* Summer 1986: 10–13.

Interviews, Profiles, and Commentary

2690. "Best-Selling Korean." *Life* 20 Mar. 1964: 125–26.
        Profile of Richard E. Kim.

2691. Japenga, Ann. "Poet's Korean Ideas Sing in English." *Los Angeles Times* 9 Jan. 1987, pt. 5: 2.
        Introduces Korean American poet Sung-yol Yi and his poetry.

2692. Nomaguchi, Debbie Murakami. "Cathy Song: 'I'm a Poet Who Happens to Be Asian American.'" *International Examiner* 2 May 1984: 9.

2693. Wade, James. "Younghill Kang's Unwritten Third Act." *Korea Journal* Apr. 1973: 57–61.
        Profile.

South Asian American Literature

Books, Theses, and Dissertations

2694. Chukwu, Augustine Emmanuel. "Home and Exile: A Study of the Fiction of Samuel Selvon." Diss. Univ. of New Brunswick, 1984.

2695. Desai, S. K. *Santha Rama Rau*. New Delhi: Arnold-Heinemann, 1975.

2696. Gemmil, Janet P. "Narrative Technique in the Novels of Raja Rao." Diss. Univ. of Wisconsin, Madison, 1973.

2697. Hines, George. *Stephen Gill and His Works*. Foreword by John Robbins. Cornwall, ON: Vesta, 1982.

2698. Itwaru, Arnold Harrichand. "The Invention of Canada: The Literary Production of Consciousness in Ten Immigrant Writers." Diss. York Univ., 1983.
    Includes two South Asian Canadian writers—Stephen Gill and Ved Devagee (Réshard Gool).

2699. Naik, M. K. *Raja Rao*. New York: Twayne, 1972.

2700. Naik, M. K., S. K. Desai, and G. S. Amur, eds. *Critical Essays on Indian Writing in English: Presented to Armando Menezes*. Dharwar: Karnatak Univ., 1972.

2701. Naik, M. K., S. K. Desai, and S. T. Kallapur, eds. *The Image of India in Western Creative Writing*. Dharwar: Karnatak UP; London: Macmillan, 1971.

2702. Narasimhaiah, C. D. *Raja Rao*. New Delhi: Arnold-Heinemann, 1973.

2703. Narasimhan, Raji. *Sensibility under Stress: Aspects of Indo-English Fiction*. New Delhi: Ashajanak Publishers, 1976.
    Includes discussions on Raja Rao and G. V. Desani.

2704. Nasta, Susheila M., ed. *Critical Perspectives on Sam Selvon*. Washington: Three Continents Press, 1987.

2705. Niven, Alastair, ed. *The Commonwealth Writer Overseas: Themes of Exile and Expatriation*. Brussels: Didier, 1976.

2706. Parameswaran, Uma. *A Study of Representative Indo-English Novelists*. New Delhi: Vikas Publishing House, 1976.
    Discusses Balachandra Rajan and Raja Rao.

2707. Russell, Peter, and Khushwant Singh. *A Note on G. V. Desani's All about H. Hatterr and Hali*. London: Karel Szeben, 1952.

2708. Sharma, Jai Prakash. *Raja Rao as a Novelist and Short Story Writer*. Meerut: n.p., 1975.

2709. Singh, Ram Sewak. *Raja Rao's Kanthapura: A Critical Study*. Delhi: Doaba House, 1973.

2710.   Sugunasiri, Suwanda H. J., ed. *The Search for Meaning: The Literature of Canadians of South Asian Origins.* Ottawa: Secretary of State, 1983. Unpublished.

2711.   Vassanji, M. G., ed. *A Meeting of Streams: South Asian Canadian Literature.* Toronto: TSAR Publications, 1985.

Articles

2712.   Ali, Ahmed. "Illusion and Reality: The Art and Philosophy of Raja Rao." *Journal of Commonwealth Literature* 5 (1968): 16–28.

2713.   Amur, G. S. "Peter Nazareth's *In a Brown Mantle*: The Novel as Revolutionary Art." *Awakened Conscience: Studies in Commonwealth Literature.* Ed. C. D. Narasimhaiah. New Delhi: Sterling Publishers, 1978. 111–17.
        Rpt. in G. S. Amur, *Images and Impressions: Essays Mainly on Contemporary Indian Literature.* Jaipur, India: Panchsheel Prakashan, 1979. 22–29.

2714.   Banerjee, N. N. "Recent Indian Writing in English." *Contemporary Indian Literature* 4.1 (1964): 12–13; 4.2 (1964): 24–26; 4.3 (1964): 11–12; 4.4 (1964): 12–13.

2715.   Beck, Brenda E. F. "Indo-Canadian Popular Culture: Should Writers Take the Lead in Its Development?" *A Meeting of Streams* [#2711] 121–32.

2716.   Belliappa, Meena. "East-West Encounter: Indian Women Writers of Fiction in English." *Literary Criterion* 7.3 (1966): 18–27.
        Rpt. in *Fiction and the Reading Public in India.* Ed. C. D. Narasimhaiah. Mysore: Univ. of Mysore, 1970. 18–27.

2717.   Bhalla, Brij M. "Quest for Identity in Raja Rao's *The Serpent and the Rope*." *Ariel* 4.4 (1973): 95–105.

2718.   Birbalsingh, Frank. "South Asian Canadian Novels in English." *A Meeting of Streams* [#2711] 49–61.

2719.   Brunton, T. D. "India in Fiction." *Critical Essays on Indian Writing in English* [#2700] 54–57.

2720.   Burjorjee, D. M. "The Dialogue in G. V. Desani's *All About H. Hatterr*." *World Literature Written in English* 13.2 (1974): 191–224.

2721.   Choi, Kim Yok. "The Concept of Love in Raja Rao's *The Serpent and the Rope*." *Triveni* 44.4 (1976): 39–47.

2722.   Dabydeen, David. "Race and Community in Anglophone Caribbean Fiction." *Toronto South Asian Review* 5.1 (1986): 139–49.

2723.   Desai, S. K. "Transplantation of English: Raja Rao's Experimentation with English in His Works of Fiction." *Experimentation with Language in Indian Writing in English.* Ed. S. K. Desai. Kohlapur: Shivaji Univ., Dept. of English, 1972. 1–32.

2724. Dey, Esha. "Hindu Critique on *The Serpent and the Rope*." *Bharati* 6.10 (1972): 27–36.

2725. Gadgil, Gangadhar. "Some Parallels in the Development of American and Indian Literature." *Western Humanities Review* 17 (1963): 107–16.

2726. Gemmil, Janet P. "Dualities and Non-Duality in Raja Rao's *The Serpent and the Rope*." *World Literature Written in English* 12.2 (1973): 247–59.

2727. ———. "Raja Rao's *The Cow of the Barricades*: Two Stories." *Journal of South Asian Literature* 13 (1977–78): 23–30.
      The two stories discussed are "Javni" and "The Client."

2728. ———. "Raja Rao: Three Tales of Independence." *World Literature Written in English* 16.1 (1976): 135–46.

2729. ———. "Rhythm in *The Cat and Shakespeare*." *Literature East and West* 13.1–2 (1969): 27–42.

2730. Globe, Alex. "Spires and Show." *Canadian Literature* 64 (1975): 118–21. On Stephen Gill.

2731. Gool, Réshard. "Back in Touch: Rienzi Crusz's Poetry." *Toronto South Asian Review* 2.1 (1983): 2+.

2732. Gowda, H. H. Annaih. "Rajan: The Serious and the Comic." *Literary Half-Yearly* 5.1 (1964): 45–46.

2733. ———. "Raja Rao's *The Serpent and the Rope*." *Literary Half-Yearly* 4.2 (1963): 36–40.

2734. Guruprasad, Thakur. "Reflections on Rama: India as Depicted in *The Serpent and the Rope*." *Journal of Indian Writing in English* 1.1 (1973): 19–28.

2735. Harrex, S. C. "Dancing in the Dark: Balachandra Rajan and T. S. Eliot." *World Literature Written in English* 14.2 (1975): 14–20.

2736. ———. "Raja Rao: Companion of Pilgrimage." *Studies in Australian and Indian Literature: Proceedings of a Seminar.* Ed. S. Nagarajan and C. D. Narasimhaiah. New Delhi: Indian Council for Cultural Relations, 1971. 257–73.

2737. Hemenway, Stephen I. "Raja Rao's *Kanthapura* and *The Serpent and the Rope*." *The Novel of India.* Calcutta: Writers Workshop, 1975. 71–109.

2738. Isaac, Shanty. "Two French Elements in *The Serpent and the Rope*." *Journal of Karnatak University (Humanities)* 18 (1974): 138–47.

2739. Iyengar, K. R. Srinivasa. "Literature as 'Sadhana': A Note on Raja Rao's *The Cat and Shakespeare*." *Aryan Path* 40.7 (1969): 301–05.

2740. Jamil, Maya. "Indian and Pakistani Writers of English Fiction." *University Studies* 1.1 (1964): 61–68.

2741. Kachru, Braj B. "Some Style Features of South Asian English." *National Identity: Papers Delivered at the Commonwealth Literature Conference, University of Queensland, Brisbane, 9th–15th August, 1968.* Ed. K. L. Goodwin. London: Heinemann, 1970. 122–37.

2742. Kantak, V. Y. "The Language of Indian Fiction in English." *Critical Essays on Indian Writing in English* [#2700] 147–59.

2743. Krishnamurthi, M. G. "Indian Fiction in English: Some Critical Problems." *Humanist Review* 1.4 (1969): 435–52.

2744. McCutchion, David. "The Novel as Sastra." *Writers Workshop Miscellany* 8 (1961): 91–99.
Rpt. in *Considerations*. Ed. Meenakshi Mukherjee. Bombay: Allied Publishers, 1977. 90–101.

2745. Mukherjee, Arun P. "South Asian Poetry in Canada: In Search of a Place." *A Meeting of Streams* [#2711] 7–25.

2746. ———. "The Sri Lankan Poets in Canada: An Alternative View." *Toronto South Asian Review* 3.2 (1984): 32–45.

2747. Mukherjee, Bharati. "Writers of the Indian Commonwealth." *Literary Review* 29.4 (1986): 400–01.

2748. Mukherjee, Meenakshi. "Literature of Exile." *Bulletin of the Association of Commonwealth Literature and Language Studies* 4.2 (1975): 27–32.

2749. ———. "Raja Rao's Shorter Fiction." *Indian Literature* 10.3 (1967): 66–76.

2750. Nagarajan, S. "A. K. Ramanujan." *Contemporary Indian Poetry in English: An Assessment and Selection*. Ed. Saleem Peeradura. Bombay: Macmillan, 1972. 18–21.

2751. ———. "An Indian Novel." *Sewanee Review* 72.3 (1964): 512–17.
Rpt. in *Considerations*. Ed. Meenakshi Mukherjee. Bombay: Allied Publishers, 1977. 84–89.

2752. ———. "A Note on Myth and Ritual in *The Serpent and the Rope*." *Journal of Commonwealth Literature* 7.1 (1972): 45–48.

2753. Naik, M. K. "The Achievement of Raja Rao." *Banasthali Patrika* 12 (1969): 44–56.

2754. ———. "*The Cat and Shakespeare*: A Study." *Indian Literature of the Past Fifty Years, 1917–1967*. Ed. C. D. Narasimhaiah. Mysore: Univ. of Mysore, 1970. 147–78.

2755. ———. "Heir to Two Worlds: Influences on Raja Rao." *Triveni* 41.1 (1972): 68–76.

2756. ———. "In Native Accents: The Juvenilia of Raja Rao." *Aryan Path* 43.2 (1972): 74–80.

2757. ———. "*Kanthapura*: The Indo-Anglian Novel as 'Legendary' History." *Journal of Karnatak University (Humanities)* 10 (1966): 26–39.

2758. ———. "The Kingdom of God Is within a 'Mew': A Study of *The Cat and Shakespeare*." *Journal of Karnatak University (Humanities)* 12 (1968): 123–50.

2759. ———. "Narrative Strategy in Raja Rao's '*The Cow of the Barricades*' and Other Stories." *Indian Writing Today* 5.3 (1972): 152–58.

2760.   ———. "Raja Rao as a Short Story Writer: '*The Cow of the Barricades.*'" *Books Abroad* 40.4 (1966): 392–96.

2761.   ———. "*The Serpent and the Rope*: The Indo-Anglian Novel as Epic Legend." *Critical Essays on Indian Writing in English* [#2700] 259–93.

2762.   Narasimhaiah, C. D. "*The Cat and Shakespeare*: An Ad-Hoc Assessment." *Literary Criterion* 8.3 (1968): 65–95.

2763.   ———. "Indian Writing in English: An Area of Promise." *Journal of Commonwealth Literature* 9.1 (1974): 35–49.

2764.   ———. "The Metaphysical Novel: *The Serpent and the Rope*." *The Swan and the Eagle*. Simla: Indian Inst. of Advanced Study, 1969. 159–202.

2765.   ———. "National Identity in Literature and Language: Its Range and Depth in the Novels of Raja Rao." *National Identity: Papers Delivered at the Commonwealth Literature Conference, University of Queensland, Brisbane, Aug. 9–15, 1968*. Ed. K. L. Goodwin. London: Heinemann, 1970. 153–69.

2766.   ———. "Raja Rao: *The Serpent and the Rope*." *Literary Criterion* 4.2 (1963): 62–89.

2767.   ———. "Raja Rao's *Kanthapura*: An Analysis." *Literary Criterion* 7.2 (1966): 54–77. Rpt. in *Critical Essays on Indian Writing in English* [#2700] 233–58; *Fiction and the Reading Public in India*. Ed. C. D. Narasimhaiah. Mysore: Univ. of Mysore, 1967. 60–83.

2768.   Narasimhan, Raji. "Desai versus Desani: Norms of Appreciation." *Indian Literature* [New Delhi] 16 (1973): 180–84.

2769.   ———. "The Strangeness of G. V. Desani." *Considerations*. Ed. Meenakshi Mukherjee. Bombay: Allied Publishers, 1977. 102–10.

2770.   Narayan, Shyamala A. "Social Concerns in the Fiction of Raja Rao." *Graybook* 3 (1973): 42–46.

2771.   Nazareth, Peter. "The Clown in the Slave Ship." *Critical Perspectives on Sam Selvon* [#2704].

2772.   ———. "Time in the Third World." *University College Quarterly* 24 (May 1979): 8–23.
         Discusses *In a Brown Mantle* [#1939].

2773.   Parameswaran, Uma. "Excelsior—Raja Rao." *A Study of Representative Indo-English Novelists*. New Delhi: Vikas, 1976. 141–70.

2774.   ———. "Ganga in the Assiniboine: Prospects for Indo-Canadian Literature." *A Meeting of Streams* [#2711] 79–93.

2775.   ———. "Karma and Work: The Allegory in Raja Rao's *The Cat and Shakespeare*." *Journal of Commonwealth Literature* 7 (1969): 107–15.

2776.   ———. "Native-aliens and Expatriates: Kamala Markandaya and Balachandra Rajan." *A Study of Representative Indo-English Novelists*. Ed. Uma Parameswaran. New Delhi: Vikas, 1976. 85–140.

2777.   ———. "Shakti in Raja Rao's Novels." *Bulletin of the Association of Commonwealth Literature and Language Studies* 9 (1972): 4027.

2778.   Parameswaran, Uma, and M. R. Parameswaran. "Singing to the Feet of the Lord: A. K. Ramanujan's *Hymns for the Drowning.*" *Journal of South Asian Literature* 19.2 (1984): 137–52.

2779.   Parthasarathy, R. "How It Strikes a Contemporary: The Poetry of A. K. Ramanujan." *Literary Criterion* 12.2–3 (1976): 187–97.
         Rpt. in *Osmania Journal of English Studies* 13.1 (1977): 187–200.

2780.   Patil, Chandrasekhar B. "The Kannada Element in Raja Rao's Prose: A Linguistic Study of *Kanthapura.*" *Journal of Karnatak University (Humanities)* 13 (1969): 143–67.

2781.   Perry, John Oliver. "Exiled by a Woman's Body: Substantial Phenomena in the Poetry of Meena Alexander." *Journal of South Asian Literature* 21.1 (1986): 125–32.

2782.   Poynting, Jeremy. "Limbo Consciousness: Between India and the Caribbean." *Toronto South Asian Review* 5.1 (1986): 205–21.
         Includes a discussion of Samuel Selvon.

2783.   Raghavacharyulu, D. V. K. "The Counterfeit Hero: Desani's Hatterr and Naipaul's Ralph Singh." *The Critical Response: Selected Essays on the American, Commonwealth, Indian and British Traditions in Literature.* Madras: Macmillan, 1980. 127–37.

2784.   Rajan, Balachandra. "Identity and Nationality." *Considerations.* Ed. Meenakshi Mukherjee. Bombay: Allied Publishers, 1977. 1–4.

2785.   Ramachandra, Ragini. "Santha Rama Rau: The Imagination of Fact." *Literary Criterion* 12.2–3 (1976): 98–114.

2786.   Ramamoorthy, P. "G. V. Desani: First Impressions." *Indian Literature of the Past Fifty Years, 1917–1967.* Ed. C. D. Narasimhaiah. Mysore: Univ. of Mysore, 1970. 203–12.

2787.   Rao, J. Srihari. "Images of Truth: A Study of Raja Rao's *The Cat and Shakespeare.*" *Journal of Indian Writing in English* 5.1 (1977): 36–41.

2788.   Rao, K. Ramachandra. "Raja Rao's *Kanthapura.*" *The Two-Fold Voice: Essays on Indian Writing in English.* Ed. D. V. K. Raghavacharyulu. Vijayawada: Navodaya Publishers, 1971. 99–113.

2789.   Rao, N. Madhava. "*Kanthapura*: An Appreciation." *Triveni* 44.3 (1975): 55–59.

2790.   Rao, Raja. "The Writer and the Word." *Literary Criterion* 7.1 (1965): 1–5.
         Rpt. in *Fiction and the Reading Public in India.* Ed. C. D. Narasimhaiah. Mysore: Univ. of Mysore, 1967. 229–31.

2791.   Ray, Robert J. "The Novels of Raja Rao." *Books Abroad* 40.4 (1966): 411–14.

2792.   Sandahl, Stella. "South Asian Literatures: A Linguistic Perspective." *A Meeting of Streams* [#2711] 133–38.

2793.   Sastry, L. S. R. Krishna. "Raja Rao." *Triveni* 36.4 (1968): 16–30.

2794.   Shahane, Vasant A. "Raja Rao and Patrick White: A Comparative Appraisal." *The Laurel Bough.* Ed. G. Nageswara Rao. Madras: Blackie, 1982. 177–89.

2795.   ———. "Raja Rao's *The Cat and Shakespeare*: A Study in the Form of Fiction." *Journal of Indian Writing in English* 3.1 (1976): 7–11.

2796.   Shepherd, Ron. "Raja Rao: Symbolism in *The Cat and Shakespeare*." *World Literature Written in English* 14.2 (1975): 347–56.

2797.   ———. "Symbolic Organization in *The Serpent and the Rope*." *Southern Review* 6.2 (1973): 93–96.

2798.   Shrivastava, M. "Love and Divorce in *The Serpent and the Rope*." *Quest* 97 (1975): 58–62.

2799.   Singh, Amritjit. "The Writer and the Critic: Notes on Creativity." *Indian Pen* 42.7–8 (1976): 3–8.

2800.   Singh, J. P. "The Serpent and the Rope Dancer." *Indian Journal of English Studies* 16 (1975–76): 53–76.

2801.   Singh, Ram Sewak. "A European Brahmin: Raja Rao." *Indian Novel in English: A Critical Study.* New Delhi: Arnold-Heinemann, 1977. 73–95.

2802.   Singh, Satyanarain. "Ramanujan and Ezekiel." *Osmania Journal of English Studies* 7.1 (1969): 67–75.
            Rpt. in *Writers Workshop Miscellany* 45 (1971): 47–56.

2803.   Srinath, C. N. "G. V. Desani: *All about H. Hatterr*." *Literary Criterion* 9.3 (1970): 40–56.

2804.   Subramanyam, Ka Naa. "On Reading Raja Rao's *The Cat and Shakespeare*." *Thought* 16 Apr. 1966: 16–17.

2805.   Sugunasiri, Suwanda H. J. "Emerging Themes in South Asian Canadian Literature." *Asianadian* 5.3 (1984): 26–28.

2806.   ———. "Forces That Shaped Sri Lankan Literature." *Toronto South Asian Review* 3.2 (1984): 2–10.

2807.   ———. "The Literature of Canadians of South Asian Origins: An Overview." *Canadian Ethnic Studies* 14.1 (1985): 1–21.

2808.   ———. "Reality and Symbolism in the Short Story." *A Meeting of Streams* [#2711] 33–48.
            Rpt. in *World Literature Written in English* 26.1 (1986): 98–107.

2809.   Sundaram, P. S. "Single and Double Vision: Anand, Raja Rao and Narayan." *Rajasthan University Studies in English* 7 (1974): 68–78.

2810.   Sutherland, Ronald. "The Caribbean Connexion in Canadian Literature." *Yearbook of English Studies* 15 (1985): 227–38.
            Discusses Réshard Gool and Sam Selvon.

2811. Taranath, Rajeev. "A Note on the Problem of Simplification." *Fiction and the Reading Public in India*. Ed. C. D. Narasimhaiah. Mysore: Univ. of Mysore, 1967. 205–12.
       On *The Serpent and the Rope*.

2812. Thieme, John. "'The World Turn Upside Down': Carnival Patterns in *The Lonely Londoners*." *Toronto South Asian Review* 5.1 (1986): 191–204.

2813. Vassanji, M. G. "The Postcolonial Writer: Myth Maker and Folk Historian." *A Meeting of Streams* [#2711] 63–68.
       Discusses works by Cyril Dabydeen, Clyde Hosein, Harold Sonny Ladoo, Lino Leitão, Peter Nazareth, Michael Ondaatje, Sam Selvon, and Shawn Hsu Wong.

2814. Vassanji, M. G., and Surjeet Kalsey. "Introduction: Panjabi Literature in Canada." *Toronto South Asian Review* 2.1 (1983): 47+.

2815. Venkatachari, K. "Raja Rao's *The Serpent and the Rope*: A Study in *Advaitic* Affirmation." *Osmania Journal of English Studies* 8.1 (1971): i–xii.

2816. Venugopal, C. V. "Raja Rao as a Short Story Writer: A Study." *Journal of Karnatak University (Humanities)* 14 (1970): 159.

2817. Verghese, C. Paul. "Raja Rao: An Assessment." *Problems of the Indian Creative Writer in English*. Bombay: Somaiya Publishers, 1971. 142–54.

2818. ———. "Raja Rao, Mulk Raj, Narayan and Others." *Indian Writing Today* 3.1 (1969): 31–38.

2819. Viswanathan, S. "The Dialect of the Tribe: Poetic Talents and Poetic License." *Contemporary Indian English Verse: An Evaluation*. Ed. Chirantan Kulshrestha. New Delhi: Arnold-Heinemann, 1980. 122–30.
       Discusses the poetry of Meena Alexander.

2820. Westbrook, Perry D. "Theme and Action in Raja Rao's *The Serpent and the Rope*." *World Literature Written in English* 14.2 (1975): 385–98.

2821. Williams, Haydn Moore. "Govindas Desani and Others." *Studies in Modern Indian Fiction in English*. Calcutta: Writers Workshop, 1973. 2: 149–75.

2822. ———. "Raja Rao: The Idea of India." *Studies in Modern Indian Fiction in English*. Calcutta: Writers Workshop, 1973. 2: 25–128.

Interviews, Profiles, and Commentary

2823. "The Art of Juggling Two Cultures." *Asiaweek* [Hong Kong] 29 June 1979: 41–43.
       Profile of Bharati Mukherjee.

2824. Carter, Alixe. "Stephen Gill: Writer, Publisher, but a Doer First." *Ottawa Journal* 29 Oct. 1977: 26.

2825. Da Silva, Ladis. "Raul Furtado (1917–1983)." *Toronto South Asian Review* 2.2 (1983): 92+.

2826. Ezekiel, Nissim. "Two Poets: A. K. Ramanujan and Keki N. Daruwalla." *Illustrated Weekly of India* 18 June 1972: 43.

2827. Flewwelling, Martin. "Hilda Woolnough and Réshard Gool." *Atlantic Advocate* Feb. 1986: 9.
    Profiles.

2828. Gallant, Doug. "Gool." *Patriot* [Charlottetown, PE] 5 Jan. 1985.
    Profile of Réshard Gool.

2829. Hamel, Guy F. Claude. "An Interview with Book Publisher and Writer: Stephen Gill." *Christian Monitor* 16 Apr. 1981: 6.

2830. Harindranath, P. S. "An Acclaimed Scholar." *Indian Express* 9 Mar. 1984: 3.
    Interview with Vasant A. Shahane.

2831. Hines, George. "A Writer on His Craft." *Writer's Lifeline* Feb. 1982: 19–22.
    Stephen Gill.

2832. "Interview: V. A. Shahane." *Deccan Chronicle* 1 Apr. 1984: 6.

2833. Irby, Charles C. "Goan Literature from Peter Nazareth: An Interview (8 November 1984)." *Explorations in Ethnic Studies* 8.1 (1985): 1–12.

2834. Nakulan. "Meeting with A. K. Ramanujan." *Thought* 21 (1964): 11–13.

2835. Narain, Laxmi. "Raja Rao: Indian Novelist in Three Languages." *Asian Student* 6 Feb. 1972: 7.

2836. O'Brien, A. P. "Meeting Raja Rao." *Prajna* 11.2 (1966): 180–84.

2837. Penny, Margaret. "Time Is True Test for Writer's Ability, Says Local Author and Publisher." *Standard-Freeholder* 19 Oct. 1976: 5.
    Stephen Gill.

2838. Rajan, Balachandra. "Writing in English." *Illustrated Weekly of India* 26 May 1963.

2839. Raman, A. S. R. "Chiaroscuro: A Meeting with Raja Rao Recalled." *Illustrated Weekly of India* 2 Oct. 1966: 13.

2841. Selvon, Samuel. "Sam Selvon Talking: A Conversation with Kenneth Ramchand." *Canadian Literature* 95 (Winter 1982): 56–66.

2842. Tharu, Susie. "A Conversation with Meena Alexander." *Chandrabhaga* 7 (Summer 1982): 69–74.

2843. "U. K. University Appoints Gool Visiting Scholar." *Guardian* 2 Mar. 1987.
    Profile of Réshard Gool.

2844. Vassanji, M. G. "A Conversation with Zulfikar Ghose." *Toronto South Asian Review* 4.3 (1986): 14–21.

2845. Vijiaraghavachari, S. V. "Raja Rao: Face to Face." *Illustrated Weekly of India* 5 Jan. 1964: 44–45.

2846. Wangu, J. L. "An Interview with a Canadian Author." *Indian Teacher* Jan.-Feb. 1979: 14–16.
    Stephen Gill.

Literature by Non-Asians about Asians and Asian Americans: Selected Books

2847. Atherton, Gertrude Franklin Horn. *The Californians*. New York: B. W. Dodge, 1898.
Contains descriptions of San Francisco Chinatown.

2848. Ayscough, Florence. *The Autobiography of a Chinese Dog*. New York: Houghton, 1926.
This dog describes life in China.

2850. Bamford, Mary Ellen. *Ti: A Story of San Francisco's Chinatown*. Chicago: David C. Cook, 1899.
Depicts Chinese immigrants.

2851. Barnes, Anna M. *The Red Miriok*. Philadelphia: American Baptist Publication Society, 1901.

2852. Barr, Pat. *Jade: A Novel of China*. New York: St. Martin's, 1982.

2853. Barrett, William E. *The Left Hand of God*. Garden City, NY: Doubleday, 1951.

2854. Bates, H. E. *The Purple Plain*. Boston: Little, 1948.
A novel of wartime Burma.

2855. Baum, Vicki. *The Weeping Wood*. Garden City, NY: Doubleday, 1943.
Set in Indonesia.

2856. Baxter, Walter. *Look Down in Mercy*. London: Heinemann, 1951.
Set in Burma, India, and Malaysia.

2857. Beach, Rex. *Son of the Gods*. New York: Harper, 1929.
A white orphan adopted by a Chinatown merchant has an irresistible urge to rebel against Asian tradition.

2858. Becker, May Lamberton, ed. *Golden Tales of the Far West*. New York: Dodd, 1935.
Seventeen regional tales.

2859. Beekman, Allan. *Hawaiian Tales*. Detroit: Harlo, 1970.
Stories about Japanese immigrants in Hawaii.

2860. ———. *The Niihau Incident: The True Story of the Japanese Fighter Pilot Who, after the Pearl Harbor Attack, Crash-Landed on the Hawaiian Island of Niihau and Terrorized the Residents*. Honolulu: Heritage Press of Pacific, 1982.
A legend set in Hawaii and Japan.

2861. Behrens, June. *Soo Ling Finds a Way*. Los Angeles: Golden Gate, 1965.
For children.

2862. Bierce, Ambrose. *The Collected Works of Ambrose Bierce.* 12 vols. New York: Neale, 1910.
Contains descriptions of Chinese immigrants in California.

2863. Biggers, Earl Derr. *Behind That Curtain.* Indianapolis: Bobbs, 1928. New York: Bantam, 1974.
All the novels by Biggers center on Charlie Chan, a Chinese American detective.

2864. ———. *The Black Camel.* New York: Grosset, 1929. New York: Bantam, 1975.

2865. ———. *Charlie Chan Carries On.* Indianapolis: Bobbs, 1930. New York: Bantam, 1975.

2866. ———. *Charlie Chan Omnibus:* The House without a Key, Behind That Curtain, Keeper of the Keys. New York: Grosset, 1925.

2867. ———. *The Chinese Parrot: A Novel.* New York: Grosset, 1926. New York: Bantam, 1974.

2868. ———. *The House without a Key.* New York: Collier, 1925.

2869. ———. *Keeper of the Keys: A Charlie Chan Story.* Indianapolis: Bobbs, 1932. New York: Bantam, 1975.

2870. Bishop, Claire Huchet, and Kurt Wiese. *The Five Chinese Brothers.* New York: Coward, 1938.
For children.

2871. Bishop, William Henry. *"Choy Susan" and Other Stories.* Boston: Houghton, 1885.
The title story concerns Chinese immigrants.

2872. Black, Monica. *Moonflete.* London: Hale, 1972.

Blessing-Eyster, Nellie. See Eyster, Nellie [Blessing].

2873. Bloom, Ursula. *The Secret Lover.* New York: Dutton, 1931.
In this secret diary a bachelor describes his affairs with several women, including a Chinese amah.

2874. Bramah, Ernest [Ernest Bramah Smith]. *Kai Lung's Golden Hours.* 1922. New York: George H. Doran, 1923.
Set in China.

2875. ———. *Kai Lung Unrolls His Mat.* Garden City, NY: Doubleday, 1928.
Set in China.

2876. ———. *The Wallet of Kai Lung.* 1900. London: Methuen, 1923.
Set in China.

2877. Breck, Vivian [Vivian Gurney Breckenfeld]. *The Two Worlds of Noriko.* Garden City, NY: Doubleday, 1966.
A romantic story of a Japanese American girl torn between her American upbringing and her parents' traditional world of strict obedience.

2878. Bromfield, Louis. *Night in Bombay.* New York: Harper, 1940.
On India.

2879. Buck, Pearl S. *Come, My Beloved*. New York: John Day, 1953.
Focuses on American missionaries in India.

2880. ———. *Dragon Seed*. New York: John Day, 1942.
On China.

2881. ———. *East Wind, West Wind*. New York: John Day, 1930.

2882. ———, ed. *Fairy Tales of the Orient*. New York: Simon, 1965.

2883. ———. *Far and Near: Stories of Japan, China, and America*. New York:
John Day, 1947.

2884. ———. *God's Men*. New York: John Day, 1951.
On China.

2885. ———. *The Good Earth*. New York: John Day, 1931.
Describes a Chinese peasant family.

2886. ———. *"Hearts Come Home" and Other Stories*. New York: Pocket,
1970.

2887. ———. *The Hidden Flower*. New York: John Day, 1952.
A love story between an American soldier and a Japanese woman.

2888. ———. *Imperial Woman*. New York: John Day, 1956.
A fictional biography of the empress dowager.

2889. ———. *Kinfolk*. New York: John Day, 1949.
Set in China.

2890. ———. *Letter from Peking*. New York: John Day, 1957.

2891. ———. *The Living Reed*. New York: John Day, 1963.
A novel about a Korean family.

2892. ———. *The Pavilion of Women*. New York: John Day, 1946.
Set in China.

2893. ———. *Peony*. New York: John Day, 1948.
Set in China.

2894. ———. *The Promise*. New York: John Day, 1943.
Set in China and Burma.

2895. ———. *Sons*. New York: John Day, 1932.
Set in China.

2896. ———. *Three Daughters of Madame Liang*. New York: John Day, 1969.
Set in China.

2897. Burke, Thomas. *Limehouse Nights*. New York: Robert McBride, 1917.
A collection of tales set in London Chinatown.

2898. ———. *More Limehouse Nights*. New York: George H. Doran, 1921.

2899. ———. *Nights in London*. New York: Holt, 1916.

2900. ———. *A Tea-Shop in Limehouse*. Boston: Little, 1931.

2901. ———. *Twinkletoes: A Tale of Limehouse*. New York: Robert McBride,
1918.

2902.   Burroughs, Edgar Rice. *The Mucker.* Chicago: A. C. McClurg, 1921.
        An Irish protagonist saves a white heroine from lascivious Chinese men.

2903.   Bushnell, O. A. *The Stone of Kannon.* Honolulu: U of Hawaii P, 1979.
        A novel about the Japanese in Hawaii.

2904.   ———. *The Water of Kane.* Honolulu: U of Hawaii P, 1980.

2905.   Butler, Robert Olen. *The Alleys of Eden.* New York: Horizon, 1961.

2906.   ———. *On Distant Ground.* New York: Knopf, 1985.

2907.   Butterworth, Hezekiah. *Little Sky-High: Or, The Surprising Doings of Washee-Washee-Wang.* New York: Crowell, 1901.
        A children's book about a Chinese boy in Boston.

2908.   Camp, William F. *Retreat, Hell.* New York: Appleton, 1943.
        On the Philippines.

2909.   Caputo, Philip. *A Rumor of War.* New York: Holt, 1978.
        A marine lieutenant's memoir of the Vietnam War.

2910.   Carpenter, Grant. *The Night Tide: A Story of Old Chinatown.* New York: H. K. Fly, 1920.

2911.   Cavanna, Betty. *Jenny Kimura.* New York: Morrow, 1964.
        The story of a child who visits Kansas and Massachusetts, comparing life in Kansas City and Cape Cod to her own home life in Tokyo.

2912.   Charyn, Jerome. *American Scrapbook.* New York: Viking, 1969.
        Describes the Japanese American internment at Manzanar during World War II.

2913.   Clavell, James. *King Rat.* Boston: Little, 1962.
        Set in Indonesia.

2914.   ———. *Noble House: A Novel of Contemporary Hong Kong.* New York: Delacorte, 1981.

2915.   ———. *Shogun: A Novel of Japan.* New York: Atheneum, 1975. New York: Dell, 1982.
        A historical novel set during the seventeenth century.

2916.   ———. *Tai-Pan: A Novel of Hong Kong.* New York: Atheneum, 1966.
        A historical novel set during the Opium War.

2917.   Conquest, Joan. *Crumbling Walls.* New York: MacCaulay, 1927.
        Set in China.

2918.   ———. *Forbidden.* New York: MacCaulay, 1927.
        A rich and handsome Chinese man is rejected by a white woman because of race.

2919.   ———. *The Street of Many Arches.* New York: MacCaulay, 1924.

2921.   Costain, Thomas. *The Black Rose.* Garden City, NY: Doubleday, 1945.
        A historical novel about an English adventurer in China.

2922.   Cronin, A. J. *The Keys of the Kingdom.* Boston: Little, 1941.
        Set in China.

2923.   Cruso, Solomon. *The Last of the Japs and the Jews.* New York: Herman W. Lefkowitz, 1933.

2924.   Cunningham, E. V. [Howard Fast]. *The Case of the Angry Actress.* New York: Dell, 1984.
        All the titles by E. V. Cunningham are part of "A Masao Masuto Mystery Series." Sergeant Masao Masuto is a Japanese American detective on the Beverly Hills police force.

2925.   ———. *The Case of the Kidnapped Angel.* New York: Delacorte, 1982.

2926.   ———. *The Case of the Murdered Mackenzie.* New York: Delacorte, 1984.

2927.   ———. *The Case of the One-Penny Orange.* New York: Holt, 1977.

2928.   ———. *The Case of the Poisoned Eclairs.* New York: Holt, 1979.

2929.   ———. *The Case of the Russian Diplomat.* New York: Holt, 1978.

2930.   ———. *The Case of the Sliding Pool.* New York: Dell, 1981.

2931.   De Bra, Lemuel. *Ways That Are Wary.* New York: Edward J. Clode, 1925.
        A collection of short stories set in San Francisco Chinatown.

2932.   De Puy, E. Spence [Edward Spence De Puy]. *Dr. Nicholas Stone.* New York: G. W. Dillingham, 1905.
        A detective novel set in San Francisco Chinatown.

2933.   Del Vecchio, John M. *The Thirteenth Valley.* New York: Bantam, 1982.

2934.   Dillon, Richard H. *The Hatchet Men: The Story of the Tong Wars in San Francisco's Chinatown.* New York: Coward, 1962.

2935.   Dobie, Charles Caldwell. *San Francisco's Chinatown.* New York: Appleton, 1936.

2936.   ———. *San Francisco Tales.* New York: Appleton, 1935.

2937.   Dodge, Ed. *Dau: A Novel of Vietnam.* New York: Macmillan, 1984.

2938.   Dooner, Pierton W. *Last Days of the Republic.* San Francisco: Alta, California Publishing House, 1880.
        Describes Chinese immigration as the Chinese government's strategy to conquer the US.

2939.   Doyle, Charles William. *The Shadow of Quong Lung.* Philadelphia: Lippincott, 1900.
        Focuses on a Chinese villain in San Francisco Chinatown.

2940.   Dressler, Albert. *California Chinese Chatter.* San Francisco: Dressler, 1927.

2941.   Edmiston, James. *Home Again.* Garden City, NY: Doubleday, 1955.
        Describes a Japanese American family.

2942.   Elegant, Robert. *Dynasty.* New York: McGraw, 1977.

2943.   ———. *Manchu.* New York: McGraw, 1980.
        On China.

2944. Emerson, Gloria. *Winners and Losers*. New York: Random, 1976.
On the Vietnam War.

2945. Eskelund, Karl. *My Chinese Wife*. Garden City, NY: Doubleday, 1945.

2946. Espey, John J. *Tales Out of School*. New York: Knopf, 1947.
Set in China.

2947. Eyster, Nellie [Blessing]. *A Chinese Quaker: An Unfictitious Novel by Nellie Blessing-Eyster*. New York: Fleming H. Revell, 1902.
Set in San Francisco Chinatown.

2948. Fales, William E. S. *Bits of Broken China*. New York: Street and Smith, 1902.
A collection of short stories about New York Chinatown.

2949. Fernald, Chester B. *"The Cat and the Cherub" and Other Stories*. New York: Century, 1896.
Contains six stories about San Francisco Chinatown.

2950. ———. *Chinatown Stories*. London: Heinemann, 1900.

2951. Fielde, Adele M. *A Corner of Cathay: Studies from Life among the Chinese*. New York: Macmillan, 1894.

2952. Fleming, Ian. *You Only Live Twice*. New York: New American Library, 1964.
Set in Japan.

2953. Ford, John. *The Tokyo Contract*. London: Angus & Robertson, 1971.

2954. Ford, Julia Ellsworth. *Consequences*. New York: Dutton, 1929.
Set in India and China.

2955. Forster, E. M. *A Passage to India*. New York: Harcourt, 1924.
Describes interaction between the British and the Indians.

2956. Frank, Pat. *Hold Back the Night*. Philadelphia: Lippincott, 1952.
Set in Korea.

2957. Fraser, Mrs. Hugh. *A Maid of Japan*. New York: Holt, 1905.

2958. Fuller, Jack. *Fragments*. New York: Morrow, 1984.
On the Vietnam War.

2959. Gale, James S. *The Vanguard: A Tale of Korea*. New York: Fleming H. Revell, 1904.

2960. Gann, Ernest K. *Soldiers of Fortune*. New York: W. Sloan Assoc., 1954.
Set in China.

2961. Garrigue, Sheila. *The Eternal Spring of Mr. Ito*. Scarsdale, NY: Bradbury Press, 1985.
For grades 5–7. A story of Japanese Canadian internment as seen by a young Caucasian girl in Vancouver.

2962. Gelzer, Jay. *The Street of a Thousand Delights*. New York: Robert M. McBride, 1921.
A collection of stories set in the Chinese quarter of Melbourne.

2963.　Gervais, Albert. *Madame Flowery Sentiment*. New York: Covici Friede, 1937.
　　　　Set in Szechwan, the novel describes a love affair between a French doctor and a Chinese woman.

2964.　Gilman, Peter. *Diamond Head*. New York: Coward, 1960.
　　　　Set in Hawaii.

2965.　Glasser, Ronald J. *365 Days*. New York: Braziller, 1971.

2966.　Glick, Carl. *The Laughing Buddha*. New York: Lothrop, 1937.
　　　　A mystery set in China.

2967.　―――. *Shake Hands with the Dragon*. New York: Whittlesey House. London: McGraw, 1941.
　　　　Memoir about New York Chinatown.

2968.　―――. *Three Times I Bow*. New York: Whittlesey House, 1943.
　　　　Memoir.

2969.　Glynn-Ward, Hilda [Hilda Glynn Howard]. *The Writing on the Wall*. Vancouver: Sun Publishing, 1921.

2970.　Godden, Jon. *The Seven Islands*. London: Chatto; New York: Knopf, 1956.
　　　　Set in India.

2971.　Godden, Rumer. *Kingfishers Catch Fire*. New York: Viking, 1953.
　　　　Set in India.

2972.　―――. *The River*. Boston: Little, 1946.
　　　　Set in India.

2973.　Gowen, Vincent H. *Sun and Moon*. Boston: Little, 1927.
　　　　Describes an Englishman in China.

2974.　Graham, Dorothy. *Lotus of the Dusk: A Romance of China*. New York: Frederick A. Stokes, 1927.

2975.　Green, Gerald. *East and West*. New York: Fine, 1986.
　　　　Novel about a Japanese family in the US during World War II.

2976.　Green, Helen. *"At the Actors' Boarding House" and Other Stories*. New York: Nevada, 1906.
　　　　Six of the stories are set in New York Chinatown.

2977.　Greene, Graham. *The Quiet American*. New York: Viking, 1955.
　　　　Describes American secret activity in Vietnam when it was a French colony.

2978.　Griggs, Veta. *Chinaman's Chance: The Life Story of Elmer Wok Wai*. New York: Exposition Press, 1969.
　　　　Biography of a Chinese man convicted of murder in the 1920s.

2979.　Gunther, John. *Inside Asia*. 1939. Rev. ed. New York: Harper, 1942.

2980.　Hackforth-Jones, Gilbert. *Yellow Peril*. London: Hodder, 1972.

2981.   Halberstam, David. *One Very Hot Day.* 1967. New York: Warner, 1984.

2982.   Hammett, Dashiell. *The Big Knockover.* New York: Random, 1966. New York: Vintage, 1972.
         Contains Chinese American and Filipino American characters.

2983.   ———. *The Continental Op.* New York: Spivak, 1945. New York: Vintage, 1975.
         Contains a Chinese ringleader.

2984.   Harte, Bret. *Writings of Bret Harte.* 20 vols. Boston: Houghton, 1896.
         Much of Harte's fiction contains descriptions of Chinese immigrants.

2985.   Hartog, Jan de. *The Spiral Road.* New York: Harper, 1957.
         On Indonesia.

2986.   Hathaway, Bo. *A World of Hurt.* New York: Taplinger, 1981.

2987.   Headland, Isaac Taylor. *The Chinese Boy and Girl.* New York: Fleming H. Revell, 1901.

2988.   Hebden, Mark [John Harris]. *A Killer for the Chairman.* London: Joseph, 1972.
         A spy thriller set mostly in China.

2989.   Hekking, Johanna M. *Pigtails.* New York: Frederick A. Stokes, 1937.
         A children's book about children in China.

2990.   Hergesheimer, Joseph. *Java Head.* New York: Knopf, 1918.
         A New England sea captain brings his Manchurian wife to his home in Salem, MA.

2991.   Herr, Michael. *Dispatches.* New York: Knopf, 1977.
         On the Vietnam War.

2992.   Hersey, John. *A Single Pebble.* New York: Knopf, 1956.
         On China.

2993.   Hilton, James. *Lost Horizon.* New York: Morrow, 1933.
         Set in Tibet.

2994.   Hittrec, Joseph G. *Son of the Moon.* New York: Harper, 1948.
         Set in India.

2995.   Hixson, Carter. *The Foreign Devil.* New York: Robert Speller, 1937.
         A Chinese villain who has graduated from an American university lusts after white women.

2996.   Hobart, Alice Tisdale. *Venture into Darkness.* New York: Longmans, 1955.
         Set in China.

2997.   Holland, Clive. *My Japanese Wife.* Westminster, Eng.: Constable, 1895.

2998.   Hosmer, Margaret. *You-Sing: The Chinaman in California: A True Story of the Sacramento Flood.* Philadelphia: Presbyterian Publication Comm., 1868.
         Centers on the relationship between a Chinese worker and a white family.

2999. Howe, Maud. *San Rosario Ranch.* 1880. Boston: Roberts Brothers, 1884.
Contains a Chinese domestic servant.

3000. Huggett, William Turner. *Body Count.* New York: Putnam's, 1973.
A novel about the Vietnam War.

3001. Irwin, Wallace. *Chinatown Ballads.* New York: Duffield, 1906.

3002. ———. *Letters of a Japanese Schoolboy.* Garden City, NY: Doubleday,
1909.

3003. ———. *Mr. Togo, Maid of All Work.* New York: Duffield, 1913.
Describes a Japanese schoolboy.

3004. ———. *Seed of the Sun.* New York: Doran, 1921. New York: Arno, 1978.
In this anti-Japanese novel, Japanese American farmers are carrying out
the wishes of the Japanese emperor.

3005. Irwin, Will [text], and Arnold Genthe [photographs]. *Old Chinatown:
A Book of Pictures.* New York: Mitchell Kennerly, 1913.

3006. Ishigo, Estelle. *Lone Heart Mountain.* Los Angeles: Anderson, Ritchie &
Simon, 1972.
Sketches about an internment camp.

3007. Itani, Frances. *No Other Lodgings.* Fredericton, NB: Fiddlehead Poetry
Books, 1978.

3008. Jacob, Heinrich Eduard. *Jacqueline and the Japanese.* Trans. S. H. Cross.
Boston: Little, 1930.

3009. Jennings, John. *The Pepper Tree.* Boston: Little, 1951.
On Indonesia.

3010. Jhabvala, Ruth Prawer. *A Backward Place.* London: Murray; New York:
Norton, 1965.
Set in India.

3011. ———. *Esmond in India: A Novel.* London: Allen; New York: Norton,
1958.

3012. ———. *An Experience of India.* New York: Norton, 1972.

3013. ———. *Get Ready for Battle.* London: Murray, 1962.
Set in India.

3014. ———. *Heat and Dust.* London: Murray, 1975. New York: Harper, 1976.
Set in India.

3015. ———. *The Householder.* New York: Norton, 1960.
Set in India.

3016. ———. *"How I Became a Holy Mother," and Other Stories.* London: Murray; New York: Harper, 1976.

3017. ———. *In Search of Love and Beauty.* London: Murray, 1983.

3018. ———. *"Like Birds, like Fishes," and Other Stories.* London: Murray,
1963. New York: Norton, 1964.

3019. ———. *The Nature of Passion*. London: Allen, 1956. New York: Norton, 1957.
Set in India.

3020. ———. *Out of India: Selected Stories*. New York: Morrow, 1986.

3021. ———. *A Stronger Climate: 9 Stories*. London: Murray; New York: Norton, 1968.

3022. ———. *Three Continents*. New York: Morrow, 1987.
Set in New York, London, and India.

3023. ———. *To Whom She Will: A Novel*. London: Allen, 1955.

3024. ———. *Travelers*. New York: Harper, 1973.
First published as *A New Dominion*. London: Murray, 1972.

3025. Johnson, Harry M. *Edith: A Story of Chinatown*. Boston: Arena, 1895.

3026. Johnson, Marjorie R. *Chinatown Stories*. New York: Dodge Publishing, 1900.

3027. Jones, Idwal. *China Boy*. Los Angeles: Primavera Press, 1936.
Includes four stories about Chinese immigrants and two stories about Japanese immigrants.

3028. Kalb, Bernard, and Marvin Kalb. *The Last Ambassador*. Boston: Little, 1981.

3029. Kaye, M[ary] M[argaret]. *The Far Pavilions*. New York: St. Martin's, 1978.
Set in India.

3030. ———. *Shadow of the Moon*. New York: J. Messner, 1956. New York: St. Martin's, 1979.
Set in India.

3031. Kehoe, Karon. *City in the Sun*. New York: Dodd, 1946.
The story of a family of Japanese Americans confined at the Maricopa Relocation Center.

3032. Keith, Agnes Newton. *Beloved Exiles*. Boston: Little, 1972.

3033. ———. *Three Came Home*. Boston: Little, 1947.
Set in Indonesia.

3034. Kim, Agnes Davis. *I Married a Korean*. New York: John Day, 1953.

3035. Kinney, Henry Walsworth. *Broken Butterflies*. Boston: Little, 1924.
The title refers to Japanese girls educated in America who must resume their conventional roles upon returning to Japan.

3036. Kipling, Rudyard. *From Sea to Sea: Letters of Travel*. Garden City, NY: Doubleday & McClure, 1899.

3037. Knox, Jessie Juliet. *In the House of the Tiger*. New York: Eaton & Mains, 1911.

3038. ———. *Little Almond Blossoms: A Book of Chinese Stories for Children*. Boston: Little, 1904.

3039. Kolpacoff, Victor. *The Prisoners of Quai Dong.* New York: New American Library, 1967.
       Describes the interrogation of a young Vietnamese suspected of being a Viet Cong soldier.

3040. Kyne, Peter B. *The Pride of Palomar.* New York: Cosmopolitan Book, 1921.
       Describes a Japanese plot to take over California.

3041. La Piere, Richard Tracy. *When the Living Strive.* New York: Harper, 1941.
       Set in San Francisco Chinatown.

3042. Lea, Homer. *Valor of Ignorance.* New York: Harper, 1909.
       Cautions against a possible Japanese conquest of America.

3043. ———. *The Vermilion Pencil: A Romance of China.* New York: McClure, 1908.
       A Breton priest attempts to elope with the wife of a Mandarin.

3044. Le Carré, John. *The Honourable Schoolboy.* New York: Knopf, 1977.
       On China.

3045. Lederer, William J., and Eugene Burdick. *The Ugly American.* New York: Norton, 1958.
       Describes Cold War politics in Southeast Asia.

3046. Leland, Charles G. *Pidgin English Sing-Song: Or, Songs and Stories in the China-English Dialect, with a Vocabulary.* London: Trubner, 1876.

3047. Leong Gor Yun [Virginia H. Ellison, with Y. K. Chu]. *Chinatown Inside Out.* New York: B. Mussey, 1936.
       A personal view of New York Chinatown. The pseudonym means "two men."

3048. Lofts, Norah. *Scent of Cloves.* Garden City, NY: Doubleday, 1957.
       Set in Indonesia.

3049. ———. *Silver Nutmeg.* Garden City, NY: Doubleday, 1947.
       Set in Indonesia.

3050. London, Jack. *Curious Fragments: Jack London's Tales of Fantasy Fiction.* Ed. Dale L. Walker. Port Washington, NY: Kennikat, 1975.
       All the titles by London contain Asian or Asian American characters.

3051. ———. *Daughter of the Snows.* Philadelphia: Lippincott, 1902.

3052. ———. *"Dutch Courage" and Other Stories.* New York: Macmillan, 1922.

3053. ———. *"Faith of Men" (and Other Stories).* New York: Macmillan, 1904.

3054. ———. *"The House of Pride" and Other Tales of Hawaii.* New York: Macmillan, 1912.

3055. ———. *The Human Drift.* New York: Macmillan, 1917.

3056. ———. *"Moon-Face" and Other Stories.* 1906. New York: MacMillan, 1929.
       Contains a "yellow peril" story entitled "The Unparalleled Invasion."

3057.   ———. *On the Makaloa Mat.* New York: Macmillan, 1919.

3058.   ———. *"Revolution" and Other Essays.* New York: Macmillan, 1910.

3059.   ———. *South Sea Tales.* New York: Macmillan, 1911.

3060.   ———. *The Star Rover.* New York: Macmillan, 1915.
Set in Korea.

3061.   ———. *Tales of the Fish Patrol.* Cleveland: International Fiction Library, 1905.

3062.   ———. *The Valley of the Moon.* New York: Macmillan, 1913.

3063.   ———. *"When God Laughs" and Other Stories.* New York: McKinley, Stone, & Mackenzie, 1911.

3064.   Long, John Luther. *Miss Cherry-Blossom of Tokyo.* Philadelphia: Lippincott, 1895.

3065.   Lustbader, Eric Van. *Dai-San.* New York: Berkley, 1981.

3066.   ———. *The Miko.* New York: Villard, 1984.

3067.   ———. *The Ninja.* New York: Evans, 1980.
On Japan.

3068.   MacKay, Margaret. *For All Men Born.* New York: John Day, 1943.
On Hawaii.

3069.   ———. *Like Water Flowing.* London: Farrar, 1938.

3070.   Madden, Maude Whitmore. *When the East Is in the West: Pacific Coast Sketches.* New York: Fleming H. Revell, 1923. San Francisco: R & E Research Assoc., 1971.
A collection of short stories centering on the experiences of a Christian worker among Japanese Americans.

3071.   Marquand, John P. *Ming Yellow.* Boston: Little, 1935. London: Robert Hale, 1942.
Focuses on Americans in China.

3072.   ———. *Mr. Moto's Three Aces: A John P. Marquand Omnibus.* Boston: Little, 1938.
Focuses on a Japanese American detective.

3073.   ———. *No Hero.* Boston: Little, 1942.
Focuses on an American aviator in the Far East.

3074.   ———. *Stopover: Tokyo.* Boston: Little, 1957.

3075.   Marshall, Edison. *Gypsy Sixpence.* New York: Farrar, 1949.

3076.   Marshall, S. L. A. [Samuel Lyman Atwood]. *Pork Chop Hill: The American Fighting Man in Action.* New York: Morrow, 1956.
On the Korean War.

3077. Martin, Mildred Crowl. *Chinatown's Angry Angel: The Story of Donaldina Cameron.* Palo Alto: Pacific, 1977.
Biography.

3078. Martin, Ralph J. *Boy from Nebraska: The Story of Ben Kuroki.* New York: Harper, 1946.
A second-generation Japanese American encounters much prejudice in the US Air Corps but emerges from the war as a hero.

3079. Mason, F. Van Wyck. *Himalayan Assignment: A Colonel North Novel.* Garden City, NY: Doubleday, 1952.
Set in Tibet and China.

3080. ———. *The Hong Kong Airbase Murders.* New York: Grosset, 1937.
Focuses on a Chinese villain.

3081. Mason, Richard Lakin. *The World of Suzie Wong.* Cleveland: World, 1957.
Describes a romance between a Hong Kong prostitute and an English painter.

3082. Masters, John. *Bhowani Junction.* New York: Viking, 1954.
Set in India, the novel describes the love affairs of an Anglo-Indian woman.

3083. ———. *Coromandel!* New York: Viking, 1955.
Set in India.

3084. ———. *Far, Far the Mountain Peak.* New York: Viking, 1957.
Set in India.

3085. ———. *The Lotus and the Wind.* New York: Viking, 1953.
Set in India.

3086. ———. *The Venus of Konpara.* New York: Harper, 1960.
A historical romance set in India.

3087. Matthews, Frances Aymar. *The Flame Dancer.* New York: G. W. Dillingham, 1908.
Set largely in the Chinatowns of New York and San Francisco.

3088. ———. *A Little Tragedy at Tien-Tsin.* New York: Robert Grier Cooke, 1904.
Set in China.

3089. Maugham, W. Somerset. *East and West: Collected Short Stories.* New York: Literary Guild, 1921. Garden City, NY: Garden City Publishing, 1932.

3090. ———. *On a Chinese Screen.* New York: George H. Doran, 1922.

3091. McCall, Sidney [Mary McNeil]. *The Breath of the Gods.* Boston: Little, 1905.

3092. McKenna, Richard. *The Sand Pebbles.* New York: Harper, 1962.
On China.

3093. McQuinn, Donald E. *Targets.* New York: Macmillan, 1980.

3094. Meagher, Maude. *White Jade*. Boston: Houghton, 1930.
A historical novel about Yang Kuei-fei, the mistress of a Chinese emperor.

3095. Michener, James A. *The Bridges at Toko-Ri*. New York: Random, 1953.
A novel of the Korean War.

3096. ———. *Hawaii*. New York: Random, 1959. London: Secker, 1976.
Describes the impact of missionaries on the Chinese, Japanese, and Filipino immigrants in Hawaii.

3097. ———. *Sayonara*. New York: Random, 1954.
Describes a love affair between an American Air Force officer and a Japanese woman.

3098. ———. *Tales of the South Pacific*. New York: Macmillan, 1947.
A series of loosely connected stories set during World War II.

3099. Miller, Joaquin. *First Fam'lies of the Sierras*. Chicago: Jansen, McClurg, and Cox, 1876.
A Chinese laundryman appears in this novel set in a mining camp.

3100. ———. *Memorie and Rime*. New York: Funk & Wagnall's, 1884.

3101. Miln, Louise Jordan. *Mr. and Mrs. Sen*. New York: Frederick A. Stokes, 1923.
Centers on the marriage between a Chinese man and an English woman.

3102. ———. *Mr. Wu*. New York: Frederick A. Stokes, 1920.

3103. ———. *Red Lily and Chinese Jade*. New York: Frederick A. Stokes, 1928.

3104. ———. *Ruben and Ivy Sen*. New York: Frederick A. Stokes, 1925.
Set mostly in China, the novel describes the conflicts faced by Eurasians.

3105. Moore, Robin. *The Green Berets*. New York: Ballantine, 1965.
On the Vietnam War.

3106. Morris, Gouverneur. *"The Footprint" and Other Stories*. New York: Scribner's, 1919.

3107. ———. *Yellow Men and Gold*. New York: Dodd, 1911.
Rival racial groups are in quest of gold in America.

3108. Muller, Marcia. *There's Nothing to Be Afraid Of*. New York: St. Martin's, 1985.
A novel about Vietnamese in San Francisco.

3109. Mundo, Oto E. *The Recovered Continent: A Tale of the Chinese Invasion*. Columbus, OH: Harper-Osgood, 1898.
The Chinese invade Southeast Asia, Europe, and America.

3110. Mydans, Shelley Smith. *The Open City*. New York: Doubleday, 1945.
On the Philippines.

3111. Newman, Shirlee Petkin. *Yellow Silk for May Lee*. New York: Bobbs, 1961.
May Lee, daughter of a San Francisco Chinatown restaurant owner, faces the differences between the older Chinese generation and the Americanized members of her family.

3112.   Norr, William. *Stories of Chinatown: Sketches from Life in the Chinese Colony of Mott, Pell and Doyers Street.* New York: privately printed, 1892.
Focuses on the relationships between white women and Chinese men.

3113.   Norris, Frank. *Blix.* Garden City, NY: Doubleday, 1899.
Contains descriptions of San Francisco Chinatown.

3114.   ———. *McTeague: A Story of San Francisco.* Garden City, NY: Doubleday, 1899.

3115.   ———. *Moran of the Lady Letty: A Story of Adventure off the Californian Coast.* Garden City, NY: Doubleday, 1898.
Describes the conflict between Chinese Americans from San Francisco Chinatown.

3116.   ———. *The Third Circle.* New York: John Lane, 1909.
A collection of short stories set in San Francisco.

3117.   Oakes, Vanya [Virginia Armstrong Oakes]. *Desert Harvest: A Story of the Japanese in California.* Philadelphia: Winston, 1953.
A historical novel for young adults.

3118.   ———. *Footprints of the Dragon: A Story of the Chinese and the Pacific Railways.* Philadelphia: Winston, 1949.
A historical novel for young adults.

3119.   O'Brien, Tim. *Going after Cacciato.* New York: Delacorte, 1978.

3120.   Packard, Frank L. *The Dragon's Jaws.* Garden City, NY: Crime Club, 1937.
A white heroine who is mistaken to be Chinese leads a group of peasants to destroy a Chinese tyrant.

3121.   Panunzio, Constantine. *The Soul of an Immigrant.* New York: Macmillan, 1922.

3122.   Paris, John [pseud.]. *Banzai.* New York: Boni, 1926.
Centers on a Japanese rogue.

3123.   ———. *Kimono.* New York: Boni, 1922.

3124.   ———. *Sayonara: Goodbye.* New York: Boni, 1924.

3125.   Pettit, Charles. *Elegant Infidelities of Madame Li Pei Fou.* New York: Horace Liveright, 1928.
Describes a Chinese adulteress.

3126.   ———. *Petal-of-the-Rose.* New York: Horace Liveright, 1930.

3127.   ———. *The Son of the Grand Eunuch.* New York: Boni, 1927.

3128.   Poole, Ernest. *Beggar's Gold.* New York: Macmillan, 1921.
A Caucasian farm boy in New York State romanticizes about China.

3129.   Porter, Hal. *"Mr. Butterfry" and Other Tales of New Japan.* Sydney: Angus & Robertson, 1970.

3130.   Powers, Tom. *Virgin with Butterflies.* New York: Bobbs, 1945.
Set in India.

3131. Pratt, John Clark. *The Laotian Fragments*. New York: Avon, 1974.

3132. Pruitt, Ida, with Ning Lao T'ai-t'ai. *A Daughter of Han: The Autobiography of a Chinese Working Woman*. New Haven: Yale UP, 1945. Rev. ed. Palo Alto: Stanford UP, 1967.

3133. Raucat, Thomas. *The Honorable Picnic*. Trans. Leonard Cline. New York: Viking, 1927.
      A foreigner tries to seduce a Japanese girl.

3134. Rideout, Henry Milner. *Tao Tales*. New York: Duffield, 1927.
      Set in China.

3135. Roark, Garland. *Wake of the Red Witch*. Boston: Little, 1946.
      On Indonesia.

3136. Robbe-Grillet, Alain. *The House of Assignation*. Trans. A. M. Sherridan Smith. London: Calder, 1970.
      Set in Hong Kong.

3137. Robertson, George Day. *The Harvest of Hate*. 1946. Forewords Moto Asakawa and Hiroshi Kamei. Introd. Arthur A. Hansen. Fullerton: Oral History Program, California State Univ., 1986.
      A novel about Poston Relocation Center.

3138. Rohmer, Sax [Arthur Sarsfield Ward]. *The Bride of Fu Manchu*. London: Cassell, 1933.
      The entire Fu Manchu series centers on a Chinese villain who tries to overthrow the white race.

3139. ———. *Daughter of Fu-Manchu*. Garden City, NY: Doubleday, for the Crime Club, 1931. New York: Pyramid, 1964.

3140. ———. *The Devil Doctor: Hitherto Unpublished Adventures in the Career of the Mysterious Dr. Fu Manchu*. London: Methuen; New York: McBride, 1916.

3141. ———. *Dope*. New York: McBride, 1919.
      Describes Chinese criminals in London Chinatown.

3142. ———. *The Drums of Fu Manchu*. Garden City, NY: Doubleday, for the Crime Club, 1939.
      Set in London.

3143. ———. *The Emperor of America*. 1927. Garden City, NY: Doubleday, for the Crime Club, 1929.

3144. ———. *Emperor Fu Manchu*. Greenwich, CT: Fawcett, 1959.

3145. ———. *Fu Manchu's Bride*. New York: A. L. Burt, 1933.

3146. ———. *The Golden Scorpion*. New York: McBride, 1920. New York: Pyramid, 1966.
      Describes Fu Manchu's secret organization.

3147. ———. *The Hand of Fu-Manchu*. New York: McBride, 1917. New York: Pyramid, 1961.

3148.   ———. *The Insidious Dr. Fu-Manchu.* New York: McBride, Nast, 1913. New York: Pyramid, 1961.

3149.   ———. *The Island of Fu Manchu.* 1940. Garden City, NY: Doubleday, for the Crime Club, 1941.
         Set in the Caribbean.

3150.   ———. *The Mask of Fu Manchu.* New York: Collier, 1932.

3151.   ———. *The Mystery of Dr. Fu-Manchu.* London: Methuen, 1913.

3152.   ———. *President Fu Manchu.* Garden City, NY: Doubleday, for the Crime Club, 1936.
         Set in America.

3153.   ———. *Re-Enter Fu Manchu.* Greenwich, CT: Fawcett, 1957. New York: Pyramid, 1968.

3154.   ———. *The Return of Dr. Fu-Manchu.* New York: McBride, 1916. New York: Pyramid, 1961.

3155.   ———. *Shadow of Fu Manchu.* Garden City, NY: Doubleday, for the Crime Club, 1948. New York: Pyramid, 1963.
         Set in New York.

3156.   ———. *The Si-Fan Mysteries.* London: Methuen, 1917.

3157.   ———. *Tales of Chinatown.* New York: McKinley, Stone, & Mackenzie, 1922.

3158.   ———. *Tales of East and West.* 1922. Garden City, NY: Doubleday, for the Crime Club, 1933.
         Describes Chinese criminals in London Chinatown.

3159.   ———. *The Trail of Fu Manchu.* Garden City, NY: Doubleday, for the Crime Club, 1934. New York: Pyramid, 1964.
         Set in London.

3160.   ———. *The Yellow Claw.* New York: McKinley, Stone & MacKenzie, 1915.
         Describes Chinese criminals in London Chinatown.

3161.   ———. *Yellow Shadows.* Garden City, NY: Doubleday, 1926.
         Describes Chinese criminals in London Chinatown.

3162.   ———. *Yu'an Hee See Laughs.* 1931. Garden City, NY: Doubleday, for the Crime Club, 1932.
         Describes Chinese mandarins in England.

3163.   Roth, Robert. *Sand in the Wind.* Boston: Little, 1973.
         A novel about the Vietnam War.

3164.   Russ, Martin. *The Last Parallel: A Marine's War Journal.* New York: Holt, 1957.
         On the Korean War.

3165.   Shears, Sarah. *Courage to Serve.* London: Elek, 1974.

3166. Shepherd, Charles Reginald. *Lim Yik Choy: The Story of a Chinese Orphan*. New York: Fleming H. Revell, 1932.
Describes an orphan at the Chung Mei Home for Chinese American boys in El Cerrito, CA.

3167. ———. *The Story of Chung Mei, Being the Authentic History of the Chung Mei Home for Chinese Boys up to Its Fifteenth Anniversary, Oct. 1938*. Philadelphia: Judson Press, 1938.

3168. ———. *The Ways of Ah Sin: A Composite Narrative of Things as They Are*. New York: Fleming H. Revell, 1923.
Set in San Francisco Chinatown.

3169. Skimin, Robert. *Chikara! A Sweeping Novel of Japan and America*. New York: St. Martin's, 1984.

3170. Smith, Steven Phillip. *American Boys*. New York: Putnam's, 1975.

3171. Sparks, Theresa A. *China Gold*. Fresno, CA: Academy Library Guild, 1954.

3172. Standish, Robert [Digby George Gerahty]. *Bonin*. New York: Macmillan, 1944.
Set in Japan.

3173. ———. *Elephant Walk*. New York: Macmillan, 1948.
Set in Sri Lanka.

3174. ———. *The Three Bamboos*. New York: Macmillan, 1942.
Set in Japan.

3175. Steinbeck, John. *Cannery Row*. New York: Viking, 1945.
Contains Chinese American characters.

3176. ———. *East of Eden*. New York: Viking, 1952.
Contains Chinese American characters.

3177. Stone, Grace Zaring. *The Bitter Tea of General Yen*. Indianapolis: Bobbs, 1930.
Focuses on the adventures of an American woman in China.

3178. Stratton-Porter, Gene. *Her Father's Daughter*. Garden City, NY: Doubleday, 1921.
An anti-Japanese novel.

3179. Strobridge, Idah Meacham. *The Land of Purple Shadows*. Los Angeles: Artemisia Bindery, 1909.

3180. Sutherland, Howard Vigne. *Songs of a City*. San Francisco: Star Press, 1904.

3181. Swinehart, Lois Hawks. *Sarangie, a Child of Chosen*. New York: Fleming H. Revell, 1926.
On Korea.

3182. Taylor, Charles M. *Winning Buddha's Smile*. Boston: Gorham Press, 1919.

3183. Templeman, Max. *Kibei: A Novel*. Kailua, HI: Daimax, 1979.

3184. Terasaki, Gwen Harold. *Bridge to the Sun.* 1957. Chapel Hill: U of North Carolina P, 1975.
Describes the marriage between a Caucasian woman and a Japanese diplomat.

3185. Teskey, Adeline M. *The Yellow Peril.* New York: George H. Doran, 1911.

3186. Townsend, Edward. *A Daughter of the Tenements.* 1895. Upper Saddle River, NJ: Literature House, 1970.
Describes Chinese immigrants in New York Chinatown.

3187. Trevanian. *Shibumi.* New York: Crown, 1979.
On Japan.

3188. Trowbridge, James [pseud.]. *Easy Victories.* Boston: Houghton, 1973.
A novel about the Vietnam War.

3189. Twain, Mark [Samuel Clemens]. *Roughing It.* 1872. New York: Harper, 1899.
Contains Chinese American characters.

3190. Ullman, James. *Windom's Way.* Philadelphia: Lippincott, 1952.
On Southeast Asia

3191. Wallace, Kathleen. *I Walk Alone.* New York: Doubleday, 1931.
Set in China.

3192. Waln, Nora. *The House of Exile.* New York: Little, 1933. New York: Penguin, 1986.
An autobiography about living in China during the twenties and thirties.

3193. Waugh, Alec. *Fuel for the Flame.* New York: Farrar, 1960.
On Malaysia.

3194. Wells, Florence. *Tama: The Diary of a Japanese School Girl.* New York: Woman's Press, 1920.

3195. West, Morris L. *The Ambassador.* New York: Morrow, 1965.
On Vietnam.

3196. Weston, Christine. *Indigo.* New York: Scribner's, 1943.
On India.

3197. Wheat, Lu. *The Third Daughter: A Story of Chinese Home Life.* Los Angeles: Oriental Publishing, 1906. Republished as *Ah Moy: The Story of a Chinese Girl.* New York: Grafton Press, 1908.
A girl is sold into slavery in China and then taken to San Francisco.

3198. White, Robin. *Elephant Hill.* New York: Harper, 1959.
Describes a romance between an Indian man and an American woman.

3199. White, Teri. *Tightrope.* New York: Mysterious, 1986.
A novel about Vietnamese in Los Angeles.

3200. White, Theodore. *The Mountain Road.* New York: W. Sloane Assoc., 1958.
Set in China.

3201. Whitney, Atwell. *Almond-Eyed: A Story of the Day*. San Francisco: Printed for the author by A. L. Bancroft, 1878.
Describes the danger of having Chinese "heathens" in America.

3202. Wiley, Hugh. *"The Copper Mask" and Other Stories*. New York: Knopf, 1932.

3203. ———. *"Jade" and Other Stories*. New York: Knopf, 1922.
Lurid tales about San Francisco Chinatown.

3204. ———. *Manchu Blood*. New York: Knopf, 1927.
The title story is about a Chinese grocer in San Francisco Chinatown.

3205. Wiley, Richard. *Soldiers in Hiding*. Boston: Atlantic Monthly Press, 1986.
A *nisei* who fought in the Japanese Army during World War II faces uncertainty in returning to the US.

3206. Woltor, Robert. *A Short and Truthful History of the Taking of California and Oregon by the Chinese in the Year A.D. 1899*. San Francisco: A. L. Bancroft. 1882.

3207. Woodworth, Herbert G. *In the Shadow of Lantern Street*. Boston: Small, Maynard, 1920.
The hero, who thinks that he is Chinese, discovers that he has a Caucasian father.

3208. Wren, Percival Christopher. *The Dark Woman*. Philadelphia: Macrae-Smith, 1943.
On India.

3209. Wright, Stephen. *Meditations in Green*. New York: Scribner's, 1983.
On the Vietnam War.

3210. Wyndham, Robert, ed. *Chinese Mother Goose*. New York: World, 1968.

Background Sources: Selected Works

3211. Aguino, Belinda A. "The History of Filipino Women in Hawaii." *Bridge* 7.1 (1979): 17–21.

3212. Alba, Jose. "Filipinos in California." *Pacific Historian* 2 (1967): 37–41.

3213. Anthony, Donald E. "Filipino Labor in Central California." *Sociology and Social Research* 16 (1931–32): 149–56.

3214. Barlow, Janelle M. "The Images of the Chinese, Japanese, and Koreans in American Secondary School Textbooks, 1900–1970." Diss. Univ. of California, Berkeley, 1972.

3215. Barth, Gunther. *Bitter Strength: A History of the Chinese in the United States 1850–1870*. Cambridge: Harvard UP, 1964.

3216. Bogardus, Emory S. "American Attitudes towards Filipinos." *Sociology and Social Research* 14.1 (1929): 59–69.

3217. ———. "Citizenship for Filipinos." *Sociology and Social Research* 29.1 (1944): 51–54.

3218. ———. "Filipino Immigrant Attitudes." *Sociology and Social Research* 14.5 (1930): 469–79.

3219. ———. "From Immigration to Exclusion." *Sociology and Social Research* 24.3 (1940): 272–78.

3220. ———. "The Filipino Immigrant Problem." *Sociology and Social Research* 13.5 (1929): 472–79.

3221. Broadfoot, Barry. *Years of Sorrow, Years of Shame: The Story of the Japanese Canadians in World War II*. Toronto: Doubleday, 1977.
    The story of the internment years is told by Japanese Canadians in their own words.

3222. Bunvand, Jan Harold. *The Choking Doberman and Other "New" Urban Legends*. New York: Norton, 1984.
    Includes urban folklore of Southeast Asian refugees.

3223. California State Board of Control. *California and the Oriental: Japanese, Chinese, and Hindus*. New York: Arno, 1922.

3224. Chadney, James G. *The Sikhs of Vancouver*. New York: AMS, 1984.

3225. Chan, Anthony B. *Gold Mountain: The Chinese in the New World*. Vancouver: New Star Books, 1983.

3226. Chan, Sucheng. *This Bittersweet Soil: The Chinese in California Agriculture, 1860–1910*. Berkeley: U of California P, 1986.

3227. Chandras, Kananur V., ed. *Racial Discrimination against Neither-White-nor-Black American Minorities: Native Americans, Chinese Americans, Japanese Americans, Mexican Americans, Puerto Ricans, and East Indian Americans.* San Francisco: R & E Research Assoc., 1978.

3228. Chandrasekhar, S., ed. *From India to Canada: A Brief History of Immigration; Problems of Discrimination, Admission and Assimilation.* La Jolla, CA: Population Review Books, 1986.

3229. Char, Tin-Yuke, comp. and ed. *The Sandalwood Mountains: Readings and Stories of the Early Chinese in Hawaii.* Honolulu: UP of Hawaii, 1975.

3230. Chen, Jack. *The Chinese of America.* San Francisco: Harper, 1980.

3231. Cheng [Hirata], Lucie. "Free, Indentured, Enslaved: Chinese Prostitutes in Nineteenth-Century America." *Signs* 5.1 (1979): 3–29.

3232. Cheng [Hirata], Lucie, and Edna Bonacich, eds. *Labor Immigration under Capitalism: Asian Immigrant Workers in the United States before World War II.* Berkeley: U of California P, 1984.

3233. Cheng [Hirata], Lucie, et al. *Linking Our Lives: Chinese American Women of Los Angeles.* A joint project of Asian American Studies Center, Univ. of California, Los Angeles, and Chinese Historical Soc. of Southern California. Los Angeles: Chinese Historical Soc. of Southern California, 1984.

3234. Chinese Historical Society of America. *The Life, Influence, and the Role of the Chinese in the United States, 1776–1960.* Proceedings/Papers of the National Conference held at the Univ. of San Francisco, 10–12 July 1975. San Francisco: Chinese Historical Soc. of America, 1976.

3235. Chinn, Thomas W., H. Mark Lai, and Philip P. Choy, eds. *A History of the Chinese in California.* San Francisco: Chinese Historical Soc. of America, 1969.

3236. Choy, Bong-Youn. *Koreans in America.* Chicago: Nelson, 1979.

3237. Con, Harry, et al. *From China to Canada: A History of the Chinese Communities in Canada.* Toronto: McClelland, in association with the Multicultural Directorate, Dept. of the Secretary of State and the Canadian Govt. Publishing Centre, Supply and Services Canada, 1982.

3238. Conner, John W. *Tradition and Change in Three Generations of Japanese Americans.* Chicago: Nelson, 1977.

3239. Conroy, Hilary. *The Japanese Frontier in Hawaii, 1868–1898.* Berkeley: U of California P, 1953. New York: Arno, 1978.

3240. Coolidge, Mary Roberts. *Chinese Immigration.* New York: Holt, 1909. New York: Arno, 1969.

3241. Coppa, Frank J., and Thomas J. Curran, eds. *The Immigrant Experience in America.* Boston: Twayne, 1976.

3242. Cordova, Fred. *Filipinos: Forgotten Asian Americans.* Dubuque, IA: Kendall/Hunt Publishing, 1983.
        Pictorial essay.

3243.   Daniels, Roger, ed. *Anti-Chinese Violence in North America*. New York: Arno, 1978.

3244.   ———. *Concentration Camps, North America: Japanese in the U.S. and Canada during World War II*. Malabar, FL: R. E. Krieger, 1981.

3245.   ———. *Concentration Camps U.S.A.: Japanese Americans and World War II*. New York: Holt, 1970.

3246.   ———. *The Decision to Relocate the Japanese Americans*. Philadelphia: Lippincott, 1975. Rev. ed. Malabar, FL: R. E. Krieger, 1986.

3247.   ———. *The Politics of Prejudice: The Anti-Japanese Movement in California and the Struggle for Japanese Exclusion*. 1962. Berkeley: U of California P, 1977.

3248.   ———. "Westerners from the East: Oriental Immigrants Reappraised." *Pacific Historical Review* 35.4 (1966): 375–78.

3249.   Daniels, Roger, and Harry H. L. Kitano. *American Racism: Exploration of the Nature of Prejudice*. Englewood Cliffs, NJ: Prentice, 1970.

3250.   Daniels, Roger, Sandra C. Taylor, and Harry H. L. Kitano, eds. *Japanese Americans: From Relocation to Redress*. Salt Lake City: U of Utah P, 1986.

3251.   DeWitt, Howard A. *Anti-Filipino Movements in California: A History, Bibliography and Study Guide*. San Francisco: R & E Research Assoc., 1976.

3252.   Dinnerstein, Leonard, and Frederic Cole Jaher, eds. *Uncertain Americans: Readings in Ethnic History*. New York: Oxford UP, 1977.

3253.   Downing, Bruce T., and Douglas P. Olney, eds. *The Hmong in the West: Observations and Reports*. Papers of the 1981 Hmong Research Conference, Univ. of Minnesota. Minneapolis: Southeast Asian Refugee Studies Project, Center for Urban and Regional Affairs, Univ. of Minnesota, 1982.

3254.   Drinnon, Richard. *Keeper of Concentration Camps: Dillon S. Myer and American Racism*. Berkeley: U of California P, 1987.
        Compares Japanese American and Native American incarceration and relocation experiences.

3256.   Duus, Masayo. *Tokyo Rose: Orphan of the Pacific*. Trans. Peter Duus. Introd. Edwin O. Reischauer. Tokyo: Kodansha, 1983.

3257.   Fessler, Loren W., ed., and China Inst. in America, comp. *Chinese in America: Stereotyped Past, Changing Present*. New York: Vantage, 1983.

3258.   Fisher, Maxine P. *The Indians of New York City: A Study of Immigrants from India*. Columbia, MO: South Asia Books, 1980.

3259.   Fuchs, Lawrence H. *Hawaii Pono: A Social History*. New York: Harcourt, 1961.

3260.   Gardiner, C. Harvey. *Pawns in a Triangle of Hate: The Peruvian Japanese and the United States*. Seattle: U of Washington P, 1981.

3261.   Gastil, Raymond D. *Cultural Regions of the United States*. Seattle: U of Washington P, 1976.

Contains information on Americans of Chinese, Japanese, and Filipino descent.

3262.   Gee, Emma. "Issei: The First Women." *Asian Women* [#84] 8–15.

Gee, Emma, et al., eds. *Counterpoint.* See #113.

3264.   Gillenkirk, Jeffrey, and James Motlow. *Bitter Melon: Stories from the Last Rural Chinatown in America.* Introd. Sucheng Chan. Seattle: U of Washington P, 1987.

3265.   Girdner, Audrie, and Anne Loftis. *The Great Betrayal: The Evacuation of the Japanese-Americans during World War II.* New York: Macmillan, 1969.

3266.   Gordon, Milton Myron. *Assimilation in American Life: The Role of Race, Religion, and National Origins.* New York: Oxford UP, 1964.

3267.   Gossett, Thomas F. *Race: The History of an Idea in America.* Dallas: Southern Methodist UP, 1963.

3268.   Gulick, Sidney L. *American Democracy and Asiatic Citizenship.* New York: Scribner's, 1918. New York: Arno, 1978.

3269.   Handlin, Oscar. *Out of Many: A Study Guide to Cultural Pluralism in the United States.* New York: Anti-Defamation League of B'nai B'rith, 1964.

3271.   Hoexler, Corinne K. *From Canton to California: The Epic of Chinese Immigration.* New York: Four Winds Press, 1976.

3272.   Holt, Hamilton, ed. *Life Stories of Undistinguished Americans as Told by Themselves.* New York: James Pott, 1906.

3273.   Hosokawa, Bill. *Nisei: The Quiet Americans.* New York: Morrow, 1969.

3274.   ———. *Thirty Five Years in the Frying Pan.* New York: McGraw, 1978.
A collection of columns originally published in *Pacific Citizen.*

3275.   Hoy, William. *The Chinese Six Companies: A Short, General Historical Resume of Its Origin, Function, and Importance in the Life of the California Chinese.* San Francisco: Chinese Consolidated Benevolent Assn. (Chinese Six Companies), 1942.

3276.   Hoyt, Edwin P. *Asians in the West.* New York: Nelson, 1974.

3277.   Hsu, Francis L. K. *Americans and Chinese—Two Ways of Life.* New York: Henry Schuman, 1953.

3278.   ———. *The Challenge of the American Dream: The Chinese in the United States.* Belmont, CA: Wadsworth, 1971.

3279.   ———. *Under the Ancestors' Shadow: Chinese Culture and Personality.* New York: Columbia UP, 1948.

3280.   Hundley, Norris, Jr., ed. *The Asian American: The Historical Experience: Essays by Roger Daniels, et al.* Introd. Akira Iriye. Santa Barbara: American Bibliographical Center, Clio Press, 1976.
A collection of essays from *Pacific Historical Review* 38.2 (1969) and 42.3–4 (1974).

3281. Hune, Shirley. *Pacific Migration to the United States: Trends and Themes in Historical and Sociological Literature*. Washington: Smithsonian Inst., 1977.

3282. Hurh, Won Moo. *Comparative Study of Korean Immigrants in the United States: A Typological Approach*. San Francisco: R & E Research Assoc., 1977.

3283. Hutchinson, E[dward] P[rince]. *Immigrants and Their Children, 1850–1950*. Census Monograph Series. New York: Wiley, 1956.

3284. Ichihashi, Yamato. *The Japanese in the United States: A Critical Study of the Problems of the Japanese Immigrants and Their Children*. Palo Alto: Stanford UP, 1932.

3285. Ichioka, Yuji. "*Amerika Nadeshiko*: Japanese Immigrant Women in the United States, 1900–1924." *Pacific Historical Review* 49.2 (1980): 339–57.

3286. ———. "Early Issei Socialists and the Japanese Community." *Amerasia Journal* 1.2 (1971): 1–25.

3287. Irons, Peter. *Justice at War*. New York: Oxford UP, 1983.
On Supreme Court cases regarding wartime treatment of Japanese Americans.

3288. Isaacs, Harold R. *Scratches on Our Minds: American Images of China and India*. New York: John Day, 1958. White Plains, NY: Sharpe, 1980.
Discusses motion pictures, best-sellers, and other forms of popular culture that gave rise to American images of China and India.

3289. Ito, Kazuo. *Issei: A History of Japanese Immigrants in North America*. Trans. Shinichiro Nakamura and Jean S. Gerard. Seattle: Japanese Community Service, 1973.

3290. Jacobs, Paul, and Saul Landau, with Eve Pell. *Colonials and Sojourners*. Vol. 2 of *To Serve the Devil*. New York: Random, 1971.

3291. Japanese Canadian Centennial Project Committee. *A Dream of Riches: The Japanese Canadians 1877–1977*. Vancouver: Japanese Canadian Centennial Project Comm., 1978.

3292. Jones, Howard Mumford. *The Age of Energy: Varieties of American Experience, 1865–1915*. New York: Viking, 1971.

3293. Kelly, Gail Paradise. *From Vietnam to America: A Chronicle of the Vietnamese Immigration to the United States*. Boulder, CO: Westview, 1977.

3294. Kikuchi, Charles. *The Kikuchi Diary: Chronicle from an American Concentration Camp*. Ed. and introd. John Modell. Urbana: U of Illinois P, 1973.
Journals written while the author was interned at Tanforan.

3295. Kikumura, Akemi. *Through Harsh Winters: The Life of a Japanese Immigrant Woman*. Novato, CA: Chandler, 1981.

3296. Kim, Bok Lim C. *The Asian American: Changing Patterns, Changing Needs*. Assn. of Korean Christian Scholars in North America Publication Series 4. Montclair, NJ: Assn. of Korean Christian Scholars in North America, 1978.

3297. Kim, Elaine H., with Janice Otani. *With Silk Wings: Asian American Women at Work*. San Francisco: Asian Women United of California, 1983.

3298. Kim, Hyung-Chan, ed. *The Korean Diaspora: Historical and Sociological Studies of Korean Immigration and Assimilation in North America*. Santa Barbara, CA: American Bibliographical Center/Clio Press, 1977.

3299. Kim, Hyung-Chan, and Wayne Patterson. *The Koreans in America, 1882–1974: A Chronology and Fact Book*. Ethnic Chronology Series 16. Dobbs Ferry, NY: Oceana, 1974.

3300. Kim, Illsoo. *New Urban Immigrants: The Korean Community in New York*. Princeton: Princeton UP, 1981.

3301. Kim, Warren Y. [Won-yong Kim]. *Koreans in America*. Seoul: Po Chin Chai Printing, 1971.

3302. Kitano, Harry H. L. *Japanese Americans: The Evolution of a Subculture*. Englewood Cliffs, NJ: Prentice, 1969.

3303. ———. *Race Relations*. 1974. 2nd ed. Englewood Cliffs, NJ: Prentice, 1980.

3304. Klass, Morton. *East Indians in Trinidad: A Study of Cultural Persistence*. New York: Columbia UP, 1961.

3305. Knoll, Tricia. *Becoming Americans: Asian Sojourners, Immigrants, and Refugees in the Western United States*. Portland, OR: Coast to Coast, 1982.
    Covers eight Asian groups in the United States: Chinese, Japanese, Filipino, Korean, Vietnamese, Laotian, Chinese from Vietnam, and Kampucheans.

3306. Kwong, Peter. *Chinatown, N.Y.: Labor and Politics, 1930–1950*. New York: Monthly Review Press, 1979.

3307. Lai, Him Mark, and Philip P. Choy. *Outlines: History of the Chinese in America*. San Francisco: Chinese-American Studies Planning Group, 1973.

3308. Lai, Him Mark, Joe Huang, and Don Wong, eds. *The Chinese of America, 1785–1980*. San Francisco: Chinese Culture Foundation, 1980.

3309. Lai, Him Mark, Ruthanne Lum McCunn, and Judy Yung, eds. *Chinese America: History and Perspectives*. San Francisco: Chinese Historical Soc. of America, 1987.

3310. Lai, Violet Lau, assisted by Kum Pui Lai. *He Was a Ram: Wong Aloiau of Hawaii*. Honolulu: U of Hawaii P, for the Hawaii History Center and the Wong Aloiau Assn., 1985.
    Biography of a plantation proprietor.

3311. Lasker, Bruno. *Filipino Immigration to Continental United States and to Hawaii*. Chicago: U of Chicago P, for the American Council, Inst. of Pacific Relations, 1931. New York: Arno, 1969.

3312. Le Xuan Khoa. "Southeast Asian Social and Cultural Customs: Similarities and Differences, Part II." *Journal of Refugee Resettlement* 1.2 (1981): 27–47.

3313. Lee, Calvin. *Chinatown U.S.A.* Garden City, NY: Doubleday, 1965.

3314. Lee, Rose Hum. *The Chinese in the United States of America*. Hong Kong: Hong Kong UP, 1960.

3315. Levine, Gene N., and Colbert Rhodes. *The Japanese American Community: A Three-Generation Study*. New York: Praeger, 1981.

3316. Light, Ivan H. *Ethnic Enterprise in America: Business and Welfare among Chinese, Japanese, and Blacks*. Berkeley: U of California P, 1972.

3317. Lim, Genny, ed. *The Chinese American Experience*. San Francisco: Chinese Historical Soc. of America and the Chinese Culture Foundation of San Francisco, 1984.

3318. Lomperis, Timothy J. *"Reading the Wind": The Literature of the Vietnam War. An Interpretative Critique by Timothy J. Lomperis with a Bibliographic Commentary by John Clark Pratt*. Durham: Duke UP, for the Asia Soc., 1987.

3319. Loosley, Allyn Campbell. *Foreign Born Population of California 1848–1920*. San Francisco: R & E Research Assoc., 1971.
Reprint of the author's thesis, completed in 1927.

3320. Lydon, Sandy. *Chinese Gold: The Chinese in the Monterey Bay Region*. Capitola, CA: Capitola Book, 1985.

3321. Lyman, Stanford M., ed. *The Asian in North America*. Santa Barbara, CA: ABC-Clio Books, 1977.

3322. ———. *The Asian in the West*. Ed. Don D. Fowler. Social Science and Humanities Publication 4. Reno: Western Studies Center, Desert Research Inst., Univ. of Nevada System, 1970.

3323. ———. *Chinatown and Little Tokyo: Power, Conflict, and Community among Chinese and Japanese Immigrants in America*. New York: Associated Faculty Press, 1986.

3324. ———. *Chinese Americans*. New York: Random, 1974.

3325. Marden, Charles, and Gladys Meyer. *Minorities in American Society*. New York: American Book, 1952.

3326. McWilliams, Carey. *Brothers under the Skin*. 1943. Rev. ed. Boston: Little, 1951.

3327. ———. *Factories in the Field: The Story of Migratory Farm Labor in California*. Hamden, CT: Shoe String Press, 1939. Salt Lake City: Peregrine Publishers, 1971.

3328. ———. *Ill Fares the Land: Migrants and Migratory Labor in the United States*. Boston: Little, 1942. New York: Arno, 1976.

3329. Melendy, H. Brett. *Asians in America: Filipinos, Koreans, and East Indians*. Boston: Twayne; New York: Hippocrene, 1977.

3330. ———. *The Oriental Americans*. New York: Twayne, 1972.

3331.   Miller, Stuart Creighton. *The Unwelcome Immigrant: The American Image of the Chinese, 1785–1882*. Berkeley: U of California P, 1969.

3332.   Mindell, Charles H., and Robert W. Habenstein, eds. *Ethnic Families in America: Patterns and Variations*. New York: Elsevier Scientific Publishing, 1976.
        Contains discussions of Chinese and Japanese American families.

3333.   Miner, Earl. *The Japanese Tradition in British and American Literature*. 1958. Westport, CT: Greenwood, 1976.

3334.   Miyamoto, S. Frank. *Social Solidarity among the Japanese in Seattle*. 1939. New introd. by author. Seattle: U of Washington P, 1984.

3335.   Montero, Darrel. *Vietnamese Americans: Patterns of Resettlement and Socioeconomic Adaptation in the United States*. Foreword Chau Kim Nhan. Boulder, CO: Westview Press, 1979.

3336.   Morton, James. *In the Sea of Sterile Mountains: The Chinese in British Columbia*. Vancouver: J. J. Douglass, 1974. Seattle: U of Washington P, 1980.

3337.   Myer, Dillon. *Uprooted Americans: The Japanese Americans and the War Relocation Authority during World War II*. Tucson: U of Arizona P, 1971.

3338.   Nagasawa, Richard. *Summer Wind: The Story of an Immigrant Chinese Politician*. Foreword Barry Goldwater et al. Tucson, AZ: Westernlore Press, 1986.
        On Yueh-ning Teng.

3339.   Nakanishi, Don T. "The Visual Panacea: Japanese-Americans in the City of Smog." *Amerasia Journal* 2.2 (1973): 32–47.

3340.   Nakanishi, Don T., and Marsha Hirano-Nakanishi, eds. *The Education of Asian and Pacific Americans: Historical Perspectives and Prescriptions for the Future*. Phoenix, AZ: Oryx, 1983.

3341.   Namias, June, comp. *First Generation: In the Words of Twentieth-Century American Immigrants*. Boston: Beacon, 1978.

3342.   Nee, Victor G., and Brett De Bary Nee. *Longtime Californ': A Documentary Study of an American Chinatown*. 1973. New York: Pantheon, 1981.

3343.   Nguyễn Dang Liem. "Vietnamese American Cross Cultural Communication." *Bilingual Resources* 3 (1980): 9–15.

3344.   Nguyễn Thanh Liem and Alan B. Henkins. "Vietnamese Refugees in the United States: Adaptation and Transitional Status." *Journal of Ethnic Studies* 9 (Winter 1982): 101–16.

3345.   Nhu Tran Tuong. "Vietnam Refugees: The Trauma of Exile." *Civil Rights Digest* 9.1 (1976): 59–62.

3346.   Noguchi, Yone. *The Spirit of Japanese Poetry*. New York: Dutton, 1914.

3347.   Nordyke, Eleanor C. *The Peopling of Hawaii*. Honolulu: UP of Hawaii, 1977.

3348. Ogawa, Dennis M. *Kodomo no tame ni, For the Sake of the Children: The Japanese American Experience in Hawaii.* Honolulu: UP of Hawaii, 1978.

3349. Patterson, Wayne K. *The Koreans in North America.* Philadelphia: Balch Inst., 1976.

3350. Pratt, John Clark, comp. *Vietnam Voices: Perspectives on the War Years, 1941–1982.* New York: Viking, 1984.

3351. Quan, Robert Seto. *Lotus among the Magnolias: The Mississippi Chinese.* Jackson: UP of Mississippi, 1982.

3352. Quinsaat, Jesse, et al., eds. *Letters in Exile: An Introductory Reader on the History of Pilipinos in America.* Los Angeles: Resource Development and Publications, Asian American Studies Center, Univ. of California, 1976.

3353. Rabaya, Violet. "Filipino Immigration: The Creation of a New Social Problem." *Roots* [#173].

3354. Reischauer, Haru Matsukata. *Samurai and Silk: A Japanese and American Heritage.* Cambridge: Belknap–Harvard UP, 1986.
   An account of the author's two grandfathers, one a samurai who played a major role in the Meiji government, the other an entrepreneur who developed the silk trade with America.

3355. Richmond, Anthony H., ed. *Readings in Race and Ethnic Relations.* Elmsford, NY: Pergamon, 1972.

3356. Samuels, Frederick. *Group Images: Racial, Ethnic, and Religious.* New Haven, CT: Coll. & Univ. Press, 1973.

3357. Sandmeyer, Elmer Clarence. *The Anti-Chinese Movement in California.* 1939. Introd. Roger Daniels. Chicago: U of Illinois P, 1973.

3358. Saran, Parmatma. *The Asian Indian Experience in the United States.* Cambridge, MA: Schenkman Publishing, 1985.

3359. ———. "Pains and Pleasures: Consequences of Migration for Asian Indians in the United States." *Journal of Ethnic Studies* 15.2 (1987): 23–46.

3360. Saran, Parmatma, and Edwin Eames, eds. *The New Ethnics: Asian Indians in the United States.* Foreword Nathan Glazer. New York: Praeger, 1980.

3361. Saxton, Alexander. *The Indispensable Enemy: Labor and the Anti-Chinese Movement in California.* Berkeley: U of California P, 1971.

3362. Siu, Paul C. P. *The Chinese Laundryman: A Study of Social Isolation.* 1953. Ed. and introd. John Kuo Wei Tchen. New York: New York UP, 1987.

3363. ———. "The Sojourner." *American Mix: The Minority Experience in America.* Ed. Morris Freedman and Carolyn Banks. New York: Lippincott, 1972. 264–78.

3364. Sowell, Thomas, ed., with Lynn D. Collins. *Essays and Data on American Ethnic Groups*. Washington: Urban Inst., 1978.

3365. Stegner, Wallace, et al. *One Nation*. Boston: Houghton, 1945.
Focuses on racial problems.

3366. Steiner, Stan. *Fusang: The Chinese Who Built America*. New York: Harper, 1979.

3367. Steinfield, Melvin, comp. *Cracks in the Melting Pot: Racism and Discrimination in American History*. 1970. 2nd ed. New York: Glencoe, 1973.

3368. Strand, Paul J., and Woodrow Jones, Jr. *Indochinese Refugees in America: Problems of Adaptation and Assimilation*. Durham: Duke UP, 1985.

3369. Strong, Edward K. *The Second-Generation Japanese Problem*. Stanford: Stanford UP, 1934. New York: Arno, 1970.

3370. Sue, Stanley, and James K. Morishima. *The Mental Health of Asian Americans: Contemporary Issues in Identifying and Treating Mental Problems*. San Francisco: Jossey, 1982.

3371. Sue, Stanley, and Nathaniel N. Wagner, eds. *Asian Americans: Psychological Perspectives*. 2 vols. Ben Lomond, CA: Science & Behavior Books, 1973–80.

3372. Sunahara, Ann Gomer. *The Politics of Racism: The Uprooting of Japanese Canadians during the Second World War*. Toronto: Lorimer, 1981.
Deals with the evacuation of Japanese in Canada during World War II.

3373. Sung, Betty Lee. *An Album of Chinese Americans*. New York: Watts, 1977.

3374. ———. *The Chinese in America*. New York: Macmillan, 1972.

3375. ———. *Mountain of Gold: The Story of the Chinese in America*. New York: Macmillan, 1967.

3376. Sunoo, Sonia S. "Korean Women Pioneers of the Pacific Northwest." *Oregon Historical Quarterly* 79.1 (1978): 51–63.
Describes six Korean women who came to the Pacific Northwest as picture brides in the 1920s.

3377. Suzuki, Peter T. *The University of California Japanese Evacuation Resettlement Study: A Prolegomenon*. Amsterdam: Elsevier Science Publishers, 1986.

Tachiki, Amy, et al., eds. *Roots*. See #173.

3378. Takaki, Ronald T. *Iron Cages: Race and Culture in Nineteenth-Century America*. New York: Knopf, 1979. Seattle: U of Washington P, 1982.

3379. ———. *Pau Hana: Plantation Life and Labor in Hawaii, 1835–1920*. Honolulu: U of Hawaii P, 1983.

3380. Thomas, Dorothy Swaine, and Richard S. Nishimoto. *The Spoilage*. Berkeley: U of California P, 1946.
On Japanese American internment camps.

3381. Tong, Ben R. "The Ghetto of the Mind: Notes on the Historical Psychology of Chinese America." *Amerasia Journal* 1.3 (1971): 1–31.

3382. Tsai, Shih-shan Henry. *China and the Overseas Chinese in the United States, 1869–1911.* Fayetteville: U of Arkansas P, 1983.

3383. ———. *The Chinese Experience in America.* Bloomington: Indiana UP, 1986.

3384. Tsuchida, Nobuya, et al., eds. *Asian and Pacific American Experiences: Women's Perspectives.* Minneapolis: Asian/Pacific American Learning Resource Center & General Coll., Univ. of Minnesota, 1982.

3385. Vallangca, Robert V., ed. *Pinoy: The First Wave.* San Francisco: Strawberry Hill Press, 1977.
       On Filipino immigrants.

3386. Vandeusen, John, et al. "Southeast Asian Social and Cultural Customs: Similarities and Differences." *Journal of Refugee Resettlement* 1.1 (1981): 20–39.

3387. Vu, Nguyễn Van, and Bob Pittman. *At Home in America.* Nashville, TN: Broadman Press, 1979.

3388. Weglyn, Michi. *Years of Infamy: The Untold Story of America's Concentration Camps.* New York: Morrow, 1976.

3389. Wilson, Robert A., and Bill Hosokawa. *East to America: A History of the Japanese in the United States.* New York: Morrow, 1980.

3390. Wong, Eugene Franklin. *On Visual Media Racism: Asians in the American Motion Pictures.* New York: Arno, 1978.

3391. Wu, Cheng-Tsu, ed. *"Chink!" A Documentary History of Anti-Chinese Prejudice in America.* Foreword Ben Fong-Torres. New York: World, 1972.

3392. Wynne, Robert Edward. *Reaction to the Chinese in the Pacific Northwest and British Columbia, 1850 to 1910.* New York: Arno, 1978.

3393. Yu, Connie Young. *Profiles of Excellence: Peninsula Chinese Americans.* Palo Alto: Stanford Chinese Club, 1986.

3394. Yu, Eui-Young, Earl H. Phillips, and Eun Sik Yang. *Koreans in Los Angeles: Prospects and Promises.* Los Angeles: Center for Korean-American and Korean Studies, California State Univ., 1982.

3395. Yung, Judy. *Chinese Women of America: A Pictorial History.* Seattle: U of Washington P, for the Chinese Cultural Federation of San Francisco, 1986.

Index of Creative Writers

Index of Authors of Secondary Materials

Indexed here are compilers of bibliographic and reference works, authors of forewords and introductions, authors of literary criticism, interviewers, and authors of background sources.

Index of Reviewers

Index of Editors, Translators, and Illustrators